COMBAT

South Africa at War Along the Angolan Frontier

Books by the same author

Battle for Angola: The End of the Cold War in Africa c1975-1989 (Helion & Company)
Lebanon: Levantine Calvary, 1958-1990 (Cold War)
Nuclear Terror: The Bomb and Other Weapons of Mass Destruction in the Wrong Hands
Al Qaeda in the Islamic Maghreb: Shadow of Terror over The Sahel, from 2007 (A History of Terror)
Underwater Africa
Under the Indian Ocean
Report on Portugal's War in Guiné-Bissau
Africa at War
The Zambezi Salient
Underwater Seychelles
Coloured: A Profile of Two Million South Africans
Africa Today
South African Handbook for Divers
The Second South African Handbook for Divers
Challenge: South Africa in the African Revolutionary Context
Underwater Mauritius
The Ultimate Handbook on Diving in South Africa
Where to Dive: In Southern Africa and off the Indian Ocean Islands
War in Angola
The Iraqi War Debrief: Why Saddam Hussein was Toppled
Iran's Nuclear Option
War Dog: Fighting Other People's Wars
Allah's Bomb: The Islamic Quest for Nuclear Weapons
Cops: Cheating Death: How One Man Saved the Lives of 3,000 Americans
How South Africa Built Six Atom Bombs
Dive South Africa
African Stories by Al Venter and Friends
Barrel of a Gun: A War Correspondent's Misspent Moments in Combat
War Stories by Al J. Venter and Friends
Gunship Ace – The Wars of Neall Ellis, Helicopter Pilot and Mercenary
Shark Stories by Al J. Venter and Friends
Portugal's Guerrilla Wars (shortlisted for the New York Military Affairs Symposium's 'Arthur Goodzeit Book Award for 2013') (Helion & Company)
Shipwreck Stories by Al Venter and Friends
South Africa's Border War (Photographs, with Willem Steenkamp) (Helion & Company)
The Chopper Boys: Helicopter Warfare in Africa (New, revised and enlarged edition Helion & Company)
Biafra's War 1967-1970: A Tribal Conflict in Nigeria That Left a Million Dead (Helion & Company)

COMBAT

South Africa at War Along the Angolan Frontier

Al J. Venter & Friends

EX MONTIBUS MEDIA

First Published in the United Kingdom in 2019 by
Helion & Company Limited
Unit 8 Amherst Business Centre
Budbrooke Road
Warwick
CV34 5WE
England
Tel. 01926 499619
Email: info@helion.co.uk
Website: www.helion.co.uk
ISBN 978-1-911628-73-6

Published in the Republic of South Africa in 2019 by
EX MONTIBUS MEDIA
26 Caledon Street,
Darling 7345.
Print edition: ISBN: 978-1-911628-73-6
Text © Al J. Venter 2018
Images © Al J. Venter or open source unless noted otherwise.

Cataloguing-in-publication data is available from the South African National Library.

For a complete list of EX MONTIBUS MEDIA titles, please contact:
Email: admin@exmontibusmedia.co.za
Telephone (27) 73 777 2745
www.exmontibusmedia.co.za

To my very dear and lovely Tillie for
making so many good things happen.

Contents

Acknowledgements

This book is appropriately credited 'By Al Venter and Friends', for the simple reason that it could never have happened without the input of so many old friends and colleagues, many of them no longer with us.

The last of those intrepid warriors to take his 'last walk' was Lieutenant General Denis Earp, erstwhile combat fighter pilot in Korea and former Chief of the South African Air Force. In his later years the general spent good time writing and some of this appears within these covers, courtesy of help from another old veteran Brigadier General Peter Stannard, who we all know as 'Crow'.

I was also able to draw on material given to me years ago by another old pal, Brigadier General Dick Lord. This is titled 'Operation Askari: Angola and Its Cuban Allies Take a Beating', (originally published in *Scientia Militaria*, South African Journal of Military Studies) and it makes for an excellent 'warts and all' assessment of how it all went down.

Dick's chapter covers 'Operation Askari', the SADFs biggest cross-border strike in the post-Savannah phase and for those not familiar, it's a bit of an eye-opener because our pilots did astonishingly well. He also warned that they were not always on top of an extremely difficult and hostile situation.

Arguably one of the most revealing chapters to emerge from that 23-year struggle came from my old friend and confidante former Lieutenant Colonel Douw Steyn who was in charge of many of the operations in which 4 Recce was involved, including the sinking of several Soviet and Cuban ships in Angolan harbours. These attacks took place 'right under the noses' of an extremely sophisticated enemy that should have been able to avoid such actions that were both bold and dangerous – but did not. Or, more likely, could not, because South African Special Forces at the time were among the best and most experienced on the planet. They achieved what the Americans were never able to do in North Vietnamese ports.

Next in line is the intrepid Brigadier General Tony Savides, a moving force behind the development of the Ratel Infantry Fighting Vehicle. He gives us the low-down on how this remarkable weapon emerged from the drawing boards and how it performed under fire.

A chapter on South Africa's own 'Puff the Magic Dragon' involving the long-serving Dakota in SAAF livery – 'Gooney Bird' in American combat vernacular – is well overdue. Keith Dell and Commandant Boy du Preez, Officer Commanding of 44 Squadron, fill in many of the gaps in Chapter Five.

That is followed by former 32 Battalion Reconnaissance Wing team second in command Piet Nortje who elaborates on a Recce Wing 'snatch' operation that might easily have been a disaster had things not worked out as planned.

My old friend Tom Cooper – together with his colleague Jonathan Kyzer (with additional details from 'Luis D' in Havana) – provide what is probably the most accurate insight to SAAF losses in Angola in Chapter Nine. They totally trashed many long-standing Cuban claims of Angolan victory.

One man has been of immense help over years while I was writing for Britain's Jane's Information Group about Iran's nuclear weapons programme and that is David Albright, no stranger to South

Africa. As head of Washington's Institute for Science and International Security he had a front-row seat in that country's nuclear weapons programme (Pretoria built six atom bombs) as well as the eventual dismantling of it all in conjunction with the International Atomic Energy Agency, a United Nations body.

It is rare that I don't consult my old oppo Neall Ellis – he made half-colonel in the SAAF – about some aspect of war in the air over African skies. He gave valuable advice on the chapter that deals with two Soviet helicopters, the Mi-17 as well as the Hind Mi-24 chopper gunship. I have flown combat with him at the controls in both these machines in several wars.

Chapter Seventeen covers a topic that goes way back in the post-World War Two history of the SAAF: the rescue of a Buccaneer crew when their bomber went down in the Atlantic during its delivery flight from Britain. SAAF Commandant 'Knoppies' Coetzer provided much of the detail. Similarly, another old friend Brigadier General Peter 'Monster' Wilkins came up with the goods with regard to the early days of Puma helicopter operations on the Border.

Walter V. Volker is another of those quiet-spoken veterans who 'did their thing' during the ongoing conflict. In a chapter headed 'Covert Communications During South Africa's Border War' he gives us an insight to this work, much of it clandestine.

Finally, my sincere thanks to both Stephen Dunkley and Manuel Ferreira. Both told about a few of the Portuguese nationals who fought in the Border War, a commendable effort that really deserves a book on its own.

The production team involved in this mini-tome did tremendous work. Leading the pack was Kim McSweeney, as well as those gathered around Duncan Rogers in putting it all together. Madelon Venter, who many years ago, helped me establish Ashanti Publishing in Johannesburg, did a final proof-read of the manuscript and as usual, she came out tops.

And last, though she deserves to be first, my lovely Gabriela who in the real world is the illustrious Tillie Harris. When not at home in Washington DC she spends her working life lecturing fellow-professors, academics, scientists, researchers and others at universities all over the globe. Without her at my side, I don't think I would have managed the challenge.

During much of the time that I spent in South Africa preparing this book, I was hosted by my 'other family' in Pretoria; Manie and Elise Troskie. We too go way back: Manie, a Parachute Battalion section leader covered my back during a heli-borne assault on the extremely well-defended Cuamato military base in South Angola. We were told it was SWAPO camp: it turned out to be an Angolan Army Special Forces base and they put up one hellova fight.

There, over two days of fairly intense combat, Parabat's Charlie Company – to which I was attached – ended up with a seven percent casualty rate, which included several of our boys KIA.

Prologue: South African 'Battle of Britain' Legends

Just up the road from where I live, in the green byways and hills of Kent sits Biggin Hill, a small town with a singular claim to fame: Royal Air Force (RAF) Station Biggin Hill – as the local air base on the outskirts of town was known during the Second World War – was arguably Britain's most important frontline air defence base against Hitler's *Luftwaffe*.

Probably because Biggin Hill is almost directly south of London, it was chosen very early on in the war as one of the principal air force bases to defend the capital, a prescient move. Squadrons operating from there shot down more German fighter planes and bombers than any other air base in Britain.

Biggin Hill has several other claims to fame, including an RAF memorial museum whose entrance is flanked by a Spitfire and a Hurricane, both of which saw war service, and the fact that it is a relatively comfortable stroll to Down House, the original family home of Charles Darwin, not far from the village of Downe.

Somebody else who lived there was a quiet-spoken, self-effacing young South African who had to struggle with the fact that his parents had given him the first name of someone who, not long after he arrived in the United Kingdom in the mid-1930s, he'd committed his life to destroy. It was not surprising then that Adolph Gysbert Malan was given the name 'Sailor' by his chums, in large part because he had spent several years in the merchant navy. His wife arbitrarily settled the matter by calling him John.

As with several other aviators who served in the Royal Air Force during the war, Biggin Hill honoured this young fellow who originally hailed from Kimberley in the Cape by naming a street after him: Malan Close.

He is in very good company because others who have been commemorated in this town include a few of the great Second World War figures like Air Chief Marshal Sir Hugh Dowding, Commander-in-Chief, RAF Fighter Command; Marshal of the RAF, Sir Arthur Tedder and the celebrated Sir Douglas Bader who continued to fly combat after losing both legs, as well as several others that made history.

Among the 'Immortal Few' who served with distinction in the RAF and who was also linked to Biggin Hill, was an eminent New Zealander who spent some time with the South African fighter ace. Air Commodore Alan Deere DSO, OBE and DFC and Bar took part in operations during the critical Dunkirk evacuation phase as well as the Battle of Britain.

Deere worked closely under, and later in the war, with Malan. Some of his comments about his South African colleague explain a lot about his approach towards the 'threatening Hun'.

It will be recalled that shortly after the Battle of Britain was initiated by the German Air Force, the South African aviator – he had been given command of No 74 Fighter Squadron with the rank of Acting Squadron Leader – published his 'Ten Rules of Air Combat' which was quickly circulated throughout the Royal Air Force.

This is what he compiled and unquestionably, it must have had a good effect on newcomers to the battling 'Fighting Elite'. In fighting German planes, he declared:

1   Wait until you see the whites of his eyes.
2   Fire short bursts of one to two seconds only when your sights are definitely 'ON'.
3   While shooting think of nothing else, brace the whole of your body: have both hands on the stick: concentrate on your ring sight.
4   Always keep a sharp lookout. 'Keep your finger out'.
5   Height gives you the initiative. Always turn and face the attack.
6   Make your decisions promptly. It is better to act quickly even though your tactics are not the best.
7   Never fly straight and level for more than 30 seconds in the combat area.
8   When diving to attack always leave a portion of your formation above to act as a top guard.
9   INITIATIVE, AGGRESSION, AIR DISCIPLINE, and TEAMWORK are words that MEAN something in Air Fighting.
10 Go in quickly – Punch hard – Get out!

Some of Deere's comments about this maverick South African who went on to achieve a high number of fighter 'kills' within the ranks of British and Commonwealth fighter aviators in the Second World War are instructive.

In his book *Nine Lives*, Alan Deere makes a number of points about air combat that, because of circumstances, radically changed the RAF approach to aerial warfare.

One of these, initiated by Malan, but only after a series of confrontations with his superiors, was that guns onboard fighter aircraft such as Spitfires and Hurricanes should not be 'harmonised' on a point 500 yards ahead of the plane, but rather, set at half that distance. This had been an issue for some time, as the South African strongly believed that in aerial combat; the closer you are to the enemy the more chance you have of bagging him …

Deere: 'The controversial question of gun harmonisation was again raised with higher authority [within the RAF] … and "Sailor" Malan, perhaps the best shot in Fighter Command, was adamant [on 250 yards]. The weight of pilot opinion in favour of adopting this course eventually won the day. Command issued instructions that point harmonisation at 250 yards was to be standard for all day operations by fighter aircraft.'

Deere also commented: 'He was the first fighter pilot in the war to do so at night: a magnificent feat by a great fighter pilot,' which was a huge step forward for somebody always considered to be extremely modest.

In fact, Malan is not thought to have been a particularly skilful or gifted pilot. But he did possess many other talents that led to success when commanding his fighter unit. His particular strengths were his superior use of tactics, an exceptional ability to shoot straight and an aggressive fighting style, as demonstrated during the historic battle.

It seems that use of these skills and the subsequent passing on of this knowledge was a recipe for victory. This was adequately summed up by another of his colleagues, John Mungo Park (who succeeded Malan as commanding officer of 74 Squadron) when he declared before he was lost in 1941: 'What I like about "Sailor" is his quiet, firm manner and his cold courage. He is gifted with uncanny eyesight and is a natural fighter pilot.'

Some of these events had taken place shortly before the Battle of Britain officially begun, though different sources give different dates: the official war history *The Fight at Odds* talks about mid-August 1940, while Deere believed it to be early July.

What is more precise is that at the end of the Dunkirk operations, RAF Fighter Command could muster only 300 serviceable Spitfires and Hurricanes. The figure improved to about 600 in the battle by mid-August. But, he warned:

The latter figure represented just half that considered by the Air Staff to be necessary for the defence of the United Kingdom when they reviewed the strategic consequences following the fall of France.

The pilot situation was still more unfavourable. Despite the invaluable intake into Fighter Command of 52 pilots on loan from the Fleet Air Arm – and what good pilots they were too – squadrons were still under strength and embarrassingly short of experienced leaders.

What of the opposition? The lull between the end of the French campaign and July had enabled Nazi forces to regroup and were now dispersed on captured and rebuilt airfields throughout the occupied territories. On 3 July, when Hitler's Armed Forces Supreme Command directive was issued, their combat strength amounted to some 3,000 aircraft of which 1,480 were fighters …

By the time the Battle of Britain got into full swing, enormous demands were being made on RAF pilots. *Luftwaffe* raids came in waves and went on for months. In a series of attacks which involved Deere's 54 Squadron, the first raid of a 'normal July 1940 day' started when a several large waves of German planes – hundreds of aircraft that included Me-110s and FW-109s, Ju-87s, Dorniers and others – crossed the Channel late one morning and the last departed English air space shortly after 1900 hours that evening after an attack on Croydon airfield.

One of the pilots recalled having been airborne six times. This took some doing because a normal sortie would last something like 40 minutes and on four of those re-arming and refuelling was necessary.

Still worse, according to the official history of the RAF, 'the replacement of casualties was the most serious aspect of the pilot problem, but it was not the only one. There was also the growing strain on those who survived … the long hours at dispersal, constant flying at high altitudes, repeated combats, the parachute descents, forced landings – all took their toll, even when the harm was not at once apparent.'

Clearly, the growing exhaustion of those who had been most actively involved was a factor which the head of RAF could neglect no more than his casualties. Significant is the fact that in 10 days of fighting over that period, 154 pilots had been killed, missing or severely wounded and only 63 new fighter pilots produced in the same period, almost all novices.

It was during one of these phases that Fighter Command – again at the behest of Malan – decided to introduce new sets of formation tactics in combat. Once the RAF had started to gain the initiative, sections of three aircraft were no longer the basis of the attack formation.

Deere: 'Malan was the first fighter leader to appreciate the advantage of basing squadron tactics on sections of four aircraft, spaced in such a way that each of the three sections, although an integral part of the squadron, had freedom of action in combat.' This was a direct copy of the tactics so effectively employed by German fighter formations.

What this meant was that during the Battle of Britain, Malan's 74 Squadron abandoned some of the RAFs outmoded doctrines. For example, he took the initiative by ending the practice of flying in a 'Vic' formation' of three aircraft in favour of the German *Schwarm* or Finger Four formation, with a 'Tail-end Charlie' to cover the flight. This configuration was later used throughout RAFs Fighter Command.

All that happened not long before RAF Biggin Hill notched up its 1,000th enemy aircraft destroyed. As Deere states: 'When that came about, the "kill" was shared by two pilots – a Canadian and a Frenchman – while a South African station commander and a New Zealand wing leader looked on … '

The big event was shared by almost all of London. A huge bash was laid on at the Dorchester Hotel opposite Hyde Park – with many of Britain's prominent names present – and scores of cabbies drove through to Biggin Hill in convoy to proudly fetch 'Sailor and his boys' and then take them home again in the early hours of the next morning. 'No charge,' the cabbies declared, 'they did what they did for us … '

Southern Africa was to produce a string of famous RAF airmen during the Second World War, names that echo immortal among the great pantheon of the 'Boys in Blue' and Group Captain Adolph 'Sailor' Malan was only one of them.

M. St. J 'Pat' Pattle, a youngster from Butterworth in the Eastern Cape who fought so valiantly in the embattled skies above Greece was another, as was Group Captain Petrus Hendrik 'Dutch' Hugo DSO, DFC from Pampoenpoort in the Cape Province who led 322 Wing during the historic Operation Torch landings in North Africa in November 1942.

Hugo, like 'Sailor' Malan and 'Pat' Pattle before him, soon received a nickname when he gained his Short Service Commission on 1 April 1939. His Afrikaans name and accent soon earned the cognomen of 'Dutch', and thus he was known to the RAF throughout his service.

The Rhodesian-born Squadron Leader Caesar Hull also made his mark, though he was to die while leading No 43 'Fighting Cocks' Squadron during the Battle of Britain.

Some of the others – in an enormous list of distinctive South Africans who made their mark in the Second World War – included Squadron Leader Albert Gerald Lewis, from Kimberley, who served so gallantly with No 249 Squadron during the Battle of Britain, winning the DFC and Bar during the war; Wing Commander Alexander Coultate Rabagliati, from Durban, who was killed while leading a 'Typhoon' wing in July 1943 and, of course, the legendary Chris le Roux, a Squadron Leader who was to serve with great distinction in France, over the skies of England, and in North Africa. He was to lose his life in September 1944 and was 26 years old when he died.

The most remarkable of them all is unquestionably Squadron Leader Pattle, DFC and Bar who, though little known and rarely mentioned today, is recognised as the top scoring British and Commonwealth fighter ace of the Second World War. *Aces High*, written by Chris Shores and Clive Williams and regarded by cognoscenti as the nearest thing to a 'Bible of RAF Aces' credits Pattle with 50 victories and two shared, while Johnnie Johnson, who is rated with the second-most RAF and Commonwealth 'kills' is given 34 victories with seven shared.

What has also since come to light is that during the final phase of the Greek campaign, most of the Allied Forces' records and paperwork (for obvious reasons) were dumped in Piraeus Harbour during the evacuation. It is generally accepted, thanks to piecing together reports from Pattle's colleagues, that this youngster from the Eastern Cape probably scored another 15 or 20 kills for which the records were lost.

Unquestionably Pattle was a most gifted flyer. He was a natural marksman who took infinite pains to hone his talents and also did routine exercises to improve distance vision and sharpen his reflexes.

His first 15 victories were in the antiquated Gloucester Gladiator, nine more victories followed in a Hurricane, and then in 33 Squadron over five-and-a-half weeks he shot down 26 enemy aircraft. Even while suffering from high fever while hopelessly trying to defend Greece during the Nazi invasion, he scored nine air kills in his last four days.

The end came on 20 April 1941, when even though sick and exhausted, he went to the aid of a fellow pilot hard pressed by a Bf-110 over Eleusis Bay. He was set upon by other 110s and killed. What he might have achieved over Europe in a Spitfire had he lived, we will never know.

Today, the illustrious Pat rests with his wrecked Hurricane in the deep ocean off Crete, somewhere south of the bay near Eleusis in the Eastern Mediterranean.

Two entries written long after the war ended are worthy of mention. Both detail the exploits of the unit led by Pattle; the first from the great Roald Dahl in his wartime reminiscences titled *Going Solo*, published in 1986. I quote *in toto* from the relevant chapter:[1]

Somebody behind a desk in Athens or Cairo had decided that for once our entire force of Hurricanes in Greece – all twelve of us – should go up together. The inhabitants of Athens, so it seemed, were getting jumpy and it was assumed that the sight of us all flying overhead would boost their morale. So on 20 April 1941, on a golden springtime morning at ten o'clock, all twelve of us took off, one after the other, and got into a tight formation over Eleusis airfield. Then we headed for Athens, which was no more than four minutes' flying time away.

Round and round Athens we went, and I was so busy trying to prevent my starboard wingtip from scraping against the plane next to me that this time I was in no mood to admire the grand view of the Parthenon or any of the other famous relics below me. Our formation was being led by Flight Lieutenant 'Pat' Pattle.

Now 'Pat' was a legend in the RAF. At least he was a legend around Egypt and the Western Desert and in the mountains of Greece. He was far and away the greatest fighter ace the Middle East was ever to see, with an astronomical number of victories to his credit.

I myself had never spoken to him and I am sure he hadn't the faintest idea who I was. I wasn't anybody. I was just a new face in a squadron whose pilots took very little notice of each other anyway. But I had observed this famous individual in the mess tent several times. He was a very small man and very soft-spoken, and he possessed the deeply wrinkled doleful face of a cat who knew that all nine of its lives had already been used up.

On that morning of 20 April, Pattle, the ace of aces, who was leading our formation of twelve Hurricanes over Athens, was evidently assuming that we could all fly as brilliantly as he could, and he led us one hell of a dance around the skies above the city.

Suddenly the whole sky around us seemed to explode with German fighters. They came down on us from high above, not only 109s but also the twin-engine 110s.

Watchers on the ground say that there cannot have been fewer than 200 of them around us that morning. I can remember seeing our tight little formation all peeling away and disappearing among the swarms of enemy aircraft, and from then on, wherever I looked I saw an endless blur of enemy fighters whizzing towards me from every side. They came from above and they came from behind and they made frontal attacks from dead ahead, and I threw my Hurricane around as best I could and whenever a Hun came into my sights, I pressed the button.

It was truly the most breathless and in a way the most exhilarating time I have ever had in my life. The sky was so full of aircraft that half my time was spent in actually avoiding collisions. I am quite sure that the German planes must have often got in each other's way because there were so many of them, and that probably saved quite a number of our skins.

I remember walking over to the little wooden Operations Room to report my return and as I made my way slowly across the grass I suddenly realised that the whole of my body and all my clothes were dripping with sweat. Then I found that my hand was shaking so much I couldn't put the flame to the end of the cigarette. The doctor, who was standing nearby, came up and lit it for me. I looked at my hands again. It was ridiculous the way they were shaking. It was embarrassing. I looked at the other pilots. They were all holding cigarettes and their

---

1   Squadron Leader D.P. Tidy: 'South African Aces of World War Two' *Military History Journal*: 1969, Volume 1, Numbers 3 and 4, 1969.

hands were all shaking as much as mine were. But I was feeling pretty good. I had stayed up there for thirty minutes and they hadn't got me.

They shot down five of the squadron's dozen Hurricanes in that battle. Among the dead was the great 'Pat' Pattle, all his lucky lives finally used up.

Edgar Baker's *Ace of Aces* provides another view of that final momentous battle over the Mediterranean:[2]

Then the skies cleared. With the situation easing, at least for the time being, Tap Jones actually planned an offensive sweep, hoping undoubtedly that this would give both the pilots and the ground crews a morale uplift. The sweep was detailed to take off at six o'clock. At five that morning the pilots gathered in the readiness hut for the briefing. 'Pat' still had a high temperature and was lying shivering on a couch, covered with blankets.

Suddenly the air raid siren sounded and a voice over the tannoy announced that more than a hundred dive-bombers and fighters had been sighted, heading directly towards the harbour. 'Pat' flung off his blankets and started for the door.

His Adjutant, George Rumsey, tried to stop him, but 'Pat' was equally determined and hurried out of the hut towards the nearest aircraft. 'Pat' felt very proud – this was typical of the spirit of his squadron – a spirit which had been engendered in every man, through the inspired and devoted efforts of their Commanding Officer.

The Hurricanes had taken off singly, but while climbing in different directions their respective pilots had managed to sort themselves out into small sections of two or three …

'Pat' had now reached the scene of the fight and was 1,000 feet above a defensive circle of 110s when he saw a lone Hurricane climbing towards them. He knew that what the Hurricane was doing was extremely foolish. Without hesitating for a single moment, he put down the nose of his fighter and dived down through the middle of the maelstrom to protect the tail of the climbing Hurricane.

The cannons of the pursuing Messerschmitt were now barking louder and nearer. Knowing that the 110s could out-dive his Hurricane, 'Pat' pulled his fighter up and round. The sky seemed full of aircraft, all of them with two engines, black crosses and cannon guns spitting red and yellow flashes.

He dived frantically into a space with no Messerschmitt in it, and almost collided with a German that was banking sharply. He pressed the gun button and just had time to see the Hun stall and fall flaming before he tugged the Hurricane away from another attack.

No one actually saw 'Pat' die except the pilots flying the attacking Messerschmitts …

It must be mentioned that the Royal Air Force has an unbroken link with several generations of South Africans over the past century. Lieutenants Kiddie, Savage, van Ryneveld, Clarke and Howe served with the squadron in 1918. Van Ryneveld's brother (later Sir Pierre van Ryneveld) was commander of XI Wing.

In the Second World War, as we have seen, South Africa's 'Sailor' Malan commanded the squadron at Biggin Hill and Bob Human, 'Tookie' Tooke and Harries followed. Once again there was South African when John Howe took over the RAF Lightnings in 1954. Jacques Kleinhans, 'Lofty' Lance and Rich Rhodes followed.

2   Baker ECR: *Ace of Aces: M. St J Pattle: Top Scoring Allied Fighter Pilot of World War ll:* Ashanti Publishers, Johannesburg, 1992. Baker's original version appeared in Britain in 1965.

Examples of three types of aircraft flown in both wars are on display at the Museum of Military History in Johannesburg together with other artefacts including the instrument panel of the *Luftwaffe* Heinkel shot down by 'Sailor', as well as all his medals and decorations.

In closing, I would be remiss not to mention another South African pilot who became the first aviator in Bomber Command to be awarded the Victoria Cross, John Nettleton VC, known to all his pals as 'Jack'.

The event followed his squadron's involvement in a 1942 daylight bombing mission planned by RAF Bomber Command against the MAN diesel engine factory at Augsburg in Bavaria, responsible for the production of half of Germany's U-boat engines. It was to be the longest low-level penetration so far made during the Second World War and the first daylight mission flown by the Command's new Avro Lancaster, only two of which are still flying today: one in Britain – which I have often viewed flying over Biggin Hill – and another in Canada.

Nettleton's citation for his Victoria Cross is quite explanatory of the attack and the rest of the story picks up from here:

> Squadron Leader Nettleton was the leader of one of two formations of six Lancaster heavy bombers detailed to deliver a low-level attack in daylight on the diesel engine factory at Augsburg in southern Germany on 17 April 1942. The enterprise was daring, the target of high military importance. To reach it and get back, some 1,000 miles had to be flown over hostile territory.
>
> Soon after crossing into enemy territory his formation was engaged by 25 to 30 fighters. A running fight ensued. His rear guns went out of action. One by one the aircraft of his formation were shot down until in the end only his and one other remained. The fighters were shaken off but the target was still far distant. There was formidable resistance to be faced.
>
> With great spirit and almost defenceless, he held his two remaining aircraft on their perilous course and after a long and arduous flight, mostly at only 50 feet above the ground, he brought them to Augsburg.
>
> Here anti-aircraft fire of great intensity and accuracy was encountered. The two aircraft came low over the rooftops. Though fired at from point-blank range, they stayed the course to drop their bombs true on the target. The second aircraft, hit by flak, burst into flames and crash-landed. The leading aircraft, though riddled with holes, flew safely back to base, the only one of the six to return.
>
> Squadron Leader Nettleton, who has successfully undertaken many other hazardous operations, displayed unflinching determination as well as leadership and valour of the highest order.

Nettleton survived the incident, his damaged Lancaster limping back to the United Kingdom, finally landing near Blackpool.

'Jack' Nettleton died on 13 July 1943, returning from a raid on Turin in Italy by 295 Lancaster bombers. He had taken off from Dunholme Lodge and was believed to have been shot down by a fighter off the Brest Peninsula. A bunch of Focke-Wulf-190s and eight Jagdgeschwader-2 – the infamous *'Richthofens'* or (JG-2s) – all scrambled from bases near Brest in the early hours of 13 July to intercept the bomber stream.

A total of eight RAF bombers were claimed, among them at least three Lancasters, one of which was Nettleton's – almost certainly shot down by the *Luftwaffe*.

His body and those of his crew were never recovered. All are commemorated on the Runnymede Memorial.

Al J. Venter, Downe, England, April 2019

Squadron Leader 'Pat' Pattle DFC and Bar was the youngster from Butterworth, South Africa who ended up the top scoring World War Two British and Commonwealth fighter ace. Roald Dahl, the famous British author who fought under his command in North Africa and over Greece said of him: '"Pat" was a legend in the RAF...he was far and away the greatest fighter ace the Middle East was ever to see.'

RAF ground crews prepare for 'Gunning-up' one of their fighters in North Africa. The air war over the desert could be intense with Pattle and his fellow pilots sometimes flying several sorties a day.

South African war artist Ron Belling captured this image in oils of an RAF fighter downing a Luftwaffe Junkers Ju88A-1 while the Spitfire Mk I K9953 / ZP-A was actually flown by Adolf 'Sailor' Malan with 74 Squadron. They were based at Hornchurch in May/June 1940, in the early stages of the Battle of Britain. The painting is now part of the author's collection.

Grainy gun camera image of an RAF fighter shooting down a German aircraft.

Unidentified RAF crew in North Africa's desert during World War Two.

Celebrating Biggin Hill's
one-thousandth 'Kill'.

Introduction

South Africa's 23-year Border War was a conflict like few others. It was a young man's war where hundreds of thousands of youngsters, fresh out of school or varsity – the majority not yet into their twenties – were put through their paces in strings of military camps dotted throughout South Africa and Namibia, or South West Africa (SWA), as it was then known.

In the process, these young men were forced to become unusually fit and strong under the watchful eyes of legions of often ruthless and uncompromising instructors, taught arcane weapons' skills and sent off for almost two years to do battle more than a thousand kilometres from home.

It was a rather extraordinary, though exacting low-key war, the likes of which future generations are unlikely to experience again. To some, it became a nightmare experience yet, curiously, once in uniform, few 'troopies' (as they were rather fondly referred to by others) absconded, though some who were due to be conscripted 'skipped bail' and headed abroad.

Talk to these veterans today, the majority well into their fifties (and showing it, in girth and gait) and they will tell you, usually without hesitation that the experience was among the best of their lives. How else in an environment where they were sent out on patrol, often under the command of a youthful officer (sometimes younger than themselves) and more often than not left to deal with problems that included skirmishes, being attacked, the occasional ambush, landmines and the rest.

They managed as best they could and invariably better than their sworn Angola-based enemies that included Cuban and Soviet troops, sometimes in great numbers.

These young men were required to handle a variety of situations for themselves, which the majority did with aplomb, some receiving medals for exceptional valour under fire.

It helped that most of the men were reasonably well educated and subliminally geared to think for themselves in difficult circumstances, which was fairly often. Such conditions in an alien environment – where the enemy was never far away – tended to create confidence, the men secure in the knowledge that if things really went haywire, they could always call for support over their field radios.

Then, in perhaps a matter of 30 minutes or so, the distant roar of an approaching pair of helicopter gunships would sound out to them across South West Africa's or Angola's Mopani-covered bush country.

Someone, very early on in the war made the comment that whirling helicopter rotors in bush country was 'the sound of freedom'.

So it was too, usually freedom from further attack or harassment. Certainly, any enemy in the vicinity would also have heard the sound of helicopters approaching and would rarely wait long enough to initiate a confrontation.

South African Air Force (SAAF) helicopters – both troop-carrying Pumas and the terrier-like Alouette gunships provided support of another kind when called upon to do so. Indeed, their roles in medical support and after-action evacuation were legendary and regarded even by their enemies as world-class, a comforting reputation the South Africans shared with the Israelis.

Although interspersed in later stages with high intensity and brutal semi-conventional operations, for most it was all pretty low key when compared to some of the more modern wars where operations are meticulously planned beforehand and orders usually come from the top.

During the course of the Border War, especially in long-range strikes deep into Angolan territory, small unit commanders were very much in control of their destiny and were expected to make good decisions, more often than not on the hop, to bring themselves and their units to safety. There were times when they went to absurd lengths in order to do so.

Case in point was a vicious battle during Operation Protea where several squadrons of Angolan T-54/55 main battle tanks were attacked by a bunch of free-ranging Ratel Infantry Combat Vehicles (ICVs). By then the South Africans had developed the relatively simple tactic of several Ratels 'ganging-up' on a single enemy tank. With better training, versatility and leadership coupled to remarkable agility, the ICVs were much more sprightly in thick African bush country than the ponderous Soviet armour facing them, letting loose an average of three armour shots each to the T-54/55's one.

At one stage, a South African infantry unit, giving close-quarter ground support to its ICVs was in radio contact with a Ratel 90 that could not see an Angolan tank concealed in a forest cluster. Despite numerous calls, the T-54/55 could not be spotted by a nearby Ratel commander, who by then was head-up in his turret and was himself under direct threat. Without ado, one of the infantrymen emerged from his shell hole, ran across open ground towards the Ratel and pointed towards the enemy tank. Half-a-minute later the enemy's turret was blasted by a 90mm armour-piercing shell.

It was during these operations that South African Special Forces played a significant role. Small reconnaissance units and radio interception teams would often be deployed close to enemy airfields, invariably deep behind the lines. The men were sometimes inserted by parachute, free-falling in HALO deployments that were rarely detected, or they would walk in carrying all their equipment with them, which could take days.

Other times Mobile Air Operations Teams (MAOTs) would be deployed up-front during ground actions to coordinate SAAF actions.

Many of these operations were perilous. The majority took place well beyond the operational range of helicopters operated by the SAAF and could not be called on for support if the newcomers were detected.

The infiltrators would then have to escape on foot, usually outrunning their pursuers and quite often, handling a few fire-fights along the way. It was dodgy work, but those efforts paid enormous dividends and as one of the old-timers long past his prime, told me recently over a country barbie (or braai, as they call it down south), 'it was a hellova war and should it happen again, I'd be first in line.'

Memories, even under the most adverse of conditions sometimes die hard ...

A South African Army patrol prepares for a counter-insurgency operation in the bush. (Author's photo)

A squad of 32 Battalion troops on patrol in Angola. (Author's photo)

Angola's Marxist leader Agostinho Neto with Cuba's Fidel Castro during the course of the war. Eventually there were more than 100,000 Cubans fighting in Angola.

As the Angolan war developed, Cuban-officered Angolan troops supplied with the most modern Soviet weapons and aircraft began to play a significant role.

Black Stalingrad – The Battle of Cuito Cuanavale, Angola where the Soviets, Cubans and Angolans took a hammering from a much smaller South African armoured force.

Chopper Casevac during Operation Hooper – Photo Willem Steenkamp.

Cuba's Che Guevara reconnoitring Angola's neighbours during Lisbon's colonial war in Africa.

Early in the conflict South African Army Eland armoured vehicles were regularly ferried across the Kavango River into Angola. (Author's photo)

Jonas Savimbi's UNITA guerrillas were great at making do with almost nothing. This primitive improvisation was supposed to fool their enemies that it resembled a tank. (Photographed by the author while heading out of the country after briefly serving with Daniel Chipenda's Chipa Esquadrao)

Portugal's guerrilla wars in Africa lasted more than a decade and its forces fought with determination against Moscow-backed insurgent armies.

Portuguese Air Force Harvards returning to Luanda after a strike in the Dembos jungles to the north. (Portuguese Air Force photo)

SADF 155mm artillery firing during Angola's 'Battle of the Lomba'.

1

Portugal: End of the Line in Africa

Portugal's wars in Angola, Mozambique and Portuguese Guinea were not 'great conflicts' in the classic, historical mould. Essentially, they were battles to survive, on both sides. Portugal, one of a dozen founding nations of the North Atlantic Treaty Organisation (NATO), was poor and ill-equipped. The guerrillas were even poorer and while they received succour and weapons from the Soviets, China, Cuba, Yugoslavia and their allies, the revolutionaries were rarely experienced enough – both mentally and physically – to use what they had to good advantage. For all that, this series of African colonial conflicts lasted 13 tough years.

Inadvertently, I had some experience of one of those wars while travelling overland through Angola in the mid-1960s. Though battles were being regularly fought in the jungles to the immediate north of Luanda, with few guerrilla attacks to the south, troops, armoured personnel carriers and warplanes were everywhere.

Afterwards, I went back as an accredited correspondent and each time things were different: sometimes the Portuguese Army was on the front foot, other times its performance was dismal. There seemed always to be a downside lurking somewhere in the eaves, more often than not involving landmines – a threat that Lisbon was never able to counter effectively.

From that initial phase I wrote my first book, as well as a multitude of disconcerting impressions about a war that seemed almost impossible to win. Both were troublesome because *The Terror Fighters* (published in 1969 by Purnell, a British company in Cape Town) was actually nothing to boast about, but in the process of putting it together, I managed to perceive something that foreshadowed some formidable problems that South Africa would face in the not-too-distant future.

On the dust jacket of the blurb I'd warned that the Angolan War, only a few hours' flying time from Johannesburg, was historically significant to all of southern Africa. My exact words were: 'It is not generally realised that on its outcome – one way or the other – may depend the future of the whole southern African sub-continent.'

As might have been expected my 'gloom and doom projections' were raised in Parliament in Cape Town and in the process I made some lasting enemies, including the loquacious Pik Botha who suggested that I had lost my mind; I had dared to challenge the perceived national perception that the security of South Africa was inviolate.

After subsequent visits to both Mozambique and Portuguese Guinea it became clear that while the guerrillas, insurgents, freedom fighters – call them what you will – while not making great inroads with their 'Liberation Wars', were very much on the ground; fighting, resisting, destabilising the status quo and intimidating those who did not share their Socialist values. Generally, it was incontrovertibly accepted that the bush combatants were getting on with the job of trying to drive the Portuguese out of their African colonies (which the Lisbon government preferred to refer to as 'overseas provinces of Portugal').

Lisbon's military forces, in turn, while coping with most of it, were having a hard time trying to get to grips with an exceedingly elusive enemy who, though not as well trained and lacking modern-day military experience, were vigorous in their revolutionary efforts.

It helped immeasurably that the guerrillas could cross borders from neighbouring territories. In contrast, the Portuguese were hardly ever allowed to go after them when they scooted back to their safe havens.

The few times that Lisbon's forces did launch cross-border attacks, the hullaballoo raised by the United Nations took ages to dissipate. Unlike the South Africans, who fought a significant part of their Border War in the country from which the South West African People's Organisation (SWAPO) – its blood enemy – operated, most times did not give a hoot what the UN or any other country thought. The Portuguese, in contrast, almost always played it by the book.

I'd covered the Portuguese wars often enough to sometimes look into my mind's crystal ball to try to envisage what would happen should the guerrillas gain the upper hand.

From day one, when the first few thousand rebels streamed into Angola from the Congo in 1961 – a country already in dreadful turmoil after being rushed into an independence for which it was woefully unprepared – the war in Angola had see-sawed back and forth. There was a lot of evidence that the barefoot fighters (they were only issued with boots a year or two into hostilities) had the fortitude to go on indefinitely while Lisbon, a poor country run by a dictator, did not; the guerrillas had absolutely nothing to lose and the Soviets knew it.

Projecting that same scenario onto what was happening just then in South Africa, it was pretty obvious that if Lisbon did not hold out in Africa, first Rhodesia and then the Pretoria government would be next in line. Not long thereafter, while covering the war in Rhodesia – where things were not going well – it became obvious that South Africa would be targeted next.

While the Rhodesians were a tough, resilient little nation and very well organised and determined to succeed in the face of extremely difficult circumstances, a few hundred thousand white settlers simply could not hold out indefinitely against a black population totalling millions. And though Rhodesia's Prime Minister Ian Smith's people were not afraid to bolster their ranks with large numbers of the selfsame African communities that had taken to opposing their presence, it became what some cognoscenti liked to refer to as 'the numbers game' – too many of them and too few of us.

In a sense, Rhodesia's African people – largely Shona and Matabele – saw cousin fighting cousin, and now and again, brother against brother, which resulted in an impossible long-term situation.

There too I sensed a succession of imbroglios. Rhodesia, with a white population roughly the size of Bournemouth, was poorly equipped to fight an extensive guerrilla war in a country fractionally smaller than Germany. Also, mixing socially with this community, it did not take long to discover that one of the consequences of a small, mobile and well-equipped force doing the fighting was that these soldiers – the majority also trying to hold down jobs when not active in the bush – were expected to do so more and more often. That meant long stretches away from home and, more salient, from earning regular incomes in Civvy Street.

Small businesses suffered while their owners were in the bush and larger firms would replace old and trusted hands with others who had little experience. It also meant that the prospects of promotion went out of the window, so it was not surprising that many of the old hands voted with their feet. Some went back to where their parents had come from; the UK, while others emigrated to Australia, New Zealand, Canada or America. The majority simply moved to South Africa.

These were all people that the Rhodesian Army and Air Force needed and I was only to find out later how bad it had become. When it was all over in that troubled land and a demagogue by the name of Robert Mugabe ensconced in State House, I visited Rhodesia's former prime minister at his home in what we once knew as Salisbury, today Harare.

During the course of many visits to cover the Rhodesian War, I had come to know Ian Smith fairly well and we could exchange the occasional confidence, which was unusual because I was a traditional hack and in the eyes of many government functionaries, not to be trusted. But on that post-independence visit in 2001, when I asked him at what stage he began to think that perhaps the country could not go on fighting, he was astonishingly candid in his reply:

> The morning I was told that we were losing a company of men a month to emigration...then
> I knew it was over. He went on to say that the British were obviously aware of those losses and
> that he'd had his feet kicked out from under him.

In many ways, Portugal suffered similar problems during the course of its three African wars.

One figure puts the number of desertions from the military at 25,000 during the course of hostilities in Africa, all active serving soldiers. It was so bad that by the time the wars ended in 1974 there was hardly a bar or restaurant in Paris that was not or had not been employing Portuguese youngsters either in their kitchens or in service roles. There was no stopping them because the frontier with Spain was all but porous: there were many places where you could just walk across the border. Many of these men had left their homes clandestinely after receiving their call-up papers, and notably, those losses were over and above the 25,000 actual deserters.

For many years the strength of the Portuguese armed forces hovered around the 80,000 mark; roughly 60,000 in the army, less than 10,000 in the navy and 12,500 in the air force. In the end, about 800,000 Portuguese men and a small number of women, mostly in medical roles, served militarily in Africa.

For Lisbon there were two additional problems. Though the country was ruled by a right-wing dictator who abhorred the left, there was no stopping individuals embracing radical political causes and as a consequence, the Portuguese Communist Party had a field day. It was actually an open secret that many members of the officer corps were hard-line socialists and there were communists within the ranks who openly espoused Marxism and slept with copies of *Das Kapital* under their pillows. While that might sound absurd, it happened.

The second problem was convincing the average young Portuguese recruit who had been called up to fight a faraway guerrilla war in Africa that he was battling for a noble cause in *protecting* his nation, something the Americans also faced during the Vietnam War. It might have worked on home soil, but stuck out in some distant malaria-ridden jungle outpost thousands of miles away from metropolitan Portugal, simply did not make sense.

Maputo, or Lourenco Marques as the capital of Mozambique was called in those days, is 8,400 kilometres from Lisbon and in today's world, a flight of almost eleven hours. In the 1960s it took three weeks or more by ship. Getting to Luanda, though closer to Europe, was also a tedious slog.

Consequently, the first question most conscripts asked on arriving in tropical Africa was: 'Why the hell are we here?'

When I tackled one young lieutenant in a camp in the north of the country, he retorted with comments like 'What's all this bullshit about? This is Africa and it's neither my home nor my country.'

All the majority of these young troops wanted was to go home, with the result that few were prepared to risk their lives while on active service.

The *raison d'être* provided by those in charge of all this largely civilian conscripted army was that Angola, Mozambique and Portuguese Guinea (as well as Lisbon's islands and far-flung outposts) were all one marvellously cohesive integral entity: in effect a single country. So, it was averred, by being posted to a military base near the Congo border or somewhere equally remote in Mozambique, you were effectively fighting for the 'motherland'. It used to be called 'fatherland' but all that changed after 1945, for obvious reasons.

Naturally, that kind of rationale had its opponents and while the majority of Lisbon's young soldiers might not have made good students or lacked the wherewithal to study further, they were not stupid.

Simply put, the jungle strongpoint of Nambuangongo in Angola's *Dembos* was not home; nor were the shores of Lake Malawi, used to good advantage by the insurgents to clandestinely infiltrate their own forces. In fact, as some of these youthful European combatants were heard to argue in the latter stages of the war, *they* – soldiers of the Portuguese Army – were the interlopers, not their purported enemy.

There were other differences in the way the South Africans and Rhodesians fought their wars, compared to the Portuguese Armed Forces.

For a start, if a South African soldier or airman was wounded, every effort would be made to airlift (casevac) him out of the bush and into hospital as quickly as was humanly possible. There might be a full-scale contact on the go involving scores, but once it got down to life-saving basics, an air force helicopter would be detached to fetch the man and rush him to where he would receive first-class medical attention. The system was similar to that employed by Israeli forces fighting their own insurgencies.

In contrast, a wounded soldier in the Portuguese Army would obviously be cared for by his buddies and clearly, if his condition was serious, a helicopter might be requested. But the chances of one being available were generally remote; not surprising, as there were three wars being fought in remote parts of Africa that cumulatively covered an area of more than two million square kilometres, almost the size of Greenland.

With a life-flight out of the question, the unit medic would do what he could while his patient was being moved overland to the closest town, but all that took time. It was not unusual that if treatment was delayed in that kind of tropical climate, a bullet or shrapnel in the torso would invariably result in septicaemia setting in, often within hours.

When I contracted malaria in Mozambique I was fortunate to have my own stock of quinine, which was the accepted treatment in those days. Without it, who knows what would have happened because most rural clinics would be blessed with only the bare essentials: doctors would make calls as and when needed.

More pertinent, landmines were always a problem in the disputed regions, with the result that the medical profession – more often than not – would be fairly circumspect about moving around on dirt roads.

Then, as I and some of my colleagues were to discover, Portuguese military hospitals were sometimes not worthy of the appellation. At one medical establishment I visited in Tete in central Mozambique with Michael Knipe, who was reporting for the London *Times* at the time – there was a soldier seriously injured in a landmine: his condition was critical because his wounds had turned gangrenous. The moment we entered the double door into the ward, the stench was overwhelming.

The poor fellow's legs were covered in blood-soaked bandages, the largest of which had already turned a mouldy green around the edges. When I pointed this out to the duty doctor, all he did was shrug and move away. The entire episode is covered on pages 393/4 of my book *Portugal's Guerrilla Wars in Africa*.[1]

The first thing both Knipe and I did was to send messages to our respective offices from the local post office – this all happened long before cell phones became the norm – that if we were wounded or injured while moving about Mozambique, a chartered plane from Salisbury would have to get to us out of the country in double-quick time.

The bottom line with this event – and others I witnessed and which were comparable – was that while the young soldier remained in hospital and was receiving only cursory treatment (and he almost certainly ended up in the unit morgue) there were others around, many of them also serving soldiers, who would have been made aware of this appalling situation by their compadres. There is no question that the full story would already have done the rounds in the local barracks and passed on to other military units, near and far.

One can only contemplate the lasting effect on army morale.

There were many other reasons for Portugal's colonial demise, all of which warrant examination. Economic issues feature prominently.

For a start, historical development of the 'Overseas Provinces' – the *Ultramar* – had always been pitifully slow and it was only in the second year of the Angolan War that Portugal's Prime Minister António de Oliveira Salazar began to address some of these issues.

In Lisbon's African colonies, the administrative accent had always been on cheap labour which, in part, meant keeping the populace relatively uneducated. While the majority of the combined populations spoke Portuguese – as they still do today more than a generation after the bloody transition – there was heavy emphasis on what was termed the 'Great Society', but little real authority vested in the provinces. Anything important was invariably referred to the 'ultimate power', which lay in Lisbon, thousands of miles away and in any event a dictatorship.

Moreover, the African colonies were subject to the bidding of legions of functionaries who – with the military or the law just outside the door – oversaw everything from local government to administration of the civil service, education, health, trade, commerce, industry, utilities and the rest.

In theory, Angola being an immensely wealthy region, there should have been more than an abundance for all its citizens, whatever their colour. In practice, members of Portugal's African population were relegated to a level of second-class citizenship that would sometimes make conditions in apartheid-ridden South Africa seemingly benevolent by comparison. Forced labour was commonplace, as were public beatings.

Government rule was not only brutal but also repressive and exploitative, coupled to heavy-handed press censorship (both in the metropolis and in the African colonies). Forced labour was exacted on a massive scale, with many of the country's roads built using either forced or prison labour.

The Portuguese secret police, the so-called International Police for the Defence of the State – or *Polícia Internacional e de Defesa do Estado (PIDE)* – later replaced by the Direção-Geral da Segurança Social – was almost a government in itself. Its methods were cruel, and in some respects, could sometimes compare with those of the Nazi SS or Iran's SAVAK during the rule of the Shah.

There was rarely any quarter afforded those suspected of colluding with the enemy, with the result that the guerrillas soon employed equally brutal tactics against anybody linked to the ruling administration.

---

1   Al J. Venter: *Portugal's Guerrilla Wars in Africa – Lisbon's Three Wars in Angola, Mozambique and Portuguese Guinea*, Helion, 2013. In Portugal: *Portugal e as Guerrilhas de África* – Clube do Autor, Lisboa, 2014.

Additionally, while everybody was supposed to be governed by a single, universal set of laws, there were different criteria for Portuguese nationals and ethnic Africans. Blacks could be arrested at the whim of the local *Chefe do Posto*, even for a trivial offence. Not paying the mandatory head tax or perhaps using bad language in the presence of a Portuguese woman could result in a jail term. Similarly, anybody encouraging labour unrest for better wages was charged with sedition and imprisoned. Since the entire country was ruled by decree, any kind of political activity by black as well as white was ruled illegal and those involved prosecuted.

Harsh laws were imposed by equally harsh and uncompromising bureaucrats. Sometimes mindlessly brutal, they were rarely made to account for their actions, even when lives were lost. Coupled to that, wages for blacks in Angola, Mozambique and Portuguese Guinea were among the lowest on the continent.

As might have been expected, living conditions throughout this expansive overseas empire were dismal, for African people especially. Lisbon would always argue that in the long term, it was better for all because nobody starved. Nor did they, but by the end of the Second World War, this political scenario was also a clear-cut recipe for revolt.

What Lisbon had not initially factored into the colonial equation was communications. What was going on elsewhere in Africa by the 1960s could obviously not fail to have an impact on the peoples of Angola and Mozambique. How else, when Lisbon suddenly had to deal with a number of former British and French colonies now in control of their own affairs, several of which were immediate neighbours of the Portuguese possessions?

These included Senegal, Malawi and Congo-Brazzaville as well as others that were passionately opposed to any kind of Portuguese presence on the continent: Guinea, Tanzania and Zambia. Some of these countries were later to support the guerrillas in their ongoing wars and permitted revolutionary groups to operate from their soil.

Even so, some Portuguese colonists believed they could deal with these imponderables and they probably might have been able to do so had those belligerent neighbours acted on their own. But the Cold War had taken effect and both Moscow and Beijing believed that ultimately, there were good prospects to be had in Africa.

It was politics that ultimately dealt the death blow to any aspirations the Portuguese might have had of holding onto their African possessions.

The vision among the country's ageing leaders to improve the political situation either at home or abroad – or to strengthen the military equation – was both blinkered and lopsided. If ever there was an example of political leadership having atrophied while in power, it could be found in Portugal, especially since Salazar had been in power since 1933. When Prime Minister Marcello Caetano succeeded Salazar in 1968, the same people who supported the dictator ended up in the Caetano cabinet. There was consequently little change in either form or content.

Of course, Africa was prominent in the minds of both Salazar and Caetano, for a rather curious reason: South Africa became the focus of attention on several occasions from the 1960s onwards. It emerged after he died that Salazar was obsessed with the threat of a Mozambique Unilateral Declaration of Independence (or as Ian Smith's Rhodesians called it, a UDI). This later became something of a mania, in part because the old man believed that there were people in Mozambique plotting with the South African government to overthrow his government in Lourenco Marques.

Matters were not helped by the many South Africans who wished to invest in the Mozambican economy. Although it was initially permitted on a small scale, it was only in 1966 that any considerable foreign investment was allowed into Angola and Mozambique … by then too late.

Angola was the one country where the possibility of independence from Portugal had been mooted for decades. Had the war not arrived, there is almost no doubt that Angola would have followed Rhodesia's example.

Douglas Porch, in his book *The Portuguese Armed Forces and the Revolution,* mentions an air force colonel in Angola who said:

> In 1965, most of us already thought that Angola should become an independent and racially mixed country like Brazil. We saw that we could not win in the colonies. It was impossible to continue. Freedom had to come gradually because the people were not prepared for it. The military would be very useful in preparing the political solution. It was a task which we could not do in two months but in six or seven years. We had to prepare the government and the local governments. The army had to maintain independence, build up the armed forces and so on ...

In direct contrast, the wisdom of the day in Lisbon was twofold: firstly, you did not negotiate with the enemy, especially not if they were in a position of strength, (which they were for much of the time while operating as an insurgent force in Guinea) and, secondly, in Mozambique where the Portuguese were stuck with inferior leadership and a terrain that was far too big to control effectively with so few troops on the ground.

As a country, Mozambique is more than 2,000 kilometres long, almost twice the size of California and interestingly, roughly the same shape.

For all that, the Portuguese Army by 1973 had about 70,000 men on the ground in a vast expanse of Africa where there was a single, reasonably maintained road that stretched from north to south. Most of the rest of the country's roads were not surfaced, which perfectly suited Frente de Libertação Moçambique (FRELIMO) minelayers.

The real downfall of Portuguese interests in Africa ultimately came from within the armed forces. To start with there was great dissatisfaction among members of the Portuguese military over service in Africa.

A two-year period of service in Africa was usually followed by six months at home and then another two years in the overseas provinces, a practice that had a crippling effect on morale in the war zones. There was also ill-feeling between regular soldiers and conscripts, particularly within the junior and middle ranks of commissioned officers.

The MFA or Armed Forces Movement that eventually organised the 1974 army mutiny recognised that no political development was taking place either in the military or in the African territories. General António de Spínola actually said as much in his book *Portugal and the Future.*

There were also powerful radical elements at work within the regular army. Many officers, as we have seen, were known to be socialist or communist orientated and espoused Marxism, yet they were allowed to continue to serve their country, partly because some of their senior officers shared their political sentiments.

Brigadier General Willem van der Waals, the penultimate South African military attaché in Luanda prior to the Portuguese leaving Africa, has his own views on developments:[2]

> The military coup in Portugal took the world, including South Africa, by surprise. To well-informed observers, however, the news was not completely unexpected. One of the general officers prominent after the coup was a member of the military junta, General Francisco da Costa Gomes. He was destined to become Portugal's second post-coup president and it was

---

2   Willem van der Waals: *Portugal's War in Angola 1961-1974,* Helion, 2013.

during his reign that Angola would slide into civil war in 1975. Eventually, the country would be left to its own fate as Portugal abandoned its responsibilities on 11 November 1975.

I worked closely with Costa Gomes after he became commander-in-chief of the armed forces in Angola in May 1970 and I found him soft-spoken, shy and a regular visitor to his troops in the field. Strange to relate – in the light of subsequent events – it was he who significantly changed the military situation in Angola. He arrived at a critical time and when he left two years later, the military crisis had dissipated so much in favour of government forces that optimists believed the war had been won. However, there were doubts in certain quarters concerning his sincerity and loyalty.

Shortly after Costa Gomes' appointment, a senior Portuguese officer said [to me] that the new commander-in-chief was a communist who had been sent to Angola to prepare the ground for a handover, but to some, his military successes dispelled the doubts. Having done some research of my own, I discovered that after the outbreak of hostilities in Angola in 1961, Costa Gomes had been involved in an abortive coup against the Salazar government, so obviously doubts persisted.

Returning from South West Africa [now Namibia] a few days after the coup, I was in contact with military intelligence in Pretoria. Two years earlier I had submitted a report forecasting the possibility of decolonisation in Angola, though at the time, it was accorded little attention. Suddenly, all that material was analysed afresh.

In particular, note was taken of a letter written in March 1972 by Costa Gomes' predecessor, General Almeida Viana, to a member of the Angolan Legislative Council in which he referred to a conspiracy in Portugal, after which Angola would be left to the 'vicissitudes of the times'.

Could the seemingly spontaneous events of the spring of 1974 have been planned two years before? There is no hard evidence to support this contention, but it is known that conservative elements of Portuguese society, including the top structure of the armed forces, were very much concerned at that time about Caetano's liberalisation of colonial policy.

He was even called Portugal's de Gaulle. Something was indeed brewing.

Significantly, some Portuguese officers (as with some South Africans) tended to equate their military efforts in Africa with the French in Algeria. Douglas Porch draws on this analogy by stating that in Portugal, as in France, circumstances for the military coup were provided by a long and exhausting colonial war.[3]

There were crucial differences between the two countries. Many French soldiers believed that they were almost within striking distance of victory. They reacted against what they believed to be a betrayal by the newly elected President de Gaulle. In contrast, some Portuguese officers felt that their country was locked in a pointless struggle to maintain a burdensome colonial empire. Also, Portugal's colonial wars sapped the country's strength and made the nation appear ridiculous in the eyes of the world and then ruined the army by flooding it with half-trained conscripts whom the government attempted to promote over the heads of long-serving regulars.

As Porch maintains, the latent resentment that gradually built up to scalding point in the officer corps was a combination of bruised national pride and wounded professional vanity, collectively an explosive mixture of sentiments which the Portuguese military establishment shared with revolutionary soldiers in Egypt and other Third World countries.

---

3   Douglas Porch: *The Portuguese Armed Forces and the Revolution* (Croom Helm, London, 1977).

The Portuguese experience also proved that increased professionalism of the armed forces can sometimes hasten its entry into the political arena rather than discourage it, as American historian Samuel Huntington has argued. Professional discontent creates a kind of 'shop floor' militancy and an army mutiny substitutes for the strike.

In retrospect, it is astonishing that Portugal never considered transferring families to the African colonies for these extended periods of anything up to five years. Their principal argument against such a step was the 'UDI Bogey'. This was a real and persistent fear that too many metropolitan Portuguese would be sent to the African colonies and then begin to think for themselves, very much as the Rhodesians had done.

Occasionally one found a member of a family in one of the African capitals, usually that of an officer, comfortably well-off and able to afford such a luxury. While I covered the war in Portuguese Guinea in 1971, the beautiful new wife of a young *alferes* (lieutenant) shared our table when her husband was in the bush. She'd been staying at the hotel for almost a year and was not dismayed by the prospect of another year in Bissau … a dreadful tropical backwater on the edge of a swamp … despite it being the only reasonably civilized place in the country.

The differences from what she was used to back home were immense. Unlike Luanda or Lourenco Marques, the population in Portuguese Guinea was almost totally black and to her, with a thoroughly European background, quite alien. There were very few of the pavement cafes that we knew in Mozambique; no good beaches (or at least none that were accessible from the capital) and no recreational parks of the kind she frequented back home. All that lay at the edge of Bissau was the jungle, the war and of course an enormous West African tropical swamp.

The hotel we all shared, the Grande, was a misnomer: it was a grim, rambling, stuccoed doss-house that was older than the century and with no air-conditioning. Only the bar showed any animation; it was raucous by midday.

Then there was the question of money. As any soldier will tell you, he can do without women, but not his beer.

Several years in Africa were not eased by the fact that a Portuguese soldier's pay was derisory. A brigadier serving in Africa in 1971 earned about US$500 a month. A private earned perhaps US$40 and perks were few. Home leave outside the period of service was almost unheard of; and anyway, who could afford a ticket back to the *metropole*? Even if he travelled steerage on one of the many Portuguese liners serving the African colonies, time was against him since the ships stopped just about everywhere on both outward and homeward legs.

Physical conditions too, especially out at the 'Sharp End', were abominable. Military camps at such remote corners of the empire as N'Requinha, Luso, Nambuangongo and Cabinda in Angola – and Zumbo, Tete and Zobue in Mozambique – or any one of the postings in Portuguese Guinea – were invariably barbarous and unhealthy. In some places, the tribesmen actually lived under better conditions than their 'protectors', especially where they were herded together in their Malayan-style protected villages or *aldeamentos*.

By the time the coup took place, there are those who maintain that for all Lisbon's problems and makeshift means to fix them, it was Portuguese Guinea that was the principal cause of the decay that set in among the Portuguese armed forces. By 1972 it had become apparent to even the most sanguine supporter of Portuguese rule in Africa that the war in this grim tropical terrain on the west coast of Africa could not be won.

After the military replaced Portugal's civilian government in 1974 in what was known as the Carnation Revolution (because of carnations shoved into the barrels of soldiers' rifles in Lisbon), Angola became the first of the three former colonial territories to make substantive changes. The respective leaders of the three political movements – civil and military – the MPLA, FNLA, and

UNITA each negotiated peace agreements with the transitional Portuguese government, but not before they had begun to seriously battle each other for control.

That was when Holden Roberto, Agostinho Neto and Jonas Savimbi met in Bakuvu, Zaire two months after the coup and agreed to negotiate with the Portuguese as a single political 'Liberation' entity. They met again in Mombasa, Kenya, on 5 January 1975, agreed to stop the fighting and further outline constitutional negotiations with the Portuguese. The third time they came together was a week later in Portugal where they signed what became known as the Alvor Agreement.

The parties agreed to hold the first assembly elections in October 1975 and from 31 January 1975 until independence, Angola would be ruled by a transitional government. That would consist of a Prime Ministerial Council (PMC) headed by the Portuguese High Commissioner, Admiral Rosa Coutinho (a card-carrying member of the Communist Party who was known as the 'Red Admiral'. His links to Havana feature prominently in *Battle for Angola*).[4]

The PMC consisted of three representatives, one from each Angolan party, and a rotating Premiership among the representatives. Every decision would require two-thirds majority support. The twelve ministries were divided equally among the Angolan parties and the Portuguese government; three representatives for each.

Of course, for all the nice words at Alvor, absolutely nothing worked as planned and the situation throughout Angola deteriorated still further.

The 'Red Admiral', we discovered only afterwards (from his clandestine communications with the Cubans), saw to that. Within weeks, a nation-wide civil war erupted that was to continue for almost 30 years and eventually involved a substantial South African mercenary force known as Executive Outcomes.[5]

While nobody is certain how many people died as a consequence, the tally is thought to be about a million.

---

4   Al J. Venter: *Battle for Africa – The End of the Cold War in Africa c.1975-1989*, Helion, 2017. See Cuba's role in the Angolan war, Chapter xx.

5   *Battle for Angola, Ibid* – Chapters One, Two and Three.

Airdrop onto a remote
Portuguese Army camp
in the Dembos jungle
perhaps 30 minutes flying
time north of Luanda.
(Author's photo)

A Puma troop-carrier
picking up troops. (Source
Portuguese Air Force)

Age-old guerrilla tactic of
blocking roads with felled
trees. (Al Venter collection)

'Ambush Alley' on the way to the Dembos. (Al Venter collection)

Angola – President Nelson Mandela with Fidel Castro. Despite protestations to the contrary, South Africa's ANC always maintained strong ties with communist Cuba.

Angolan paratroopers during a counter-insurgency bush operation.

Angola's Rio Lue Bridge in the jungle near the Congo border: during the war, road communications were always tenuous.

Chopper and Ground forces during a bush operation. (Al Venter collection)

Convoy on the road into the Dembos with a Panhard APC for back-up. These armoured vehicles travelled front and rear. (Author's photo)

Few Commando operations took place without helicopter gunship support, because they were customarily given the toughest counter-insurgency nuts to crack. (Photo Associação de Comandos)

Guerrilla leader Agostinho Neto reviews his troops. (MPLA photo)

An insurgent squad laying landmines in the Angolan interior, something the Portuguese Army was never able to effectively counter.

Hammer and Sickle Angolan Flag: once in control in Angola, the country quickly became a Soviet surrogate state. (Author's photo taken in Luanda)

Helicopter gunship over the Dembos, north of the capital. (Author's photo)

In order to recapture Nambuangongo from the rebels early in the war – after they had invaded Angola from the Congo – the government had to send in armour from Luanda to reverse the tide. (Photo Revista Militar)

Landmine control-detonated along a jungle road. (Photo Revista Militar)

Much of Africa where Portuguese ground and air forces fought their wars was primeval jungle – always a difficult terrain in which to operate. (Author's photo)

Not always given to half measures, Portuguese Special Forces were tough and resilient in the bush. (Photo Revista Militar)

Portuguese Air Force Harvards were a defensive mainstay in ground support operations for many years. (Source Portuguese Air Force)

Portuguese Army convoy in Angola's interior. These troop-carrying Unimog vehicles were not mine-protected and the exposed troops vulnerable to ambush attacks. The South Africans went on to field the much more effective Buffel troop carrier.

The army on parade in Luanda, Angola's capital city during one of the author's visits.

Portuguese Army Panhard AML-60 armoured car, similar to the SA Army Eland. (Al Venter collection)

Portuguese paratroopers man a strongpoint at the end of the war. (Author's photo)

Portuguese Fuzileiros (Marines) prepare for action in a difficult jungle area. (Sourced to John P. Cann)

Puma in Angola's eastern quadrant picking up a mixed patrol of flechas and infantry.

The bazooka device home-produced by the Portuguese. It fired a 37mm air-to-ground French-supplied SNEB rocket. (Author's photo)

Two guerrilla adversaries travel by plane to a conference venue – future Angolan President Agostinho Neto on the left and UNITA's Jonah Savimbi. (Al Venter collection)

2

A Contrasting View of South Africa's Border War

Syria, Iraq, Afghanistan, Northern Ireland and Yemen have hugged the headlines for decades. In contrast, South Africa's efforts to combat insurgency in what not long ago was South West Africa – and ultimately Angola – received sparse attention beyond that country's own frontiers.

There are several long-standing misapprehensions relating to the Border War that still need to be clarified decades after that conflict ended. The first involves SWAPO guerrillas who managed to keep what many regard as a minor or low-intensity conflict on the boil for almost a quarter century.

For decades the consensus – almost throughout the South African Defence Force (SADF) and among politicians back home – was that the average enemy fighter in the region was little more than an ill-trained, modestly-equipped subversive acting almost solely on the whims of his Soviet-trained commissars.

In reality, these rugged combatants were anything but. While the majority of fighters attached to the People's Liberation Army of Namibia (PLAN) were the kind of ordinary-rated soldiers likely to be encountered in any army, there were specialist SWAPO combatants who managed to give the SADF a right runabout and, now and again, a bloodied proboscis.

Some of these guerrilla strike forces – most were quite modest in number, perhaps a couple of dozen combatants at a time – would enter from Angola and it would sometimes take the SADF weeks to flush them out. And that in spite of the enemy having no air cover, very little logistical back-up, almost no medical facilities for their wounded and an adversary that was eventually rated as one of the most competent counter-insurgency forces on the globe.

Matters were compounded by the fact that unlike forest-clad Vietnam with its jungles and guerrilla tunnel links, the region in which the fighting was taking place in Angola was sparse: in most areas the terrain is as flat as the proverbial pancake with little ground cover, coupled to the reality that with all the disadvantages facing SWAPO, its cadres went on to become masters of some of the arcane disciplines of landmine warfare.

Many of the former guerrillas who were captured were given the option of serving in Koevoet, the South African Police counter-insurgency unit and, almost to a man they distinguished themselves, even though they were battling their old comrades.

Koevoet's 'kill rate' during the course of the war was significantly higher than any comparable South African Army unit, in large part because its components, black and white, were well-focused, efficient and committed.

Take one example: Frans Conradie, with a nominal force of half a dozen Casspirs and perhaps 20 men, was Koevoet's top scorer in combat for three years before he was killed in a motor vehicle accident. He and his group notched up 98 kills in 1981, more than 80 in 1982 and by August the following year when he died, it had already topped the 60-mark.

I was on ops with Frans several times and he always credited his black troops – some of whom he had personally taken prisoner – with remarkable fighting prowess.

Essentially, had this enemy been anywhere as inferior as many of our senior commanders suggested, the Border War – and linked Angolan misadventures – would never have lasted over two decades …

And yet, much of what took place in this remote region of Africa remained in the shadows because there were more extensive wars going on elsewhere (Vietnam) and an extremely effective programme on Pretoria's part of non-disclosure of what was actually taking place in the disputed regions. Rigorous press censorship coupled to a skilful programme of disinformation also played a role.

Which begs the question: Were the South African and South West African/Namibian soldiers better than the SWAPO insurgents? The answer is an unqualified 'yes' and one must understand why this was so.

It was not about courage or cowardice, but about better organisation, more astute planning and utilisation of resources and, above all, superb basic training. These attributes went all the way through to the most advanced military-related disciplines that involved fieldwork, retaliation, transport, armour, close-air support, the always-urgent evacuation of casualties and the kind of clandestine work that involved South Africa's Special Forces.

Most importantly, the South Africans understood something that seems to elude some Western military thinkers: time is not automatically on the insurgent's side – it *can* be on the insurgent's if he accepts that he is in for the long haul and tailors his tactics accordingly. The South Africans did exactly that and eventually the war ended in successful negotiations for a democratic Namibia.

If that war proved anything, it was that although most insurgencies end in political solutions, he who has lost the penultimate military phase has no voice when the armed struggle concludes, not with a bang, but with the rustle of papers being shuffled around the conference table.

American military historian Robert Goldich phrased it well in a recent assessment widely circulated in United States and European military circles and easily accessed on Google.

Writing in the prestigious American magazine *Foreign Policy*, Goldich – who retired from the United States Congressional Research Service as their senior military manpower analyst in 2005 – declared that South Africa enjoyed immense superiority in several areas.

Its advantages, he declared, lay in the ability of the South Africans to manoeuvre operationally, combined arms operations, superior command and control growing out of the standard Western types of doctrinal development, military training centres, as well as a highly professional military education structure.

So much for the dismissive comments of a few commentators who maintained, in print, that some of our senior military commanders were not properly educated in the art of war. That might have been true early on when some senior men were politically appointed, but as the threat factor escalated, only the best of the leadership pool got to the top.

There are numerous examples of some of these men reaching senior positions in subsequent conflicts in Iraq and Afghanistan and, as we go to print, Chris du Toit is just back from years of running military affairs in a large part of South Sudan, a country bigger than Botswana. His role was that of principal military adviser to the UN.

Another example is former deputy head of the South African Army Major General Roland de Vries – dubbed 'South Africa's Rommel' by his fellow commanders – who successfully nurtured the concept of 'mobile warfare'. In a succession of armoured onslaughts his modest ranks of 'thin-skinned' Ratel Infantry Fighting Vehicles, tackled Soviet main battle tanks and thrashed them. After he retired he was linked to the Australian Command and Staff College in the Australian capital.

Goldich goes on:

> To make things far worse for South Africa, and potentially the West in general, the Soviet Union committed huge amounts of military hardware and military advisers/trainers for the Angolan Army – known as FAPLA, the acronym for Forças Armadas Populares de Libertação de Angola.
>
> Cuba made an even more massive military investment in that African conflict. It ultimately dispatched an expeditionary force to Angola which reached a maximum strength of about 55,000 (more recent evidence out of Havana points to a figure in excess of 100,000) with a total of almost 380,000 Cuban military personnel serving in the country from 1975 through 1991.
>
> If SWAPO took over or destabilised South West Africa (now Namibia), whether or not Angolan or Cuban troops moved into SWA, the front line would have shifted south all the way to the Orange River and no question, quite a few South African cities would have been directly affected.

A notable element in South Africa's success in being able to counter a hugely disproportionate enemy force thrusting southwards from Angola was the arms and equipment used to counter these efforts.

With South Africa under a United Nations arms embargo, most of the country's needs came 'home-made' and what an impressive array it eventually became. Items produced locally ranged from basic R4 and R5 infantry rifles, heavy calibre weapons, troop-carrying vehicles all the way through to multiple rocket launchers (MRLs), advanced anti-aircraft missiles and trackers and, under licence from the Israelis, naval strike craft.

The South Africans even managed to upgrade the French-built Puma helicopter into the Oryx, still in service in the SAAF today.

It was in anti-landmine technology that the country became a world leader, so much so that several of the mine-protected vehicles developed during the war years still offer good service in many of the world's trouble spots, with the Casspir – designed for the South African Police unit Koevoet by Pretoria scientist Dr Vernon Joynt (who subsequently became an adviser to the US Department of Defence in counter-mining techniques) – taking the lead.

What has never been properly acknowledged is the enormous role played by Special Forces units such as the Reconnaissance Regiment or 32 Battalion – the latter a comparatively small unit which drew most of its manpower resources from former enemy units – including the Angolan FNLA.

As with the Recces, 32 Battalion's tasks often ranged well beyond enemy lines and considering its modest numbers, the unit ended with a better average success rate per operation than any equivalent American military unit deployed in either Iraq or Afghanistan.

South Africa is also the only relatively small nation to have beaten the Soviet Union at its own game. With all the resources at its disposal, Moscow and its allies never once managed to penetrate the defences of South African ports long enough to cause damage.

The crack maritime combat unit, 4 Recce, whose operational side was headed by a still-youthful Colonel Douw Steyn, trained for underwater warfare at Langebaan on South Africa's west coast and he ended up taking a group of his frogmen on several raids into Angolan ports.

There, in June 1986, 4 Recce squads blew up two Soviet freighters, the *Kapitan Chirkov* (16,000 tons) and the *Kapitan Vislobokov* (12,000 tons) as well as the *Habana*, a 6,000-ton Cuban ship loaded with arms. The entire strike was completed in a single night raid on Namibe harbour.

Prior to that, they sank two cargo ships in Luanda harbour and crippled one of the largest oil refineries in West Africa: all that in spite of the presence of a huge Soviet naval presence that included a 3,500-ton Soviet Kashin-class guided missile destroyer. I deal with those attacks in some detail in *Battle for Angola*.

In truth, South Africa emerged from the Border War with more unsung honours than most other countries facing conflagrations. And while casualties were modest, the troops and the civilian population took some heavy knocks.

Take one example: Northern Ireland's 'Troubles'. In 30 years of hostilities, there were more than 3,600 people killed and thousands more injured in Northern Ireland.

South Africa lost an estimated 700 security force personnel as well as 1,000-plus SWA/Namibian civilians in its 23-year-long Border War. Add to that several thousand guerrillas killed while fighting for SWAPO and who knows how many thousands more Cubans, Angolan Army and UNITA troops.

The fact is that Pretoria was faced with an expansive unconventional conflict that steadily escalated into a full-blown series of military confrontations and several times, conventional battles that would not have been of place in the Second World War. Had it not been halted by the joint efforts of US Under-Secretary of State for Africa, Chester Crocker and his Soviet counterpart, it might well have gone nuclear after the Angolan Army had misfired (failed to detonate) the first of their chemical weapon projectiles.

When that occurred, the South African cabinet decided it was time to act. The SAAF was ordered to prepare for a strike – possibly on Luanda – that would almost certainly have involved the deployment of one of the six atom bombs that were held in storage at the Circle facility on Pretoria's outskirts. It was that close, details of which are contained in my book *How South Africa Built Six Atom Bombs*, published in 2007.

Interestingly, those involved with South Africa's nuclear weapons programme have always declared that they never had any intention of actually using that weapon of mass destruction, but then that kind of response is hardly feasible when contrasted with original intent.

Until the first quarter of 1974, the support of Prime Minister Marcelo Caetano's regime in Portugal had been of great value to Pretoria in its counter-insurgency campaign in South West Africa. While the Portuguese Army was still around, PLAN could not freely use southern Angola as a sanctuary, training-ground and jumping-off place for infiltrations into that country's southern neighbour.

By 1974 however, after more than a decade of combating several simultaneous insurgencies in all three of Lisbon's African provinces, cumulative financial and manpower demands brought Portugal, the poorest country in Europe, to the brink of financial and spiritual collapse. The bottom line was that while this European nation financed its wars on its own, with little extraneous support from its NATO allies, its enemies got all their military hardware from the Soviet Union free.

In late 1974 alone, an estimated $6 million US dollars' worth of heavy Russian weaponry – including 122mm BM-21 multiple rocket launchers, (obsolescent weapons perhaps, but highly effective against unsophisticated African troops) – were moved to remote rural MPLA depots either from Dar es Salaam (through Zambia) or more directly via Congo-Brazzaville. Soviet outlay eventually inched up towards billions of dollars expended in Moscow's African wars, never mind what Afghanistan was costing.

The author was dropped into action with Parachute Battalion's Charlie Company in the south Angolan two-day Battle for Cuamato. That attack resulted in several South African dead as well as quite a few of the men wounded. All photos by Al J. Venter.

Additionally, large numbers of MPLA officers were flown to Eastern Europe and elsewhere for training, though in fairness, this only took place after Red China had sent the FNLA instructors and 450 tons of light arms through Zaire in June of that year. That was followed by another weapons' shipment from Romania.

In addition, more Cuban military advisers and instructors were quietly slipping into Luanda, and from then on, they kept coming...

For years SWAPO and MPLA sympathisers and fellow travellers, both inside and outside South Africa, claimed that Cubans started arriving in Angola only in late 1975 (after independence from Portugal) *because* of South African aggression. In fact, there was an old relationship between Agostinho Neto and President Fidel Castro, with Cuba providing the Angolan president with a huge body of instructors and a personal bodyguard since 1966.

With dismaying speed, Angola began to slide into full-scale chaos as the three contenders battled it out – for survival in the case of Savimbi – and for supremacy in respect of Neto and Holden Roberto.

In July 1975 the MPLA won the first round by throwing both the FNLA and the small UNITA presence out of Luanda and establishing the Marxist party (which displayed its allegiance to the Soviet hammer and sickle on the country's national flag) in almost every sizeable population centre between the capital and the South West African border.

To the South Africans it was obvious that an already serious and deteriorating situation had become critical. Refugees, by now streaming southwards over the border in their thousands, had started bringing word of the close Cuban involvement with the MPLA. Independent proof of Fidel Castro's role in the escalating war – and possible future plans – was revealed when one of the numerous small hot pursuits launched by the South Africans over the ever more irrelevant border turned up Cuban-origin ammunition and weapons dumps which, as one official spokesman later said, 'placed the security situation of southern Angola in a completely different light.'

The Americans' grasp of these issues does not seem to have been very strong if one is to believe John Stockwell, who headed out to Africa from the disaster in Saigon to be made head of the operation the CIA hastily set up in Angola in 1975. In a 1984 television documentary, Stockwell – who by then had severed his ties with Langley to become one of its most outspoken critics – described the first briefing on Angola to be delivered by the head of the CIA to the National Security Council, effectively US President Gerald Ford's inner cabinet.

The CIA director (said): 'Gentlemen, this is a map of Africa, and here is Angola. In Angola there are three liberation movements. There is the FNLA, headed by Holden Roberto, they're the good guys. There is the MPLA, headed by Neto, who's a drunken psychotic poet with a Marxist background and they are the bad guys.' As Stockwell later explained, that was exactly the kind of terminology employed: 'good guys' and 'bad guys', so that those people on the National Security Council could get it straight what the game was and who was involved.

The reason why Savimbi did not get a mention at this stage was undoubtedly the fact that (as Stockwell himself noted), 'nobody knew much about Savimbi ... he didn't hit the international cocktail circuit the way FNLA and MPLA activists and leaders did. Instead, the UNITA leader stayed in Angola, tending to his business.'

The fact is that throughout the crucial first six months of 1975 (after the Portuguese had pulled all their forces out of Africa) the US government was virtually inert as far as Angola was concerned. No doubt the Americans' deeply ingrained parochialism was partly to blame and, in addition, the United States was not only still too deeply mired in its post-Vietnam nervous breakdown to take positive action but was entering its traditional pre-presidential election paralysis.

And so South Africa was sucked into the burgeoning war, a conflict that went on for another 15 years.

Pretoria's military involvement in Angola has been attributed to everything from blatant racism to out-and-out neo-imperialist expansion, and Stockwell's theory is that the South Africans' main reason for giving in to the American urgings was because they sensed a lever which they could use to force the US to support their policies.

The Border War, in contrast, was still of very low intensity, but an intermittent dribble of contacts, mine explosions and shoot-and-scoot rocket and mortar bombardments inexorably pushed up the casualty rate. For SWAPO's insurgent wing – known as PLAN or People's Liberation Army of Namibia – and operating on their home ground against relatively inexperienced enemies, the environment was still comparatively favourable; the SADFs immediate reaction was to mount intensive counter-insurgency operations.

Meanwhile, South West Africa's northern conflict showed no signs of abating. Insurgents often operated in increasingly larger groups and did not hesitate to fight if contacts resulted. In certain sectors of the South African public, the erroneous conclusion was reached that PLAN cadres tended to run if attacked. In fact, this tactic was usually the only one that made sense and in any event, they were constantly 'on the run'. At the same time, the guerrillas were certainly not afraid to exchange blows.

A typical contact consisted of a short, fierce fire-fight, after which the guerrilla group usually gave way and headed for the Angolan border or dispersed into Ovamboland's endless stretches of sparsely foliated bush country. To do otherwise would provide targets for the SADFs helicopters and reaction-force units.

During the course of the 23-year-long Border War, cost became a significant and often inhibiting factor. If material losses of all the participants are counted, it came to billions in any reputable currency on both sides of the front and ended up affecting the lives of millions, especially in Angola.

Total casualties will probably never be established: South African sources gave 'known deaths' by November 1988 as 715 security force soldiers; 1,087 SWA/Namibian civilians and 11,291 insurgents and Angolan soldiers.

It is quite possible that many more PLAN fighters were killed, given the fact that they did not have recourse to the sophisticated medical backup enjoyed by the South Africans. These figures do not include thousands of deaths suffered by UNITA, or by the Cubans and their Angolan allies, never mind huge numbers of civilians caught in the crossfire.

Cuba alone is believed to have lost more than 10,000 troops during the course of both the border and the civil war that followed, about a third from non-combative causes (road accidents, tropical diseases and in later stages, from AIDS). It got so bad towards the end that Cuban troops infected with AIDS were shipped off to a remote island to avoid them infecting the rest of the population, something that was kept very low key until fairly recently.

The number of dead and permanently disabled is possibly not impressive when measured against the ghastly losses suffered in some of the greater more wars Middle East and Central Asian (Afghanistan) wars. By the standards of southern Africa however, where countries are spread across vast regions but populations are small, it becomes a heavy toll. Angola will be a long time recovering from the loss of its precious blood and treasure.

An interesting avenue of speculation is this: was it necessary for SWAPO to embark on its 'armed struggle' in 1962? Might it not have been better advised to fight for an independent Namibia on the national and international political battlefield rather than take up arms in its own backyard?

The answer is a possible 'no' to the first part and 'yes' to the second, but that said, the question should be examined within the context of its times.

The early post-war period and thereafter was the era of the 'Freedom Fighter' and not the negotiator,[1] and in any case, the South African government of the time was little disposed towards negotiations with an openly revolutionary organisation which maintained solid links with Moscow. What is also certain is that most of those conflicts would never have happened had Moscow not played a seminal role in fostering their version of revolutionary wars.

An intriguing idea some observers play around with is the theory that perhaps the war did not hasten South West Africa's progress towards independence but actually delayed it. True or false? It is difficult to say, for there is no clear answer.

An interesting question is this: Should the South African government of the time have gone to war against the South West African insurgents?

The answer is probably that, apart from personal inclinations, they had no real alternative, especially once it had become apparent that the insurgency was not a nine days' wonder. To many – possibly most – of their white voters, the Pretoria government would have been regarded as 'hands-uppers' or worse.

The consequences of Operation Savannah and the arrival of thousands of Cubans in Angola sealed the matter, especially after it became clear that Castro had been clandestinely infiltrating Cuban troops into the country even before the ink on Lisbon's handover was dry.

After 1976, when the insurgency became really viable (because Angola's new Marxist masters threw their support behind SWAPO) there was no turning back. An irony here is that the seeds of the SWAPO movement were already sown as far back as in the 1940s and 1950s, but did not come to fruition till late in the 1960s. That was when attitudes had begun to change towards a more militant approach.

Period history teaches us a great lot. Angola's disastrous slide into chaos was largely due to the Soviet Union's undermining of the post-Caetano era in Portugal. It might well be that the Russians were not working to a pre-determined plan but were merely seizing a handy opportunity. But that does not alter Moscow's culpability (and the 'opportunity' theory is suspect in any case when one considers that Moscow, Cuba and the likes of Rosa Coutinho had already started working in 1974 to manoeuvre the MPLA into power).

Then there is the matter of the true victims of the Angolan war – the ordinary people, unquestionably the greatest victims of all. Yet, to a large extent, the Angolan government could be said to have brought its troubles on itself for seizing power in the first place instead of promised universal elections.

South Africa had a different but related set of problems. There have been many statements that thousands of young whites left the country to avoid service in SWA/Namibia, but this has not been backed up by any conclusive research. Many of those who went abroad did so because they considered that two years of full-time conscription coupled to 720 days of part-time service was simply too onerous a burden on their careers and personal lives and on this, one cannot argue. There was also a moral issue.

Angola was certainly not South Africa's Vietnam in the sense that SADF actions were circumscribed by either the guerrillas or the Angolan Army (FAPLA) like the Americans were in their

---

1   These include revolutionary wars, uprisings following army mutinies and coups, tribal differences (Biafra) and disaffected minorities in countries like Algeria, Somalia, Ethiopia, Eritrea, Rhodesia, both Congos, Cabinda, Angola, Nigeria, the Cassamance Province of Senegal, Mozambique, Uganda, Chad, Libya and others.

South East Asian war.[2] Well into the 1980s the South Africans did pretty much as they pleased in southern Angola and scored many victories at little cost to themselves. If Angola was anybody's Vietnam, it was Cuba's.

Another popular misconception was that the Border War destroyed the 'myth of South African military superiority'. This was (and remains) a handy phrase readily bandied about by both the present-day government in Pretoria, Havana and their radical supporters abroad but in reality, the converse is true. South African military superiority was anything but myth, then or later.

Unlike almost every other southern African army, the SADF was a long-established body, forged by six decades of independent development and two bloody world wars into the best-organised, best-trained fighting force in Africa. What Savannah did prove at the start of it was that the SADF was not in good shape after 30 years of peace; its equipment was outdated and there was a good deal of dead wood – both in personnel and in doctrine – and that needed to be lopped off, which it was.

To the South Africans' credit, they took this lesson to heart, with the border war supplying a handy training-ground. As a result, the SADF emerged with a standard of operational expertise which surpassed that of some of the most famous armed forces in the world – and the self-confidence that went with it.

Were the South African and SWA/Namibian soldiers better than the SWAPO insurgents? The quick answer is 'yes' – but one must understand why that was so. It was not about courage or cowardice but about better organisation, superior planning and utilisation of resources and, above all, good training.

If the war proved anything, it was that although most insurgencies end in political solutions, which rarely satisfy those who were involved.

To those who did not know better – and to some who did, but found it more convenient to avoid facing the facts – the Border War was a simple confrontation between racist whites and oppressed blacks. But the men and women who fought in it knew better: probably no other southern African war has ever featured such a motley, many-tongued, multi-hued array of combatants driven by such a variety of motives – patriotism, political beliefs, a hunger for vengeance, a desire for money, obedience to the authorities, and so on.

For some, it satisfied a thirst for adventure for the simple reason that the Border War, in a sense, was a fighting man's conflict, in that most of the action in it was Mark One face-to-face soldiering at whites-of-the-eyes range rather than the impersonal killing of enemies at long distance.

It has also been called a 'colonial' war, but in at least one important aspect it was not. Where it differed from most such conflagrations was that almost none of the bush fighters were foreigners, in the sense of coming to the battle zone from distant lands, like the Americans in Vietnam and the British in Malaya.

All were southern Africans of one race or another and did not experience real difficulty in coming to terms with what faced them.

---

2   As the war progressed and the effect of a mandatory United Nations arms embargo began to make an impact, Pretoria was never able to match some of the more sophisticated weapons given to opposing forces by the Kremlin. Long before the cease-fire was signed between the belligerents, the SAAF had lost its air superiority to some of the most modern fighter aircraft of the time, including MiG-23s, Sukhoi-27s and a range of sophisticated helicopters, none of which Pretoria was able to either match or counter.

A ragged bunch of South African troopies proudly display one of their battle trophies – a Soviet main battle tank knocked out by 'soft-skinned' Ratel infantry combat vehicles in one of many confrontations in south Angola.

A shirtless Colonel Jan Breytenbach with friends during Operation Savannah.

… after action, satisfaction … (Photo sourced to Roland de Vries)

Alouette gunship pilot's-eye-view of one of the front line camps (Author's photo, taken while embedded with South African forces)

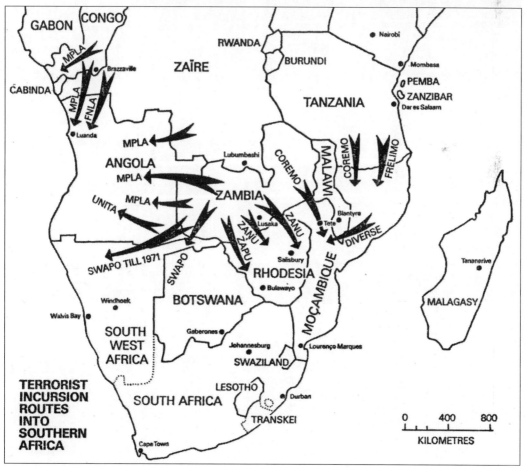

Border War – the threat from several neighbouring states.

Large supplies of captured Soviet anti-tank mines recovered during one of the cross-border onslaughts. (Author's photo)

Ratel crew after pre-attack briefing deep inside Angola during one of the major incursions to halt Angolan and Cuban forces in their march towards UNITA's Jamba headquarters. (Author's photo)

SWAPO combatant killed in a contact with a Koevoet 'search and destroy squad'. Seen here, members prepare to strap the body onto a Casspir mudguard, so it could be taken back to Oshakati for possible identification. (Author's photo)

Parabats bringing back 'one of our own', KIA in one of a series of major battles in south Angola.

SA Olifant main battle tanks go into action against Soviet-supplied armour in south Angola.

Spoils of war – captured Soviet hardware in Angola. (Photo Roland de Vries)

South African armoured units move ahead into Angola.

Soviet-supplied helicopter 'taken out' by UNITA with an American Stinger SAM missile.
Washington's largesse came with company-strength military instructors who taught Savimbi's men
how to use the weapons.

SWA-Spes operations team being briefed prior to deployment close to the Angolan border. (Author's photo)

Youthful Lieutenant Johan Louw, commanding a mounted unit on border operations, 'talks turkey'
to SWA Spes-Ops officers. (Author's photo)

3

An Intrusive Operational Backdrop – Given to an Erstwhile Soviet Adversary

Attack combat diver Lieutenant Colonel Douw Steyn, former operations commander of 4 Reconnaissance Regiment (4 Recce in the argot) is a man of many secrets. During the Border War, his frogmen teams successfully sabotaged and sank half a dozen Soviet and Cuban ships at their moorings in Angolan harbours; three in a single night's work in the southern Angolan port of Namibe. The Soviets could never accept that it might have been South African Special Forces working on their own or have the ability to cause that measure of destruction, something that the Americans never achieved on a similar scale in the Vietnam War. Decades later, on a visit to Moscow, Steyn was interviewed by one of the Soviet commanders originally deployed in Angola.

Part 1

Q. *In the history of the world's Special Forces there are many pages describing unique, masterly operations in which persistence and decisiveness of just a few people tipped the scales in favour of one of the contending parties. Undoubtedly, one such operation which took place in 1987 was 4 Reconnaissance Regiment's Operation Coolidge, which was aimed to destroy the Cuito River bridge. What can you say about the event?*

A. Yes indeed, this was arguably one of the most unusual operations conducted by 4 Recce during the course of the 23-year Border War.[1] The diving teams entered the Cuito River, unit-by-unit

---

1   Editor/translator's note: The information above is likely to shock even the most experienced scuba-diving professional – swims totalling 40 kilometres with fins – even when drifting with the current (which becomes stronger in the rainy season and which was when the operation was carried out). Then the actual dive and dangerous bottom work: installation of the bombs in conditions of zero-visibility coupled to very powerful currents and in total darkness. The launching of the operation was fraught: no kayaks, no underwater scooters. In the kind of wetsuits we had a quarter century or more ago, together with the additional gear like heavy re-breathers, our weapons and bombs on neutral-buoyancy buoys, only extremely well-trained operators could manage it.

   In this respect says Douw Steyn: 'You must remember we did that while we were young and very, very fit – now we are only young.' Then he adds, 'The flow of the river was powerful and most of the time we just drifted along keeping direction with our fins and trying to avoid the crocodiles.'

at last light about 40 kilometres upstream from the bridge. They swam most of the way above the water, dived at the bridge, planted the bombs and were then required to swim another 20 kilometres to a point where they were picked up by a helicopter. I was not part of that raiding team but I initially did a reconnaissance of the bridge and surrounding areas. I also assisted in the planning of the operation and the final training of the team in rivers in South Africa and Namibia.

A brief clarification is called for: The Cuito River flows from the north southwards, towards the Namibian frontier. The distance between the target bridge and the Namibian border is about 300 kilometres. How did the South African divers make it to the starting point which is 40 kilometres upstream from the bridge, well into Angolan territory? The answer to this question quite simply is with the help of UNITA – using the so-called 'Savimbi Trail'. Our interviewee refrained from denying this assumption. On the contrary, he fully confirmed it, 'You are 100 percent correct – that is how we infiltrated. Remember the old saying: time spent on reconnaissance is never wasted. After our initial reconnaissance, we would also involve ourselves in very detailed planning.'

Q. *Will you please share with us what you know about the act of sabotage that took place in the port of Luanda June 30, 1984, when unrecognised operators blew up East Germany's 7,000-ton commercial ship* Arendsee *and the Angolan vessel* Lundoge? *Was it an operation of 4 Recce? Can you tell us about the planning and execution?*

A. It was one of 4 Recce's first diving operations, launched from one of our Daphne Class submarines that had surfaced close to the harbour mouth with two rubber boats and eight divers.

Q. *June 5, 1986, at night, in the port of Namibe, Soviet dry-cargo freighters* Captain Chirkov *(16,000 tons) and* Captain Vislobokov *(12,000 tons) that had delivered about 20 thousand tons of war* materiel *for FAPLA, SWAPO and the ANC, as well as the Cuban steamer* Habana *(6,000 tons) with a cargo of food supplies, were blown up. South Africa said at the time that it had nothing to do with it. But combat divers of the Soviet Black Sea Fleet managed to disarm one of the dud mines. The mine had 'DD' marking and bore the serial number 13. Its design and mix of parts allowed us to conclude unambiguously that it had been made in a country that possessed a high level of technology. According to the Intelligence Directorate of the Soviet Navy, in those days in southern Africa, an operation of such level and scale could only be carried out by professionals from SADF Special Forces specialising in maritime sabotage. Of course, that must have been the Recces. Was that an operation of 4 Recce? Did you take direct part in it and can you give us more details?*

A. Yes, it was a 4 Recce operation, and it also was the first operation where we jointly deployed a land sabotage team as well as a diving team together. We did the operation with two naval strike crafts, each carrying two ski-boats; the diving team on one ship and the land sabotage team on the other. Each boat team consisted of two members per ski-boat and the entire operation was synchronised by time. On all our operations we never talked to each other, except in extreme cases – then we would only use Afrikaans. The story told by Riaan Labuchagne is quite true, and I did get many problems because I did sabotage targets that were not on my list. As in some of your writings, the divers never left the water to attack the ships. They swam above the water after they were dropped off by our ski-boats (Barracudas), and on coming close to their respective targets they dived in order to attach their limpet mines.

All the special equipment we used, including all sabotage bombs, were created by ourselves and made by a company called EMLC. This was a company specially working for our Special Forces; they performed research and designed and manufactured almost all our equipment.

Q. *In 1981, I, Sergei Kolomnin, was in Luanda when Petrangol Oil Refinery was blasted – I remember this incident very well. I take it that that was a 4 Recce operation? Were you involved there as well?*

A. Yes, this was also a 4 Recce operation. To be honest, it was our second operation in Angola – the first one was on the oil installations in the Port of Lobito in 1980. I was the commander in that operation and did all the planning and training. I had four teams each of two or three men that infiltrated the target, with me stationed at a command post just outside the refinery, once again coordinating the op by time only. One team consisting of three soldiers was commanded by Captain de Kock – when he attached a bomb to one of the tanks the bomb exploded and blew him – he was totally gone. The other two guys were seriously injured but with very good training in emergencies, we recovered both those guys while the Angolans were all over us. On the next day, there were propaganda photos published with a piece of his foot – that was the only part of him that was recovered. It was a very sad day in my military career because he was my very close friend.

This operation was also executed by two of our navy's strike craft. They launched us about 15 kilometres from the harbour mouth. The story in *Silent War* is a true reflection of this operation, as well as the book written by Jack Greeff. He was the person who had also done close reconnaissance of the refinery two nights before we attacked it.

It turned out to be one of our greatest operations in the history of 4 Recce and in the process, confirmed the enormous value of the unit. It is necessary to understand that the General Staff of our army did not believe in us because they did not or could not understand how to use us to maximum advantage.

On the other hand, our politicians always had the last say in all our operations and to be honest, that would make our soldiers furious.

Q. *November 8, 1982, roughly 12 kilometres north of Namibe, a strategic railway bridge was destroyed. That bridge had played an important role in supplying weapons and materiel to FAPLA and Cuban troops deployed in the interior, and in particular, carrying out combat operations in Angola's Cunene and Cuando Cubango provinces. At the same time, approximately 400 metres up the river a local road bridge was partly destroyed. According to the investigation performed by Soviet officers who were then working in Namibe, on the 7th of November, again at night, a seaborne assault group was landed from several powerboats. Retreating, the raiding party abandoned one faulty twin-engine boat (two 25-hp kicker motors) and 15 empty gasoline cans. On top of that, in the landing area (on the shore and in the sea) more than 2,000 empty fluorescent-painted plastic bottles were found – presumably, they had helped the raiders to orientate themselves. Was that also a 4 Recce operation and were you involved?*

A. Yes, that too was a 4 Recce operation, but I was not involved. Wynand du Toit was in command. I never could understand why this operation really took place. The good thing that emerged from this operation was that we altered all our ski-boat techniques, like how and where to approach the beach and put our operators ashore. You must understand we made mistakes due to lack of experience or lack of contacts who might be able to train us in this type of operation. In the end, we learnt the hard way, but we never gave up. We actually only became better after each operation.

Q. *In 1970-80s, the areas of the central and southern Atlantic adjacent to Angola and Namibia were patrolled by 30 Operational Squadron of the Soviet Navy, comprising up to 30 capital ships and submarines. One of the main tasks of those ships was to protect commercial vessels coming to the port of Luanda, as well as themselves against combat divers. To counter underwater sabotage, the ships' crews used 'preventive grenade throwing'. Also, most dangerous areas were swept with the use of rocket grenade launchers, etc. Have any of South African combat divers ever encountered such measures? Have there been any casualties caused by them? And how were those measures countered by members of SA Special Forces? Have South African submarines ever encountered Soviet submarine hunters?*

A. This is a very big surprise to my friends from the navy and me as well. In fact, we never knew about it. Had we been aware we would have made totally different plans. Also, our divers never encountered any such measures you mention. While we did submarine reconnaissance along the coast of Angola, we saw many Russian ships in the harbour. And I remember, once at the entrance to Luanda harbour, we spotted a Russian ship that was probably looking for us. But we were using Daphne-class diesel submarines – we went deeper into the sea and dived to 300 metres and switched off everything; the entire submarine was in total darkness. We actually heard the Asdic pings from your ships, but luckily they missed us. Or possibly they did not think it was a boat.

Q. *Ironically, the best-known operations that we are certain were carried out by South African seaborne forces are those which failed. One that eventually became general knowledge was the attempt to destroy Gulf Oil's oil storage units in Angola's Cabinda province in May 1985, an operation codenamed Argon. The refinery's guards discovered the raiders and managed to kill two of them, after which the raiding party's leader, Captain Wynand du Toit was taken prisoner. Who was in charge of this operation? Was it Colonel Hannes Venter, then commander of 4 Recce? Also, what do you think about it all and were there other objectives other than the destruction of the storage tanks?*

A. As I said before, I was only a soldier executing those operations that were handed to me. But with the Cabinda operation, I must confess I really did not understand it; until today nobody has been able to give me a reason why it actually took place. Yes, Colonel Hannes Venter was in charge, with Wynand on the ground in command. And yes, the operators went in by submarine. But at the time I was in command of another operation south of Luanda. The plan was for me and my men to execute our operation at exactly the same time as what was going on in Cabinda, the idea being to divert attention. The various stories you got are all true, but the one thing that should be remembered is that in all our operations we had a series of emergency escape and evasion plans, just in case anybody got caught, and essentially, to provide opportunity and time for others to make a getaway. That was about the only good thing about that operation because the escape and evasion side of things worked perfectly.

Q. *Can you share with us any information about the super-secret Recce operation of the early 1970s which is known to some historians as the raid on Dar-es-Salaam? Then the Daphne-class submarine the SAS Emily Hobhouse under command of Lieutenant Commander Woodburn took a group of Recces into Tanzanian waters and they went ashore. Is it true that the raid on the Tanzanian capital was intended to overthrow Tanzanian President Julius Nyerere? Also, what was the group's objectives? Is it true that in order to make it to the shore and then return to the submarine the raiders used two-seater Klepper kayaks?*

A. The only info I got is the same you get from Peter Stiff's book. Admiral Woodburn later became Special Forces Senior Staff Naval Operation and after that he was appointed Chief of the Navy. We wanted to interview him but his health is very bad because of Alzheimer's, which makes it very difficult to speak to him.

Q. *What can you tell us about SA Special Forces' operation in Maputo 17-18 October 1983 – code-named Operation Vine? To what extent were 4 Recce and units of the South African Navy involved?*

A. Yes, indeed that was a 4 Recce operation. The navy transported us there onboard their strike crafts. The base that we used to train and prepare was in Durban, below 1 Recce headquarters on the Bluff. We also used 1 Reconnaissance Regiment to assist us.

Part 2

Q. *We are aware that South African Special Forces' selection procedures were extremely tough, if not cruel. Did these procedures have any specific features in 4 Recce? What was the most important aspect for candidates to become members of your unit: physical fitness, mental conditioning, stamina or anything else? Also, what proportion of those involved in selection ended up being 'filtered out', and how many eventually became members of your maritime unit?*

A. The Recce selection process was never cruel, but it certainly was not for chancers and jack-asses – or what we term in Afrikaans, *windgatte*. We did have a selection procedure early at the beginning of the unit's existence where we concentrated more on the physical side of the aspirant and this selection lasted 21 days.

In 1980, we converted the selection process to three days and designed a course where we tried to identify certain qualities in a soldier to make sure that he could be trained to become a Special Forces operator. Once that had been completed and he was selected to carry on with training, he started a lengthy eight-month course to learn all the basic tactics of a specialist soldier. Thereafter, he was expected to execute an operation and specialise in a certain direction. Only after the newcomers had successfully taken part an actual operation against the enemy did we actually accept him within our ranks.

That done, he then underwent another six-month training course by 4 Recce and this would involve a three-month dive course and a special sabotage course that lasted a couple of months where he was expected to become qualified to do seaborne raids.

One thing to remember, we developed every aspect of our training courses ourselves – all the doctrines and books were written by us and were based on experiences gained in operations. 4 Recce never had more than 45 qualified operators in its ranks, which made it quite a small but absolutely top class group.

Q. *What was your unit's ethnic mix? Who prevailed – Afrikaners or English? Were there any blacks or coloureds in 4 Recce? Could ethnic or cultural differences somehow affect the unit's life?*

A. We were all South African youngsters from both language groups, but our day-to-day communication was in Afrikaans at all times. In 1979-80, we decided to recruit six Portuguese soldiers from 32 Battalion, but it took them quite a time to get them used to the maritime side of things, though in the end it worked out very well. We used them mainly for their language skills on operations in Angola and Mozambique, where the lingua franca was Portuguese and where we had previously encountered problems. Ultimately, it was a huge success.

There were no South African black soldiers in the unit because the majority, to put it simply, were not water-orientated. This was not something unique to us: it is encountered by almost all maritime-linked Special Forces units like American SEAL teams or Britain's Special Boat Service (SBS).

Q. *The Afrikaners are known as very religious people. Former SA Special Forces members often write in their reminiscences that they always carried a pocket-sized Bible in their packs. Some people even talk of having a Bible on them during combat operations. What role did religion play in the life the average 4 Recce operator?*

A. Yes, we are strong Christians and we always had the Bible on hand in our day-to-day work when training. When we went on a special operation, we would read Scriptures and pray before we set out, as we did on our return. While on ops we did not take Bibles with us as a matter of course but would leave them at the point of departure or on board the ship that ferried us to the strike point.

Q. *The life of any military man, especially if he is a Special Forces' member, is usually confined to numerous limits and denials. How did your members' families cope with the fact that very often they had to be away from home? Were the wives to know or presume to know where their husbands were, and what they were doing? Did the service in one of the most secret and most danger-exposed units affect members' family life?*

A. The effect on our family lives was devastating – 99 percent of us got divorced after the war, including me. I had three children who really did not know their father at all. The families were never aware of what we were doing and we actually lived double lives. When we were at our base in Langebaan on the west coast, we only trained at night and never during the day. As soldiers, we were based on an island called Donkergat, a restricted area even for our families.

Q. *Apart from training, planning and executing combat operations, any military unit has daily routines. What was life like in 4 Recce? Did it have anything in common with other (non-Recce) SADF units? Also, did your members have much leisure time, and if so, what did they do during such time?*

A. We lived a totally different lifestyle to any other unit. As I said, we trained at night and did most of our preparation during the day. There was no real leisure time, but if we got a bit of free time we would spend it with our families. Our drinking habits were also reasonably good, and our favourite drink was Red Heart rum and coke … a really great drink!

Q. *There is a popular myth that in the mid-1980s somewhere in the southern Atlantic there was real underwater combat between Soviet and South African combat divers. Outcome descriptions come in different flavours – some people claim that the South Africans were killed by the Soviet Spetsnaz divers, while the others insist that it was a draw. Have you heard anything about it? Have you ever met Soviet citizens in Angola face to face?*

A. No, nothing like that ever happened. I was involved with seaborne operations from 1979 onwards and while it might sound fascinating; I never met any Russians in Angola.

Q. *For SADF personnel involved in the Border War, including the members of Special Forces, it was no big secret that FAPLA planned and carried out its operations with the help of Soviet military advisers and specialists. What was your unit members' attitude towards that presence in Angola? Did you feel any hatred towards us 'Russkies' and 'Godless Bolsheviks'? Or did you consider the USSR as a dangerous enemy? In your personal opinion, how serious was the 'Red Threat' or in your own language, 'Rooi Gevaar'?*

A. We always respected the fact that there were Russians in Angola and we knew very well what they were capable of, which is why, as previously mentioned, our greatest fear was to get caught and to be interrogated by you Russians. In our unit we had a joke – if I get caught [by Russians], I will tell them, 'Stop the aggressiveness – bring me a rum and coke, and I'll tell you everything you want to know.' Luckily, it never happened to most of us (though Captain Wynand du Toit was wounded and taken prisoner on the Cabinda raid and he was held for seven years before release). I can remember when I went to do promotion courses with conventional soldiers, we did a lot of battle appreciation on the Russians because you were a very big threat to us all with all your equipment. We also knew that things were not all that easy for you in Angola: you had a constant battle to get FAPLA troops up to speed, just to get them to do what you wanted them to do, very much as we had problems with UNITA.

Q. *Former 1 Reconnaissance Regiment operator Harry McCallion in his book* Killing Zone *mentions Operation Milk Float, a seaborne assault operation carried out by SA Special Forces together with Rhodesian armed forces. That operation comprised several phases, one of which was the destruction of the Beira bulk-oil terminal by Rhodesian SAS operators in 1979. What was the role of 4 Recce in that operation and what were the other phases of Operation Milk Float? I ask because apart from the Beira strike, McCallion suggests that there were other targets.*

A. I was not involved at all in that operation but I knew about it and that it was also one of the first SAS operations when they amalgamated with the SADF. 4 Recce was still in the research phase, and this operation was done on inflatable boats handled by 4 Recce.

Q. *It is mentioned in literature that South African Special Forces cooperated a good deal with the armed forces of Israel, namely that there were regular exchanges of experiences between 4 Recce and Israeli Flotilla 13 or IDF Shayetet Commandos. Is it true that there was such cooperation? In which period did it exist? How intensive was it?*

A. This cooperation was on a pretty low level. In fact, we never exchanged ideas on training, but they did support us in getting us some vital special weapons that could be put to good use in water, like the Heckler and Koch MP 5.

Q. *Before 1981, the most secret SADF unit was 32 Battalion (the leaders of SADF only admitted it existed after Corporal Edwards deserted and disclosed information about it to the global press). What kind of 'hush-hush' precautions existed in 4 Recce and how classified was information about the unit?*

A. A very good question. There were no special procedures in place – apart from the obvious – to keep our unit's classified information secret. We had implicit faith in the integrity, honesty, and loyalty of individuals to their fellow soldiers and to themselves. All of us knew that if we disclosed anything untoward, the lives of our comrades would be at risk, the surprise factor would evaporate and it would make things extremely dangerous in any mission we launched.

The rest of the SADF and the general public did not know what we were doing, and they were not very interested either, mainly because they did not understand what we were doing. This mutual agreement worked and still works today. In fact, it is quite difficult to make some soldiers admit that they actually served in the unit. I have also found it difficult to discover that some of my old friends have been unwilling to talk to me about their exploits, but then that is how it goes in Special Forces ranks.

Before I wrote my book, absolutely nothing was known about the unit or the role of the navy that assisted us in the years 1978-89. I personally decided to write about those years because they were the most active and hard years of the unit. All the equipment and personal [things] that we used in that time do not exist anymore, and that includes all the ships and submarines on which we were deployed.

Part 3

Q. *What was your personal experience with the South African Army and Special Forces? How did it all start? What kind of background did you have before the army service (family, education and so on)?*

A. I grew up in a relatively small town called Klerksdorp in what was then known as the Western Transvaal and was the middle child of a family of five kids. My father was a miner in the goldmines; I enjoyed my sport and left school for the army in 1973 after graduating. Like most other youngsters my age, we were called up for national service and I was posted to the School of Engineers where I qualified as an officer and a military engineer. The rest you know, as you have already shown me on clips from the Internet, but to put it in chronological order, the following dates were important in my life:

First the wars: In 1976 I served in Angola, after which I joined 1 Recce, at a time when this unit initiated the most intense demolition training in the whole of Special Forces. I also helped to put together the first raiding groups to attack from the sea.

In 1980, I was transferred to the newly established 4 Recce where I was involved in establishing sabotage groups. By that time, we had already attacked Luanda and Lobito from the sea by using my raiding parties from 1 Recce and 4 Recce as boats' crews. After my senior officer course in 1989, I was transferred as the Senior Staff Officer Research and Development in Pretoria at Special Forces HQ. This was at my request because by then I was exhausted and wanted to start a new family again.

I got divorced and married again in 1998 with a lady who served as a lieutenant colonel in Signals. I retired from the SADF in 1996 and moved to Durban because I love the sea. Now I spend my time in a security unit as a national manager.

Q. *Were the orders that you received from your commanders always in line with your personal ideas and ideals? How did you cope with the situations when they were not?*

A. I did not really have any such problems because I was not politically motivated or driven in that direction. Essentially I was a soldier and wanted to do things for which I was trained. What I did not appreciate was when they gave us a mission which we planned and prepared for, always in considerable detail – which would always include a lot of long hours and tough training and then have the mission aborted. This made me – and the others – furious, because the psychological effect could sometimes be much greater than our commanders realised.

Q. *Despite the regiment motto 'We fear nought but God', what was your major concern in dealing with a foe armed with Soviet weapons and helped by Soviet advisers as well as Cuban troops? What kind of counter-action or warfare did you find the most dangerous and effective?*

A. As I said before, we in 4 Reconnaissance Regiment did not encounter situations like that, but there was no question that we had a good appreciation both of your role and your influence should things go wrong (as it sometimes did in Cabinda). We had the greatest respect for you people because we knew your capabilities as a Super Power. It was always our greatest fear to be caught and interrogated by the Soviets.

The Cubans, we found out fairly soon, were normal soldiers, and we did not fear them. However, as an officer that underwent many courses in SADF with conventional army officers, I should mention that they were most concerned about your presence in Angola and all the excellent equipment supplied by Moscow to the Cubans and FAPLA. The motto 'We fear nought but God' is the motto of 5 Recce, and this unit was mainly black soldiers with a lot of pseudo operational background. Mostly they fought in Angola on the landward side and crossed swords quite often with Cubans. This specific unit was better equipped and trained than 32 Battalion.

Q. *What was your experience after the end of apartheid? Did you stay in the army and Special Forces? What were your relations with the new ANC authorities?*

A. As I said, I am a soldier and know little about politics. Nor am I interested. I left SADF in 1996 with very good memories and excellent friends.

Q. *It is known that you have visited Russia and are personally familiar with the Russian military. What do you think about Soviet and Russian combat capability – then and now?*

A. I was fortunate to be invited to go to Russia – what a beautiful country with great people. My first impression when I saw your soldiers, equipment and aircraft was to thank God that I was never caught or attacked by Russian troops. The quality of your soldiers and your people is commendable: you make for a tough bunch of fighters. The life of a normal soldier in Russia is not unlike where most of our unit's soldiers came from, and what we got in common is that when we grew up there was no money for luxuries. The result is that learn to survive from the beginning.

Sinking Soviet Ships in Angola

The number of operations conducted by various SADF Special Forces units over three decades runs into hundreds. Most of these remain secret and one of the problems facing anybody wishing to write about them invariably results in the scribe coming up against the proverbial 'blank wall'.

In preparing his own book *Iron Fist from the Sea* for publication, former Lieutenant Colonel Douw Steyn, founder member of 4 Reconnaissance Regiment – the equivalent to Britain's ultra-exclusive Special Boat Service or the United States SEALS – told me it did not take him long to discover that many of those involved in these clandestine operations simply refused to talk about what they did during the course of the war, even though he was one of their own.

As he records in his own book, 'while most, if not all, [of our] covert operations, especially maritime ones, were classified Top Secret (and with a few notable exceptions, were never made public) there were always a considerable number of serving members, especially naval personnel and other supporting services, who were involved and well aware of 4 Recce participation but sworn to secrecy.'

One of the most fascinating – and ultimately historically important events of the Border War – involved 4 Recce blowing the bridge at Cuito Cuanavale, an enormously strategic military Angolan army and air force base in south-central Angola. By knocking out the bridge, it followed that several divisions of Soviet-Cuban-Angolan armour would be stranded on the east bank of a fast flowing river and would have had no means to reach the safety of Cuito.

All that hardware – many millions of dollars' worth of military hardware (some of it high-tech) – was abandoned within a day or two and those involved fled, usually discarding their uniforms and rifles along the way.

Soviet and Cuban commanders directly involved in what is now known as the Lomba Battle had sensed disaster approaching even before the bridge was destroyed; the majority were air-lifted out of the combat zone a day or two before the entire front collapsed in disarray. It was no secret that they left their Angolan 'compadres' and many of their fellow officers in the lurch, the majority subsequently hunted down and killed in the aftermath of the battle.

Codenamed Operation Coolidge, the battles waged in that region have become the subject of a great deal of controversy.

Essentially, the Battle of Cuito Cuanavale was a series of engagements between the Cuban-backed Angolan Army (FAPLA) and the South Africans – as well as conventional and guerrilla forces – near the important town of Cuito Cuanavale during the latter part of the Angolan Civil War.

Wikipedia spells it out in simple terms, which centre on FAPLA forces initially being deployed to eliminate the UNITA position at Jamba and Mavinga (where they had established their primary operating bases).

Following a number of failed attempts to take the settlement in 1986, eight FAPLA brigades (five to six thousand men) mustered for a final offensive – *Operação Saludando Octubre* (as the Cubans called it) – in August 1987 'with extensive auxiliary support from one of Angola's closest military allies, the Soviet Union.'

They were joined by a number of Castro's armoured and motorised units that had become more directly committed to the fighting for the first time during Havana's lengthy intervention. Soviet weapon deliveries to FAPLA were also accelerated, including over a hundred T-62 main battle tanks and strike aircraft seconded from the Warsaw Pact's strategic reserve.

South Africa, which shared a common border with Angola through South West Africa, was determined to prevent those forces from gaining control of Jamba (Savimbi's headquarters) and allow guerrillas of the Marxist South West African People's Organisation (SWAPO) to operate in the region.

Saludando Octubre prompted the South African military to underpin the defence of Jamba and launch Operation Modular with the objective of stopping FAPLA's offensive. At the same time, the Angolan government and its Soviet advisory personnel had failed to make contingency plans for South African intervention.

The campaign which followed culminated in the largest battle involving armour on African soil since the Second World War and, according to some accounts, the second largest clash of African military forces in history. There is no question that the very well-equipped Angolan forces were poorly disciplined, even though Cuban air power proved to have a decisive advantage over the SAAF. Nevertheless, advancing FAPLA forces were frequently encircled and destroyed in running clashes with the much nimbler South African Ratel infantry fighting vehicles: effectively Soviet tanks battling South African 'thin-skinned' vehicles. The Angolan offensive was halted with heavy casualties and abandoned shortly afterwards.

Notably, the SADF had a political imperative to avoid casualties wherever possible and had orders to avoid taking the town unless it fell into their hands without a fight. Consequently, the South Africans made no attempt to follow up on its advantage and to capture Cuito Cuanavale.

It is notable that by the mid-1980s, the Angolan armed forces had received a massive amount of modern Soviet equipment and had built up their forces in the south.

In 1985, with some 30,000 Cuban troops in support, numerous Soviet advisers deployed at all levels within all the various Angolan brigades involved. This included a sophisticated Soviet air defence umbrella to deter the SAAF and with all those preparations in hand, they were ready to attack and defeat UNITA in its stronghold in the south-east of Angola.

The two-pronged offensive, drawn up by the senior Soviet adviser to Angola, with planning input from the Cuban and Soviet advisers on the ground, was named *Congresso II* and commenced in 1985…

This offensive motivated the successful Reconnaissance Regiment attack on Namibe by South African Special Forces the following year, code-named Operation Drosdy. As a result of the destruction of fuel supplies in the port, the advance on Mavinga from Cuito Cuanavale in 1986 was halted and eventually cancelled as UNITA then had the opportunity to attack Cuito Cuanavale and destroy further supplies.

A short while later, mid-1986, the Reconnaissance Regiment launched its most ambitious cross-border raid of the war, underscoring the enormously important role this unit played in the struggle.

In retrospect, it was one of the most decisive South African military strikes since the end of the Second World War and the ramifications were felt all the way back to the Kremlin. It also resulted in, if not ending Soviet navy involvement in the South Atlantic, then substantially limiting it.

Until then, much to Washington's consternation, the Soviet navy had been a major player in the region, with Luanda hosting a variety of key Eastern Bloc ships over the years, including major units such as the fixed-wing aircraft carrier (with cruiser armament) the *Minsk*, the Soviet anti-submarine helicopter carrier *Moskva* as well as a full range of other large Russian warships like the *Talinn*, a guided-missile cruiser. All underscored Moscow's long-term interest in what was going on in southern Africa at the time.

Aware that the port of Namibe in Angola's 'deep south' was being used to supply the Angolan Army and its Soviet and Cuban cohorts in a succession of thrusts eastwards in bids to cripple its allies, Pretoria examined ways of halting the flow of both weapons and fuel from this strategic deep-water harbour.

The planners eventually settled on Operation Drosdy, the biggest single Special Forces operation ever launched by the South Africans: that was to sink several Soviet or Cuban ships in Angolan ports, something even the Americans had not been able to do in Haiphong during the Vietnam War.

There were 58 Recce operators in several teams involved, most from 4 Reconnaissance Regiment. The contingent included quite a few specialist operators.

South Africa's navy played a critical role, with the French-built Daphne-class submarine *Johanna van der Merwe* doing much of the legwork over several days in the approaches to the target – most times at periscope level. Also involved were three strike craft and the supply ship SAS *Tafelberg*, with a pair of SAAF Puma helicopters taken on board for liaison and emergencies. To avoid detection, the Tafelberg remained far out in the south Atlantic but could come in at short notice should it have the need to

Strike craft involved were SAS *Kobie Coetzee*, SAS *Hendrik Mentz* and P1561, later renamed SAS *Jan Smuts*. Naval Task Force Commander was Commander 'Jock' Deacon, a strike craft veteran.

The raid was a remarkable success with no South African losses. This was all the more surprising because the attack spanned several nights with reconnaissance teams going in after dark and emerging intact well before sun-up. Using small craft, they remained undetected and managed to conduct their surveys unopposed, though there were some close shaves.

In the actual attack, a lot of damage was caused ashore by the South African operators blowing up three of four large fuel tanks as well as a host of electrical installations and the sinking of three ships at their moorings.

Because the limpet mines used were fitted with anti-lifting devices, it took months to make things safe and the *Vislobokov* was so badly damaged it was eventually scuppered.

The Soviets took an intense interest in the maritime attack because it was believed in Moscow that South Africa was not sophisticated or experienced enough to launch something quite so successful. For a long time, the Soviets believed the attack was initiated by a mobile land force and they took it very seriously by sending a string of naval craft to Namibe.

A couple of interesting asides emerged much later. Because the actual attack was put back one day because of technical problems (Steyn's reconnaissance teams had already been ashore the previous night) there was quite a bit of shipping movement in and around Namibe harbour.

This was fortuitous because two of the three ships sunk were not yet at their berths: they were held up by a Greek and an Italian freighter that took an unusually long time to unload their cargoes. Only after they got underway were the *Habana* and the *Kapitan Chirkov* able to come alongside.

Additionally, the initial attack team had earlier reported the presence of a liquid petroleum gas tanker tied up at the harbour's iron ore quay. Curiously, it departed Namibe at 2200 hours, just as the strike force was heading in from deep water in their rubber boats, both totally unaware of each others' presence. In fact, they must have passed each other in the dark and it would have been a very different story had contact been made.

Attack team onboard one of the South African Navy's French-built Daphne-class submarines. The men are all blacked up, prior to one of 4 Reconnaissance Regiment's attacks on ships lying in Luanda harbour. (Source Douw Steyn)

One of Douw Steyn's men preparing at sunset for clandestine ops against Soviet and Cuban ships in an Angolan port on the deck of a South African Navy submarine.

Behind-the-lines landmine sabotage of Angola's Benguela rail link – another 4 Recce operation organised from Langebaan and sourced to Douw Steyn.

Cuban freighter sunk by limpet mines in Angola's Mocamades harbour. (today, the port of Namibe) by Douw Steyn's 4 Recce.

Douw Steyn in a 4 Reconnaissance Regiment maritime pre-strike briefing.

SA Navy fleet tanker refuelling one of the frigates involved in the operation.

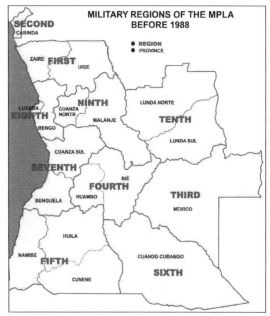

Angola's military regions as delineated by the Luanda regime during the Border War period.

Cuban anti-SADF propaganda leaflet.

Pre-operational preparations with Strike Craft 'gunning up' in Langebaan harbour north of the Cape Town.

Periscope view off the Angolan coast. (Douw Steyn)

Mobile unit launching anti-tank missile against Cuban T-54/55 armour in Angola. (SADF photo)

Recce maritime operations often ranged well into the interior of Africa, and sometimes included Lake Kariba. (Douw Steyn)

The Angolan town of Ongiva changed hands several times during the war. Observe an aerial view of the many Soviet-style defences around the buildings that include mortar pits and trench lines. (Photo sourced to Douw Steyn)

4

The Ratel – Infantry Combat Vehicle Extraordinary

The South African Border War was primarily a counter-insurgency (COIN) conflict, characterised from 1978 onwards by a number of cross-border operations involving mechanised forces with the South African Air Force (SAAF) in full support. This culminated in what is sometimes referred to as the 'Conventional Phase' in 1987-88, during which, for the first time the army deployed its own Infantry Combat Vehicles (ICVs). Brigadier General Tony Savides, one of the brains behind the development of this remarkable machine tells us how the weapon was developed and how it performed under fire.

The details of the many cross-border operations and the conventional phase which came in the latter part of the 1980s are well documented elsewhere and not necessarily discussed further here, except that they collectively provide the scenario in which one of the SADFs most formidable and successful landward weapon systems – the Ratel Infantry Combat Vehicle (ICV) – was deployed.

It may well be argued that had the Ratel not been available at the time, the SADF might never have undertaken a succession of deep penetration operations that saw South African ground forces reach over 200 kilometres into Angola. Similarly, without the Ratel, another of the SADFs most formidable and successful combat systems, the 155mm G-5 artillery system, may never have been placed in the position where it could prove (as it so often did) to be the proverbial match-winner.

But top of the list here is the Ratel (ICV) which weighs in at almost 20 tons. With a Büssing D 3256 BTXF six-cylinder turbocharged diesel engine, it was fielded in the Angolan war as one of the most distinctive locally-produced armoured fighting vehicles yet built in Africa.

The Ratel, of which almost 1,500 have been built, some of which have subsequently seen active service in Somalia, the Western Sahara War, Libya, Yemen, the Central African Republic and in Nigeria against Boko Haram quickly established a reputation for user-friendliness, reliability and versatility. Over several decades, it has been matched by few and become the envy of many.

It was remarkable in many ways, not least that its performance somewhat defied the logic of its design (and in conditions for which it had not really been developed including a combat range of 1,000 kilometres over any kind of terrain), from the deserts of the Sahara to Yemen's mountainous terrain.

However, despite its phenomenal successes in the Border War, the Ratel was neither designed for nor intended to be deployed in that largely Angolan conflict. In fact, its primary role was to operate in conjunction with South Africa's main battle tanks in the country's conventional forces.

As it happened, for the first nine years of its participation along the border, Ratels were mainly involved in secondary roles. Its primary role only emerged during 1987-88 when the conflict turned conventional (armour against armour) – and where these machines operated in close tandem with the Olifant main battle tank with G-5 and G-6 155mm artillery providing support.

Background

Origin of the Infantry Combat Vehicle requirement
In the late 1960s, the SADF realised that its ground forces, doctrine and equipment were inadequate for a move towards more mobile forces and operations and, specifically for mobile warfare in southern Africa.

Emerging from various studies was (among others) a requirement in 1970 for an infantry combat vehicle which was addressed by 1974 when the Ratel entered production as the South African Army's ICV of choice.

The formal requirement included the need that it should be a wheeled (as opposed to a tracked) vehicle with significant protection and firepower.

The evaluation of several foreign contenders followed with a locally-adapted, six-wheeled infantry fighting vehicle concept named Buffel (based on a German design) joining the competition later. This version of Buffel – not to be confused with subsequent development of the Buffel mine-protected troop-carrying vehicle – proved to be a far superior machine compared to some of the foreign offerings and was eventually accepted as the basis for further development. From that emerged the Ratel as we know it today.

Operation Savannah (The SADF intervention in Angola in 1975)
The SADFs intervention in the Angolan civil war demonstrated South Africa's willingness to project its forces beyond its borders if conditions were considered expedient. At the same time, it had no direct influence on the Ratel ICV programme, other than to confirm the urgent requirement for such a fighting vehicle and for armoured command vehicles at various levels.

There is a misconception that the Ratel came about as a direct consequence of Operation Savannah, but the ICV was already in production when that cross-border raid took place. Similarly, while the lessons from this operation were certainly taken into consideration, there were no direct changes to its requirement, or indeed to the vehicle itself.

Another misconception about the Ratel is that it was developed for the Border War (the COIN war as it was in the early to mid-1970s and into the 1980s).

The army had indeed accepted that a new generation of protected vehicles was required for both mobility and protection during COIN operations and for this reason, a number of mine-protected vehicles (MPVs) were developed. Many of these were fairly rudimentary during the early stages, but the Buffel and Casspir mine-protected APCs and the Kwêvoël and other logistic MPVs proved as successful and effective in their roles – and at their level of operations – as the Ratel would be in subsequent roles.

Unchartered waters

The need for an ICV saw the South African Army entering relatively unchartered waters because the country's infantry up to that stage had been motorised. Now it had to be mechanised.

The original British designed and built Saracen armoured personnel carrier (APC) did provide a measure of protection, but with limited safeguards and cross-country ability. Indeed, there was no capability for infantry to actually go into combat in vehicles or carry on through towards an objective, one of the basic requirements of what has since been termed 'mobile operations' or 'mobile warfare'.

It is not surprising then that, given the situation at the time, the initial requirement in 1970 laid down 'desired' characteristics rather than 'detailed' user specifications. The latter were also defined (and later refined several times) but what set the scene was the need for the envisaged ICV to either be or have:

- Unsophisticated
- Devoid of luxury equipment
- Simple driving technique
- Minimum maintenance and servicing
- Lightweight with low silhouette
- All-wheel drive with drive disengaging facilities from the driver's compartment
- Manual differential locks provided
- Simple replacement of assemblies
- Suspension providing maximum comfort for passengers
- Suitably powered engine, preferably diesel; mounted to allow easy manning and debussing
- All systems preferably conventional, e.g. no pre-selector gearbox or electronically operated clutch
- Synchromesh gears
- Efficient brakes
- 24-volt electrical system with a high charging capacity

In total, this was an extremely demanding series of requirements. Evaluating the Ratel later, it is clear that this machine met or exceeded all these expectations with the possible exception of 'low silhouette'.

Why 'Ratel'?

The Ratel ICV was named after the African ratel or honey badger (*melivoracapensus*) – a ferocious and extremely tenacious creature that gave rise to the Afrikaans saying *'so taai soos 'n ratel'* (as tough as a honey badger). It certainly lived up to that reputation throughout its most demanding years – just over a decade of intense combat operations in the operational area astride the borders of the then South West Africa (now Namibia) and Angola.

The New ICV and a new breed of infantryman: the transition to mechanised infantry

Essentially, the switch to mobile warfare and mobile operations necessitated mechanised infantry.

It was soon accepted that a major change in the doctrine and employment of infantry would be at section and platoon level; primarily because the existing doctrine of the South African Army and the battle-handling of the average infantry company and battalion were still adequate – as long as the infantry could be provided with similar mobility, protection, firepower and manoeuvrability as the armour with which they would be deployed.

That said, the basic tenet remained focused on the need, as phrased by one pundit, for all infantry 'to close with and neutralise the enemy'.

The doctrine

From an infantry perspective, with the Ratel already introduced into service, a new form of battle doctrine was in the process of being formulated by the South African Army.

Infantry doctrine and battle-handling at the time were merged with the tried-and-tested battle-handling of the South African Armoured Corps and then mixed in with a bit of doctrine 'borrowed' from other sources, coupled to a healthy dose of 'mobile thinking' – the idea being to produce the initial mechanised infantry battle-handling and related manuals.

Combined arms training

Emerging from all of this was a fresh appreciation of the need for and value of combined arms training and operations. This involved mechanised infantry and armour (tanks and armoured cars) and artillery merging into effective combat teams with combat groups and other linked support arms. In this make-up, there were also elements of the South African Air Force, medics and the proverbial 'everyone in-between'.

A great potential – but 'in waiting'

The initial result was that towards the end of 1975 and the middle of 1976 the army had a potentially-formidable, yet untried brand new combat vehicle coupled to a similarly new and untried doctrine as well as a growing number of mechanised infantrymen.

All the while, from 1975 on, Ratel production steadily increased. This momentum was unencumbered by the ongoing COIN war on the border, except that trained mechanised soldiers would experience service in the COIN war without their Ratels, sometimes making their mine-protected APCs their best substitute.

However, as the need for cross-border mechanised operations evolved the priorities of both the Ratel project and the development of mechanised infantry evolved.

The leaders

Initially, Junior Leaders (JLs) for mechanised infantry were trained at the Infantry School and then transferred to 1 South African Infantry Battalion (1 SAI) for mechanised orientation and then marrying up with their platoons.

This programme had two drawbacks, the first being that there was hardly sufficient time for orientation, let alone marrying-up before they were deployed operationally and secondly, the troops were by that stage far more seasoned in the 'mechanical way of life', having been put through their paces with Ratels almost immediately after basic training.

The obvious solution was for the JLs to be trained in parallel with the troops. Thus the 'Mechanised Leader Wing' came into being at 1 SAI for both JL training as well as 'mechanisation' of Permanent Force personnel.

By 1980 1 SAI Battalion was effectively the 'mechanised infantry hub' where co-location with 1 Special Service Battalion (1 SSB) and the School of Armour facilitated combined training with armoured car and tank elements.

Ratel enters the Border War

By early 1978 the SADF had realised that in order to effectively disrupt and destroy enemy forces, it would be necessary to attack their bases across the border where they were made to feel secure, in large part because of the proximity of Angolan forces. The availability of the Ratel enabled this concept, but the transition was not simple.

An operation against enemy bases some 30 or 50 kilometres inside Angola was already being planned by early 1978 and 1 SAI Battalion was tasked to evaluate the feasibility of mechanised operations in the bush.

Initial trials showed that the Ratel did indeed have the potential to be used in cross-border operations (albeit with several limitations) and Battle Group Juliet was raised with two Ratel mechanised companies, an Eland armoured car squadron and a battery of 140mm guns; plus supporting elements.

It also became clear that the Ratel ICV, not having been designed for 'bush warfare', would have limitations in that rugged environment and would not really be fully operational as a total system before the mid- to late-1980s.

However, a few weeks later an ad hoc dash across the border was launched to rescue a South African soldier abducted by the enemy. The search proved fruitless, but in the process, the Ratels executed their first concerted strike on enemy positions during an assault on a base at Ohipeto in southern Angola.

In the process, there were many lessons learnt and several (further) shortcomings of both the Ratel and the fledgling mechanised doctrine exposed. These were analysed and converted into 'Lessons Learned', which was just as well because eight weeks later the first full mechanised operation was launched with Battle Group Juliet as the main ground assault force in Operation Reindeer.

Operation Reindeer

This assault against SWAPO bases at and near Chetequera in May 1978 is often overshadowed in the media and other literature by the simultaneous airborne assault against Cassinga. In the broader historic shape of things, the importance of that landward operation cannot be overstated.

Battle Group Juliet executed an extremely effective assault after a march of over 100 kilometres across extremely difficult terrain that included dense bush.

It was achieved with equipment that was not exactly 'designed-to-task', in part because the group consisted of untested Ratel ICVs, the nuggety yet bush-challenged Eland armoured cars and a variety of towed artillery and soft-skinned logistic vehicles. However, despite its shortcomings, the Ratel exceeded even the most optimistic expectations, while its advanced mechanised battle-handling was rapidly adapted to new circumstances.

61 Mechanised Battalion Group (61 Mech)

A major turning point in Ratel deployment emerged early 1979 when 61 Mech was established as a full-time, all-arms mechanised combat unit – with time and space to develop both doctrine and the ICV into a true and properly-integrated mechanised combat system. More importantly, a system of Standard Operating Procedures (SOPs) that honed the doctrine and the vehicle to fit the specific requirements of the Bush War was also established.

A total support system was also developed, one that became critical to the deployment of Ratels in battle.

These were constantly improved to ensure the uninterrupted availability of each component and of the unit for as long as required. On the other hand, early 1979, because the Ratel had been prematurely deployed, there were major shortages of spares and ammunition types and still no essentials as run-flat tyres. 61 Mech had never featured in the original Ratel planning concept so priorities were adjusted to provide this new unit with both its Ratels and essential technical and logistic support systems.

How did the Ratel fare in operations during the Bush War?

The overall significance of the Ratel

When assessing the operational combat systems of the South African ground forces, it becomes evident that with the possible exception of artillery, mechanised elements such as the Ratel played pivotal roles in the majority of successful cross-border operations.

This ICV's ability to strike deep, effectively and relatively silently into the heart of enemy-held territory – coupled to its combat power (through a variety of weapon 'mixes' and almost unbelievable agility in combat) allowed mechanised forces to successfully engage and destroy or neutralise a wide variety of targets. These ranged from infantry emplacements through anti-aircraft systems to modern-day Soviet main battle tanks.

It was arguably this long-range strike capability of Ratel that best allowed the optimal exploitation of the weapon's full strike potential linked to other key elements such as artillery and air power.

In the conventional battle for which the Ratel was initially designed (and for which the initial tactics and drills were developed), longer engagement ranges, less-dense bush and other factors might well have been the norm. But in the Bush War, drills and tactics were rapidly adapted or new ones developed; while the nature of 'conventional' deployments and battles that characterised Operations Modular, Hooper, Packer and other extended bush confrontations in 1977-78 were also adapted.

These tended to exercise a mix of conventional and unconventional drills, as well as battle-handling and tactics; together with a great deal of 'bush-savvy' improvisation which has always characterised the way South Africans fought their wars.

Shortcomings and overcoming them

Despite the Ratel's success as a combat system, one must speculate how this was possible given the shortcomings referred to above.

Besides the capabilities of the commanders and men who served in Ratels, there must surely be other factors that contributed to overcoming these shortcomings. So too there were …

Those criticising the performance of the Ratel ICV under battle conditions at face value often highlighted several shortcomings.

These included:

- Axles instead of independent suspension
- Uneven spacing of the axles
- Height of the vehicle
- No large rear door/ramp
- Punctures by the score
- 'Inadequate' armour protection

Axles

While independent suspension might well have had specific advantages, not least of which a 'clean' underside, the so-called beam axles proved to be extremely robust for both 'bundu-bashing' and mine detonations.

One drawback of the beam axles was that Ratels could sometimes get stuck if the vehicle's front axle rode up onto an obstacle such as a tree stump. This was eliminated by sound tactics and drills such as simply avoiding such obstacles, or possibly approaching them at a lower speed or dismounting infantry to scan for them.

Obviously, under fire or during mounted assaults, it was sometimes necessary to take chances and trust that 'the gods of war' were smiling.

Uneven axle spacing

This was a specific challenge, primarily when negotiating obstacles such as trenches. In most cases though, due to the soft under-wheel conditions, Ratels could often just barge their way through using the full 6x6, full-differential-lock combination, coupled to the power of the driveline, momentum, and sheer brute force.

As operations progressed and lessons were learnt, specific drills were developed to avoid, negotiate or occasionally be extracted from such obstacles.

Height

While the height of the Ratel was initially thought by some to be a drawback, it turned out to be a major advantage when operating under primitive conditions. Depending on whether the undergrowth or branches of trees were impeding vision, either the driver or crew commander and gunner in the turret, would invariably have the best 'view' and be able to guide the movement.

Specific drills were employed even to the extent of drivers sometimes giving fire control indications to their gunners when either the view of the gunner or commander was restricted. In low bush and scrub, superior height sometimes enabled commanders and gunners to see and engage targets that were invisible at lower heights and which, similarly, could not see and engage the Ratels.

In more open terrain, as was to be expected, Ratels did present distinctly attractive targets to enemy tanks and anti-armour weapons such as the RPG-7. But again, this was often negated by sound tactics, drills and mutual support.

It is notable that during the conventional phase of the Bush War, both the Ratel 90 and Olifant main battle tanks often had an advantage over enemy T-54/55 tanks by being able to see and engage in low, thick bush; while the enemy tank commanders and gunners were severely hampered by the restricted view.

The rear door

While the original user requirement specified a rear door, this was not possible with the prototype upon which the Ratel was based; consequently, the army accepted the two side door concept as an acceptable alternative. In the end, the side doors proved to be both efficient and effective; allowing simultaneous dismounting on either side or selective dismounting on one side only. In truth, little time, if any, was spent on discussing how much better a rear door and ramp might have been; but the focus was rather on how best to use what was available. Mounting and dismounting drills and other battle-handling procedures ensured effective results.

Punctures

This, probably more than any other impediment, was the bane of the Ratel crews' lives – drivers especially. In thick bush, hard scrub would often break or split under the wheels of vehicles, leaving thick, sharp spikes that would penetrate tyres – especially their sidewalls. Once again drills and experience helped alleviate the problem somewhat, but two later innovations certainly helped.

The first was the introduction of run-flat tyres which made it possible for actions to be completed even with one or more (and sometimes even all six) wheels punctured. The second (uniquely South African) innovation was the development of the 'bush radial' tyre. While radial-ply tyres provided better flotation and thus better overall mobility, their soft and bulging sidewalls were literally 'soft targets' for all manner of sharp objects.

Cross-ply tyres were tougher and could withstand more because their sidewalls were thicker, but they were less advantageous in soft sand and mud. The bush radial, quite simply, provided most of the flotation of radial-ply tyres – but with the toughness of the cross-ply version.

Originally a requirement of the Ratel project, bush radials were introduced by the Rooikat armoured car project and were able to enter service before the Rooikat.

Successes

Given all these 'inadequacies' coupled with the fact that it was prematurely deployed in a war for which it was not intended, one might well ask how the Ratel ICV managed to attain such an astonishing success rate.

Getting the basics right

While the deployment of the Ratel ICV struggled in many ways in the beginning is clear, that it progressed rapidly into a solid, trustworthy, user-friendly and formidable combat system was borne out by its successes under fire and of course lives saved.

Quite simply, the answer lay in two factors: firstly, a reliable and effective vehicle and secondly, a new generation of combat soldiers in the South African Army whose ability, training and confidence allowed them to operate at full potential.

A reliable and effective Infantry Combat Vehicle

The Ratel had many of the characteristics and capabilities of a true ICV, but also a few other traits emerged that were strictly Ratel-orientated and part of most of the South African-developed military equipment of the era. These included:

- user-friendliness (in operation, maintenance and support)
- economy in operation (cost to run)
- a solid, reliable and robust vehicle
- a high COTS (commercial-off-the-shelf) content
- wheels instead of tracks (for strategic mobility), and
- a (surprisingly effective) degree of mine protection

Simple, yet effective

The Ratel ICV was and still is (in conflicts where it continues to be operationally deployed) a simple, wheeled armoured vehicle based on a commercial driveline; developed for deployment with tanks in a conventional warfare scenario and force structure. Yet, it was extremely successful in a bush war scenario without the formal organisation and support of conventional brigades or divisions, and in the kinds of terrain that could generally be described as 'armour-unfriendly'.

At worst this kind of environment was 'non-armour' terrain.

The variants

In conforming to the expectations ('characteristics' and later 'user requirements'), the Ratel proved extremely adaptable and easy to transform into a truly bush-capable system. There were often minor adjustments and modifications, many of which were implemented in the field at first- and second-line level.

Furthermore, a whole family of variants emerged – not merely based on, but physically built onto the same or slightly adapted body and driveline – that offered commanders ease of support and commonality that was both enviable and effective.

Where some seven variants of this infantry fighting machine were originally envisaged, the final count was well over a dozen. As a consequence, the Ratel proved to be not merely indispensable, but also much sought-after by those in the combat zone, ranging from infantry and armour to medics, signallers, technical personnel, gunners, air force forward air controllers and a host of others. Many of the 'non-project' variants were simply modified versions of the original machines produced.

Three of the variants that warrant specific mention are the Ratel 90 (with a 90mm cannon mounted on a turret) which effectively replaced the Eland 90 as the South African Army's combat armoured car during the Bush War, the Ratel 60 ICV and the Ratel Command.

These three variants, supported by the many others, helped to rapidly promote the mobile warfare concept in that the armour component (Ratel 90) had the same mobility as its infantry partners; while the command vehicle enabled mechanised commanders to maintain command and control while on the move and in combat.

The Ratel 60 was an interesting phenomenon as it came about primarily due to a shortage of the F2 (GI2) 20mm cannon. The solution was even simpler than with the Ratel 90 as it meant, quite simply, placing some of the several hundred turrets of obsolete Eland 60s onto standard Ratel 20 ICV hulls. The Ratel 60 was primarily issued to the army's mechanised platoon commanders.

The role, usefulness and effectiveness of all the other variants should not be underestimated.

As new equipment and other innovations became necessary and available for operations, all found an able carrier in the Ratel. Of the 1,321 Ratels produced in South African armament factories, 649 were ICVs, 154 were Ratel 90s, 268 were command variants, 90 were Ratel ZT-3s (anti-tank missile) and 160 were designated Ratel 81mm mortar.

This excludes 30 each Ratel 20 and Ratel 90 produced for Morocco in 1979-80.

The new generation of mechanised soldiers

That the Ratel was effective is clear, but the ICV and its variants – and the men who commanded and manned them were only a part of the equation. Another was the new generation of mechanised thinkers and doers; commanders who studied the art of war and specifically the art of fighting a war in the African bush.

Those involved not only improved battle-handling and drills on an ongoing basis and developed and honed new drills and skills at every level, but they also devised and employed new tactics. These would centre on the deployment of integrated combat groups and teams, invariably devised, trained and rehearsed to a state of near-perfection.

Also, some of the physical shortcomings of the Ratel were overcome through innovative thinking and execution rather than a formal engineering and industrial approach.

A learning culture

Lessons learned from each successive operation while the Border War lasted were adapted or used to modify and improve the SOPs to ensure that in future operations the same mistakes would not be repeated. Similarly, additional tactics, as well as field modifications and improvements, created a much more effective and formidable Ratel ICV as a fighting machine.

Maintaining efficiency

Another key factor was that while the bulk of unit personnel of 61 Mech (and later 62 and 63 Mech) were national servicemen, they were trained, prepared for combat and then led in combat by extremely competent Permanent Force (PF) officers, warrant officers and non-commissioned officers (NCOs).

National Service Junior Leaders (both officers and NCOs) – and more often than not, the PF element that had trained a specific national service intake – deployed into battle with their charges. As a result, learning curves and honing of skills were continually upgraded.

Integration with other units as well as the transfer of Permanent Force personnel between units ensured that the mechanisation process expanded effectively and widely. When it became necessary for certain operations to use additional mechanised elements, there was a ready pool of competent leaders and commanders available at all levels. Successive intakes of national servicemen were trained and within twelve months were committed to their respective combat units as well-trained, eager and competent crews.

Essentially, these modern day gladiators were a mix of seasoned PF veterans and among the best national service JLs in service.

Protection

There were relatively few incidents where multiple casualties were sustained in single actions in which Ratels were severely damaged or even destroyed. In retrospect, most crewmen will tell of how secure they felt within their armoured, but comparatively light-skinned 'cocoons' (when compared to main battle tanks that they engaged in combat) and where the decision to remain mounted or to dismount could be a blessing or a curse within a second or two.

Remaining in their ICVs when they faced enemy artillery, mortars and other munitions was comforting, but things could instantaneously change whenever a Ratel took a hit from Soviet-built anti-armour weapons and occasionally their T-54/55 tanks. Though Angolan and Cuban forces rarely scored hits, casualties did happen from time to time. Landmines also took a toll.

There are no recorded incidents where crews that manned Ratels were either killed or seriously wounded by weapons against which the Ratel was specifically designed to protect (the so-called 'within-specification' weapons). These included tank mines, tank cannons, RPG-7s as well as 14.5mm and 23mm quick-firing heavier automatic weapons.

While always feared, they were most times countered by the superior training, drills and discipline of the SADF. There is only one recorded incident of a Ratel crewman being killed in a mine detonation.

Punching above its weight

Stories abound in many books and articles of the Ratel's incredible resilience, adaptability and ability to protect its crews under the most difficult and threatening terrain and circumstances.
Accolades are commonplace when veterans of the Bush War gather to share their stories and memories; from how the Ratel stood up to long arduous periods of unbroken bush-bashing, to close-in combat (mounted and dismounted) against pretty formidable odds.

However, the greatest accolade must surely go to the Ratel for how it stood up time again to the Soviet T-54/55 main battle tanks crewed by Cubans and Angolans. Given the discrepancy in armour protection and firepower, the fact that these infantry combat vehicles even dared to oppose Soviet armour, let alone take them on, speaks volumes.

Even though specifically developed to counter tanks, the Ratel 90 was seriously outgunned. But it made up for any shortcomings by such tactics as 'swarming' with a number of vehicles tackling a single tank and by fairly new-fangled 'dog-fighting' tactics, with Ratel 90s literarily running circles around the heavily encumbered tanks in thick bush terrain to score hits on their vulnerable backsides.

In the process, several Ratel 90s were knocked out but many more tanks were destroyed by Ratels than anyone considered possible.

There are also recorded incidents of Ratel 20s (with 20mm cannon) taking on the T-54/55s when the proverbial chips were down and there was no alternative but to retaliate in numbers.

On at least two occasions, enemy tanks were literally 'brewed-up' by a constant stream of 20mm armour-piercing rounds that eventually pierced their armour and ignited ammunition. There were also two recorded incidents of infantrymen willing to take on the tanks with hand grenades and assault rifles …

Ratel's final combat of the Border War

When SWAPO's military wing (PLAN) launched its illegal incursion into SWA-Namibia on 1 April 1989, the combined South African and South West African forces unleashed a variety of units, weapons and equipment, including Ratels.

Within less than a week the invasion had been routed and conditions on the ground totally reversed. The issue culminated in a major battle six days later when Ratels of 63 Mechanised Battalion Group together with Casspirs and Wolf MPVs from a Koevoet counter-insurgency unit of the SWA Police (SWAPOL) dealt SWAPO its final blow in the ongoing guerrilla war.

Although one Ratel 90 was lost to enemy fire, with a single crewman seriously injured, SWAPO dissidents, apparently unaware of the effect of the ICVs 90mm canister shot had few opportunities to retaliate. In the words of the then commander of Sector 10 in which the combat occurred:

> … it was the Ratel with a 90mm gun mounted and loaded with canister shot which made the difference. It not only did the morale of SWAPOL – which at a stage was under severe strain – a lot of good but also led to there being sufficient short-range fire support and shock-action available. This 'super shotgun' simply blasted PLAN out of the war. From Koevoet interrogations of captured guerrillas, it is clear that the Ratel 90 was seen as the most feared and successful weapon in the counter-offensive.

The South African Air Force was also involved. Alouette helicopter gunships and Impala ground-attack aircraft played a pivotal role in providing back-up to the Ratels' 81mm mortars, 20mm cannon and mechanised infantrymen of 63 Mech, backed by the trackers and fighters of the Koevoet anti-terror police unit.

This was the only incident during the Border War when SAAF aircraft dropped bombs on an enemy inside South West Africa.

Those were also the last and decisive series of operations where a South African Army force involving Ratels saw combat in the Border War.

A Soviet T55 main battle tank
destroyed by South African armour
during Operation Hooper.

Crossing the bridge at Xangongo
in a northwards sweep on 25
August 1981. (sourced to Roland
de Vries)

Giving the salute during the mechanised parade on 4 May 1988 at the commencement of Operation Reindeer.

Mechanised South African armour and infantry returning to base.

A Ratel combat squad, still neat and relatively tidy, prior to going into battle. (Photo Ariel Hugo)

Part of the process –
field repairs to a Ratel
during Angolan external
operations.

Ratel infantry combat
vehicle. (Diagram courtesy
of Lieutenant Colonel
William Marshall)

SA Army's Ratel 90 in one
of the forward operational
bases.

Ratel column deep into
Angola looking for a scrap
with Angolan tanks.

The author went into action in south Angola during Operation Daisy in Lieutenant Ariël Hugo's
Command Ratel.

5

South African Air Force's Own 'Puff the Magic Dragon'

Known variously as 'Puff the Magic Dragon', 'Dragonship' or more popularly 'Spooky', the Dakota AC-47 gunship with its broadside battery of Gatlings and heavy machine guns changed the course of quite a few battles in Vietnam. It was said that no village or hamlet under 'Spooky's' protection was ever lost to the enemy. As South Africa's Border War developed, the SAAF developed its own 'Killer-in-the-Sky' with a mounted .50 calibre Browning. They called it 'Dragon'.

There were quite a few differences between the American and South African versions of these tactical airborne weapons.

According to Keith Dell, originally assigned as an Armscor Project Manager to the programme, Pretoria had hoped that their fixed-wing gunship would be armed with the distinctive American multi-barrelled Gatlings in 7.62mm NATO calibre (as were those deployed in Vietnam).

So Commandant Boy du Preez, Officer Commanding of 44 Squadron – the new weapon would operate under his auspices – sent him off to Israel to arrange for a discreet but legitimate 'buy-in' of the American weapons. Jerusalem was receptive to the request, he recalled when I contacted him.

There was good reason why South Africa was eager to acquire these advanced weapons systems. As Chris Eager of guns.com tells us in his assessment of the plane, ' "Spooky" was a sight to behold.'

He explains that in 1965 – with American troops on the ground in the Vietnam War in great numbers and needing as much persistent close air support as could be spared – the United States Air Force converted a handful of Second World War and Korean-era C-47 transports for the task. Some surplus SAAF Dakotas were actually sold to Washington for this purpose.

The first C-47s converted as actual 'gunships' flew in Vietnam in December 1964 and their controversial start immediately had a number of successes in areas where the Viet Cong – who obviously bitterly opposed the American presence – could attack or ambush almost at will.

These twin-engine planes that had played such a vital role in the Berlin Air Lift – and by then already antiquated – were fitted with three laterally-mounted General Electric GAU-2/M134 mini-guns arranged to fire through the port-side cargo hatch of the plane. They could fire selectively, either 50 or 100 rounds a second.

Cruising in an overhead orbit at 120 knots at an altitude of roughly 3,000 feet, a converted AC-47 could put a high explosive or glowing red incendiary bullet into every square metre of a rugby field-sized target in three seconds.

Clearly, it was a formidable weapon and the North Vietnamese had no counter until they acquired MANPADs – hand-held, shoulder-fired anti-aircraft missiles.

In the attacking mode, the pilot would start a narrow orbit of his aircraft, circling in a pylon turn over an enemy presence that had earlier been detected by US ground troops. The firing action was triggered by the captain who used the left-side propeller hub and wing insert space tip for aiming, tracers giving him visual sight of hits in the target area below.

The mini-guns with six electrically-driven revolving barrels pumped out between 3,000 and 6,000 rounds per minute and could continue to do this intermittently while loitering over the target, sometimes for hours. As one commentator observed, 'the effect of such a hefty "ammo hailstorm" was similar to that of a giant aerial shotgun used in a combat scene where there was no cover or concrete bunkers.'

The AC-47 had a seven-man crew and carried up to 24,000 rounds of ammo on board, with a payload of over 2.5 tons. Obviously, firing was in short bursts and never continuous or the barrels would quickly burn out. And should it be necessary, the Dak could quickly recharge its magazines at a nearby friendly airbase.

To maximise effectiveness and minimise risk to the planes, Washington's GlobalSecurity.org is more specific. The aircraft typically flew at night with the call-signs of either 'Spooky' or 'Puff', for obvious reasons. Only about 50 of these aircraft were converted and of these – as a testament to their hard use – a dozen were lost in combat. There is no mention as to whether crews survived.

'Puff's' first significant victory occurred on the night of 23 December 1964. An FC-47 (designated for fighter-cargo) arrived over the hard-pressed Special Forces outpost at Tranh Yend in the Mekong Delta less than 40 minutes after an air support request had come in. The plane fired 4,500 rounds of ammunition and unsurprisingly, broke the Viet Cong attack.

That aircraft was then called to assist a second outpost at Trung Hung, about 30 kilometres away, also under serious threat, this time of possibly being overrun. Again, the aircraft forced a retreat. Between 15 and 26 December, all the FC-47s – involved in 16 separate combat sorties – were successful.

Then, on 8 February 1965, an FC-47 flying over the Bong Son area of Vietnam's Central Highlands demonstrated its capabilities in the process of blunting a concerted Viet Cong offensive. For over four hours, it fired 20,500 rounds into a VC hilltop position, killing an estimated 300 enemy troops.

Under the name 'Spooky' the aircraft's striking ability soon became a legend in South East Asia where it remained in operation for five years. It was eventually supplanted by the much larger, four-engine Hercules AC-130 'Spectre', which could also mount a cannon.

Like 'Spooky', initially operating only at night and cruising at 7,000 feet, 'Spectre' was armed with two 20mm M61 Vulcan cannons, a Bofors 40mm cannon and a single 105mm M102 howitzer, which could cumulatively deliver a series of withering salvoes.

Subsequently, the Americans upgraded their AC-130U and it now has a single 25mm GAU-12 Equalizer cannon in place of 'Spectre's' pair of 20mm cannons, later supplanted for deployment against Islamic State in Iraq and Syria by one 30mm Bushmaster cannon. Also fitted afterwards were AGM-176 Griffin missiles as well as small diameter bombs.

As Keith Dell recalls, his Israeli 'shopping trip' yielded no results because Washington would not agree to their Gatlings being sold to the SAAF (following a demand from the Israelis for an end-user certificate). 'That was when we decided on the 20mm cannon instead,' he states.

He makes the point that this installation involved the C-47 and not the DC-3-configured Dakota – the C-47 being the cargo version with a wide rear door capable of loading a Willys Jeep. It also allowed for a much wider arc of fire for the gunner.

Dell's opposite number at 44 Squadron was Major (later Brigadier General) Thinus du Toit who had joined the project at roughly the same time. Dell remembers working together with this officer, 'though his liaison was more with Defence Headquarters, while mine was with Armscor.'

He also explained why the gunship eventually became a priority, though it was never properly followed through, in large part because of ground fire and the potential of SAMs which the Soviets supplied to the guerrillas half-way through the Border War.

Throughout that conflict, most ground operations were centred the basic concept of what were termed either Fire Force or Hot Pursuit Operations, similar to the way the Rhodesians had oper-ated, though under totally different conditions: south Angola being largely flat, arid and feature-less. Rhodesian terrain in places like Operation Hurricane ran the gambit between hills, great river valleys (the Zambezi) and heavily foliaged bush country.

Fundamentally, Fire Force along the Angolan frontier or across the border into Angola itself consisted (with variations according to requirements) of two basic components: a ground force element (either South African Army or SA Police Koevoet units) operating on foot or from their vehicles. Secondly, there was an operational SAAF element.

The normal support given by the air force would come from a pair of Alouette III helicopter gunships flying in tandem. If required, a light plane in the role of a spotter might be called upon to assist and as we are now aware, this simple combination evolved into a formidable strike force that accounted for many successes.

There was one problem, however, that often plagued extended operations in that vast African region that extended over hundreds of kilometres. Due to the weight of the 20mm cannon, an Alouette could not take on board enough fuel to stay airborne for much longer than between 60 to 90 minutes. Weight limitations also meant it could only load just so much ammunition, which might be quickly expended in the event of concerted retaliation by the enemy.

And, as Murphy's Law would sometimes have it, one or both Alouettes would sometimes run low on fuel at a critical moment of the fire-fight. This meant that both guns, as well as eyes-in-the-sky, would have to pull back to base to refuel and gun up. In turn, the guerrillas more often than not would use this opportunity to escape, perhaps laying a clutch of anti-personnel mines to deter effective follow-up. Obviously, a solution had to be found.

What was required was an aircraft that provided back-up to ground forces at critical moments with a 20mm gun, lots of ammunition and remain airborne for a couple of hours at a stretch, as in the Vietnam War with the Americans. The Dakota was the obvious answer and as we have seen, proved extremely effective. Moreover, the SAAF had them in abundance, so that old timer simply had to be the obvious choice.

Curiously, it took a while – some years, in fact – for the operational configuration of the DC-3/AC-47 in its new role to take effect.

Thus, in July 1983, with Commandant Boy du Preez as Officer Commanding, 44 Squadron – which was dormant at the time – was revived. By then too, all technical aspects regarding the installation of the gun were completed. The system was cleared and certified for installation and all that remained was to work out was flight profiles and Standard Operating Procedures (SOPs).

That task was given to Major Thinus du Toit, an ex-chopper pilot with 14 years of combat expe-rience, which included a lot of time spent operationally on gunships. He joined 44 Squadron in January 1983 and immediately had his task cut out, looking at some of the problems that had to be solved.

For a start, the aircraft had to be flown in such a way that the gunner would be able to keep the target in view at all times. With the weapon mounted in the cargo and passenger door on the port-side, it was obvious that the flight profile would be a left-hand orbit. But the gun had certain limitations in its horizontal and vertical travel distances.

Too much or too little bank would mean that the gunner would lose sight of his target. And to fly at a predetermined fixed angle of bank was neither viable nor practical: that would have meant the pilot had to fly at a mathematically calculated distance *away* from the target and this too was not feasible. Essentially, a more practical solution had to be managed.

It was found that if the pilot was seated in the co-pilot's seat (on the right-hand side of the aircraft because of the attack configuration) and did the flying, at the same time keeping the target in the frame of the small window on the left-hand side (the commander's customary side) of the cockpit, the gunner had no problem fixing onto the target. Occasionally the pilot would be obliged to use his left hand to keep the other pilot's head out of the way for him to have a clearer view of the target area.

Another problem was linked to air force culture and tradition, which goes back a long way. The Dakota, being a freighter, was customarily flown by transport pilots, most of whom played an indispensable and valuable role throughout the war. However, coming under direct fire from the ground was not part of their daily routine: it happened in the operational area of course, but rarely.

Yet, the threat was real. The enemy on the ground carried the usual Soviet-Bloc squad weapons centred on the AK but included the full range of light machine guns, RPG-7 rocket grenades – which could do a lot of damage to low-flying aircraft (it has a 900 metre self-destruct radius) – and quite often SAM-7/Strela heat-seeking missiles. Neall Ellis had three of these supersonic missiles fired at his helicopter during Operation Super but all missed because he either took evasive action or those firing them were not that well trained.

Heavy-calibre anti-aircraft guns were rarely a threat because the AC-47 gunship would never be used in an attack on an enemy base or fixed targets. They were around of course, and there was cognisance of that threat as well.

So, a few calculations were made. Considering the average height at which the aircraft flew, coupled to the distance from the target, the average speed of the aircraft and the muzzle-velocity of an AK-47 bullet (and an RPG-7 missile) it was easy to determine that for the enemy to fire at the aircraft and strike it, the enemy marksman would have to lead by between seven to eleven aircraft lengths.

A lot of thought was put into this work and it was finally believed that it would be unlikely that the guerrillas on the ground had either the understanding or ability to be successful. Certainly, they were not trained for it.

While the SAM-7 ground-to-air missile was a threat at the start of the war and previously against Portugal's air force, the guerrillas downed several aircraft, after which missile counter-measures were soon made effective. Also, SAMs were not deployed all that extensively by the enemy, one reason being that Cuban and Angolan pilots feared being brought down by 'friendly fire'.

Eventually, a second dimension was added to the DC-3 gunship concept: it was decided to install a 'Skyshout' sound amplification system that would be utilised in a psychological warfare role and which later proved to be quite effective.

Finally, it became time for lift-off. Majors Thinus du Toit and Len Haasbroek – together with Flight Sergeant Daantjie Marneweck – did a 30-minute flight on 15 July 1983 in the gunship Dakota 6859, the intent being to test all systems. Four more flights followed, this time headed by Major du Toit, assisted in later stages by Major Wessel Worst and Captains Carlos da Silveira and Melt Pienaar.

Early August 1983 the first Dakota gunship with Commandant du Preez at the controls left for Air Force Base Ondangua in a six-and-a-half hour flight. It had barely touched down when it was scrambled.

Mission L52W took off operationally and apart from aircrew, they had on board a Koevoet member to operate 'Skyshout'. Radio contact was made with ground forces and shortly afterwards a bunch of Casspir infantry fighting vehicles – hot on the trail of a guerrilla squad – came into view.

Because it was not customary for ground forces to use the aircraft mission number in their radio comms with aircraft – in this case L52W – the first question asked by the ground commander was a simple 'What's your call sign?'

Obviously, 'gunship' was inappropriate because it had already been claimed operationally by Alouette crews (by then also in on the scene). The pilot hesitated a moment and came back like a flash: thus 'Dragon' became the accepted appellation for armed SAAF Dakotas.

On this sortie, 'Dragon' went into an orbit at a thousand feet, the altitude thought to be the most suitable for these kinds of strikes. Simultaneously, a pair of Alouettes – operating anywhere between 50 and 800 feet were doing their thing. The direction in which these opposing columns were moving – as well the probable direction of the enemy – was quickly established. Shortly afterwards, the Koevoet team started to approach an area of thick vegetation, always a risky option.

Once there, experience in the past had proved that the enemy would use as much of the heavy foliage around them to establish an ambush position. Commandant du Preez decided to play his hand.

With 'Skyshout' on full blast urging the guerrillas below to surrender or be killed, Flight Sergeant Marneweck delivered a burst of flushing fire into some thick vegetation ahead of the advancing ground force. This was effective because a couple of minutes later the ground force commander reported that the burst had sprayed an area close to the enemy and that there had been some casualties, an observation made by some of the police trackers on the ground.

The next moment everything changed, with some of the enemy careering out of clusters of thick vegetation into an open clearing, followed by several Casspirs. With the enemy in full view of four sets of gunners – the helicopter gunships, the Casspirs and 'Dragon', the outcome was brief but bloody. The episode was described later as a 'textbook' operation and an entire guerrilla contingent that had been active in the area for weeks was eliminated.

'Dragon' was subsequently also deployed to enforce a regional after-dark curfew adjacent to the Angolan border and again 'Skyshout' played its part.

Keith Dell came into this picture after a long stint on Puma helicopters, having been active in the Rhodesian War, cross-border raids into Mozambique as well as hostilities fringing south Angola (more often than not into that former Portuguese territory after Lisbon had withdrawn her forces).

Having been downed in Angola by enemy 12.7mm anti-aircraft fire while at the controls of a Puma in 1982, he was posted to 44 Squadron a year later. Prior to that, he recalls, he had been on a maintenance test pilot course at TFDC, which was actually training for project management and maintenance test flying.

As he declared, 'My main experiments during this phase involved night interdiction of enemy convoys bringing resupplies to SWAPO guerrilla units. They kind of preferred the dark hours for pretty obvious reasons, so we used night vision goggles (NVGs) while the commander and the gunner had laser designators (these were not issued by the SADF, but, as he told me, the equipment had to be bought with their own money from a gun shop in Pretoria).

Keith Dell continues:

> On board the Dakota while in flight operationally over potentially hostile terrain, we were initially faced with the problem of communications between the cockpit and the gunner. It did not help that the pilot had to indicate where the target was situated: he had to actually

physically show him, which was difficult in the dark because the two were separated by a gap of approximately a dozen metres.

To counter this, the commander would point his laser designator at a specific selected target below. The gunner would then light up and move his laser designator beam over the same target as the commander and then wait for the instruction to fire.

Typically, we would try to 'box-in' a convoy on the sand roads by initially disabling both the lead and last vehicles. Other trucks in the group would usually rush off the road and try to secrete themselves under whatever trees were nearby, some getting stuck in the sand and as a result, making for fairly easy targets. But it was fruitless because with our NVGs we could clearly see the hopefully hidden trucks, almost as plain as day.

We were successful quite a few times, but I think ultimately the scenario in Angola started to become increasingly dangerous for our slow transport aircraft. The Soviets were pumping more and more anti-aircraft weapons into the country and some of it was quite deadly, like the twin- or four-barrelled ZSUs. And of course there was any number of RPG-7s that began to proliferate at an astonishing pace, never mind SAM-7s. The 'Dragon' crews were especially vulnerable because we did not fully trust the counter-Strela modifications on our Daks.

Finally, in 1983, Captain Colin Green was hit in the elevator of his DC-3 while flying over Ovamboland on a run out towards Ruacana – he was lucky that he didn't have his tail removed but managed to limp back to base.

It was a powerful MANPAD blast, and by some miracle, Green managed to bring the plane in safely into Ondangua, made all the more dramatic because several senior SADF generals – as well as the commander of Sector 10 – were on board.

That was the catalyst, reckoned Dell, that started restricting 'Dragon' operations in Angola, and in retrospect, he reckons, it was a sensible choice.

It is worth mentioning that all SAAF DC-3s – as well as DC-4 electronic intelligence (ELINT) operations – involved a fairly small pool of pilots and flight engineers, the majority of whom had a background of combat in helicopters.

Obviously, secrecy was paramount and nobody spoke about what they did. As a result, not all SAAF Dakota pilots were aware of these events and a few have even queried their authenticity.

They no longer have that need because it is all here, chapter and verse …

.50 Browning on the SAAF Dragon Gunship. It worked well but the planes became too vulnerable. (Source Peter 'Crow' Stannard)

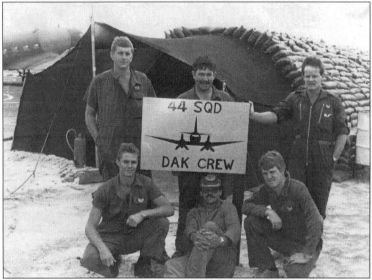

Air crew from 44 Squadron at Ondangua Air Force base. (Sourced to Keith Dell)

An American AC-47 in Vietnam, which subsequently inspired the use of this destructive weapon in one of several Central American guerrilla wars. (Al Venter's collection)

Dakota air and ground crews gather for a group photo. (Sourced to Keith Dell)

The AC-47 was adapted for various gun platforms in a variety of 20th Century wars, from Vietnam to Central America.

Dak 'Dragon' gunner ready for action.

Weapons mounted on 'Spooky' Douglas AC-47Ds similar to those deployed in El Salvador.

44 Squadron crew back at base.

Basic four-barrelled Gatling fitted to the Dakota.

Deadly – an American Spooky-AC-47 Gunship deployed in Vietnam.

El Salvador's 'Spooky' AC-47 Gunship. (Al Venter collection, taken while he was operational in El Salvador's guerrilla war)

6

Angola's War in the Air: A Commanding Perspective from the late Lieutenant General Denis Earp

Brigadier Peter Stannard – known to his friends as 'Crow' – spent a lot of time on combat duties flying helicopters during the course of the Border War. He is a good friend of Lieutenant General Earp who, prior to becoming head of the SAAF, flew fighter planes against Communist Chinese forces in Korea and after being shot down, spent two years as a prisoner of war. 'Stannard's book on the life of General Denis Earp is titled *Beyond the Edge of the Sky* and this excerpt details some of the events during the course of the Angolan War, as related by the general himself.

Our military operations against SWAPO[1] in South West Africa (SWA) and Angola cover a very long period. Starting in 1966 and going on right through until 1989 – almost a quarter century or more than twice as long as the Portuguese fought their colonial wars in Africa.

My personal involvement started in 1968 and continued until I retired as Chief of the Air Force in June 1988. This military involvement cost me a great deal of energy and tragically, would also lead to the death of my son, Michael, when he was shot down in a Puma helicopter in January 1982.

In 1968 the SAAF started helping the Portuguese in Angola, and to achieve this we based our main air operations centre at Rundu in South West Africa. This support operation was classified as top secret in those days, and it was really the beginning of the days that we often referred to as '*mag-nie-sê-nie*' (may not say, nor talk about).

Pilots and aircrew that operated from Rundu wore Portuguese uniforms, and were not allowed to take photographs, nor were they permitted to make any compromising entries in their flying logbooks. Ultimately, this decision – not to allow these aviators to record their missions – led to a lot of historical data being lost forever.

---

1   SWAPO is the acronym for South West Africa People's Organisation, a guerrilla force backed by the Soviet Union and Cuban forces. It was founded in April 1960 as the successor to the Ovamboland People's Organisation. There was also SWAPO's military wing, the People's Liberation Army of Namibia (PLAN). Most prominent among its founders was Sam Nujoma, who renamed the party to show that it represented all the people of South West Africa (renamed Namibia after the Border War ended). During the conflict, the organisation had its base largely among the Ovambo people of northern Namibia, who constituted nearly half the country's total population.

The first person to go up to Rundu as head of the Air Component was Larry Eagar, from June to mid-July 1968. He was followed by Mike Muller, mid-July to August, and I was dispatched to Rundu as his relief.

In theory, all I was supposed to do was to ensure that our helicopters – all French-built Alouette IIIs – were allocated correctly to the Portuguese and not misused. But again, because of my interest in counter-insurgency warfare (which is what was seriously troubling the Portuguese at the time and ended up as an 11-year long guerrilla war), I started to get involved in some of the planning of those operations. I would attend planning sessions with Ben Roos, then an army commandant or 'half colonel'.

Ben later featured in Operation Savannah as a brigadier, when he operated out of a small town north of Luanda. Because he could speak Portuguese, he was appointed liaison officer and stationed at Serpa Pinto; a modest town in the south of the country and in the process was in direct contact with a Colonel Neves Pedro, the army commander of the area.

Nothing was ever clear-cut with the Portuguese because Neves Pedro, in turn, fell under the command of the governor of the district, who was a naval Lieutenant Commander ...

The colonel was from the old school Portuguese Army. He did not know much about Africa and I don't think that he particularly wanted to know too much. Typically, the average Portuguese senior officer would look at the terrain where an operation was scheduled to take place, and then they'd say: 'It's impossible, we cannot go in there. Only terrorists can operate there!'

I knew that soldiers could operate in that area, and so did Ben Roos. As a result, between us, we involved ourselves in the setting up of Portuguese operations and figured out how to manipulate Neves Pedro. Basically, we did this by talking around and around the point, and then suddenly saying to him, 'We think that's a brilliant idea colonel; we think that your idea will work!'

He would look a little puzzled and then because everybody would applaud, he really thought that it was his idea!

Operations thereafter became slightly more successful, but we were always saddled with one basic problem, namely the lack of good tactical intelligence. We just did not seem to be able to catch the enemy in his camp and take him by surprise. Sometimes, when the soldiers arrived at a specific place that we had information about, they could see that the insurgents had left in haste some minutes before.

While I was working in Rundu, Ken Smith, a man from my squadron, was the person seconded to liaise with the Portuguese in Cuito Cuanavale, and General Fraser, then General Officer Commanding Joint Combat Forces (BGGGM)[2], wanted to know from us: 'What is the quality of the Portuguese troops?'

We explained that the Portuguese had saturated Angola with a real hotchpotch of troops and combatants. There were the poor conscripted national servicemen who definitely did not want to be in Angola (or anywhere in Africa for that matter). They dreaded the possibility of getting into a scrap, and maybe being wounded, or worse still – killed. Good medical attention was always a long way from the combat areas and there was never any certainty of getting a quick evacuation. Their officers were career appointees but they were definitely not motivated.

There were the also forces that belonged to PIDE[3], the security police as well as Flechas (Arrows) which was a fairly successful unit controlled by the PIDE/DBS and composed of Bushmen and other indigenous people. These units specialised in tracking, reconnaissance and pseudo-terrorist

---

2   In Afrikaans: *Bevelvoerende Generaal Gesaamlike Gevegs Magte.*
3   The *Polícia Internacional e de Defesa do Estado* or PIDE (International and State Defence Police), was the main tool of political oppression used by the authoritarian regime of António de Oliveira Salazar in Portugal.

operations and were also deployed in Mozambique. Then there were the paratroopers, who were actually air force troops as well as commandos.

So I said to Ken: 'We need to make an assessment on the ground as to the capabilities of the Portuguese – basically to see whether there are any operations that you can get me onto so that I can go see how they are doing.' Ken managed to set this up, and so I put on a Portuguese uniform, without rank of course, and went in with the troops to assess their effectiveness. This gave me the opportunity to make a realistic appreciation. I reported back to General Fraser on the quality of the troops – how they operated and what was going wrong with their operations.

The bad news that emerged from this assessment was that the Portuguese were really slaughtering the civilians. When the Flechas went through a village, they left absolutely nothing alive. The Portuguese didn't understand that to win this insurgency they had to start, as Mao put it, by winning 'hearts and minds'. But that never came into play. They simply thought that if there was a chance that there were insurgents in the vicinity, or the people merely knew of their operations, they had to be killed.

Moreover, if guerrillas were found to be hidden in a village, then the whole village must have known that they were there, and everybody was simply wiped out. I refused to accept this approach, and after some altercation, I reached the point where I refused permission for the SAAF helicopters to take part. At that point, all hell broke loose: the Portuguese were furious, they ranted and raved and referred the matter all the way up to Luanda.

I realised that I had opened a hornet's nest and very soon afterwards, General Fraser said to me: 'Come, you are going with me. We are going to Luanda.'

Knowing that there was going to be a bit of trouble, I discussed it with General Fraser on the flight to the Angolan capital.

'How do you want to play it?' I asked. 'We could handle it diplomatically which, I would suggest, is the best way. You can say that there has been a misunderstanding. You can blame me if you wish, but you don't have to if you don't wish to do that. Then again, you could make it very clear that if there is any doubt, your commander on the ground will have the final decision.'

In the end, the meeting was more fruitful than expected. We discussed the problem and then had a round-the-table think-scrum about how best to get on top of the situation, and achieve a better kill rate. After much discussion, we sold the idea that maybe photo-reconnaissance might help them to get better results.

General Fraser then asked me if I would extend my tour because there were some big operations coming off. This meant staying in Rundu in Caprivi through September and October where the weather was usually most unpleasant. It was hot and dry, and the air was filled with that fine dust that tended to wear out an electric razor in a couple of days. I agreed to stay on, and shortly thereafter Ben Roos and I influenced a particular operation which, by Portuguese standards, was very successful.

Of course Colonel Neves Pedro got all the credit, which one might think was a good thing for him but in reality, it wasn't. Some years later I bumped into him in Nampula, in Mozambique. We greeted each other like long lost friends and later Neves Pedro and I got very much under the weather. He started to cry openly because, as a result of the success of this operation in Angola, they had posted him to Mozambique, to carry on the good work, so to speak. They sent him to the Mueda Plateau, way up in the north, adjacent to the Tanzanian frontier where the war was extremely active, obviously the worst place for operations in the whole country and certainly the last place that he wanted to be. And so the wheel turns, and that was his ultimate reward.

From a military point of view, during the war along the border and in Angola, we never lost sight of the military objective which was: 'Destroy SWAPO'.

However, it is necessary to put everything into perspective and explain how the conflict developed, and for that I need to go back to the Portuguese Revolution. As mentioned, up until the army mutiny in Lisbon in 1974, our air force had been supporting the Portuguese in their efforts to fight two guerrilla armies; the Marxist MPLA and Jonas Savimbi's UNITA. Our helicopters and light and medium transport were continually giving their armed forces a hand; not very successfully I'm afraid, as far as results are concerned.

Initially, on the political front was the Commanding General from Portuguese Guinea (later Guiné-Bissau), General António de Spínola. Colonel Red Mac, from Joint Combat Forces and I had met him when we went up to see how Lisbon was approaching that insurgency and it says a lot that General Spínola later took over control of Portugal for a short time when Prime Minister Caetano refused to surrender to anybody else but Spínola.

In those earlier days, we had talked him into reading General Fraser's book on Counter-insurgency which, in essence, said that after using all the means of fighting counter-insurgency, the end result must be achieved through political means and not through military force. Spínola then wrote a book along similar lines titled *Portugal e o Futuro* (Portugal and the Future) and that annoyed the hell out of the Portuguese political establishment.

Later, in March 1975 General Spínola became involved in a right-wing coup attempt and fled the country after its failure. Irrelevant as it is today, he was eventually rehabilitated and in 1981 promoted to the highest rank in the Portuguese Armed Forces, namely Field Marshal.

While the colonial war in Africa lasted, Lisbon wanted desperately to rid itself of the continual economic drain of its African military operations, but the government's main goal in negotiations was to prevent the mass emigration of white Angolans. Paradoxically, the agreement only allowed the black political parties – MPLA, FNLA, and UNITA – to nominate candidates to the first assembly elections, thus deliberately disenfranchising Cabindans and almost the entire white population, which ran into hundreds of thousands.

The Portuguese reasoned, stupidly, that European Angolans would join the separatist movements and the separatists would have to moderate their platforms to expand their political bases: ergo, end of Lisbon's political control.

By the time all that came about in the mid-1970s, there were quite a few Portuguese soldiers who were tired of the war. Also, they lacked equipment, motivation and commitment. The Angolan nationalists meanwhile, though getting all the hardware they needed from the Soviets, were antagonistic towards each other and sadly lacked proper military training.

At this stage, western international influence lay crippled by ineptitude. The Americans were totally unprepared: they had not yet recovered from Vietnam and all that they were prepared to do was to deploy a CIA man to check on the ground and report what was happening. He was totally out of his depth, and he simply said that the MPLA was a communist movement and that it appeared to him that the MPLA was likely to win.

The French, the Americans and the British, all indicated to South Africa, not on an open government forum, but through agents, that South Africa should support UNITA and try to stop the Marxist MPLA guerrilla group from taking over completely. High Commissioner Admiral Rosa Coutinho – a committed communist – now openly gave Portuguese military equipment to the MPLA forces.

South Africa by then had been suckered by the Western Powers into helping them out and it was enormously frustrating. As military men, we could not get a clear political directive from Pretoria. It was always: 'Let's keep it all secret. Don't let these developments in Angola get to the public.'

More importantly, in our own war against SWAPO and in helping Portuguese forces in south Angola, we were ordered not to lose any troops … but 'you have got to stop this …!'

Abroad, the public knew what was happening; in South Africa however, nothing was made public. Our politicians were reluctant to commit our air force in any great measure, so only the army on the Angolan border went on the full offensive and the SAAF role was largely restricted to logistic support.

With Operation Savannah, South Africa's Blitzkrieg-type advance astonished everybody. The army moved northwards from the South West African border into Angola taking town after town, sometimes with commandeered vegetable trucks and anything else that could drive and haul men and weapons. Afterwards, we worked out that their rate of advance was somewhat faster than the most famous rapid advance in history up to date: the armoured attack of the Germans that ended in Dunkirk during the Second World War.

We reached the outskirts of Luanda, but still we did not get the political go-ahead to take the city. Holden Roberto's Washington-backed FNLA moved in from the Congo and ended up with his troops backed up against a river heading south towards Luanda, and then requested South African assistance.

Brigadier Ben Roos was deployed up in the north at the town of Ambrize. The SAAF flew in field guns with its C-130 transports and they were assembled to assist Roberto in his advance. We also deployed some Canberra bombers to drop bombs at a given time and place.

As it happened, on the day of the attack, the weather was cloudy but the Canberras were tasked for high altitude bombing because we weren't supposed to be there ...

One of the Canberras had a bomb hang-up and the other two dropped their ordnance way off target. Regardless, the artillery barrage began and once it stopped, Roberto's troops were scheduled to follow up immediately. But of course, being Africa, his army first had to stop for breakfast and then had to re-muster. When this huge, disorganised mass of troops finally went in, they were slaughtered by the MPLA who were very effectively backed by a large Cuban force that had been surreptitiously smuggled into Angola's north by the Soviets.

And that was the end of that. The FNLA withdrew and they virtually disappeared from the political and military scene of Angola.

While all this was happening, the Americans started muttering on the political stage. South Africa wasn't equipped for a war and although the United States made all sorts of assurances of support, Pretoria got none of the promised weaponry. Before long, the American Senate was convinced by a Senator Clarke that the Americans should have nothing to do with this battle in Africa because it was none of their business. Therefore, the Clarke Amendment was passed which said simply that there would be no more support to anybody.

The South Africans withdrew, the MPLA advanced and UNITA was up the creek without a paddle. This created the ideal opportunity for SWAPO: if that guerrilla force was left unhindered, Sam Nujoma's army could move freely all the way through Angola, which left us with 1,500 kilometres of frontier to protect. In truth, which only the secretive military knew, we really did not have the troops to cover such an expanse of frontier, even with helicopter support.

UNITA then came up with an offer to keep SWAPO out of the area south of their main base if we would give them military support. That meant that we could restrict SWAPO to operations centred largely in Ovamboland and further towards the west. We believed that maybe we could muster enough troops to cover that area.

To ensure any form of success against SWAPO, we had to continually close them down deep inside Angola. Had we not done that, they would have moved their bases further and further south towards the frontier and once close enough, and militarily prepared – again with Soviet help – they could send detachments across the border to do whatever damage they could. Their ultimate target was to drive all the farmers off their lands and to establish a new frontline ten or twelve hours' drive further south, on the Orange River and directly on the South African border.

This was not a good scenario for the morale of our people. It also meant that we needed to have the ability to deploy rapidly within the contested areas adjacent to the frontier with Angola in order to hunt down the encroaching insurgents. The closer SWAPO bases in Angola were to the border of SWA, the more reactive we had to be. In other words, if we were not proactive and did not strike the enemy in the deep, we would have to sit and wait until they had effectively penetrated our defences and crossed the border. This kind of situation clearly made it extremely difficult to deploy our troops and very expensive on helicopters.

With the departure of the Portuguese army and air force back to Europe, FAPLA[4] became the official military element of the MPLA. Their secondary role was to protect SWAPO guerrillas trying to infiltrate southwards into what is Namibia today.

It did not take us long to establish that they were fully integrated with Cuban forces that had arrived in Angola in very substantial numbers and, later, with Russian military personnel, both of which included aviators flying Angolan warplanes. At that point, the SWAPO high command started to press for more and more movement towards the east and Caprivi in order to penetrate down that front as well. They moved into Zambia and with the support of the Zambian army, struck at our positions in the Caprivi Strip and Katima Mulilo, the biggest town in the strip.

In 1978, SWAPO launched rocket attacks on Katima Mulilo. They also ambushed a vehicle in which Bill Poole, who was up there on a road engineering task, was killed. We reacted immediately and sent troops into Zambia, cleaning up any opposition we could find. In the process, we hammered the hell out of SWAPO.

When our troops withdrew from Zambia, a lot of the Zambians wanted to come out with them. They thought that we were their liberators but we had to stop them at the border and say: 'No! You must stay in your country.' That was virtually the end of the SWAPO story in Zambia. President Kenneth Kaunda reckoned it was not worth the internal disruption of their country, with the result that SWAPO eventually retired from that front.

The guerrillas still wanted access to that eastern region of Angola, from Ovamboland, all the way through to Kongola, and we therefore thought that it was best to keep giving good support to UNITA because Savimbi could keep SWAPO out of that area.

This plan was very successful but in contrast, the guerrilla presence on the western front was expanding. Our intelligence clearly indicated that big bases were being prepared, the majority fairly close to the SWA border. SWAPO would periodically operate from these bases, cross the border, kidnap a bunch of students from a school, and force-march them back into Angola to be trained and indoctrinated as PLAN soldiers.

We finally convinced Pretoria that this had to stop and the only way to do it would be to clean out the SWAPO bases to keep insurgent logistic lines as far-reaching as possible; in other words, hamper their logistics chain and prevent the easy movement of weapons towards the front. Our politicians, by now under duress, agreed and we went across the unmarked frontier and attacked bases. So, for a while, things went quiet.

But SWAPO now changed their strategy and established several larger military bases, more deeply located in the Angolan interior and heavily protected with some very sophisticated anti-aircraft artillery, trenches and minefields. They also integrated their protection with Angola's FAPLA military, as well as with the Cubans. In effect, they became an extension of the Angolan military.

---

4   People's Armed Forces for the Liberation of Angola – *Forças Armadas Populares de Libertação de Angola* – was originally the armed wing of the MPLA movement but later became the country's official armed forces when the MPLA (which adopted the Soviet hammer and sickle on the country's national flag) took control of the government.

An example of this was the big military base at Cassinga. When we received intelligence about the place – it was a regional headquarters, intelligence centre and gathering point of SWAPO cadres – it seemed like a very promising target for our people.

At that stage I was at Air Force Headquarters as SSO Ops, transitioning over to D Ops, Air Force. The intelligence was reasonably good, we had aerial photos, but the problem was that there was also a large body of Angolan troops as well as a Cuban presence in the area, mostly gathered at the nearby town of Tetchamutete.

When we finally went in for the strike – on Cassinga and several other big bases – it became a massive operation and we ended up killing a huge number of SWAPO. We'll never know how many, but the initial estimate was something like 600 fatalities at Cassinga alone, with about three times as many wounded. But that was only the beginning of a series of attacks and raids against SWAPO and as hostilities escalated, we started getting mixed up in scraps with the Angolan Army and occasionally with Cuban troops.

SWAPO was now forced to pull back even further north if only to remain under the anti-aircraft cover of FAPLA and Cuba. This meant that it was harder for them to infiltrate southwards.

On the other hand, if we received indications that they were going to launch an attack, we also had to try and strike deep into Angola in bids to take them out at their bases before they dispersed, which of course meant that we needed a stronger and stronger conventional capability. It was not that we escalated the war; the circumstances essentially forced increased force levels on our part.

In the second half of the 1980s, South Africa was heavily involved in two big operations in Angola. First, there was the big attack in 1985 when the Soviets – certain that they could for once and for all clean up UNITA – convinced Fidel Castro that it was a worthwhile undertaking.

As things developed, a large Angolan military force was mobilised by the Cubans, and under duress, even SWAPO was persuaded that their guerrillas had to be part of a joint force to strike at Savimbi's insurgent army. Had Sam Nujoma's people not done so, he was warned, his forces would not be accorded the protection they had been given before. It was also stressed that the campaign was to be SWAPO's priority task.

Meanwhile, intelligence told us that the offensive was coming, and the build-up continued through Serpa Pinto and Cuito Cuanavale. So it went until the combined Cuban, Angolan and SWAPO forces had a significant military line-up that was also backed by strong Angolan Air Force support. Notably, South Africa's ANC was somehow also coerced to get involved and in the process, Nelson Mandela's supporters lost some very good men.

The aim of this combined operation was to cross the Cuito River in south Angola, head further down towards the Lomba River, cross that and push on to Mavinga which would have compromised UNITA. Another line of attack was destined to swing towards the north and close in on Savimbi from there.

As usual, we did not at the time have a clear strategic directive from Pretoria which should have ordered us to stop the Angolan advance. We should have been told halt that whole build-up. However, it was not until enemy forces were virtually on the doorstep of the Lomba River and Mavinga – close to the UNITA homeland – that Dr Jonas Savimbi flew south and spoke to President P.W. Botha and urgently called for help.

Our government responded to us: 'Fine, help them, but don't lose any of our troops. Also, don't lose any of our planes and let's just keep it all as quiet as we can.'

However, what was taking place in Angola had suddenly become a major issue. Indeed, it was a very significant Angolan offensive and well into the interior of the country. That made it extremely difficult for our air force because our radar cover did not extend as far as Cuito Cuanavale, not even into the operational area near the upper reaches of the Lomba River.

In contrast, the enemy had excellent radar cover and some really fine fighter aircraft. These included Soviet MiG-21s, MiG-23s and Sukhoi-27s, which, because of a United Nations arms embargo against South Africa, were superior to our ageing attack fleet of Mirages and Impala trainers.

And at that moment we were faced with the problem of trying to counter this air dominance, particularly the enemy's attack helicopters, mainly Mi-24 Hind gunships. With solid perseverance, we quickly found a way when we deployed our special forces to carry out round-the-clock surveillance on the airfields at Cuito Cuanavale as well as Lubango, the two major Angolan military bases in the region.

Under extremely dangerous conditions, these Special Force operators, under the very noses of their adversaries, inveigled themselves into several positions in difficult bush country and would then let us know when the Angolan choppers went airborne so that we could then work out how long it would take them to get to where their troops were deployed. We could then also work out how long it would take us, with our Impala jet fighter-trainers, to get to the same spot.

Using this type of *'Jakkals Operasies'[5]* and having briefed the Impala pilots to stay low to try to get the choppers silhouetted against the skyline, they managed to shoot down one or two Soviet helicopters. Then, on a single day, we bagged four, which included Mi-17 armed transport helicopters (NATO-designated Hips) as well as Hinds.

Our successes in a remote part of Angola where there weren't supposed to be any South African military aircraft had a remarkable effect both on the Angolan campaign to destroy Savimbi and especially on the morale of the Angolan and Cuban pilots. An immediate result was that they refused to fly operationally in what was now regarded as an extremely dangerous region. Their reasoning was perfectly sound: they argued that their helicopters would go out on operations and they would never be heard or seen again. Their attitude obviously fringed on mutiny and several rebellious pilots were arrested. I am not sure if they were brought to court-martial, but they certainly got locked up.

Notably, to jump to the next major Angolan operation – also against UNITA forces in 1987 – the Angolans had to pull some of those pilots out of jail to get them to fly again because they were suddenly short of helicopter aviators.

The entire saga of the South African Air Force destroying a number of Angolan helicopters while transiting south Angola features in Chapter 19 of Al Venter's *The Chopper Boys*, published in Britain by Helion in 2016.

During the course of air operations in 1985 it was not a matter of simply flying into Angola whenever we wanted to; we had to wait until the enemy fighters had returned to their bases, and only then could we deploy our planes to attack their ground formations.

Our cannon and our multiple rocket launchers added to the slaughter, and though it took a huge amount of effort and time, the Angolans – like the Portuguese before them – eventually tired of this African war and all went home.

But here again we did not have a clear, strategic direction from the top. We were aware of the objective: destroy SWAPO and stop the Angolans annihilating UNITA, but there was never anything specific laid down. We were always asking what exactly our political leaders expected us to do.

To me, as a professional air force aviator, this was the start of my having to learn another basic principle of war, apart from the traditional ten principles that are in the book. This one, succinctly

---

5   Afrikaans: 'Sly fox' operations.

put, is: 'If you do not have the political will, then don't even start.' And the bottom line, as long the war lasted, was that we did not have a clear political will.

We had ministers in the cabinet like Pik Botha who talked too much. He would drone on any and every occasion as long as he was the centre of attention, including disclosing, inadvertently or not, confidential and quite often, secret information. In my opinion, he had always been an untrustworthy individual holding a senior government position and I was not the only senior officer or government functionary who shared that opinion.

In fact, I never allowed him to be briefed on what we were doing, or proposed to do until it was too late for him to warn the enemy. Curiously the same sort of thing also took place when we worked with the Rhodesians: the stage for a particular operation or attack would be set, but by the time that the strike went in, the enemy had gone. And the question always arose: Why? Who? Each time we asked these questions the suspicion fell squarely on South Africa's Foreign Affairs. That was a thoroughly indoctrinated political body that would probably have done justice to the KGB in the duplicitous manner it ran things.

Pik Botha's chosen few did not believe in aggression and maybe they even felt that what we were doing was wrong. In fact, I really do not believe they were ever solidly behind us. It seemed that at the time, other government departments neither knew nor cared, the logic of them all being along the lines that 'the army must take care of it.'

We restricted our use of Buccaneers and Canberras to those operations about which we had solid intelligence, usually having been confirmed by aerial reconnaissance, which meant sending in a Mirage III RZ. Quite often, combat intelligence was so complete that we were able to be quite explicit: 'Here is the enemy!'

Then, provided that the air situation allowed, we would use conventional offensive air power. But we did not have sufficient conventional air capability to tackle the enemy head-on. Also, we had few reserves and could not afford to lose aircrew. If we could sucker the enemy into a situation where we could attack, we did.

A good example came when we 'neutered' the Angolan Air Force's MiG-21s. In one attack, after they had come out of their cover and we went in at very low level. By using Mark I eyeballs, we picked them up and knocked them out with our guns, not missiles. The situation was not conducive to classical air power implementation and we could only use our offensive air power on a day-to-day basis, and then only if circumstances allowed.

During the 1985 and 1987 attacks on Angola's FAPLA army and the Cubans, we successfully applied conventional air power with the use of the cluster bombs that were known in the lingo as 'Tiekie'. They had a mass of 120 kilograms and had an enormously destructive effect on lightly-armoured vehicles. By timing it exactly right and aware that the enemy did not have any significant air defence, we struck at them with great success.

After one of the attacks on the Lomba, I went in by air to assess the situation and reckoned that our forces had accounted for something like five or six thousand enemy killed or wounded. While this was only an estimate – and a cursory one at that, because my observations were from the air and covered many miles of raw African terrain – it was obvious that enemy losses were shattering. More to the point, without medical support and unable to recover their casualties, wounded soldiers caught out there in the open were almost certainly going to die. In the tropics, an untended gut wound almost always results in septicaemia setting in after about six or eight hours.

Admittedly our artillery played a seminal role in South Africa's successes, but our air power was extremely effective under those conditions. Unfortunately we couldn't go in whenever we wanted to, and of course our politicians were reluctant to authorise the use of offensive air power, so most times it was a Catch-22 situation. If the political will had been there at the beginning of each action, it might have been different, but we were forced to consider political implications at all times. Understandably, that made for very rigid parameters in the use of air force capability.

This was one of the most persistent frustrations of those heady days, not always understood by our own people.

After their defeat in the 1985 battle, Angola's FAPLA army was not at all keen to get involved again, neither with us nor with Jonas Savimbi's UNITA. Actually, in the 1987 offensive, it was the Russians that ultimately pushed them into some kind of action.

We gathered afterwards that it was the Kremlin that mercilessly put pressure on the Cubans and on Castro's direct orders, they in turn pushed the FAPLA into action. They would coax them by saying something along the lines of 'this time, we are going to do it right!' And so the next huge drive to try to destroy UNITA would start all over again.

In getting that far, there was no question that their military build-up in troops and hardware was considerable, all of it financed and supplied by the Soviets. Each time a strong conventional force would emerge, with tanks, troop carriers, thousands of trucks carrying supplies, all of it supported by a series of sophisticated mobile anti-aircraft missiles.

Those in the know might recall that after one of those actions, Johan Lehman was instrumental in South African forces capturing a complete SA-8 missile system – a design which nobody in the West had ever seen before. I knew our intelligence people were eager to get their hands on it because they were sure they could swap it with the Americans or the British or even the French. However, we did not want to trade it, we wanted to analyse it with the purpose of building, by a process of reverse engineering, a similar system for ourselves.

In the process, we also captured a number of the more advanced shoulder-launched SAM-16s.

The Angolan military might that we came up against on those immense assaults was huge by any standards. The Soviet equipment was of a very high standard and more importantly, there was an awful lot of it. It says a lot that – despite the lack of a clear directive from Pretoria when they started building up their forces – we managed to whip the enemy every time.

To me, as Chief of the Air Force, the successes of our operations in 1985 and again in 1987 were the real highlights of my role in the Border War; this, after all, is the purpose of an air force. None of the operations was straight-forward; in fact, far from it. Nor were they conventional in the sense of classic air operations because, as mentioned before, we could not afford to lose lives. Nor could we lose aeroplanes.

Add to that the fact that we did not have the kind of sophisticated Soviet weaponry that they fielded, nor their level of radar cover. Most salient, we did not even have the 'all aspect' air-to-air missiles fired by Angolan Air Force fighters (in most cases, flown by Russians and Cubans). Our missiles were 'rear-aspect'. If we met an enemy fighter head on, we were in trouble, because his missile could take us out from up-front whereas our pilots needed to try to get into a quarter attack position.

When Arthur Piercy's aircraft was hit by a missile, he brought his stricken plane back safely and put it down at Rundu. Unfortunately, he could not stop the damaged aircraft, and he ran off the end of the runway whereupon the ejection seat fired, leaving him a paraplegic. This was a tragic accident that need not have happened because very much earlier we had told Pretoria that we needed Rundu to be a fully operational base. The answer that came back was: 'No, it is only temporary.'

We had added a gravel over-run to the runway, but it did not have the requisite barrier that would almost certainly have saved him.

Which brings us to one other issue which, of necessity, needs to be addressed. Quite often people are heard to say: 'Why did you go to Angola? You didn't even win!'

I would usually reply along the lines that while I and my colleagues were fighting a major war – which as we have already seen, went on for many years – it became clear quite early on that there was no clear political will in Pretoria to win. We were actually fighting something that could best be described as a rearguard action against SWAPO, one of the best guerrilla armies of the period.

In reality, there was a political option that was open for us to possibly have turned our back on South West Africa and walk away. Had we done that, we would have had a Russian dominated country in South Africa today, which would have been a serious threat to us all.

In battling SWAPO from what was then South West Africa, we managed to hold out until after the collapse of the Berlin Wall and the disintegration of the Soviet Union as a major international role player. We'd seen Rhodesia fall and Mozambique had already gone Marxist. If South West Africa had gone that way too, then Botswana would have been next and we would have been on our knees. Had that happened, we could definitely not have resisted.

As a consequence, the long rearguard action against SWAPO was really what the war was all about. Even the large conventional operations in 1985 and 1987 were aimed at stopping SWAPO, although we were doing it indirectly by helping UNITA who, in turn, was denying the insurgents access to Angola's eastern flank.

SAAF Impala fighter-trainer that Pretoria bought in quantity from Italy and ended up taking part in numerous ground-support actions during the war in Angola. (Photo Herman Potgieter)

Heavy machine-gun mounted on a SAAF Alouette gunship on the border. (Author's photo)

Versatile and deadly – the Soviet SA-6 Gainful anti-aircraft missile was deployed in numbers with Angolan forces and got its modest share of 'kills'. SAAF operational tactics soon blunted the efficacy of the weapon by always flying at treetop level. (Pierre Louw Victor)

A Portuguese Air Force Dakota hit by a Strela SAM-7 missile towards the end of the war in Mozambique. (Sourced to John P. Cann)

French-built SAAF Mirage jet fighters being prepared for action.

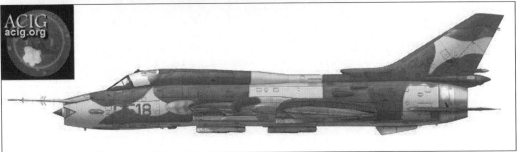

In the late 1980s the Soviet Union delivered 14 Su-22M-4Ks and two Su-22UM-3Ks to Angola. (Tom Cooper image)

The illustrious SAAF emblem.

Impala jet trainers in peacetime livery. They only adopted camouflage once the air war intensified. (Author's photo)

Lisbon never had enough helicopter gunships, like this one in south Angola, so the SAAF offered a hand in the latter stages of Portugal's colonial war in Angola.

Because of a UN-imposed arms embargo, Angolan Air Force MiG-23 'Floggers' were superior to anything the SAAF was able to send into combat. These sophisticated fighters were eventually flown operationally by South African mercenary pilots, usually out of Luanda International Airport. (Sourced to Pierre Louw Victor)

The Bosbok spotter did useful work in that war, but this aircraft was not really suited for this kind of warfare and several were downed by Angolan SAMs.

Fierce storms would often lash the border regions making flying hazardous. (Author's photo)

Tigercat Missiles eventually found their way to South Africa's border defences, courtesy of a friendly Arab anti-Soviet nation.

7

32 Battalion Reconnaissance Wing Mission

Former 32 Battalion Reconnaissance Wing second in command Piet Nortje elaborates on a Recce Wing 'snatch' operation that might easily have been a disaster had things not worked out as planned. He recalls events as they took place.

Calais and Derico, two small towns in south Angola that lay on the banks of the Kavango River were occupied by the Angolan Army, or as it was officially termed, FAPLA (Forças Armadas Populares de Libertação de Angola).

The South African Army's Military Intelligence Division had advised UNITA command to capture both towns. They told Dr Jonas Savimbi, the rebel leader, that that would result not only in expanding his influence in the area but also prevent SWAPO guerrillas from achieving a foothold.

Were that to happen, they told the man who, by then had become a staunch ally, the insurgent force headed by Sam Nujoma would be able to open a new military front in the Kavango and Caprivi regions of South West Africa (Namibia today), which would cause big problems both for UNITA and Pretoria. The reason was simple: South Africa simply did not have the additional manpower to cope with any kind of expansion of hostilities, never mind open a totally new frontline in the Caprivi Strip.

In line with Major General Geldenhuys's earlier instructions, plans had already been formulated to expel FAPLA from several other towns along the border. But the first problem encountered was that there was little information about Angolan army strength, nor about their defence structure in the region.

Consequently, the intelligence boffins approached Commandant Deon Ferreira, head of 32 Battalion to send two of his reconnaissance squads on so-called 'snatch' operations to Calais and Derico, the idea being to get information from one or more captured Angolan soldiers so that broader attacks in the south could be planned.

The request from 32 Battalion headquarters for two Recce teams from Omauni to report to Rundu was welcomed. For several weeks some of those specialist operators had been sitting on their thumbs in Omauni waiting for orders. There was something happening, that much they were aware of, and when the order came for some of the men to go to Rundu, the Kavango and west Caprivi regional headquarters, spirits were lifted. They were also told that specialised equipment would be issued to a bunch of 32 Battalion men for some cross-border strikes.

Early in the morning of 7 January 1980, two six-man teams left Omauni for Rundu in a couple of Buffel mine-protected troop carriers. Team members were reservedly excited about what lay in store for them but they were also uncertain about detail.

When it became clear that there were going to be two attacks in enemy territory and not only one, they were also made aware that both would differ radically from what had been undertaken before. It added to the mystique that headquarters needed some prisoners to talk to and that could only happen if they were taken alive. Notice of the impending operation had been short, and the fact that everything was being planned in Rundu was not only top secret but added a measure of subterfuge to the impending mission that was both puzzling and intriguing.

The groups arrived at the Rundu headquarters late in the afternoon. Little time was wasted on briefing except that the intelligence officer went into some detail about the need to snatch an enemy soldier – two if possible – from one of the FAPLA army bases and bring him (or rather, them) back across the river for interrogation.

As far as Derico (the main FAPLA target) was concerned, the officer heading the briefing was more specific. He actually wanted its commander captured and that was obviously a very different ball game. Certainly, it would be no easy task.

The officer told the men from 32 Battalion that the intended target lived in a tin shack close to the town's water tower, almost in the centre of the village. That would be their first obstacle; penetrating FAPLA's town defences.

He reckoned that it was to be surmised that by not living in one of the comfortable old colonial houses in Derico itself, that the commander was lying low and was trying to avoid being pinpointed by SADF aerial reconnaissance missions. But somebody was obviously onto him, thus details about his residence emerged, together with aerial photos showing its exact location.

After the briefing, the two recce teams left for a secure location on the outskirts of Rundu where they remained for a few days of intense rehearsals before they separated to plan individual operations. They intended optimising for the raid in a period with a full-moon and cloudless skies, which meant only two days of preparation.

Late on the last afternoon, the teams returned to Rundu for kitting out and by now, the gravity of the mission had taken hold.

Every one of the men knew that their biggest weapon would be to be able to make sharp tactical changes at a moment's notice and that they had to plan for any eventuality. Since the intention was to penetrate a heavily defended town where the Angolan Army was in total control, they would need a healthy dollop of luck.

The Derico Snatch

The plan to approach and penetrate Derico was relatively simple. The men opted to cross the river directly south of the village, loop around its western outskirts and navigate into town along the main road running through its centre.

By following this route, they believed they might be able to avoid the enemy's outer defences to the north. The south and the west were not as intensively defended because both were covered by the river. Job done, they reckoned, they would use the shortest escape route and that would mean heading out towards the south again, though plans also included a westward escape route involving several potential emergency rendezvous (RV) points. There they would be able to regroup if they were forced to 'bombshell' (which mean fleeing in all directions).

For the first time since the existence of 32's Recce Wing, it would be an 'all white' team that would was to deploy and would be led by Lieutenant Paul 'Zack' Garret.

Lieutenant Theuns Marais was responsible for the actual snatch. The signaller was Lieutenant Erick Rabie and Lieutenant Steph Naude carried the RPD machine gun with about 2,000 rounds of ammunition. Bringing up the rear was the medic, Sergeant Kevin Sydow. The only Portuguese member was Corporal Manuel Gaspar; his presence was essential since the enemy presumably spoke no English.

Manuel, a white Portuguese originally from Portugal, had been part of a team that had destroyed part of the Soviet embassy in Lisbon in 1976. He had fled to Mozambique, where he was captured and imprisoned. After escaping three years later, he crossed the border into South Africa and joined the SADF where 32 Battalion grabbed him. In the war with Angola, the ability to speak the language was always an asset.

Lieutenant Marais, the designated 'snatcher' was armed only with a 9mm pistol. His main weapon curiously was a 40cm lead pipe padded with surgical plaster and painted black. It might have been crude, but it was adequate for its intended purpose which was immobilising the Angolan Army commander, so he had his work cut out for him.

Weighing in at 68 kilograms himself, Marais was understandably apprehensive about the size of the intended prisoner.

Marais explains:

> During rehearsals, I rather nervously joked about the possibility that the officer we were after – the Derico army commander – might well be some kind of body-builder with a bad attitude. The last thing I needed was for the man to kick up a racket. That would immediately put paid to our being able to whisk the commander away. Obviously, we could not expect his full cooperation: the opposite, in fact, since being taken by force to a destination unknown to him – and by a bunch of heavily armed white men who spoke the wrong language – was probably not on.

Apart from the Recce group, another mixed bunch was involved but on the South West African, or 'friendly' side of the river. They were Lieutenant Jim Ross, Second Lieutenant 'Smoothy' Baumeister, Sergeant Jim Freeman, and a late addition, a black Portuguese soldier, again for language purposes.

Ross and Freeman would set up a command post on the banks of the Kavango, but because of the short distance and duration of the operation which was expected to last perhaps an hour or two, only VHF radios were issued. But Ross also had an HF radio to communicate to headquarters in Rundu.

At 2300 hours, Baumeister and the Portuguese soldier accompanied the team crossing the Kavango River in a Zodiac rubber boat. They would remain on the hostile bank of the river for as long it took the infiltrators to find a lay-up spot to the west of Derico. That took only an hour.

What they found was a position with Derico in clear view in the bright moonlight but eerily quiet. It was strange, the watchers said afterwards because there were no lights and no movement or sound in the town itself.

By then the Recce snatch team were all huddled close together in the sparse vegetation.

Old hands at clandestine work, total inactivity in Derico worried the attackers. No activity in the town spelled one of two things: either the enemy was on high alert or they were expecting an attack, which would have meant that the South African squad had been compromised.

Wary and acutely alert of their surroundings, the team laid-up and waited for H-hour, scheduled for 0200 hours to coincide with what the other 32 strike team had planned for Calais.

For the next hour or so the only sound was that of Gaspar's suppressed bouts of a dry cough that he had developed. Had they known what effect this cough would have later in the operation, they would probably have left him behind when they finally went in. The night remained silent and the town totally inactive.

About 45 minutes before they were scheduled to move into the attack, some of the team members started becoming restless, fiddling with their kit and checking that nothing would be left behind or get lost. It was not uncommon for the men to react this way: there were some serious events waiting.

By 0130 hours, they had set up their requisite single file and slowly headed towards the town. Naude's RPD light machine gun, behind Garret and Gaspar, was the only real firepower they had, and it was to be used both for support and cover fire.

Keeping deathly silent and covering a long stretch of soft sand and short and sparse vegetation, which helped, they moved in. Visibility was excellent with moonlight reflecting off the white sand.

Wary of security patrols on the outer perimeter of the town – which was essentially a military base – progress was excruciatingly slow. It surprised the men that there were no signs of defensive positions; no trenches or foxholes were encountered en route. This was little consolation though because aerial photos of the town's defences, carefully perused before setting out, had shown that they were moving between a fairly extensive enemy trench system to the north of the main road and the main FAPLA headquarters a few hundred metres away.

When they reached the middle of the town, their first real test came when the men had to cross the main road. It was the only way to get close to the enemy's headquarters, sprawled under the trees near the water tower. They began by moving stealthily on along its northern side of the main road and only making a move to cross it in the middle of town. That would avoid what they knew were several enemy defence positions in the vicinity, and for this purpose several buildings to the south afforded good cover to within about 100 metres of the target.

The downside however, and powerful factor indeed, was that whatever they did would be illuminated in brilliant moonlight. If there was somebody watching, they wouldn't be missed.

With Marais moving in the middle of the group for protection, they moved quickly towards the far side of the main road in single file. Marias explains:

> Just as we reached the middle of the road Corporal Gaspar started coughing and it was quite sudden. He managed to quickly get it under control, but the damage was done. Hunched over forward with knees bent and moving somewhat faster, we reached the curb of the road and took up a linear position behind a garden wall. Barely 30cms high, it offered minimal cover against a direct line of sight and fire, or so we thought. From our new vantage position, it soon became clear that a guard hut, perched on top of the water tower, had a perfect all-round vision. The only chance we had of not being detected since entering Derico, would have been that the man was either asleep or the hut was not manned.

Two of the attackers cautiously approached the water tower with the objective of establishing whether there was any indication whether that high point, the only one in town, was active. Soon they returned with the news that there was a set of one-way boot tracks that did indeed lead to the tower, but there were none that indicated that anybody had returned. The squad now had to face the possibility that they had been spotted and that there was a good chance that problems might soon start. They did not have to wait long. Marais continues:

> Laying low behind the wall we confirmed the next move towards the tin shack, but it was not to be. Suddenly, a voice directly ahead shouted out *quem são voceis* (who are you?). The call came from about 15 or 16 silhouettes facing us a few metres away … we did not move. A few moments later, one of the silhouettes started walking towards the gate leading to the wall and behind which we had taken cover. Once there, he peered towards the left, half his torso sticking out behind the gate pillar. Obviously, he had good reason to want to know to see what was going on behind the wall.

Steeped in covert and secret operations, soldiers generally do not take well to being discovered during operations and it was the last time that this man peered to the left. A single shot rang out, sending him reeling. A single command came for the men to deliver maximum fire.

At that moment, all hell broke loose as they exchanged fire with the enemy patrol. A hand grenade hurled by one of the team members exploded under a tree close to where the silhouettes had been spotted moments before. A body came crashing through the branches and hit the ground. The thud was pronounced enough for all to hear. It was later believed that this Angolan soldier had climbed into the tree to get a better arc of fire.

A second later Gaspar doubled up where he was crouched as a ricochet bullet from his AK-47 magazine hit his arm and lodged in his shoulder. By now, the place was alive with the enemy either firing wildly into the night or making a dash for their trenches. By then the Angolan troops also needed to assess the position and the volume of fire slightly decreased. The leader of the South African squad whispered a hurried order for the men to withdraw and bombshell and that was when Naude realised that their only chance of survival was the support fire he was providing with his LMG. He explains:

> I confirmed with Zack and Theuns by radio that the operation was aborted. The next moment, FAPLA started shouting slogans like: 'Puppets', 'Racists' and 'We're coming to kill you' and from what we could hear of a large number of assault weapons being cocked, the Angolans were ready for us. Still worse, we were surrounded and soon it would be the moment of now or never. During Minor Tactics Training back home, Andre Diedericks would often warn us that only you will know when it is time to break out of an encirclement and when that happens, he would stress, 'Do not hesitate!'
>
> Meantime, I was kind of 'digging in' between the pavement and the street, trying to get a good arc of fire at the approaching enemy, when the RPDFs bipod malfunctioned. So I folded it and waited until the first of the FAPLA sections was about 20 metres away. I opened fire and saw four of them were hit and then directed my attention towards where shots were heading towards us from the tin building.
>
> Obviously, I must have neutralised that threat because there was no return fire, which prompted me to 'go now' or stay forever. I just managed to take cover when the enemy opened fire when more shots came in at us from another direction.
>
> After changing drums, I returned fire and made a dash for the pre-planned rendezvous and as I dashed towards buildings on the other side of the road there was plaster flying all over the place as their as bullets hit the walls of buildings around me. Then, at the rendezvous point, there was nobody around, so I stayed for a while, thinking that the rest would soon arrive so I set about to secure the new position.

With the enemy directly ahead and an open road behind them, the team was still left in a precarious position.

To make matters more critical for the strike team, a Soviet 14.5mm anti-aircraft gun joined the fray. With its barrel depressed into a ground attack role, it started to deliver rapid fire from a short distance away to the east of the main FAPLA position. Effectively, it cut off any possibility of escape in that direction.

There was no other choice for the remaining members of the team but to withdraw across the road and go straight over the Angolan Army trench line. That was when they turned and started to run. Garret was halfway across the road when he went down, but only momentarily; an enemy projectile had grazed his right leg but it was a flesh wound so he got up and continued running. Marais was also nearly knocked down by RPG fire:

I headed straight for cover behind one of the houses across the road. As I reached the house, an RPG-7 grenade detonated against the wall just above my head and I crashed to the ground and pieces of the wall came raining down. I thought then that that was it!

A group of enemy soldiers in pursuit or running for the safety of the trenches saw me drop and started to shout: 'aqua – aqua' (here he is – here he is). I went for my pistol, only to discover that it had fallen out of my holster, probably when I had turned to run.

While shots were being exchanged at close range, Marais jumped up and disappeared around the back of the house, now heading south-west towards the planned second emergency rendezvous, the first being out of the question.

But now, with both Recce team members and the enemy all running in the same direction towards the south and the trenches and not being able to recognise each other, the situation suddenly became confused, with the result that small-arms fire slowly subsided. But the difference was that most the enemy sought refuge in their trenches while the South Africans simply carried on running. Meanwhile, Naude was still waiting at the first emergency rendezvous, but he did not stay for long:

> When I reached that RV there was nobody around, so I stayed for a while thinking that the rest would still arrive and even managed to temporarily secure the position. But things changed once large numbers of FAPLA troops were ordered to deploy all over the area, and looking at my watch, I realised that it was time – 10 minutes – to move to the main emergency rendezvous point. What was peculiar was that the Angolans were now also firing their mortars, but these were all detonating in the opposite direction from where we were, towards the bridge.
>
> Arriving there, I ran into Zack and Theuns – armed only with the lead pipe. Jim's pistol was apparently lost during the withdrawal. Gaspar seemingly refused to go with them, and there had been no sight or sound of Erick and Kevin. Jim tried to raise them on the radio, but there was no response.

At the main emergency rendezvous, the Recce team members arrived, one after the other, ragged, disconsolate and with a few of them wounded. It didn't take long to discover that Rabie and Gaspar were missing. On the basis that they were hopelessly outnumbered and that the target area was alert, the rest of the group decided to head for the final rendezvous and wait there for the previously arranged connection. Only a while later was a radio message received which confirmed that Rabie and Gaspar had in fact escaped; they were heading for the last grid reference. Naude recalls:

> After about 10 to 15 minutes, radio silence was broken by Erick's faint voice and we couldn't believe it – the boys were actually alive!
>
> More importantly, they hadn't been captured, but (as it emerged in the debrief back at base) it had been an incredibly close call. He told us to stand by and when we spotted white phosphorous that told us they were approaching, we sent a message to Jim and moved forward to welcome them.
>
> Using white phosphorous to signal was actually not a good idea. Moments later there were FAPLA soldiers just about everywhere, some emerging from dugouts, others falling out of trees and just about every one of them screaming. There was chaos within their ranks as we were to learn subsequently they had about 20 of their number dead or wounded.
>
> 'Smoothy's' party was ready when we reached the riverbank and we paddled across the Kavango River to the tactical headquarters.

On the back on their way to 32 Battalion headquarters, the group was told of Erick Rabie's heroics. A small man in stature, he had saved the life of the wounded Gaspar by picking him up and carrying him on his not overly broad shoulders to safety. There were a few other problems during the firefight, including Rabie noticing that Gaspar had been inordinately slow to react to the command to retreat.

Probably because of blood loss and shock, Gaspar had been unable to get up and run. So Rabie helped the man to his feet, slung him over his shoulders and under heavy fire, hauled the man him to safety over an open road. It was something of a miracle that the pair eventually made the RV point.

What made Rabie's feat even more remarkable was that few understood how he had managed to pick up and carry a man twice his size over all that distance.

Later in his career, while working at FAPLA's Joint Aerial Reconnaissance Centre, Marais found aerial photos revealing a minefield to the north of the trenches at Derico. By some merciful coincidence, not a single mine was detonated by the South Africans.

By the high standards of the SADF and despite recommendations for an *Honoris Crux* decoration for bravery in the face of the enemy, Rabie was denied a medal for bravery.

For his efforts, Lieutenant Theuns Marais was fined R420 for losing the pistol.

The Calais Snatch

The plan was that Lieutenant Dave Thompson, one of the company members, would take a six-man strike force in a Zodiac rubber duck across the Kavango River and drop them well to the east of Calais town, also manned by a large Angolan Army contingent.

The team would then approach the enemy base from the north because it was surmised that the FAPLA commanders would hardly expect anybody coming to attack them from that direction, never mind grab the first man they encountered. The operation was directly controlled from the Rundu HQ because, as the crow flies, it was a relatively short distance away.

During rehearsals at Buffalo base, Lieutenant Frans Fourie, the team leader, appointed Sergeants Pieter van Eeden and Cornelius 'Tabo' Maree to do the physical snatch. The Buffalo's sickbay doctor made up a concoction that could be injected and said it would immobilise whoever was taken, which, in turn, would make it easy for the team to carry the prisoner to the boat.

Van Eeden also had a baton, similar to the one that had been made for the Derico team and that would come into play if all else failed.

The team was dropped without any complications and after laying up for a while, they proceeded with the infiltration. Van Eeden and Maree, using night vision goggles, led the men through a stretch of Kavango River swamps to the bush lane, which was visible at a distance. There was no thought given to encountering crocodiles along the way, though all knew that the river was thick with them.

After the tiny strike force had reached land running through the bush on the far side of the river – they were now on enemy soil – they found a two-track road running parallel with the Kavango. Opposite the road, Maree saw a cluster of huts and told Fourie and his team to stay south of the road while he and van Eeden went forward to have a look.

Maree explained how they successfully captured their enemy which, looking back, was like a walk in the park in comparison with the Derico fiasco:

> We had just crossed the road when we heard people heading towards us. They were walking west, towards the enemy base. So Piet and I moved back to the road and took up position

behind a large bush alongside the road. The rest of the team had been placed in an ambush position parallel with the track.

After waiting a short while, the first bloke walked past our position – an armed FAPLA soldier. Behind him there was another and neither of the men was aware of our presence. Piet and I looked at each other in the moonlight and our faces said it all: it was now or never. In a sharp co-ordinated movement we jumped from behind the bush and dived onto the enemy soldier. He yelled when he was surprised by a pair of 'ghosts' that had jumped out of the bush and grabbed him. At that moment, we completely forgot about the injection and the baton and Piet hit him with his AK rifle butt against his head and he was out of the fight.

The second FAPLA man, his rifle slung behind his back, was trying to get his weapon ready to fire at us interlopers when the rest of the team opened fire, killing him.

Fourie gave the order to withdraw, Maree and van Eeden grabbed the prisoner, who by now realised that he had to cooperate and, followed by the rest of the team, made their way to the river.

Once there, the men went into an all-round defence position, obviously expecting that there would be some kind of retaliation from the Angolan Army. They also called Thompson for the pick-up. Yet, by the time he arrived not long afterwards, everything was still quiet. Most significantly, the Calais 'Snatch' group had their prisoner.

Commandant Deon Ferreira was happy with the operation, except for the shooting that took place. His mood soon changed when he was told that Marais had lost his South African produced Star pistol during the struggle with the prisoner because the men were not supposed to have anything South African with them, which meant equipment or weapons.

It was anticipated that the Luanda would believe that the attacks were UNITA inspired.

Calais and Derico Attack

As a result of these actions and the moderate success enjoyed by one of them, a combined Recce Commando and UNITA operation was then planned to attack Calais.

32 Battalion was given the mission of attacking the military base and airfield at Derico and also to demolish the bridge spanning the Cuito River which lay to the east of Derico.

In support, a mortar group from 32 Battalion was attached to Staff Sergeant Jack Greef, which also turned out to be something of a success.

Commandant Ferreira's plan for the attack on Derico was simple. A Recce team – consisting of Lieutenant Willem Ratte, Sergeant Piet van Eeden, a now revitalised Corporal Manuel Gaspar, and Rifleman Pedro Kasoma would infiltrate the enemy town by Klepper kayaks, do a reconnaissance and place demolition charges on the bridge to destroy it so as to cut off all possible support to Derico from east of the river. Derico's only support would have to arrive from the east, and across the bridge but with no bridge there would be no support.

The rest of the Recce Wing would infiltrate by both the kayaks and zodiacs, applying their recently acquired skills to set up stopper groups in order to cut off fleeing FAPLA troops.

Sergeant John Botha's Recce Team, comprising Corporal Kevin Sydow and Riflemen Pedrito and Castico (nicknamed 'Sandsak'), would feint a deception attack prior to a mortar bombardment: that would be followed by the main attack.

When Commandants Marius 'Mo' Oelschig and Blignaut and Major Des Lynch arrived at the Buffalo tactical headquarters on 11 February 1980, the assault force was already in laying up positions south of the river: they were waiting to cross the river when the command came to stand down. Word had reached Oelschig that FAPLA had abandoned their base.

To confirm this, Captain Daan de la Rey, the 32 intelligence boffin, 2nd Lieutenant Paul 'Zack' Garret, and Corporal Rick Lobb (who had just finished the Recce Wing selection and training) were sent by Ferreira to infiltrate the base area.

It was Lobb's first reconnaissance operation and, as it turned out, a rather unusual experience. He explains:

> At nightfall, around 2300 hours, we were dropped on the Angolan side by the deployment team. We proceeded tentatively and with extreme caution on foot towards the MPLA base. After a few hours of careful walking, we approached the perimeter of the base where we lay for a while, quietly watching and listening for any signs of activity and also to establish where there was a guarding routine (there was none implemented).
>
> After an hour or so of observation, we carefully entered the base from the western side to establish what the headcount was and whether the main FAPLA force had in fact all fled to avoid the scheduled 32 Battalion assault on their base.
>
> Once inside the base, we soon realised that there was only a skeleton force present and that they were all asleep. In addition, we also spotted a 14.5mm heavy machine gun which under any circumstances was a pretty heavy piece. This one had an unlimited 180 degrees fire-arc in the direction of the river from where we had just come.
>
> During our movements and observations inside the base, Captain de la Rey quietly told Zack and me to string together any boots, weapons, and other equipment while he went to work by silently removing the HMGs breechblock.
>
> Just as his task was completed, our luck ran out when one of the sleeping MPLA soldiers woke up and started shouting, which obviously aroused everyone else.
>
> With that, we took off at top speed, running down the hill towards the river. But it was difficult to run at full tilt in the darkness, and as we scurried away, a few of the FAPLA troops had managed to untangle their boots and other equipment because some of them opened fire in our direction: there were tracers galore over our heads.
>
> Once away from the base, we initiated anti-tracking skills and took extra care when we back-tracked in order to avoid being followed, which we knew would happen at first light.
>
> We continued with our anti-tracking until we found a position to the south-east of the base in tremendously thick bush, very much to our advantage. Very carefully we back-tracked into this thicket, taking care to remove all signs that we were near the thicket where we lay for the day, We would be picked up after dark by the rubber duck deployment team.
>
> Throughout the day we could hear the FAPLA troops shouting at each other in their search for us. It was tense.
>
> At about 2100 hours that evening, we liaised with the deployment team by radio, were picked up and ferried back across the border.

Following the fall of both Derico and Calais, only Cuangar remained occupied by a small group of FAPLA.

32 Battalion Reconnaissance unit. (Sourced to Paul Els)

Tough times for 32 Battalion cross-border patrol. (Photo sourced to Paul Els)

Squads of 32 Battalion troops being briefed prior to launching an attack.

His friends called him 'Piet Boer' – a part-time soldier from Vryheid in Natal where he farmed and in true Boer fashion, he did part-time service as and when he could. He was recognised by his peers as one of the best combatants of the war. (Author's photo)

32 Battalion combatant Peter Williams, then not yet 20 years old and having already been in action in the Angolan bush for more than a year. (Author's photo)

32 Battalion Lieutenant T T de Abreu – one of the best of the unconventional operators. (Photo Paul Els)

Early morning uplift in the Angolan bush – squads of 32 Battalion combatants – most of them former Angolan Army dissidents – prepare for action. (Author's photo)

A large 32 Battalion contingent took part in the battle for Cuamato where some of the men were airlifted by Puma helicopters. (Author's photo)

32 Battalion troopies on patrol. (Author's photo)

One of the biggest successes enjoyed by 32 Battalion was Operation Super, where 300 SWAPO insurgents were killed in a single morning's action. Neall Ellis, then a SAAF major, led the air strike.

Most of the white officers and NCOs operational with 32 Battalion, often deep behind the lines were youngsters still in their teens. They were a committed bunch! (Author's photo)

8

The Boys on Their Bikes on the Border

We heard them coming before we saw them, snaking their way through the long grass and growling like demons,' said the man with an emphatic wave of his arm. 'Then they were on us and a man next to me was shot ... I saw another comrade drop and after that, nothing, which was when I threw my gun aside and ran for my life ...

The man spoke quietly, his black skin glistening under the hot Ovambo sun as he recalled the contact that separated him from his SWAPO buddies. He was picked up by a South African security force patrol a few hours later.

'They were like lions ... they were everywhere,' he added a short while later, after which he went quiet for a while.

I knew him only as Timoteo and was amused when he gesticulated with one hand as he made a cut-throat gesture across his throat to emphasise a point. Then he sat back in the hard wooden chair to which he was led from his prison cell, cleared his throat and continued.

'I knew they were *motorfietse* (Afrikaans for motorcycles) because I had seen those machines in Windhoek before I was recruited for the cause of the comrades ... I was sent to Angola for training. But this time it was different because these were soldiers riding them ... and they were shooting at us.' Timoteo's eyes narrowed.

The exchange of fire referred to by this former SWAPO guerrilla – surprisingly erudite for someone who had received only a rudimentary education – took place in the early 1980s, during an extended counter-insurgency operation to the east of Oshikati, the SADFs main operational base in northern South West Africa (now Namibia).

As he explained, his group of about 20 guerrillas had been on the run for four or five days and in that time they had done quite a bit of damage. They had managed to lay quite a few mines, attacked one of the army control points, murdered several headmen who were thought to be cooperating with the government and then continued to head south.

Their tracks were discovered and lost again several times by army patrols until finally, elements of South West Africa's crack specialist unit, more colloquially known as South West African Specialist Unit (SWASpes), operating from Otavi, picked them up again.

Firstly, there were horses that followed his team's tracks, after one of its members had killed another local headman, claiming in leaflets left behind that the dead man had close ties with the 'Racist Boer regime'. Then SWASpes took over. What the guerrillas did not say at the time was that the headman had visited Oshikati a month before to enquire about getting his son into the local high school.

On the hunt for the killers, however, the trail again disappeared after cattle and goats were used to obliterate tracks. Local tribesmen – or as the boys in uniform liked to call them 'local pops', had apparently been coerced to follow instructions: it was that kind of war.

Once again tracks were picked up, this time about 35 kilometres to the south of the original position. Sector 10 Command at Oshakati lost no time in bringing another element of the Specialist Unit into play – the recently formed motorcycle detachment.

When the unit set out, together with a tracker support unit early in the day, the spoor (Afrikaans word for 'track') was already half-a-day old. Before the sun had reached its apogee, they had narrowed that gap to less than 90 minutes. At that stage, the insurgents ran into a well-prepared squad that had been deployed from a Puma as a stopper group ahead of the anticipated route that the SWAPO fighters were expected to take.

But the guerrillas turned and doubled back the way they had come and the bike squad's specially-adapted 350cc motorcycles were onto them before they were able to prepare an ambush against this new threat.

While actual casualties suffered by this SWAPO strike force is unknown, SWASpes members were clearly pleased with results when I spoke to the young lieutenant who had been leading them back at his base. He was happy too that none of his men had been injured in the firefight that followed.

The role of the 'Boys on their Bikes' in South Africa's Border War was a novel contribution to that country's 23-year-long conflict along the Angolan border, a totally new concept in a counter-insurgency campaign that was contested largely in Ovamboland, but sometimes extended into adjacent regions and a few times across the badly demarcated border into Angola itself.

There was good reason why a motorcycle combat unit had been formed. Following Operation Savannah, where a relatively small South African military force penetrated deep into Angola and eventually became involved in a series of battles on the outskirts of Luanda, it became clear to military planners in Pretoria that if the SADF was going to effectively control a region that stretched from the Atlantic Ocean all the way to the north-west extremity of Zimbabwe – a distance of about 1,600 kilometres – they would require light and mobile forces to operate with little logistical support. This was something closely followed by several other countries that kept tabs on what was happening in Africa at the time.

One also needs to bear in mind that not all that long before, Portugal had faced a spate of guerrilla wars in all three its three African territories, Angola, Mozambique and Portuguese Guinea (now Guiné-Bissau). Thereafter the Rhodesians were tackling similar problems and eventually had to yield to British efforts and a fast-shrinking white population to halt the fighting. The Border War followed, in the words of former Tanzanian President Julius Nyerere, 'to drive the white settler communities out of Africa.'[1]

The combat motorcycle concept actually resulted in a case study that was used by American military planners and theoreticians as well as quite a few other countries to model the idea of 'light and mobile' forces (the US in Afghanistan) of the 1990s and beyond.

But launching a bunch of armed hell riders into the African bush to harry insurgents was never going to be a simple matter. The terrain of South West Africa is mostly covered by a featureless and flat terrain, mostly bush country. This sometimes makes navigating at ground level – with no

---

1   Al Venter's book *Portugal's Guerrilla Wars in Africa* published by Helion in 2015 covers these conflicts in detail. And that, despite the fact that Portugal had been settled in its African colonies for almost five centuries and whites communities in South Africa since 1652. The difference between 20th-century wars and earlier uprisings and insurrections was the enormous amount of support given to the so-called African Freedom Fighters by the Soviet Union and its allies.

markers like hills or anything else visible – especially since a large part of it is semi-desert during the dry months. When the summer rains arrive the countryside becomes a quagmire.

As one foreign correspondent covering the war on the South African side stated, all this happened before GPS, and even compasses were not accurate due to magnetic interference in the soil substrata which is mostly loose and sandy. Thick bush is only encountered along rivers and the further north or east one goes into Angola, he observed.

Towards the end, it became obvious to somebody at Defence Headquarters in Pretoria that one of the answers might be the use of motorcycles. Light machines, not men on foot (though foot patrols were always paramount to maintain a presence on the ground) could cope with long distances, a relatively sparse population, little or no water, flat, featureless terrain, loose sand and dust, thick bush and dust; in fact, everything that made this kind of guerrilla conflagration difficult, including more dust.

Also, it was not the first time that two-wheelers had been used in modern conflicts, but the South African specialist unit revolutionised its combat role.

It is worth noting that motorbikes were seen on the battlefronts of both the First and Second World Wars. During the Great War, both the Germans and their adversaries allocated more than 300 machines to each division at the front. This figure was cut by 90 percent during the Second World War.

On both occasions – and during the Korean War of the 1950s – they were deployed primarily in communications and control roles, delivering messages between various units or assisting in traffic movement, especially on the Western European front. There were also motorcycles with Soviet fighting units.

In contrast, South Africa was the first nation to deploy bikes in a fully combatant mode, but only just. It is significant that a month after the first motorcycle evaluation tests were started in the SADF, United States Military Command began its own revised two-wheeled programme. Tests were conducted by the First Cavalry Division at Fort Hood, supported by CDC Infantry Agency at the famous Special Forces, North Carolina.

Like the South Africans, the Americans were reported to be reasonably pleased with preliminary results and intended for use in the Vietnam War. But that ended before Washington was effectively able to deploy their military motorcycle machine for real.

In finding the manpower to ride the bikes to war, instructors attached to SWASpes units maintain that while they favoured applicants who had experience in motocross or off-road motorcycle riding, this was not essential. Indeed, a number of successful applicants had little two-wheel experience apart from cycling.

As one of the bike squad instructors said, 'We can train a man from scratch, but obviously, if a fellow has been spending every weekend for the past year racing bikes or involved with mountain bikes in difficult terrain, then he is going to have an edge on anyone who prefers the golf course … it's as simple as that.'

That NCO knew what he was talking about; he had been with the unit on almost all its operational ventures.

The one characteristic he and others involved in the development phase looked for in their recruiting programme was perseverance. 'We want aggression – a man has got to be demonstrably hostile if he is going to survive in this game,' were his words.

'Put it this way,' the sergeant said. 'This is about the toughest course of this type that there is. We had 400 applicants try to enter the unit last year, but only 40 were successful and that makes it one in ten. Most aspiring bike riders fell out because the going was too tough – they just were not up to it.'

Those who did survive came from all four corners of South Africa. Corporal Pieter Olivier was born and raised on a Kalahari farm; Rifleman Bruce Allen came from Cape Town as did his friend and associate Peter Holt of Fish Hoek. Another of their buddies, Ian Grant, was an Empangeni resident from what was then Natal, while Corporal Hans Duvenhage was from Krugersdorp. The men were about equally divided between English and Afrikaans speakers.

Conditions to which motorcycle unit aspirants were subjected were uncompromisingly tough. It involved a three-day bike ride across some of the most difficult bush country in Africa, the men remaining on the move from dawn to dusk, as would be the norm on full military operations.

Also, there was nothing desultory about getting from A to B. Just before I arrived at the Specialist Unit HQ, a detachment had covered 760 kilometres in less than three days, almost all of it across difficult thorn-tree speckled Ovamboland terrain that was mostly sandy.

As somebody commented, if you run out of ammo during a fire-fight, there aren't even rocks to throw at the enemy.

Also, this might be a dry country, but the bush can get thick. 'So it's nothing to have a man pulled off his machine by a thorn tree branch,' the Sergeant declared

Luckily most injuries in that kind of terrain were not serious. Injuries suffered included a broken arm or two and very occasionally, a dislocated collar bone. There were some head injuries that required a few stitches and lots of minor scrapes and cuts. 'But that is all part of the game,' said the little man with the kind of military moustache that intimidates novices.

The sergeant admitted that one of the biggest problems in any extended bike operation was exhaustion.

'The body takes tremendous punishment and it is not unusual to find some of the bikers arriving at a temporary base and simply collapsing next to their machines the moment they are able to dismount. I usually leave them there to sleep – they can eat when they want to – their choice,' he reckoned.

Training in the bike unit followed a specific pattern after basics had been completed. Riders were first put through a platoon weapons-training course with the main emphasis on the intricacies of conventional warfare. They were then taught motorcycle driving and maintenance care, after which each candidate was expected to cope with fixing his machine should the need arise. Another time they were taught to take their bikes apart and put them all together again, which would invariably come handy in bush repairs.

According to some of these warriors, all that training was invaluable, the more so after they left the army.

Training in counter-insurgency warfare followed – first back at the home base and then in full operations in a part of the country adjacent to Angola. Everything was done under simulated battle conditions with live ammunition, a month on foot as normal infantry, then two weeks on a machine.

The sergeant told me that by the time all that had been done, he thought he had produced a pretty accomplished motorised fighter: 'You can take it from me that by then they are bloody good because only the toughest and the fittest survived the course!'

Most of the specialist unit motorcyclists to whom I spoke admitted that one of the attractions of the bike unit was that no two days were ever the same.

'There is always something different, whether it is getting ourselves involved in follow-up operations, being deployed as a cut-off group or even as part of a reaction force – sometimes we would leapfrog into a forward tracking position,' explained Corporal Lonnie Leschger of Randburg.

Many times the men operated as contact patrols and their roles could be as diverse as delivering a set of operational maps to a field commander deep into a chase or a new set of batteries to a pursuit squad hot on the tracks of an insurgent group.

Most times though, the unit worked closely with trackers attached to SWASpes whose job it was to find a trail and stay on it to the point where a contact is made and by then there would also be helicopter gunships involved.

That would often be done in conjunction with Koevoet, the crack police counter-insurgent unit that went to war in their mine-protected Casspir fighting vehicles, almost always with gunship top cover when needed.

At the time I spoke to the sergeant he was pleased with one recent development. 'We have learned to work very closely with the air force, and that's important when some of the boys have come under direct fire.

'Also, it's comforting to know that if a man is hit, it takes only minutes from the time he is wounded to lift-off by chopper hovering nearby, though obviously distance also plays a role there if they still have to bring a helicopter in to take a wounded man out.'

Historian Egon Mendel makes some interesting observations in an article he wrote for South Africa's *Military History Journal*.

Titled 'British Motorcycles in Khaki', he made reference to their use by South Africa's Union Defence Forces in World War Two.[2] I quote him at length:

> Although Harley-Davidsons were almost synonymous with motorcycles used by the Union Defence Forces in the Second World War, British bikes used by the UDF merit some attention, also having played a role in the war, albeit in a more limited way.
>
> These machines took their place with front-line troops and were used in ensuring the smooth running of convoys, the sign-posting of roads and deviations, and the rounding up of prisoners. They were particularly useful for reconnaissance, despatch riding and signalling related duties.
>
> After the outbreak of hostilities in September 1939, motorcycles belonging to private individuals in South Africa were commandeered by the UDF, compensated for, and put into service. These were almost all of British manufacture and makes such as the BSA, Norton, Ariel, AJS, Matchless, Royal Enfield and Triumph made up the majority of the machines in the motley collection at the outset of the war.
>
> Shortly before, in 1937 the South African Defence Force had ordered only ten Nortons. That was followed in 1938 by 24 BSAs and in 1939, 177 (M20) BSAs.
>
> In 1940, 101 BSAs were purchased from the South African Police and an additional 110 Matchlesses came from England. In the same year, American Harley-Davidsons were also ordered and began to appear on the scene.
>
> Being at war herself, Britain could no longer afford to supply motorcycles for export and the production of civilian bikes had already ceased when the war started.
>
> Thousands of BSAs, Matchlesses, Nortons, Triumphs and Royal Enfields, among others, were manufactured for use by the British forces in various theatres of the war. The manufacturers had accepted that, in wartime, a tough and simple machine was essential; one which could withstand rigorous service use and required the least possible maintenance (as riders would often have to improvise in difficult situations).
>
> Fortunately, most manufacturers were able to produce this type of motorcycle and simple single-cylinder machines were those in highest demand. In this context, it is interesting to note some details of the various British marques, as well as the comparatively large number of military models that were developed and manufactured during the war.
>
> Britain was committed to providing her armies with motorcycles and therefore could hardly be expected to fulfil outside orders. Therefore, these British motorcycles differed substantially from those produced for South Africa.

2   Egon Mendel: *Military History Journal*, Vol. 10 No. 6, June 1995.

In July 1940, 96 newly-ordered BSA motorcycles with sidecars arrived at Voortrekkerhoogte for training. These formed part of No 1 Motorcycle Company whose personnel, after strenuous training, were ready to leave for the frontline.

Unfortunately, very few spare parts were available for the company's impressed second-hand machines. The South African Police had also supplied some units to No 1 Motorcycle Company.

Early in 1940, No's 2 and 3 Motorcycle companies were raised as Active Citizen Force units, later to be formed into two companies in June 1940, with No 3 being considered as a reinforcement pool.

No 1 Company travelled by train to Durban and, in August 1940, they left for East Africa by ship. From Mombasa they travelled by train to Gil Gil in Kenya, where they remained for a month, carrying out further orientation, long cross-country rides (where elephant, rhino and lion were commonplace) and then manoeuvres. In September, the company left for Marsabit in the Northern Frontier District, a terrible journey as there were no proper roads and those that there were with deep sand and rocks. On many a stretch, they covered less than four kilometres in an hour.

At times, those riding solo had to hobble along with their machines between their legs. Others had to ride 35 metres apart because of the immense clouds of dust that were created. In the process, there were many collisions.

With the advent of autumn and the area's torrential rains, machines became bogged down in the mud and the men were all but washed out of their camp, forcing them to move to higher ground.

They struggled for days to extricate their motorcycles from the mud. Machines with sidecars, laden with Bren guns, anti-tank rifles and ammunition sometimes required the effort of the entire patrol to move them. They could sometimes not be ridden, conditions were so severe.

In November 1940, the company moved to the Abyssinian frontier and North Horr, some 200 kilometres away, and then on to Dukana, a further 140km away, all of this once again on bad roads and in trying conditions with extreme heat and wind and driving dust storms.

It was soon realised that motorcycles were not suitable for that type of terrain, but the riders persevered, braving difficult weather conditions and riding to the best of their ability, hoping for a chance of a scrap. Many suffered from heat fatigue and other tropical ailments. Inadequate supplies of decent food (rations were extremely limited), as well as the occasional cutting back on water, added to the problems. Kenya and Abyssinia (Ethiopia today) was then indeed a very tough country.

By March 1941 the company had made its way to Mega, once again through a morass of mud and six motorcycles were abandoned.

Nevertheless, the journey continued and 800km was covered in seven days over extremely difficult terrain. Further orders were received for 60 motorcycles to be railed from Mombasa for shipment to Mogadishu (in Somalia, which had then been captured from the Italians), whereas other vehicles (including motorcycles) reached their destination in Ethiopia by completing the 1,600-kilometre journey by road. Again, a tough experience ...

From Mogadishu, the whole company continued on a 1,800-kilometre journey via Modun, Tijiga, Harar, Auasc to the capital of Ethiopia, Addis Ababa (which had, by then, had also been captured from the Italians), where they arrived in May 1941.

Quartered in Addis Ababa for four months, the company's duties were to police and patrol the town and to maintain law and order. This, No 1 SA Motorcycle Company did admirably, laying the foundation for the newly formed Ethiopian Police Force that subsequently took over.

August 1941 was to see an end to No 1 Motorcycle Company's spell in Addis Ababa when patrolling was taken over by the Civil Police to whom its drab khaki-painted British motorcycles were presented.

The military achievements created with the help of motorcycle companies in the unforgiving wastes of Kenya's northern frontier and in the deserts and mountains of Abyssinia in the first two years of the Second World War were an important milestone in the annals of the history of the UDF.

No 1 Motorcycle Company subsequently embarked for the Middle East in August 1941. Once there, it was disbanded and its personnel transferred to the 3rd South African Armoured Car Battalion to do battle with Rommel.

That ended the somewhat short saga of the use of British motorcycles by South Africans in the war against Hitler and Mussolini. These machines were not used by South Africans in the epic battles of the Western Desert – this was left to the stronger, more rugged and imposing Harley-Davidsons of that era.

The American Version, by Robin Heid

Rapid deployment versatility marks the US Army's approach to motorcycle combat.

The 4th Squadron, 9th Cavalry, at Fort Hood, Texas, usually deploys its bikes in two-man reconnaissance teams, supported by helicopters. The bikes are strapped to racks mounted on the sides of UH-1H Huey helicopters and ferried to a location near the recon area, where the team unloads its machines (a 30-second operation) and embarks on patrol.

Armed with M-16s and equipped with PRC-77 radios mounted on the front forks, bikers report on enemy presence and movements, secure landing zones, and direct unit attack choppers to their targets. When the mission is completed, the team returns to the insertion helicopter and flies back to the main unit area.

Recon Platoon Sergeant Greg Fitzhugh explained: 'We use the bikes because they are an asset to us in an air combat unit. The bikes are quick, quietly manoeuvrable and adaptable to terrain and weather.'

Indeed, the motorcycle teams give the 4/9th Cavalry an all-weather reconnaissance capability, for they can operate in weather conditions that prevent aerial observation or keep aircraft on the ground. In addition to their primary mission of reconnaissance, the teams are also used as convoy scout escorts, messengers, and forward observers.

Training for the unit is tough. Like their South African counterparts, riders go through rigorous cross-country riding to familiarise themselves with their machines and the terrain in which they will be operating. That completed, training centres on recon technique and other missions useful to the unit. There are also support personnel who assist the riders in caring for their machines, but the primary responsibility for maintenance falls on the bikers themselves.

'We are very picky about whom we choose to ride. We want a biker who is already experienced in riding and repairing,' says Fitzhugh.

For that reason, the unit is invariably short of riders, but the platoon sergeant does not see any lowering of standards to ease matters. 'We do not want any wild men on these bikes,' he says.

The motorcycle unit has other problems. The stock Suzuki TS 185s used by the recon teams are nearly ten years old and they break down all too often these days. They are also underpowered – as a result, some kinds of terrain are difficult in which to operate effectively.

Another problem is the availability of parts. In typical fashion, the army has neglected to include motorcycle parts in its inventory, so the unit must purchase what it needs from a local motorcycle shop.

Motorcycle warfare in the African bush – ready for action. (Author's photo)

A brief rest stop during bush patrol.

Bike squad's detailed unit briefing. (Author's photo)

The South Africans were not the first to use motorcycles in warfare: Motorized *Wehrmacht* bikes and, seen here, Krupp Protze bike in Russia.

The bike squad was fast, mobile, well-trained and equipped, but too noisy for effective counter-insurgency operations. (Author's photo)

Bush confab.

American soldiers trained to fight in the Second World War with Thompson submachine-guns on
their Harley-Davidson WLA motorcycles.

The Germans made good use of their two-wheelers, even in the worst conditions.

The bikers operated closely with elements of SWA Spes – bush-briefing prior to night attack. (Author's photo)

A bike squad commander questions a suspect in an area where the enemy had been encountered. (Author's photo)

9

Claims and Reality about South African Air Losses in Angola

Much has been asserted about South African aircraft losses during the war in Angola, with Luanda and Cuban sources frequently fabricating evidence for downed SAAF Mirages and other operational planes. The practice became widespread after hostilities ended, with several instances of falsified narratives from Cuban pilots who had flown combat missions in that war. This report by Tom Cooper and Jonathan Kyzer, with additional details from 'Luis D' in Havana, provides more accurate details.

Since 1975, when the South Africans were directly involved militarily in the war in Angola for the first time, there were many claims about South African Air Force (SAAF) fighters, light aircraft, transports or helicopters having been shot down over that country, always to high acclaim by Angolan media.

This was to have been expected since exaggerated claims have been – and will continue to be – a feature of all air wars.

However, some Cuban, Angolan, Russian and Ukrainian assertions in these matters need to be carefully examined because most are exaggerated or totally false. Losses there were, of that there is no doubt: how many is another matter.

Claims relating to the Angolan war are discussed below, but it must be stressed that disinformation in wartime is a two-edged sword, with the Cubans and Angolans often purposely misled by the South African Defence Force. In this regard, the country's intelligence services also played a useful role.

There are reports, for example, that the South Africans would send two aircraft into Angolan air space, one of which would 'suddenly disappear'; that is, drop to a low level and leaving the area undetected, thus appearing to have been destroyed. The Cubans and Angolans would later find a dummy crash-site set up by SADF special operations teams.

There were other reasons. In 1979 a SAAF French-built Mirage III RZ was indeed shot down near Ongiva, in south Angola. The wreckage of the aircraft was recovered by the Angolans and repeatedly displayed until 1987 to international media as the 'wreckage of a downed Mirage'– each time, of course, as 'confirmation' for a brand new claim. Reporters unaware of the SAAF loss from 1979 were certainly left in no doubt by Luanda's people about the wreckage they saw as being authentic 'recent' kills.

Pretoria also became quite accomplished in constructing decoys: extremely realistic fakes of Mirage F.1AZs are known to have been built and deployed on airfields in northern South West Africa for unknown purposes. But neither the Angolans nor the Cubans ever attacked these planes, while SWAPO only made a few attempts, most of which failed. Nonetheless, time and again the SAAF would leave the 'burned wreck' of such a decoy to be seen by SWAPO – resulting in a report of a 'success'.

It is essential to accept that there were numerous authors and journalists who mixed with the various forces opposed to Luanda, including UNITA, various SADF units, SWAPOL (the Police Force of South West Africa) Koevoet and the rest – especially when it came to losses. While SADF and SWAPOL losses were made public – those of UNITA was never promulgated.

According to routine procedures, families of South African soldiers had to be notified first, and in most cases, this was done within 24 hours.

Following the end of the Border War in 1989, a number of publications appeared in South Africa, many detailing losses from this extended conflict that lasted 23 years. With UNITA however, a strictly Angolan organisation, nothing like that was possible, nor were South Africans responsible for publishing UNITA's losses: if at all, this would have been the task of the UNITA command and that simply did not happen.

Besides, South Africa was not the only party supporting UNITA. While the SADF was militarily involved with this guerrilla movement during the 1980s, countries like USA, China, Zambia, Morocco and the Ivory Coast were frequently much more active in supporting the rebels than they ever revealed, even if they never deployed their armed forces into Angola as South Africa did.

Still, even when the SADF deployed into Angola in any strength, this was not necessarily in support of UNITA. During the 1970s and 1980s the SADF was fighting a major counter-insurgency against SWAPO – the South West African guerrilla organisation that was supported by Luanda's Marxist regime, the Cubans and the Soviets.

In fact, especially in the air war in Angola, it was not only Cuban and South African pilots who were matching skills. Thousands of Soviet, East German, Polish, Romanian, Bulgarian and other East European aviators and technicians were involved on the Angolan side over more than a decade, which made for an extremely hefty input against the South Africans who were on their own.

There were even some former Portuguese army and air force regulars – including pilots (all defectors who were revolutionary orientated) and who had defected to the Luanda regime.

The Americans – through Langley's efforts as we have already seen, gave good support to UNITA, including supplying Savimbi's forces with substantial supplies of sophisticated Stinger supersonic ground-to-air missiles that downed a host of enemy aircraft, the same missiles being issued to anti-Soviet Mujahadeen in Afghanistan while that war raged. Washington also provided technicians who were sent to clandestine bases in Eastern Angola to train UNITA specialists in the use of this equipment. As we will see later, they did a remarkable job because Angolan losses in aircraft and aviators had the appropriate effect. It was rare to see one of the Angolan jets at low level in any of the combat zones.

The CIA supported UNITA extensively during the late 1980s, regularly flying supplies into rebel-held territory, particularly to Jamba, Savimbi's headquarters in south-east Angola. Most of it arrived on board Lockheed L-100 aircraft (the civilian version of the C-130 Hercules transport) owned by American-backed front companies.

Consequently, when the Angolans claimed to have shot down a 'South African Hercules', they might have been right about a C-130 being downed – except when those flying the aircraft were identified, not an easy task while hostilities lasted.

It is instructive that the SAAF never lost any of its C-130Bs over Angola, irrespective of the fact that between September 1987 and April 1988 those sturdy aircraft flew more than 400 missions, almost all at night. And that, too, while Cuban and Angolan fighter-aircraft had battlefield air superiority.

In addition, South African Air Force C-160 Transalls were also active in these nightly escapades, bringing military supplies into Jamba on 169 additional sorties during the same period, also without loss.

Details about losses to some CIA front companies remain vague because those operators were not only flying L-100s for UNITA but on occasion, also for the Angolan government and obviously there must have been CIA security considerations for that to have taken place.

There are several other related issues still unclear. An Angolan Yak-40FG was shot down near Cuamato at one point, reportedly 'by a missile from a foreign aircraft.' Some sources claim the 'foreign aircraft' was a Zambian J-6 jet fighter, but it could also have been a Cuban-flown MiG-21; after all, there were persistent rumours that a Cuban pilot shot down one of its own transport aircraft over Angolan air space with many of their own officers on board, some quite senior. All had attempted to defect from Angola, possibly to Zambia

Still more cases remain unresolved, quite a few of which have surfaced on the internet, especially in Russian and Ukrainian social media.

Consequently, to appreciate many of the more obscure events that took place in Angola, one needs careful research, without any bias. Case in point is the Cuban and Angolan claim that they downed or destroyed on the ground many more South African Mirage fighter aircraft than were ever delivered to the SAAF. The real tally of SAAF Mirage losses in that war was a modest four of the jet fighters.

When such claims are then accepted at face value by people claiming to be experts (and absolutely nothing solid in the way of evidence presented to back veracity) truth suffers.

Indeed, in recent years many 'additional' spurious claims have emerged, the majority also dubious and that, in turn, makes any kind of serious assessment of what took place during this lengthy war problematic. These are the best-known examples:

Legend of Cuban MiG-23s in Angola

Probably the best-known examples for exaggerated Cuban and Angolan claims against the SAAF are those linked to the deployment of Cuban MiG-23 pilots and technicians in Angola. Some (unofficial) Cuban, Ukrainian, and Russian sources describe this deployment as a totally disproportionate success. Indeed, they maintain that many South African military aircraft and helicopters were shot down by Soviet MiG-23s but a closer examination of most of those claims simply do not stand up.

Obviously, Cuban MiG-23 operations were a fascinating aspect of the war but some of the stories linked to the deployment of these aircraft and the claims of successes are distinctly wonky.

What we do know is that the *Defensa Anti-Aérea y Fuerza Aérea Revolucionaria* (DAAFAR) – the Cuban Air Force – did not operate any MiG-23s in other African wars in which that country was involved.

Certainly, there were Cuban aviators involved in the Ogaden War in Africa's Horn – a bitter struggle fought between Ethiopia and Somalia in 1977 and 1978 and which cost hundreds of thousands of lives. But it was also made clear to military planners in both Moscow and Havana that aircraft with better capabilities than MiG-17s and MiG-21s were badly needed. That resulted in the delivery of squadrons of MiG-23s to Angola.

At least 24 MiG-23BNs and six MiG-23UBs were supplied to Cuba by Moscow in mid-1978; only months after fighting in Ogaden had ended. The new aircraft entered service with two units: the 2661 *Esadron de Caza-Bombardeo,* and one other, unknown squadron. Both were based at Santa Clara, and subordinated to *Comando Aereo Tactico* (Tactical Air Command) of the *Zona Aerea Central.*

All those aircraft became operational in time for the American intervention in Grenada in October 1983 and, in part, due also to Soviet concerns that the United States was preparing for a third world war (especially in the aftermath of intensive US exercises worldwide in 1982). That was followed by a military intervention in Lebanon.

What we know today is that these Soviet fighters sent to Cuba were actually prepared for eventual counter-strikes against a variety of different targets in Trinidad, Venezuela and Florida.

In the end, Cuba remained passive in response to developments on Grenada, which was probably just as well as they would have been trounced by the Americans. Instead, Castro reacted by requesting additional advanced interceptors from the USSR and in 1984 a dozen more fighter jets, including MiG-23MFs were supplied to Havana. They formed the basis of an obscure *Escuadron de Caza* of the 1779 *Regimento de Caza*, stationed at San Antonio de los Banos and subordinated to *Comando de Defensa Aerea* (Air Defence Command).

Interestingly, Cuban units deployed in Angola by then were already equipped with MiG-23MLs (contrary to what is usually reported) and we know this we have documentary proof supplied by a defector who fled to the United States.

The first of 55 MiG-23MLs had already reached Luanda in 1984 (and not three years later as some pundits aver). Both the 12th and 13th Fighter Squadrons FAPA-DAA (both units were almost entirely manned by Cubans, but there were also East German, a few Soviet and some Romanian pilots, until 1987) were equipped with them. All these planes were vastly superior to anything the SAAF was even able to field, which meant the playing fields, as far as Pretoria was concerned, were hardly level.

Originally, Angola's 12th Squadron FAPA-DAA was a transport unit, organised in mid-1976 and flying two ex-Portuguese C-47s, two Noratlas transporters and a pair of Fokker F-27s. Once equipped with MiG-23MLs, both squadrons were integrated into the 25th Air Combat Fighter Regiment FAPA-DAA and headquartered in Luanda. From time to time, when the situation demanded, they would also be put under control of the 24th and 26th Regiments.

As a consequence, while the Angolan Air Force was well-equipped with MiG-23MLs, the DAAFAR was never allowed to have more than a dozen MiG-23MFs at any given time. Usual reports that there were two squadrons of these aircraft, of which one should have been based at San Julian air force base, are also wrong.

In fact, the DAAFAR barely had enough MiG-23MFs to equip a single squadron at home. Later, this unit was disbanded: survivors of this version were then merged into a newly-established squadron of 1779 *Regimento de Caza*, equipped with twelve MiG-23MLs, and based at San Antonio de los Banos air base.

Meanwhile, the Angolan 9th Fighter-Training Squadron FAPA-DAA was equipped with at least ten MiG-23UBs, figured mainly for conversion training. Until 1987 however, aviators converted were almost entirely Cuban, with hardly any Angolan pilots involved in the fighting and not without good reason. Soviet aircraft were all top of the range and proved much more complex to fly and maintain than Luanda's senior military staff expected. As it was, many Soviet MiGs sent to Angola were lost in mishaps, especially early on in the war following their introduction into service and alcohol was sometimes part of it.

In later years, once the civil war went fully operational with the introduction by Luanda of South African mercenaries in the pay of Executive Outcomes, there were quite a few instances of drunk Angolan pilots taking their choppers aloft and coming short.

Operations would be planned and if the African pilots were not stone cold sober, the men would refuse to board the Hips. Some of this is detailed in my book *Battle for Angola*, the first three chapters of which detail mercenary involvement in that country.

There were other problems. For example, in August 1984, two MiG-23s from the 9th Fighter Training Squadron and four MiG-23MLs from the 12th Fighter Squadron – led by Major Antonio Rojas – became lost during a training flight in bad weather. The outcome was that a MiG-21bis, a MiG-23UB (flown by Major Marrero), and two MiG-23MLs crashed, while two other MiG-23MLs made emergency landings in Luena. That was a write-off of six aircraft, but it bothered nobody in Angola because it was accepted that the Kremlin was paying. In reality, Moscow was not: Angola had to fork out heavily for its military purchases.

And contrary to Cuban reports, the Angolans never purchased any MiG-23BNs, even if it was obvious that they had need of the ground-attack version very much more than interceptors. The purpose of deploying MiG-23MLs in Angola was to tackle South African air superiority over the southern battlefields.

For this task, the FAPA-DAA and its Cuban allies needed an aircraft that could outfly and outfight the SAAF's Mirage F.1CZs and F.1AZs. Consequently, the main role of the Cuban-manned 12th and 13th Fighter Squadrons was interception, even if – with time – they were to become increasingly involved in ground fighting as well.

All that, despite some obvious limitations, like problems with simultaneous carriage of a single drop tank under the centreline and bombs on hard points beneath intakes, or the lack of chaff and flare dispensers for defence against Stinger MANPADs (by then effectively deployed by UNITA cadres following missile instruction by the US).

In fact, in the face of considerable losses to UNITA man-portable air defences – meanwhile equipped with FIM-92A Stinger and SA-14 MANPADs through the CIA and South Africans – the Angolans by late 1987 were forced to purchase still more MiG-23MLs. That brought the eventual total to around 80 aircraft (barely 50 percent of which were ever operational at any one time).

The main base of the 12th and 13th Squadrons in Angola was Serpa Pinto near Menongue, a large, well-developed airfield with a number of blast-pens, a long runway, several early warning radars and a local ground-control centre, defended by two SA-3 missile sites and numerous 23mm anti-aircraft guns.

The 'Angolan' MiG-23MLs became operational in early 1984, but these planes were not to be involved in support of any offensive operations of the Angolan Army before 1987, when – under command of Soviet General Shagnovich – the Angolan Army launched a major two-pronged offensive from Luena towards the Cazombo Panhandle. From there it was intended to move from Cuito Cuanavale towards Mavinga in a bid to cripple the main body of Dr Jonas Savimbi's guerrilla might. These operations were eventually to form a backdrop to the culmination of this long war.

Alarmed by the every burgeoning onslaught, UNITA requested urgent help from South Africa, and the SADF started deploying its mechanised forces into southern Angola, as well as a squadron of Mirages to Rundu airfield in Caprivi.

In the views of some observers, the sudden appearance of MiG-23s in Angolan skies should have caused more than a few problems for the SAAF. On the contrary, however: due to intensive training in air-to-air combat (especially in high-speed manoeuvring), the South Africans actually looked forward to engaging the enemy.

As a result, the SAAF continued flying operational sorties over battlefields, despite the rather obvious fact that the MiG-23ML had a distinct advantage over the Mirage F.1CZ and F.1AZ: the former was armed with R-24 (ASCC-code AA-7 Apex) medium-range, all-aspect air-to-air missiles with an engagement envelope that reached out to 24km at levels above 15,000ft.

The South Africans had nothing to counter the R-24. Their best air-to-air missile was the Kukri, a licensed version of the early Matra R.550 Magic Mk.1.

From the start, those involved with this problem in the SAAF were aware that the Kukri was much too short-ranged for this sort of combat, especially against aircraft operating at such high speeds like the MiG-23s. The French-built fighters also lacked structure capable of surviving manoeuvres at anything over 4Gs; confirmed in several instances where Kukris disintegrated after the aircraft carrying them pulled tight manoeuvres.

Nonetheless, the R-24 had nothing like an effective range of up to 40km, as was usually claimed. In fact, the average maximal range from which they could be launched against low-flying SAAF fighters – even from the forward hemisphere – was only between seven and ten kilometres.

We are today also aware that the MiG-23ML – as delivered to Angola – had only a minimal look-down/shoot-down capability, and their pilots rarely flew low because of the MANPAD threat.

For all that, the Soviet R-24 was always a threat to South African Mirages because the SAAF had no air-to-air missile in their arsenal that could be fired from similar ranges, nor a missile capable of attacks from the forward hemisphere (or, as it is termed in some quarters, the front envelope).

Further comparisons between the Mirage F.1 and MiG-23 showed that the Mirage was originally designed as a medium- and high-altitude interceptor, and that its small wings and good thrust-to-weight ratio made it a very good low-level interdictor. The MiG-23 was developed for flying fast at low levels and delivering 'slash' attacks from the rear hemisphere. Essentially, neither was a true 'dogfighter' – both were at their best at high subsonic speeds and medium levels.

What also became clear as the Angolan war progressed, was that SAAF pilots expertly matched the capabilities of their aircraft; they often flew at altitudes of around 15 metres over the completely flat terrain of southern Angola (which allowed roughly five metres for a reasonably sparse bush cover, though the pilots had to keep a keen eye open for the occasional over-tall bit of forest).

In the face of the ongoing MiG-23ML threat, they continued with intensive combat operations against enemy targets up to 300km inside enemy territory.

Most such strikes were never detected by any of more than 70 Angolan and Cuban monitoring stations deployed in southern Angola, even less so by either Angolan and Cuban radars or FAPA-DAA's interceptors. Conversely, while the Cubans and Angolans were experts of all technical aspects of their aircraft, they both lacked realistic interception training and time and again proved dismal in tactics.

In theory at least, neither the Cubans nor Angolans needed to be excellent pilots (despite the demanding aircraft they flew). Moscow did expect the average pilot's role in flying a MiG-23 to be minimal because the plane, to function properly, had a highly automated weapons system but was heavily dependent on proper ground support.

Additionally, Angolan radar should have caused the South Africans some grave problems. With intensive Soviet and East German support, the Angolans developed an excellent radar control system in their country during the 1980s, but in truth, even this was not enough to properly cover the enormous battlefield that comprised almost all of southern Angola. Besides, the South Africans were such experts in low-level operations – the 'pancake flat' terrain of southern Angola being ideal for ultra-low-level flying – the systems installed by Luanda proved only marginally useful.

Consequently, the Cubans and Angolans were not really in a position to use the supposed advantage of their extensive radar coverage over the battlefield.

Also, neither the Mirage F.1 nor the MiG-23 were good 'dogfighters'. Both lacked solid, reliable multi-function airborne-intercept radars with long detection range. Their initial and sustained turning capabilities were poor compared to several new fighters that emerged in the 1980s. But in the hands of good pilots both were still very potent fighters and under specific conditions, the MiG-23 could out-turn even the vaunted MiG-21.

In a direct comparison, the Mirage had some advantage in corner velocity and was therefore more likely to win a turning fight. The MiG-23, in contrast, had superb acceleration and speed in combat configuration, and more than likely could dictate the engagement.

Over Angola, pilots of both aircraft suffered from poor situational awareness and while having radar stations in central and southern Angola, the FAPA-DAA were not really able to detect or track the low-flying South African jets. In turn, the South Africans lacked any kind of advanced radar coverage over their sectors of the battlefield because this was moving away from South West African borders and, with time, further into Angola's interior.

Both sides were frequently operating on the verge of their combat range and pilots invariably had one eye glued on their fuel gauges.

It is notable that the Angolan Air Force never had a sufficient number of MiG-23MLs in operational condition to fly in larger formations – as originally envisaged for this type of fighter. It was not only that attrition in combat and service was sobering; the MANPAD threat fielded by Savimbi's people was formidable enough to cause Cuban pilots to fly at medium- to high-levels. From there, they were expected to perform effective 'slash' attacks and then use their performance to either disengage or outdistance the opponent.

Obviously, this was never intended to work, but who could argue? At least Cuban pilots were not dying.

Due to their extensive and extremely thorough training, pilots of both the Cuban MiG-23MLs and those of SAAF Mirages did not appear to be fazed by any of these shortcomings.

By all accounts, as we have already seen, they were actually looking forward to aerial confrontations. And while it may surprise those not familiar with what was going on in Angolan air space at the time, the SAAF even deployed its Mirage F.1AZ – the ground-attack version – for air-to-air tasks, something that Lieutenant Colonel Dolf Prinsloo explained in an interview for *Air Forces Monthly* magazine, published in December 1994:

> During this time we did a lot of ACM camps and I would say that our air-to-air was better than our air-to-ground. The situation was such, namely, that the SAAF was preparing Mirage F.1CZs for retirement, while the third main fighter-jet unit of the air force, the No 2 Squadron, was converting to the Cheetah. Consequently, the Mirage F.1AZs had to act as interceptors.

Once the Angolans launched their main ground operations against UNITA in late summer 1987, the two sides did not have to wait long to make contact.

The first clash between MiG-23MLs and Mirages occurred on 10 September that year, a few days after a small SADF task force – supported by long-range artillery – thrashed the Angolan Army's 21 Brigade on the Lomba River.

Approaching at a very low level, SAAF fighters first surprised and then out-manoeuvred two Cuban MiGs that came out of Menongue. The R.550 missile fired by Captain Anton van Rensburg exploded in the heat plume behind a MiG-23ML from the 13th Fighter Squadron FAPA-DAA causing no damage. Van Rensburg then fired another, but it also failed.

A day later South African Army units hit FAPLA's 59 Brigade while it was crossing the Lomba River and mauled it as well. The next FAPLA unit, the 47 Brigade, was also neutralised as a fighting unit only days later. By 16 September, all SADF ground units in the area launched a joint offensive against the Angolans, again on the Lomba River and once more supported by heavy 155mm artillery. SAAF Mirages then added to the carnage by pounding the enemy with a series of precise strikes. Angolan planes hit back in force, limiting the manoeuvrability of SADF units on the ground, but not preventing them from mauling three Angolan brigades in the following days.

Observing some concerted activity by the FAPA-DAA on the morning of 27 September, the South Africans attempted to set up a trap for the MiGs by dispatching three pairs of Mirage F.1CZs at low-level over the battlefield.

The first pair airborne over Angola was vectored towards two MiG-23MLs flown by Major Alberto Ley Rivas and First Lieutenant Juan Carlos Chavez Godoy, who were on a mission escorting several helicopters. All were obviously well-prepared for a scrap.

The two Mirages, flown by Captains Carlo Gagiano and Arthur Piercey did achieve a surprise: Rivas detected one of the French-built jets only as it climbed and approached. But, the Mirages ended slightly aside and on an opposite course from the MiGs.

As both pairs turned back to engage, Major Rivas fired a pair of R-23R missiles at Piercey's Mirage, while Godoy fired either an R-23 or an R-60 against Gagiano. Captain Gagiano could only watch as the weapon flashed over his canopy without detonating.

However, one of the other two missiles detonated while passing to the left of Piercey's Mirage, spraying its tailpipe with shrapnel. In fact, after the missile exploded, Piercey – followed by Gagiano – dived hard for the deck, but the explosion had damaged Piercey's tail and wing, causing its breaking parachute to pop. But the worst damage was caused to the hydraulic system, which powered flight controls.

Piercey managed to nurse his aircraft back to Rundu, but while attempting to land the aircraft he veered off the runway and crashed, collapsing his front gear in the process. The force of the impact caused his ejection seat to activate, hurling Piercey out of his jet. As there was neither time nor space for the parachute to deploy, Piercey hit the ground extremely hard and ended up paralysed.

The fuselage of his aircraft, F.1CZ 206 was subsequently used to repair Mirage F.1CZ 205, which had been out of service after an engine fire for some time.

Interestingly, specific Cuban, Ukrainian, and Russian sources credit Rivas with 1.5 and Godoy with 0.5 kills – that is, with two (and not one) Mirages shot down on 27 September 1987.

In an interview to the Cuban military reporter Cesar Gómez Chacón, published in the book *Cuito Cuanavale: Viaje al Centro de Los Heroes*, in 1989, Major Alberto Ley Rivas described this engagement in detail, stressing that he was not really sure about scoring any kind of a hit on SAAF Mirages, until – several seconds after the contact – he heard his wingman's shouts of joy about a 'Mirage falling in flames.'

Still, Rivas would not believe the Mirage was shot down until several days later he heard on the South African radio about the loss of an aircraft and its injured pilot. Furthermore, Rivas explained, any other pilot in his unit – including his wingman – could have done the same that he did, clearly indicating that only one Mirage was indeed hit.

Consequently, Rivas is not claiming a second kill being scored and Godoy is not doing anything similar either, but his statements in that interview to a reporter who won an award by the Cuban Defence Ministry, clearly suggests that the DAAFAR and the Cuban authorities have a completely different view of that engagement compared to numerous invalid reports in specialised Cuban, Ukrainian, and Russian media.

Obviously, there is no reason to believe that the FAPA-DAA or DAAFAR 'forgot' to mention 'shooting down' the second Mirage to the highest Angolan and Cuban authorities, which means that the book *Cuito Cuanavale: Viaje al Centro de Los Heroes* was written in a 'politically-correct' manner, turning every little success of Cuban forces in Angola into a major victory.

The Mirage F.1CZ flown by Captain Carlo Gagiano was certainly not 'blown up' during this combat as claimed by unofficial Cuban sources, otherwise it would have been impossible for it to bring back a gun-camera video showing one of the missiles passing low over the cockpit. Even more so, given the place where this engagement occurred, it would be impossible for Captain Gagiano to have evaded capture, and even less so to continue a highly successful career with the SAAF, eventually becoming Chief of the SAAF.

Then, the same Cuban, Ukrainian, and Russian sources also claim the FAPA-DAA MiG-23MLs shot down a SAAF Puma helicopter on 27 September 1987, supposedly using a single R-60. Peculiarly, no such claim was published in Chacón's book, despite supposedly happening on the same day of Piercey's Mirage misadventure.

Obviously, the reporter sent by the Cuban officials to Angola to 'uncover the truth', relating to these events appears to have 'forgotten' to report it to anybody. More salient, Dick Lord in his excellent book *Vlamgat* – mentions nothing of such a loss for the day in question.

On the contrary, all the losses of SAAF SA.330 Pumas during the war in Angola – and during the 'externals' into Mozambique – are well known:

22 December 1975
SAAF Puma flown by Captain John Millbank was hit by Cuban AAA about 20 kilometres west of Cela in south Angola. The crew executed a safe emergency landing and evaded capture by returning to own lines.

6 September 1979
Puma flown by Captain Paul Vellerman was hit by AAA over Mozambique while attacking an ANC camp there. All onboard were killed.

5 January 1982
Puma flown by Captain John Robinson was hit by SMAF, the helicopter turned turtle and hit the ground, killing all occupants.

In addition, quite a number of Pumas (and other SAAF helicopters) were damaged by SMAF during the course of the war, while still more suffered operational mishaps but were recovered and repaired. This includes one Puma (155) which crashed near Cassinga in southern Angola on an unknown date before 1987 and was certainly not brought down by MiG-23s.

How many SAAF Mirages were actually lost?

Much has also been said about other 'possible' air combats involving both Angolan MiG-21s and MiG-23s pitted against South African fighter aircraft.

A persistent rumour is that in 1985 SAAF Mirages shot down a FAPA-DAA MiG-21 during one of several strikes deep into Angolan territory and held secret until today. Cuban, Russian, and Ukrainian sources are persistent in their claims for additional SAAF Mirages – and even Impala strike-fighters as well as helicopters – being taken out by Cuban-flown MiG-23MLs.

On several internet websites it is claimed that Lieutenant Colonel Eduardo Gonzales Sarria, a Cuban MiG-23ML pilot who participated in the fighting in Angola downed a SAAF Mirage. It is not entirely clear when should this have happened. Several articles in the magazine *Aviyatsiya & Vremya* – as well as internet publications – have declared that Cuban-flown Angolan MiG-23s shot down a SAAF Mirage F.1AZ 'during the first part of 1987 in the north of Namibia.' They mention that 'South Africa admitted losing a Mirage F.1AZ but claimed it was hit by an IR SAM, probably a SA-7 or SA-9.'

Most likely these claims are based on a reader's letter published in *Air Forces Monthly* magazine, volume January 2000, in which it was said that the SAAF Mirage F.1CZ '206' was shot down by an R-60 missile fired from an Angolan MiG-23.

In truth, the South African Air Force lost no Mirage F.1s over Angola in 1987, and even more unlikely over Namibia.

As detailed above, Angola's 12th and 13th Fighter Squadrons FAPA-DAA in the early 1987 period were still in the process of converting to newly acquired MiG-23MLs. Consequently, these aircraft were simply not flying any kind of combat operations. In fact, comprehensive details about all SAAF Mirage and other losses have since been published and while it could be said that one or two minor facts are missing, it is at least a clear picture of what was lost when, where, and for which reason.

More salient, most of the aviators are still alive and they would be the first to correct errors of fact with regard to the SAAF.

What is actually missing are specific details about some SAAF operations deep into Angola, about which all SAAF personnel contacted so far have been peculiarly quiet, obviously for security reasons and to protect their own identities in the 'new' South Africa. Details about which we are aware, however, do not include any SAAF losses. Instead, there are several unconfirmed claims of shooting down of Angolan, Cuban, and Soviet aircraft.

Given the fact that neither the Cubans nor the Angolans – and even less so the Russians or the Ukrainians – have proved to be able to offer any kind of serious evidence of the contrary, the following list of SAAF Mirage F.1 losses in the 1980s – compiled by Jonathan Kyzer on the basis of private research and the book *Vlamgat*, by former SAAF Mirage F.1-pilot Colonel Dick Lord – should be considered the most complete published so far:

(Note: SAAF Mirage F.1AZs were numbered 216–247, Mirage F.1CZs were numbered 200–215.)

15 February 1979
F.1AZ 246 flown by Captain Wassie Wasserman
Engine flame-out near Cullinan in South Africa, pilot ejected safely and crash confirmed by local residents and *Vlamgat*;

F.1CZ 200 flown by Major Chris Brits: Went down after a slow flypast on the crash scene of 246, pilot ejected but seat failed to deploy in time. This plane was certainly not lost over Angola as indicated elsewhere on this forum (where it appeared). The incident, which took place only two minutes after that of the 246, was confirmed by local residents and two non-involved pilots, as well as *Vlamgat*;

(Note: despite numerous eyewitnesses and publications mentioning these two accidents, unofficial Cuban sources claim that the Mirage F.1CZ '200' was shot down over Angola – completely ignoring the fact that it is impossible for any SAAF Mirage F.1s to have been lost in Angola at the time as the SAAF only started deploying that type in theatre from June 1980 onwards.)

7 June 1980
F.1AZ 234 flown by Major Frans Pretorius: Damaged by SA-3 near Lubango, Angola. Recovered successfully to Ondangua despite engine flame-out some 40km from the base.

F.1AZ 237 flown by Captain I.C. du Plessis: Damaged by a Soviet SA-3 ground-to-air missile, recovered safely to Ruacana and landed without nose-wheel; Captain du Plessis was decorated for saving that plane. A photo of the aircraft, taken after it had landed is available for verification.

4 November 1980
F.1CZ 208 flown by Captain Les Bennett: Crashed after full upwards runway trim near Groblersdal (South Africa), pilot ejected safely.

13 March 1984
F.1AZ 228 flown by Captain Digby Holdsworth: Crashed in bad weather near Lydenburg (South Africa), pilot ejected safely.

8 February 1985
F.1CZ 205 flown by Captain Pierre du Plessis: Engine fire during DACM sortie over Langebaan (South Africa), recovered safely, fire extinguished; confirmed by two former SAAF pilots and members of the local fire brigade.

4 April 1985
F.1AZ 222 flown by Major Jan Henning: Crashed at Hoedspruit Air Base, pilot ejected safely.

23 July 1985
F.1AZ 221 flown by Captain Rickus de Beer: Fuel pipe problems during a training flight, crashed onto a threshold while attempting to land at Hoedspruit Air Base (South Africa); crash confirmed by former members of the local fire brigade.

28 December 1986
F.1CZ 215 flown by Captain John Sinclair: Struck a mountain ridge while on a low-level navigation training exercise over eastern Transvaal (South Africa); pilot ejected safely (see *Vlamgat*, page 165).

(Note: this is another Mirage claimed by unofficial Cuban sources to have been shot down in Angola – supposedly by FAPA-DAA MiG-23MLs. This aircraft was certainly not lost over Angola because the pilot was at a low-level training sortie deep over South Africa, busy monitoring his maps when he suddenly realised the hill was in front of him. A last moment evasion manoeuvre was initiated, but this helped only in so far that the plane hit the top of the hill with its tail. The pilot ejected safely. Due to the date, it is likely that the loss was reported as occurring in 1987).

27 September 1987
F.1CZ 206 flown by Captain Arthur Piercey: Hit by R-23 or R-60 during engagement with MiG-23MLs inside Angola (see above). On recovery in Rundu overshot the runway, pilot inadvertently ejected and was badly injured; tail section fitted to F.1CZ 205 and returned to service; results of engagement confirmed by photos taken by Al J. Venter.

20 February 1988
F.1AZ 245 flown by Major Ed Every: Hit by Soviet SA-9 and crashed in Angola, pilot KIA. The kill was confirmed both by Angolan and Cuban sources, as well as reports from a SADF

reconnaissance team, which reported the presence of a SA-9-squad near the wreckage.

The Impala Claim

Finally, the same sources also credit a loss of a SAAF Impala strike jet to Cuban/Angolan MiG-23s. The basis of this is unknown when neither a date, place nor even a weapon with which this 'success' should have been achieved are mentioned. All SAAF Impala losses for the whole war in Angola and the reasons for these are known in detail.

18 October 1979
Impala Mk.II '1033', flown by Major Aubrey Bell, shot down by AAA during armed recce mission near Omapande; pilot recovered by Alouette III flown by Major Polla Kruger (the helicopter itself was struck by 22 AK bullets).

24 January 1980
Impala Mk.II '1056', flown by Captain Leon Burger, hit by SA-7 while on armed recce mission near Aanhanca; pilot flew successfully back to Ondangua but was forced to eject due to damage on the loss of his entire vertical fin (which, of course, reduced directional control), darkness and an airfield packed with other aircraft.

23 March 1980
Impala Mk.II '1050', flown by Captain Sarel Smal, lost due to fuel system being contaminated by sand. Pilot ejected and was recovered. Angolans claimed to have shot this plane down and killed Captain J.H. Henning because his name was painted on the canopy rail of Impala '1050'. Captain Henning, however, is still very much alive.

25 April 1980
Impala Mk.II '1029', flown by Lieutenant Pete Hollis, shot down while on armed recce over Angola. Pilot ejected but his neck was broken when his head struck the canopy.

20 June 1980
Impala Mk.II '1037', flown by Lieutenant Neil Thomas, shot down by 23mm AAA while on CAS mission for Operation Smokeshell. Pilot ejected safely and was recovered by an Alouette helicopter. The aircraft was also recovered by a SAAF Super Frelon helicopter and was subsequently repaired.

10 October 1980
Impala Mk.II '1042', flown by Lieutenant Steve Volkerz, shot down by a SA-7 missile some 20km south-west of Mupa. Volkerz ejected safely and waved to his wingman (Lieutenant Skinner) from the ground; intercepted radio messages indicated that he was subsequently captured and killed by SWAPO.

1 June 1981
Impala Mk.II '1052', flown by Major Gene Kotze, shot down by AAA over Angola and pilot KIA.

Despite this type of trainer jet aircraft being deployed extensively during the fighting in Angola – and flying hundreds of close-air-support sorties between 1979 and 1988 – no other Impalas were lost during the rest of the war. There were several damaged by Angolan SAMs.

For example, on 23 December 1983, during a strike against targets in Mulondo area (in the Operation Askari timeframe) one Impala was hit by SA-7. The plane was considerably damaged, but the pilot flew back safely to Ondangua air force base.

Another Impala was damaged by a SA-9 during the same operation, but it also managed to return to Ongiva air base in south Angola (then in South African hands). It brought back with it the seeker-head of the SAM missile, tidily embedded in the fuselage of the aircraft.

No Impalas were ever engaged in combat by Angolan or Cuban MiGs. On the contrary: in 1985 the SAAF used them to intercept and shoot down several Cuban and Soviet Mi-8 and Mi-24 helicopters deep over Angola, in turn stopping one of the offensives against UNITA. These sorties appear in detail in Al Venter's book *The Chopper Boys*, a marvellous account of subterfuge and intrigue.

Meanwhile, exact details about every single operational and combat loss of SAAF aircraft and helicopters in the last 30 years has been published, and none came anywhere near confirming any of the Cuban and Russian claims.

For example, in addition to Mirage and Impala losses mentioned above, on 3 September 1987, the SAAF lost Bosbok '934' to an Angolan SA-8 during a night artillery spotting mission south of the Lomba River, in Angola. Lieutenant Richard Glynn and Colonel Pax (an artillery officer), were killed when the plane went down.

Yet, such facts are ignored. On the contrary, quite a number of Russian and Ukrainian – as well as Cuban sources – are basing their claims on events where almost nothing is known about South African operational accidents, the majority of which occurred at least 1,500km – and two borders – distant from Angola.

Even if a revelation of full details about the involvement of Cuban MiG-21 and MiG-23 units is not to be expected before the end of the communist regime in Havana, it can already be concluded that the Mirage F.1CZ 206, flown by Captain Arthur Piercey, was the only South African aircraft ever to have been hit either by the Cuban or Angolan MiG-21s or MiG-23s.

Besides, absolutely nothing has been published about Cuba's DAAFAR contingent in Angola, aside from unit designations (and unit histories) and their equipment as well as few names. Meanwhile, a good deal more is known about losses of Cuban-flown Angolan aircraft in the 1980s.

For example, we are aware of:

- Two MiG-23MLs lost during a training flight near Luena on 9 August 1984 were flown by Captain Pedro Zequeiras and First Lieutenant Alberto Olivares Horta;
- MiG-23ML shot down near Menongue on 12 March 1985 was flown by Captain Lino Cabrera Viera;
- MiG-23ML shot down near Menongue on 25 July 1986 was flown by Captain Jorge Gonzalez Perez;
- MiG-23ML shot down near Menongue on 13 September 1986 was flown by Captain Jose A. Garcia Flores;
- MiG-23ML shot down near Menongue on 14 January 1988 by UNITA MANPAD was flown by Captain Francisco A. Doval;
- MiG-23ML shot down near Menongue on 21 January 1988 was flown by Captain Carlos Rodriguez Perez;
- MiG-23ML lost on 15 February 1988 near Cuito was flown by Captain Juan P. Rodriguez;
- MiG-23ML shot down near Menongue on 17 March 1988 (probably the same claimed as shot down on 23 April by SADF Ystervark 20mm AAA) was flown by pilot named Ernesto Chavez.

Exact details about some 60 additional losses of Cuban and Angolan aircraft during this war are also on record. More in-depth research is currently being done and additional data – especially about the Cuban involvement in this war with appear under the author's name: Tom Cooper.

Soviet MiGs Broke Nobody's Hearts

One of the most obscure legends about the air war over Angola is that surrounding the strike by 12 Cuban Air Force MiG-23MLs against the hydroelectric dam at Ruacana-Caleque, a story which deserves to be described in detail.

During January 1988, the Cuban-Angolan garrison in the city of Cuito Cuanavale was surrounded by UNITA troops and the local airfield was put out of action by SADF artillery. FAPA-DAA MiG-21 and MiG-23 strikes did succeed in containing the siege, partially with the help of heavy rains, despite suffering losses to American Stinger MANPADs.

A month later the frontlines stabilised as the South Africans stopped their advance in the face of the garrison in Cuito being considerably reinforced and put under the command of a Cuban general. Fighting once again intensified and aircraft on both sides of the front were now flying up to three sorties a day.

Due to the threat of hand-held missiles (MANPADs) however, most Cuban air strikes were delivered from medium levels and lacked precision.

By this time, the MiG-21MF and MiG-21bis were almost exclusively used in fighter-bomber roles, together with Mi-24/25/35 helicopters. MiG-23MLs played their intended role – that of battlefield interceptors.

Operating at medium levels, and due to the lack of an effective look-down/shoot-down capability, they were never effective against numerous SAAF aircraft flying at extremely low levels of barely 15 metres (some, when bush covering allowed, down to ten metres, something the enemy would not even contemplate).

In the face of the MiG as well as SAM threats, SAAF aircraft began operating by night, something that neither the Cubans nor the Angolans were doing. Attacking by night, the Mirages initially delivered several heavy blows, but on 20 February the F.1AZ flown by Major Ed Every was shot down by SA-13s shortly after releasing his bombs.

The SAAF unit to which this Mirage was attached, 1st Squadron, was then ordered to provide a presence over South African troops involved inside Angola, despite the fact that the battlefield was on the very edge of effective range of its aircraft. This led to a new series of engagements with Cuban-flown MiG-23s but also culminated in a direct confrontation between the Cubans and South Africans.

On 25 February, the Cuban ground control advised First Lieutenant Eladio Avila from the 12th Fighter Squadron, underway for an air-to-ground sortie, about the appearance of the two SAAF Mirages. Avila initiated a pursuit and his opponents were apparently not aware of his presence. But short of reaching his maximum engagement range – a control light in the cockpit warned him about his fast depleting fuel status.

After turning away, Avila was finally forced to land at Cuito Cuanavale airfield, even though the town was under almost constant bombardment from South African G-5 and G-6 long-range 155mm calibre guns. Remarkably, ground crews managed to refuel the aircraft and Avila took off again without any further incident.

Several hours later, Captain Orlando Carbo and his wingman were vectored to intercept three Mirage F.1AZs flown by Commandant Johan Rankin, Major Frans Coetzee and Captain Trompie Nel. The approaching MiGs were detected by the SAAF control station monitoring enemy radio traffic, and then only after the MiG pilots had established visual contact.

Warned about the MiGs, Captain Rankin swung his jet around to counter-attack and positioned himself behind Carbo's MiG-23. In turn, having been warned by his ground controller, the Cuban pilot accelerated while doing several reverses in order to shake off the Mirage. Rankin fired two missiles and also his 30mm cannons. But with the Angolan fighter accelerating away, he missed.

This was the last known air-to-air engagement involving Angolan MiGs and the SAAF. The Soviet surrogates were to take part in a number of additional combat sorties flown against UNITA and SADF troops for the rest of the year, but most of those events are not as well documented.

For example, Lieutenant Colonel Dolf Prinsloo, who took over command of No 1 Squadron SAAF, also participated in an engagement with a FAPA-DAA/DAAFAR MiG-23ML and years later met up with one of the senior Angolan MiG-23 pilots. He told him that that confrontation was the best thing that had ever happened to him as he 'learned more in a couple of minutes than a million words could have ever taught him.'

A single exception might be the attack of a SADF mechanised force against Tumpo in March 1988, which had its impetus checked by a combination of minefields, Angolan artillery barrages and numerous air strikes by MiG-21s and MiG-23s. The South Africans lost two Olifant main battle tanks as well as two Ratel Infantry Combat Vehicles. Three troops were killed in the fighting. The Cubans went on to use the wrecks of the two Olifants captured extensively for propaganda purposes.

By this time, the Soviets, Cubans and the MPLA were very much aware that they would never win the war, as was South Africa's military command even though Pretoria's politicians – their heads perpetually in the clouds and totally out of touch with real life – believed otherwise.

With the Soviets, stretched to the limit in Afghanistan and signalling their decision to pull out of Angola in early May 1988, Castro indicated to his senior commanders that the time had come to prepare for a pull-out. Obviously, a face-saving measure was needed to avoid the withdrawal looking like a defeat and also to raise the morale of the soldiers. It was essential that all Cuban forces return home as 'victorious'.

As the SADF was now disengaging towards the south, their movements were explained to the Cuban populace as a 'defeat of the Boers in the battle of Cuito Cuanavale' which never happened. By 23 May that year, the Cubans had about 50,000 troops in Angola (down from something like 110,000 at best), of which some 10,000 were advancing towards the northern border of South West Africa.

Bringing the airfield at Xangongo into shape in order to accept MiG-23MLs, the Cuban Air Force was able to start sending patrols even further south and the SAAF – ill-equipped to counter this threat because of lower-ranking air power – had to be restrained, even if the majority of their aviators were all systems go …

A rather inevitable final confrontation had to take place. By 26 June, three columns of the Cuban 50th Mechanised Division, covered by mobile SA-6 SAMs, advanced towards the hydro-electric dam at Ruacana-Caleque. There a battalion-sized SADF armoured and mechanised force was waiting for its turn to cross the Cunene River back into South West Africa.

The South Africans confronted the oncoming enemy, hitting the over-confident Cubans with heavy artillery. Suffering losses, Castro's soldiers continued their assault, threatening to outflank. SADF armoured columns then swiftly manoeuvred to hit the enemy's central positions causing additional heavy losses, while heavy 155mm artillery pounded the Angolan western column before forcing it to pull back.

In the end, the Cubans left at least 30 damaged and destroyed tanks and APCs, as well as 300 killed and injured troops on the battlefield. For all that, both sides disengaged in good order.

While the result of this clash tended to discourage Cuban and Angolan commanders to again engage the SADF on the ground, the Cuban Air Force in Angola was ordered to prepare for one last counter-attack. On 27 June 1988, a dozen MiG-23MLs – eight armed with FAB-250 bombs – were sent in to attack the hydroelectric dam at Ruacana-Caleque within the borders of South West Africa. Most bombs missed, but one bounced off the dam, causing some damage, while another – purely by accident – fell directly near a SADF fighting vehicle, killing 12 SADF soldiers. In turn, SADF anti-aircraft guns shot down one of the MiGs.

The results of this attack and several threatening manoeuvres by Cuban troops along the border with South West Africa were trumpeted by the Cuban propaganda machine, which in turn enabled Castro to pull his forces out of Angola without losing face.

Havana declared Techipa as an immense victory, and the overextended success of the MiG-23-strike against the Ruacana-Caleque dam became one of the major Cuban propaganda campaigns of the war. An argument used to 'confirm' an overwhelming Cuban victory during this final series of clashes is a photo supposedly showing an inscription left behind by the SADF troops on some wall of the Ruacana-Caleque dam. It read: 'MIK23 sak van die hart', whatever that was supposed to mean.

Looking back, it is clear that during the Angolan campaigns of 1987 and 1988, FAPA-DAA and DAAFAR contingents in Angola suffered a confirmed loss of eight MiG-23MLs, four MiG-21s as well as two Su-20Ms shot down (but also seven SA-8, five SA-13, and three SA-9 vehicles captured).

The best documented of these occurred on 28 October 1987, when two high-ranking Cuban officers, Lieutenant Colonel Rocas Garcias and Captain Ramos Cacadas, were captured after their MiG-21UM was shot down by Stinger missiles in UNITA hands. In addition, Angolan ground units lost most of the equipment of four of their brigades, as well as almost three dozen SA-14 MANPADs, which – together with remaining stocks of CIA-supplied FIM-92A Stingers – were used by UNITA forces over the next two years to cause extensive losses.

Total Cuban and Angolan losses during the campaigns between September 1987 and June 1988 included 4,785 soldiers killed while the number of deserters and injured remains unknown. In contrast, the SADF lost 31 men killed. UNITA losses remain unknown.

Consequently, it can only be concluded that most of the recently published claims about South African Air Force losses during the war in Angola should actually be seen as the continuation of Havana's efforts to present their actions in 1988 as a 'Final Victory'. What these distortions did provide was a reason for Cuba's withdrawal from Angola.

In his book *Continent Ablaze; The Insurgency Wars in Africa, 1960 to the Present*: Arms and Armour Press 1998, John W. Turner sets the record straight:

> The fighting from August of 1987 to July of 1988 was in many ways the climax of the Super Power involvement in the war. It was marked by extensive South African ground and air intervention to assist UNITA in repelling the most ambitious FAPLA offensive yet to be launched against insurgent-held areas of Cuando Cubango and Moxico provinces.
>
> During the course of the fighting FAPLA suffered one of the worst defeats to befall an army since the Second World War. The SADF intervention (Operation Modular) began modestly as UNITA attempted to stiffen its resistance to the invaders in Cuando Cubango in August, and picked up through September as South African artillery repelled two attempts by FAPLA to cross the Lomba River. Finally, South African mechanised forces intervened to annihilate one of the FAPLA task forces in battles which took place over two days, 3 and 4 October.
>
> This defeat was followed by the FAPLA withdrawal toward Cuito Cuanavale, which was put under siege by UNITA and bombarded by South Africans (Operations Hooper and Packer). At the same time, UNITA made considerable gains in the central plateau area and on the CFB, most of which was later regained by FAPLA at great cost.

Frustrated in attempts to remedy the situation in Angola's central and eastern regions, FAPLA and the Cubans redeployed their forces in south-western Angola towards the Namibian border. There they sparred with the SADF until being decisively checked on 26-27 June at Techipa in Cunene province.

Following this battle, the Cubans were convinced that further military confrontation with the SADF would not succeed but launched a major propaganda and diplomatic campaign to cover their setbacks and losses.

They also apparently decided to leave the MPLA to its fate, accepting the joint proposal by Washington, Moscow and Lisbon that led to total Cuban troop withdrawal from Angola and Namibia's independence.

The situation in mid-1988

The results of a year of South African involvement inside Angola were profound. The armed intervention by the SADF decisively changed the course of the war and despite massive Soviet, Cuban and MPLA propaganda to the contrary, FAPLA and its supporters were effectively beaten.

FAPLA casualties included at least a fifth of its ground forces either killed or wounded in action. At least a quarter of its available equipment was either destroyed or captured. Much equipment in the latter category wound up in UNITA hands to be very fielded against its original owners.

It was the battle at Techipa that took place late June 1988, with its high Cuban casualties that discouraged Havana from further engaging South African forces. Castro agreed to withdraw his troops and aviators from Angola in a linkage with the implementation of United Nations Resolution 435, which began the independence process for Namibia.

As history has shown, this represented a major policy defeat for the Angolan ruling MPLA, the Cubans as well as the Soviet Union, because after the foreign contingents pulled out, the civil war continued for another decade.

It took a tough, well experienced and professional bunch of South African mercenaries (almost all former SADF Special Forces and operating under the auspices of Executive Outcomes) to bring an end to it all.

Acknowledgement from Tom Cooper

Special thanks to Tom N. for sharing his extensive database on the Angolan Air Force as well as to Luis D., for revealing exclusive details about correct unit designations of the Cuban Air Force, based on his close contacts with local sources. Finally, special thanks to Grant Barclay for reminding us about the loss of the Bosbok from No 42 Squadron, shot down by an Angolan SA-8 in September 1987.

Pumas played an invaluable role throughout the war. (Willem Steenkamp photo)

SAAF Mirage jet fighters lined up at Waterkloof Air Force base in Pretoria. Many of these French-built aircraft saw good service in Angola. On a one-to-one basis though, were no match when trying to counter more advanced Soviet combat aircraft like the Soviet MiG-23.

A trio of SAAF Impala ground-support jets in wartime camouflage livery over the ocean.

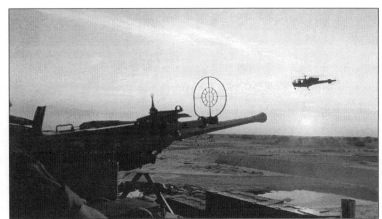

SAAF Alouette helicopter gunship returns to base at sunset, offset by one of the unit's anti-aircraft guns in the foreground. (Author's photo)

Hand-held MANPAD supersonic anti-aircraft missile of the kind that both FAPLA and UNITA used in Angola. (Image Pierre Louw Victor)

South African pilots overflying Angolan positions had to contend with Soviet anti-aircraft missiles, as had government planes. This Angolan Hind was brought down by UNITA who were fielding American Stinger missiles.

Tried and trusted in many major wars for the past 70 or more years – from World War II, almost to the present day – the venerable old Douglas Dakota served the South African Air Force throughout the Border War's 23 years.

Forward operational air base adjacent to the Angolan border. (Author's photo)

SAAF Buccaneer bomber, of which several were bought from Britain before sanctions began to make serious inroads in South Africa's ability to acquire modern military aircraft.

A squadron of SAAF Puma helicopters in flight.

Dean Wingrin took this classic of a SAAF Hercules transport aircraft taxiing in preparation for take-off.

10

What Happened to South Africa's Secret Atom Bomb Project?

David Albright is no stranger to South Africa. As head of Washington's Institute for Science and International Security – or ISIS (the *real* ISIS) as he likes to stress – he was one of the first on the scene both before and after Pretoria decided to dispose of its six atom bombs. As one of the leading authorities on nuclear weapons proliferation, he is often seen on CNN, Fox News, the BBC and others. One of his recent books is *Revisiting South Africa's Nuclear Weapons Program*, published in the United States in 2016.[1]

President F.W. de Klerk's announcement in March 1993 that South Africa had secretly (and very successfully) developed a small nuclear arsenal – and then junked it – was startling in its candour. The news that the nation had actually built atom bombs emerged some time afterwards. Nevertheless, de Klerk's formal announcement left many questions unanswered, including the scope and sophistication of the programme, as well as its rationale. Decades later, some questions linger. Others can be answered, including the fact that one stage this African nation had nuclear weapons in its arsenal and that Pretoria would have used them had it needed to do so …

Nuclear Blackmail

The bedrock question, of course, is why South Africa developed and built fission weapons in the first place. It is not yet possible for an outsider to answer that question with full confidence. One can only report what South African scientists, engineers, and policy-makers say, on the record and off. To a man, they claim that the weapons were never intended for military use.

According to these sources, the weapons came out of a technological 'can-do' mentality that coincided with South Africa's increasing international isolation in the 1970s and 1980s. The country's leaders believed that using nuclear weapons would have been akin to committing suicide. Instead, they say, the government gradually developed a strategy that involved using South Africa's bombs for 'political' purposes.

The emerging strategy was designed to bring Western governments to South Africa's aid in the event of an overwhelming attack by Soviet-inspired military forces then in southern Africa. At a

---

1   David H. Albright and Andrea Stricker: *Revisiting South Africa's Nuclear Weapons Program – Its History, Dismantling and Lessons for Today*, CreateSpace Independent Publishing Platform, USA, 2016.

moment of crisis, the government would have declared or 'demonstrated' the weapons. An official who described this 'strategy of uncertainty' said that Pretoria would have revealed its nuclear capability only if 'the country found itself with its back to the wall.'

Because its strategy of uncertainty required secrecy to work, South Africa kept its weapons production infrastructure extremely secret. As a consequence, the programme could not depend on outside assistance as much as expected.

Also, there are ANC members who believe the apartheid government would have dropped nuclear bombs on black Africans to defend the Afrikaner way of life.

The African National Congress's Roger Jardine disagrees. He describes apartheid South Africa as a high-tech *laager* guaranteed by nuclear weapons. Jardine, national coordinator of the ANCs Science and Technology Policy Division is only one of many.

In any case, in the late 1980s, the end of the Cold War reduced tensions in Africa and many in the government came to believe that nuclear weapons were unnecessary. Shortly after F.W. de Klerk became president in 1989, he ordered a halt to the nuclear weapons programme in anticipation of acceding to the Nuclear Non-Proliferation Treaty (NPT). On 10 July 1991, South Africa became a member of the NPT.

Coming Clean

It was not until 24 March 1993, four years after ordering their destruction, that de Klerk publicly acknowledged South Africa's nuclear weapons. According to Waldo Stumpf, chief executive officer of the state-controlled Atomic Energy Corporation (AEC), the government feared that revealing the fact of its nuclear arsenal earlier could have led to confrontational inspections similar to those then (taking place) in Iraq. Stumpf also believes that South Africa's political strife made it difficult to acknowledge the programme.

When it acceded to the NPT in 1991, South Africa was under no obligation to reveal past nuclear weapons activities. The NPT essentially looks forward, although it requires extensive accounting of a nation's nuclear material and facilities when the treaty takes effect.

However, soon after International Atomic Energy Agency (IAEA) inspectors began to visit South Africa's nuclear facilities in 1991, they suspected that there had been a nuclear weapons programme. Their suspicions centred on a large inventory of weapons-grade uranium metal stored at the AECs Pelindaba Nuclear Research Centre, 25 kilometres west of Pretoria. This stockpile had been declared to the IAEA as part of the accounting of the nuclear material.

But the IAEA kept its suspicions to itself – the IAEA charter prevents it from sharing confidential safeguard information with the public. In addition, the South African government insisted that the IAEA maintain a strict level of confidentiality.

Still, leaks about the IAEAs inspection activities began immediately and led the public and the ANC to learn something about the nuclear programme. First, the press reported the existence of the stockpiled weapons-grade uranium. Later press reports estimated its size and described old nuclear weapons production facilities at Pelindaba.

In late 1992, the ANC intensified its efforts to uncover the nuclear weapons programme, charging that the government might have hidden some weapons-grade material from the IAEA. De Klerk acknowledged the effect of ANC and other efforts in his March 1993 announcement, saying that charges were 'regularly taken up by both the local and international press', and, that they were 'beginning to take on the dimensions of a campaign.'

Although the ANC welcomed the public disclosure of the bomb programme, it greeted de Klerk's announcement with suspicion and it continues to raise questions about the programme.

While doubts still linger, a great deal of information about the nuclear weapons programme has been made public. Disclosures by Armscor and the AEC – the South African government's weapons and nuclear agencies – as well as the IAEA have led to a more complete picture of the South African nuclear weapons programme.

Pulling the Pieces Together

The South African nuclear weapons programme demonstrated perseverance, patience, and technical competence. The scale of the programme was small at its peak it could produce only one or two weapons a year. Its total cost was also small, only a tiny fraction of South Africa's total defence budget.

From the 1960s until the programme was cancelled in 1989, South Africa made steady progress toward safe, secure, and deliverable nuclear weapons. When the program was cancelled, it was poised to develop more advanced weapons including warheads for ballistic missiles.

Like other threshold countries with nuclear weapons programmes, South Africa procured many important items overseas. Its imports were also aimed at creating indigenous nuclear capabilities. Because of its technological capabilities, however, South Africa depended less on imports than Iraq or Pakistan.

In the 1950s and 1960s, South Africa's civilian nuclear programme received extensive assistance from abroad. Staff members were sent to Europe and the United States for training in various nuclear fields with the result that South Africa was able to build a solid nuclear infrastructure. This foundation was undoubtedly important in its efforts to obtain nuclear weapons.

During this period, the United States supplied South Africa with the Safari-1 research reactor, commissioned in 1965 at the Pelindaba Nuclear Research Centre and subjected to IAEA safeguards. Over the next ten years, the United States also supplied the reactor with about 100 kilograms of weapons-grade uranium fuel.

However, when the international community began instituting international sanctions against the apartheid government in the 1970s, South Africa's nuclear programme was one of its first targets. In 1975, the United States suspended additional shipments of fuel to the Safari reactor.

Faced with UN sanctions, South Africa began to organise clandestine procurement networks in Europe and the United States, and a long, secret collaboration with Israel. These secret dealings for technology, knowledge, material, and equipment were designed to meet South Africa's armaments needs as effectively and economically as possible.

A common question is whether Israel provided South Africa with weapons design assistance, although available evidence argues against significant cooperation. In any case, Armscor is unlikely to have used Israeli assistance in developing its nuclear devices.

By the end of the 1980s, South Africa had imported machine tools, furnaces, and other equipment for the programme. Most of these items were not proscribed by international nuclear export controls but were imported in violation of international sanctions imposed on the apartheid regime.

Fissile Material

The hardest part of building a nuclear explosive is acquiring an adequate supply of separated plutonium or highly enriched uranium (HEU). The Atomic Energy Board (AEB), the predecessor to the AEC, started researching methods of producing both materials in the 1960s. The programme initially focused on uranium enrichment and a locally designed power reactor to produce plutonium.

Plutonium

The power reactor programme, aimed at producing plutonium, first attempted to develop heavy water moderated, natural uranium-fuelled, sodium-cooled reactor. The indigenously built Pelinduna critical facility, which depended on a US supply of 606 kilograms of two percent enriched uranium and 5.4 metric tons of heavy water, went critical in 1967. Because it was not competitive with light water reactors and was draining resources from the enrichment programme, both the critical facility and this reactor type were abandoned in 1969. Before the enriched uranium was returned to the United States in 1971, the slightly irradiated fuel produced at Pelinduna was sent to Britain for reprocessing.

Enriched Uranium

The uranium enrichment programme, which ran parallel to the plutonium programme, made steady progress throughout the 1960s. It started secretly, in a small warehouse in central Pretoria. As more sophisticated experiments and stricter security measures were needed, the project moved in the mid-1960s to the Pelindaba Nuclear Research Centre. By the end of 1967, the enrichment programme had succeeded in enriching uranium on a laboratory scale. After an external review of the process, the government decided in early 1969 to build a pilot plant. As more organisations and individuals learned of the project, the government decided that the enrichment programme's existence could no longer be kept secret. But the underlying purpose of the programme remained highly classified, hidden behind declarations that its purpose was to enrich uranium for commercial applications.

In 1970, the government publicly announced that it intended to build the Y-Plant at Valindaba, next to the Pelindaba Research Centre. It also created a separate state corporation, the Uranium Enrichment Corporation (UCOR) to build the enrichment programme. (UCOR and the AEB, were merged into the AEC in 1982.)

The South African enrichment process uses an aerodynamic technique similar to a stationary wall centrifuge. Uranium hexafluoride and hydrogen gas spin inside a small stationary tube and centrifugal effects created by rapid spinning causes the uranium separation. The mixture enters at high speed through holes in the side of the tube and spirals toward the ends of the tube. When the mixture reaches the holes at the ends of the tube, its radius of curvature is reduced several fold, significantly increasing the separation of uranium isotopes. The heavy fraction, containing more uranium-238, exits to the side. The lighter fraction, which contains more uranium-235, exits straight out the end.

Foreign Assistance

Press reports and members of the ANC often assert that the enrichment programme depends almost totally on the Becker nozzle process which was developed in Germany in the 1960s. Not enough is known about the history of the enrichment programme to determine if this is true, but the available information strongly suggests that assertions about the importance of the Becker nozzle process are exaggerated.

Undoubtedly, the South Africans learned about the Becker nozzle programme from published sources. But the separating elements in the South African process are not the same as Becker nozzle elements. According to participants and Western government experts, the Y-Plant's success depended principally on the skill and initiative of its scientists and technicians. They went through years of trial and error before producing significant amounts of enriched uranium. Behind this talent was the government's willingness to provide adequate funding to solve complicated problems. Because the Y-Plant was a vital part of the nuclear explosives programme, it received enough funding to overcome glitches in the enrichment process and in the mass production of high-precision components.

Nevertheless, many components and materials for the enrichment programme were acquired abroad. Important instrumentation and valves were imported via circuitous routes and small quantities of unsafeguarded uranium hexafluoride were imported from France.

However, the programme was unable to get everything it wanted. For example, in the South African process, it is particularly difficult to seal the area where a rotating shaft enters a compressor. Unable to get foreign items, personnel were forced to solve this problem on their own, which they eventually did.

The Y-Plant

The Y-Plant began commissioning in 1974 and began producing highly enriched uranium (HEU) in 1978. After overcoming several technical and chemical problems, the plant was able to produce a steady output of HEU for the weapons programme. In addition, the plant produced 45 percent enriched uranium for the Safari research reactor, low-enriched uranium (LEU) test assemblies for the Koeberg nuclear power reactors near Cape Town, and LEU blending stock. The blending stock was mixed with imported, unsafeguarded LEU from China and this mix of low-enriched uranium was used for fuel at Koeberg.

The Y-Plant was originally designed to produce about 10-15,000 separative work units (SWUs) a year, but design improvements increased its potential annual output to 20,000. Chemical reactions and inefficient mechanical processes ('mixing') caused losses in the enriched uranium output, and the plant never achieved its design output. Assuming that it averaged about 10,000 SWUs per year, the plant could have produced about 60 kilograms of 90 percent enriched uranium a year, or roughly enough for one of the devices of South African design. Because the plant was also producing enriched uranium for reactor fuel, it never produced weapons-grade uranium at that rate. During its lifetime, the Y-Plant produced a total of about 400 kilograms of uranium enriched above 80 percent, the minimum enrichment used in South Africa's nuclear weapons. The Y-Plant closed in 1990 – the first official hint that the still-secret weapons programme had ended.

'Peaceful Nuclear Explosives'

The effort to build nuclear explosive devices had its origins in the 1960s under the auspices of a 'peaceful nuclear explosives' (PNEs) programme. According to the AEC's Waldo Stumpf, early investigations were modest and limited to studies of the literature. In 1969, the AEB established an internal committee to investigate the economic and technical aspects of using PNEs in mining.

In 1971, with a source of HEU in sight, the AEB received permission from the minister of mines to begin secret research and development work on nuclear explosive devices for peaceful purposes. These investigations were based on literature studies, theoretical calculations, and preliminary studies of the ballistics of gun-type devices. In addition, limited theoretical studies of implosion devices were conducted, according to J.W. de Villiers, chairman of the AEC, who is widely believed to have headed the nuclear explosive programme in the 1970s. He said that only three engineers were involved in the ballistics research and theoretical implosion work.

Because the AEB lacked adequate facilities at Pelindaba, in 1972 and 1973, a small team of AEB personnel worked under tight security at a propulsion laboratory at the Somchem establishment near Cape Town. An Armscor official said recently he doubts that the management of Somchem knew what the team was working on. (Until the early 1990s, Somchem was an Armscor facility involved in the development and manufacture of explosives and propellants, and later, rocket launchers. Somchem is now a division of Denel Limited.)

At Somchem, AEB personnel worked on the mechanical and pyrotechnic subsystems for a gun-type device. The team designed a scale model which, with a projectile constructed of non-nuclear material, was tested at Somchem in May 1974.

This test convinced the AEB that a nuclear explosive was feasible. In 1974, Prime Minister John Vorster approved the development of a limited nuclear explosive capability and the construction of an underground test site.

During the next three years, the AEB developed internal ballistic and neutronic computer programmes, conducted experiments to determine properties of the materials in the devices, designed and constructed a critical facility in Building 5000 at Pelindaba and experimented with propellants for a gun-type device. The team working at Somchem tested the first full-scale model of the gun-type device using a natural uranium projectile in 1976. This test proved the mechanical integrity of the design.

The Test Site and First Device

Meanwhile, the AEB selected a test site in the Kalahari Desert, the Vastrap testing range north of Upington. Two test shafts were completed in 1976 and 1977. One was 385 metres deep and the other was 216 metres deep.

In 1977, the AEB established its own high-security weapons research and development facilities at Pelindaba, and during that year the programme was transferred from Somchem to Pelindaba. Later that year the AEB produced a gun-type device-without an HEU core. The Y-Plant was operating by this time, but it had not yet produced enough weapons-grade uranium for a device. As has happened in programmes in other nations, the development of the devices outpaced the production of the fissile material.

AEC officials say that a 'cold test' (a test without uranium-235) was planned for August 1977. An Armscor official who was not involved at the time said that the test would have been a fully instrumented underground test with a dummy core. Its major purpose was to test the logistical plans for an actual detonation.

How that test was cancelled has been well publicised. That summer, Soviet intelligence detected test preparations and, in early August, alerted Washington. US intelligence quickly confirmed the existence of the test site and on August 28, the *Washington Post* quoted a US official: 'I'd say we were 99 percent certain that the construction was preparation for an atomic test.'

The Soviet and Western governments were convinced that South Africa was preparing for a full-scale nuclear test. During the next two weeks in August, they strongly pressed South Africa not to test. The French foreign minister warned of 'grave consequences' for French–South African relations. Although he did not elaborate, his statement implied that France was willing to cancel its contract to provide South Africa with the Koeberg nuclear power reactors.

Looking back, the South African explanation of a planned 'cold test' at the Kalahari site is plausible. Perhaps the AEB believed the site would not be discovered. In any case, in the summer of 1993, de Villiers told me that when the test site was exposed, he ordered its immediate shutdown. The site was abandoned and the holes sealed.

Of significance here is the fact that Commodore Dieter Gerhardt, the commander of the Simonstown Naval Base near Cape Town who was arrested as a KGB spy in 1982, says that the

Soviets expressed their concern to the United States a year earlier. He declared in an interview that a Russian told him that the Soviet Union and the United States met about the South African weapons programme in 1976 and during this meeting, the Soviets presented evidence of South Africa's nuclear programme and asked for US cooperation in stopping it. Gerhardt said that one of several options mentioned by the Russians was a pre-emptive military strike on the Y-Plant and added that the United States rejected that option.)

Although the test was cancelled, the nuclear explosive programme continued unabated. In 1978, the AEB built a second, smaller device. This device was designed to be rapidly deployed for a fully instrumented underground nuclear test at the Kalahari site.

This second device was still not loaded with fissile material. The Y-Plant had produced its first HEU, but it was not until the second half of 1979 that the plant would produce enough for a device, about 55 kilograms of material. This first batch of HEU was only about 80 percent enriched. The device was designed to use weapons-grade uranium (greater than 90 percent enriched), but the principal effect of the lower enrichment would have been a lower [explosive] yield. According to the IAEA, this device was kept for demonstration purposes throughout the programme and was never converted into a deliverable weapon. Its code name was reported to be 'Melba'.

Building 5000

When the Y-Plant had produced enough HEU, the material was converted into metal and sent to the recently completed critical assembly facility in Building 5000. This tall grey building sits in a valley on the south-western portion of the Pelindaba site, away from the main complex. Building 5000 was operated by the Reactor Development Group.

While there, I drove to Building 5000, which is in a small compound inside a security fence about five minutes by car from the main research site. The building is empty except for some old equipment and waste barrels from other parts of the Pelindaba site.

In the late 1970s, this building tested the gun-type device. For a brief moment, the HEU metal went critical, providing confidence that the device would work as predicted by theoretical calculations. When the Manhattan Project scientists conducted this dangerous experiment, they called it 'tickling the dragon's tail.'

Several other buildings with addresses such as 5100 or 5200 are also located in this valley and were dedicated to developing a nuclear explosive. The Atomic Energy Board had the capability to develop propellants for gun-type devices and high explosives for implosion weapons. Today, these facilities are either abandoned or dedicated to non-nuclear uses.

According to an AEC official, after the first test, the critical facility was never loaded with HEU again, even for civilian experiments.

Within a few years, Pelindaba's weapons manufacturing capabilities were replaced by new Armscor facilities several kilometres away. The critical facility, however, was not replaced. Since the basic 'physics package' of South Africa's device remained unchanged, a single experiment was apparently considered adequate.

When the IAEA began its inspections in 1991, South Africa was not obligated to reveal the existence of the critical facility or the other buildings in the valley. The NPT requires only that nuclear facilities existing at the time of signing the treaty be declared. The IAEA however, had learned of Building 5000 from Western intelligence, asked for and was granted permission to inspect it.

From Explosives to the Bomb

All South African officials agree that the shift in emphasis from peaceful nuclear explosives to strategic deterrence was in response to South Africa's deteriorating security situation.

The apartheid regime feared Soviet expansionist policies in southern Africa and was alarmed by the build-up of Cuban forces in Angola starting in 1975. (This fear was not unfounded because recent disclosures by a defector to the United States disclosed that the Cuban army and air forces increased to more than 100,000 personnel by the time the Angolan war ended.)

Increasingly isolated, the South African government was convinced that outside assistance was unlikely in the event of an attack.

There is some disagreement, however, about when officials adopted a military justification for South Africa's nuclear explosives programme. President de Klerk said in his March 1993 announcement that the decision to develop a limited nuclear deterrent capability was taken as early as 1974, and de Villiers agrees. In contrast, Stumpf says that the programme was not military in nature until 1977. The shift may have been stimulated by the episode in the Kalahari. Stumpf says that the prime minister's formal approval of a deterrent strategy came only in April 1978.

Armscor, which agrees with Stumpf, says that the formal shift occurred in 1978. One Armscor official characterised the entire AEB nuclear explosive programme as civilian. The AEB, he said, did not 'fly' anything and was apparently referring to the inability of the nuclear establishment to produce a deliverable weapon which, in Armscor's view, was necessary for a credible deterrent.

The deterrent strategy that began to emerge in this period was ultimately based on three phases, the final aim of which was to obtain Western assistance in the case of an overwhelming military threat. The First Phase was a 'strategic uncertainty' during which South Africa's nuclear capability would be neither acknowledged nor denied.

If the country were threatened militarily, it would move to Phase Two. The government would covertly acknowledge the existence of its nuclear weapons to leading Western governments, particularly to the United States. If that failed to persuade the international community to come to South Africa's assistance, the government would move to Phase Three: it would publicly acknowledge its capability or demonstrate it with an underground test.

That said, this policy did require a credible nuclear weapon and according to Armscor officials, credibility required deliverability. They declared that if the government had decided to show its nuclear devices to a Western power as part of Phase Two, the devices would have had to have been deliverable. If the nuclear devices were only test devices, the Western powers might not take South Africa's threat seriously enough to intervene on its behalf.

According to the de Klerk government, the weapons were never intended for actual use and were never deployed militarily or integrated into the country's military doctrine. In essence, the weapons were the last card in a political bluff intended to blackmail the United States or other Western powers. Whether it would have worked is impossible to determine.

Armscor Takes Over

With the shift to strategic deterrence in 1979 the government gave Armscor the job of manufacturing additional nuclear devices. The AEC was charged with providing nuclear materials, health physics support as well as theoretical studies and development work in more advanced nuclear weapons technology.

The Armscor-run nuclear weapons programme had three main components:

- development and production of a number of deliverable gun-type devices;
- studies of implosion and thermonuclear technology, including 'boosted' devices. (Boosting increases the explosive yield of a fission device. In such a device, the thermonuclear reaction of tritium and deuterium produces a spike of neutrons that fission significantly more plutonium or highly enriched uranium);
- and research and development of production and recovery of plutonium and tritium, and production of lithium.

The Circle building where Armscor was involved in the nuclear programme lies about 15 kilometres east of Pelindaba. (This site was later renamed Advena). Armscor's chief responsibility was the manufacture of deliverable gun-type devices and the Circle building essentially duplicated (under one roof) most of the development and manufacturing capabilities at Pelindaba.

Circle was built in 1980 and commissioned in May 1981. The facility essentially comprised the Circle building and a nearby environmental test facility that was involved in the development and integration of cannon type devices.

Circle was built deep within another Armscor site, Gerotek. This site tests vehicles at high speeds and on various types of road surfaces and grades. The turn-off to Circle, marked only with a sign that says 'Workshop', is several minutes' drive inside Gerotek's main gate. The entire site is hilly and on the hillsides are many graded tracks for testing vehicles.

The exterior of the Circle building is nondescript. Inside are two floors with a total of 8,000 square metres of floor space. The lower floor was dedicated to making nuclear devices. The top floor contained mostly offices and conference rooms. The only external clue to the potential importance of the building was a large embankment built next to the building to block prying eyes from seeing the building from a nearby road deep within the Gerotek compound. Advena's managers also blocked proposals to place sophisticated communications on the roof to avoid a 'signature' that might attract the attention of intelligence agencies.

The first floor of the Circle building had conventional workshops for making mechanical and electrical equipment. There were also storage rooms, uranium casting and machining workshops, a large vault, integration rooms where portions of the devices were assembled as well as eight 'cells' for testing internal ballistics, propellants, igniters, and small quantities of high explosives for self-destruct mechanisms.

An explosive test chamber located in one of the cells could handle up to 2.5 kilograms of high explosive. It was also used to conduct plane-wave experiments with shaped charges and to develop high-speed instrumentation for preliminary work on implosion designs. Another cell contained the 'pigsty', a wood enclosure where projectile tests were done for the gun-type device.

The designers put a 'plenum' or large room above these cells. In the event of an accident, this room would serve to dissipate the overpressure from an explosion, preventing the collapse of the roof or the walls. Holes at one end of the room would allow the explosion to vent. From the outside, the holes were disguised as ventilation ducts.

Manufacturing HEU shapes for the devices generated scrap and nuclear waste, which were sent back to the AEC for recovery or disposal and all shipments despatched at night to minimise detection.

In the early 1980s, the programme employed about 100 people, of which only about 40 were directly involved in the weapons programme and only 20 actually built the devices. The rest were involved in administrative support and security. By the time the programme was cancelled in 1989, the workforce had risen to 300, with about half directly involved in weapons work.

The Armscor Approach

Armscor approached the problem of building nuclear weapons very differently than the AEB. Comprised principally of engineers and employed by the military, Armscor's philosophy differed from that of the AEC, which was essentially a civilian scientific organisation.

Armscor considered the AEBs November 1979 device to be an unqualified design that could not meet the rigid safety, security and reliability specifications then under development by Circle engineers. Moreover, the first device was not deliverable and the AEB device was transferred to Circle and placed in a special vault. It had been temporarily stored in an abandoned coal mine at Witbank, a former military ammunition depot.

Armscor manufactured its first device in April 1982, which it considered a 'pre-qualification' model. According to an Armscor official, it could be 'kicked out the back of a plane.'

Throughout, South African engineers involved emphasised reliability, safety and security. The system engineering department at Circle developed very strict qualification specifications. In addition, extraordinary secrecy requirements forced Circle to make many items in-house. As a result, according to Armscor, design refinement and re-qualification of the hardware took several years.

Many difficulties were encountered in the early years at Circle. Some of the development and production problems concerned repeatability of projectile velocity as well as repeatability of symmetry requirements when the projectile is injected; the density of the neutron reflectors; the plating of uranium components with nickel; and the reliability of arming and safing devices.

Ultimately though, Armscor's design was highly reliable – it had redundancy built into the system whenever possible and it was thoroughly qualified in terms of its internal ballistics and mechanical arming and safing operations.

Security

Armscor emphasised the physical security of both the devices and the HEU. A special high-security vault with many smaller vaults inside was installed inside the Circle building and access was tightly controlled.

Each nuclear device was divided into two sections, a front and a back. With the HEU distributed between the two halves, the design minimised the possibility of accidental detonation or unauthorised use.

According to an Armscor official, a front and a back end were never worked on simultaneously. Both ends could leave the vault at the same time only after three top ministers and the head of government inserted their separate sections of the code into the vault. No one person had the complete code.

The Highly Enriched Uranium involved was also tightly controlled. At the beginning of each work day, the HEU scheduled for use in a manufacturing area was carefully weighed to the nearest 0.1 gram before being checked out of the vault. At the end of each day, the material was removed from the processing and manufacturing areas and weighed again to a similar precision before being returned to the vault. HEU was not stored in process lines.

Circle personnel needed top secret security clearances. Only native-born South African citizens with no other citizenship could receive the necessary security clearance.

Safety

Circle engineers carefully studied failure modes and effects and conducted criticality analysis under a range of postulated storage, delivery and accident scenarios. According to Armscor, the devices exceeded safety requirements for this type of device, and 'subsystems were subjected to strenuous tests to ensure that reliability and safety criteria were met.'

A common safety concern with gun-type devices is that the propellant will accidentally fire, sending the projectile into the fixed end, causing a nuclear explosion. Another danger is that the projectile will accidentally slide down the barrel. At a minimum, this would cause a criticality accident, risking workers and contaminating the adjacent area.

To prevent such accidents, each device had mechanical safing mechanisms that blocked the projectile from reaching the other end and dissipated the pressure caused by the propellant firing. The first attempt at the safing mechanism did not work adequately, but later versions performed well.

Although implosion designs were never a high priority, safety considerations were already being factored into them. An implosion device poses a risk that an accidental detonation of high explosives will trigger a nuclear explosion. To reduce this risk, Circle engineers begin producing small quantities of TATB, an 'insensitive' high explosive in 1988.

Insensitive explosives ignite at higher temperatures than ordinary explosives and firing a bullet into TATB will not cause it to detonate.

Producing More Devices

With such stringent specifications, nuclear weapons production was slow. The first 'qualified' gun-type device was not completed until August 1987. This model could be delivered by a modified Buccaneer bomber and by the time the programme was cancelled; three more deliverable devices had been completed. The HEU core and some non-nuclear components for a seventh device had also been manufactured. This last device was intended as a second test device, more advanced than the first.

According to Armscor, 'all the devices were identical' in principle, but detail changes were made to enhance reliability.' Parts of some earlier models were recycled during the years of production.

The total mass of a completed device was about one metric ton. It had a diameter of nearly 65 centimetres and was about 1.8 metres long. Each device contained an estimated 55 kilograms of HEU. The cores of the second-through-seventh contained weapons-grade uranium. The reflector was made of tungsten and the calculated yield of each device was about 10 to 18 kilotons when the core had weapons-grade uranium. Using 80 percent enriched material halved the expected yield.

By the end of the programme, according to an Armscor official, they could have routinely manufactured these devices. At that point, the annual operating expenditures were about 20 to 25 million rand (roughly $5.9 to $7.4 million at the ruling exchange rate when the book was published).

In the early 1980s, the annual budget was about 10 million rand, then about $2.9 million.

Boosted Devices

Although Armscor took over most of the weapons portfolio, the AEC remained in charge of several important aspects. However, its scientists became increasingly discouraged by their role and began to leave the programme.

The AEC was charged with developing more advanced weapons. One result was that the AEC evaluated the use of tritium to boost gun-assembled devices. Apparently, the purpose would have been to boost the explosive yield from less than 18 to roughly 100 kilotons. According to the International Atomic Energy Agency, AEC officials said that this work did not involve the use of tritium, although the AEC had obtained a small stock of tritium in the mid-1970s from Israel and other sources (which one source said was never used).

The work was theoretical and did not involve any hardware, according to an Armscor official.

Armscor had little interest in the AECs work on boosted gun-type devices. Its weapons programme was simply not ready for such an advanced concept. Circle did not have any facilities to handle tritium, which is very radioactive and difficult to handle. In addition, Armscor officials said recently, if the purpose of the bomb programme was to demonstrate capability, so why would yield matter? The goal was a workable device.

- **Plutonium and Tritium Production:** The AEC was also responsible for evaluating methods to produce and recover plutonium and tritium. The AEC concentrated on the design of a reactor to be built at Gouriqua (not far from the mouth of the Gouritz River) near Mossel Bay in the Cape Province. They planned to build a 150-megawatt pressurised-water research and development reactor that could also produce plutonium and tritium, but the site was never developed beyond some rudimentary civil engineering preparations. In 1985, the weapons programme stopped funding the reactor programme and the AEC was unable to sustain the programme with its own funds. The AEC tried unsuccessfully to turn the reactor into a test facility for pressurised-water reactor fuel, but the programme ended in 1989 or 1990.
- **Neutron Initiators:** A unique feature of South Africa's gun-type design is that it did not use a neutron initiator – a device that generates neutrons to start the chain reaction in the super-critical material. South African devices were designed to use background, or stray, neutrons to initiate the chain reaction. Calculations showed that the chain reaction would start within a few microseconds after the HEU projectile hit the fixed HEU component. As long as the device was intended for an underground test or an airburst with an imprecise height, the lack of an initiator did not matter. Implosion devices, however, typically require a neutron initiator. As a result, the AEC began developing a miniaturised neutron generator based on accelerating deuterium into a tritium target. Only minute quantities of tritium and deuterium are required for a generator, and small quantities can be easily bought or produced.

Cutbacks

In September 1985, the government decided to limit the scope of the weapons programme. According to an AEC official, de Klerk's predecessor, Prime Minister P.W. Botha, recognised that the cost of the weapons programme could escalate significantly.

The government limited the programme to the seven gun-type weapons, stopped all work related to plutonium devices, halted efforts to produce plutonium and tritium for weapons and limited the production of lithium-6. But implosion development and theoretical work on more advanced devices continued.

Despite the cutbacks, the weapons programme was not ending as most of the weapons were manufactured after 1987. One Circle employee said that this period was one of considerable stress for employees at Advena.

In the mid-1980s, tensions in the southern African region were high. At that stage already, there were about 50,000 Cuban troops in Angola (soon to grow in strength to more than 100,000 according to recently disclosed documents out of Havana). According to one official, if the Soviet Union had made a greater effort in Angola, South Africa could not have stopped them. He said that the bush war in Angola had reached in parts reached a 'semi-conventional state.'

South Africa's nuclear 'strategy of uncertainty' was reaffirmed in the mid-1980s and the government wanted to know how long it would take to conduct an underground test. Before answering, Armscor wanted to assure itself that the underground test shafts could be used in a timely manner. According to Armscor, it needed to check the condition of at least one of the shafts in the Kalahari. To minimise the risk of exposure, Armscor built a shed over a shaft. The military conducted target shooting at the same time to provide a plausible cover for the operation.

In the desert, the water pumped out of the shaft could not be dumped on the ground without possibly tipping off intelligence agencies to what was happening. As a result, the water was put into containers and hauled off the site. Thereafter, technicians lowered a specially designed inspection probe that determined that the shaft was still intact.

Some South African officials have said that they believe that Western or Soviet intelligence discovered the shed and that this exercise convinced the Western powers that South Africa was serious about nuclear weapons. This, in turn, led them to start putting pressure on the Soviet Union and Cuba to withdraw from Angola. Whatever the case, during the mid-1980s the South African nuclear weapons programme was under the twin pressures of budget cuts and heightened requirements. As a result, the government decided to fund a new facility.

1990s: The Advena Central Laboratories

The government approved plans to build a new complex, the Advena Central Laboratories, which were about five minutes away from the Circle building.

The Advena buildings were just being completed when the programme was cancelled in 1989. The total cost of the new complex and upgrading the Circle building was 36 million rand.

Although Advena would have had many capabilities for advanced nuclear weapons work, its rate of weapons production would have been modest. Each year, it could have produced two to three weapons. According to Armscor, the 'occupation of the new Advena facilities started during 1988 and the process of commissioning was still underway when the programme was terminated.'

Armscor also said that the Circle building 'would have been used for the maintenance of the seven cannon-type devices' after the expansion to Advena.

After the programme was cancelled, both facilities were converted to commercial enterprises operated by Denel. The commercial programme continued to use the Advena and Circle facilities for a while, though on a smaller scale than originally envisaged.

In the late 1980s, Armscor had been preparing to upgrade the seven gun-type devices. Armscor said it planned to 'replace the seven cannon-type devices with seven up-graded devices when they reached the end of their estimated life by the year 2000.' The replacement devices would have been deliverable by aircraft and most likely also by ballistic missile, although a final decision about missiles had not yet been made.

The decision to build new facilities was motivated by several factors. Armscor needed more modern and sophisticated facilities for its long-term goals. It was going to replace the gun-type devices and conduct nuclear-weapons development work on advanced gun-type and implosion-type devices. At the same time, Armscor was diversifying into conventional military pyrotechnics and missile control components, such as 'jet vanes'.

Also, the programme had outgrown the Circle building. The labour force had increased from 100 to 300, and more space was needed. Workers were tired of being confined to limited space in the Circle building. They expressed relief that the new buildings were better lighted than Circle which had no windows and felt claustrophobic.

In addition, the Circle building had been designed so that only project participants could enter the building. The new site made it possible to host visitors without divulging the true purpose of the programme.

Advena had an extensive array of nuclear weapons manufacturing capabilities aimed at advanced designs. It had sophisticated capabilities in high explosives, theoretical calculations, metallurgy, high-speed electronics, environmental and reliability testing, and ultra high-speed diagnostics.

Implosion

Although research on implosion-type devices had been conducted since the beginning of South Africa's nuclear explosives programme, implosion research was never a priority. One possible reason is that the designers did not believe that an implosion weapon was really needed unless South Africa decided to build a thermonuclear weapon (Hydrogen bomb). The weapon scientists, however, never appeared serious about building thermonuclear devices.

According to Armscor, its implosion programme started in the mid-1980s. In the beginning, the goal was not strictly the development of an implosion design. The purpose was to help maintain a technology base for the maintenance of gun-type devices. According to an Armscor official, work on more advanced systems, such as implosion, helped to keep the weapons scientists and technicians interested in their work on gun-type systems.

The primary focus of the implosion effort, according to Armscor, 'was on the development of measurement systems which could be used during the 1990s.'

Armscor said that 'no implosion tests were done up to the time that the nuclear programme was terminated by the head of the government and no prototypes were constructed.' Only a couple of concepts were on the table.

However, Advena was equipped with the capability to develop and manufacture implosion-type devices. It is unclear whether Armscor would have built such weapons as replacements for the gun-type devices. Armscor engineers might not have been able to produce an implosion weapon manufactured to the same level of demanding safety, security, and reliability specifications as the gun-type device without conducting a full-scale nuclear test.

According to an Armscor official, a decision on building implosion weapons was still ten years away when the weapons programme was cancelled. He said that in any case, an implosion-weapon programme would have required a full-scale cold test of the implosion system with a natural uranium core. Such a test, he said 'would have caused contamination which was not acceptable to Armscor and would have posed risks with regard to detection.'

If Armscor had decided to build a closed arena large enough to contain the detonation of large quantities of high explosives in a cold test, the arena would have cost about 12 million rand. This sum, he said, was considerable – and perhaps prohibitive – for the Advena programme.

Although P.W. Botha limited the number of weapons to seven in 1985 (six were completed) preliminary estimates suggested that the seven gun-type devices had enough HEU for 14 implosion weapons.

Missile Warhead

The design of Advena's integration building implies that South Africa, in the long term, was thinking of an enhanced weapon. The building had sufficient space to load a warhead onto a ballistic missile and new storage vaults contained space suitable for one small re-entry body.

An unusual feature of the South African programme is that if the government had deployed nuclear-tipped ballistic missiles, the warheads might have used gun-type devices, not implosion warheads as is often thought necessary. Also, Armscor might have preferred a gun-type warhead because it was within reach of the existing design, although it would have required further development. The existing design was not symmetrical enough for a missile warhead. Developing an acceptable design was seen as well within Armscor's capabilities.

It might have been difficult to build an implosion weapon that simultaneously met rigorous specifications while remaining small enough to fit on the end of a missile. The relatively small missile diameters would have placed a tremendous constraint on Armscor's implosion system.

Dismantling the Programme

Before the weapons programme could occupy Advena, the security situation in southern Africa eased. In December 1988, South Africa, Angola, and Cuba signed a tripartite agreement for a phased withdrawal of Cuban troops in Angola. In April 1989, Namibia was granted independence and at the end of 1989, the Berlin Wall fell, signalling the end of the Cold War and superpower rivalry in Africa.

In September 1989, F.W. de Klerk was elected president. He immediately took steps to bring about fundamental political reforms aimed at ending apartheid and creating a democratic South Africa. Within a short time, the country's nuclear weapons programme had become a liability: it stood in the way of South Africa rejoining the international community. In November 1989, the government decided to stop the production of nuclear weapons.

On 26 February 1990, de Klerk issued written instructions to terminate the nuclear weapons programme and dismantle all existing weapons. The nuclear materials were to be melted down and returned to the AEC in preparation for South Africa's accession to the NPT.

The government also decided that it would not admit to the existence of the nuclear weapons programme before accession to the NPT. As a result, the dismantling project – like the weapons project – remained top secret.

Dismantling started in July 1990. By 6 September 1991, all of the HEU had been removed from the weapons, melted down, and sent back to the AEC for storage. During the dismantlement process at Circle, criticality-safe shelves were installed in one vault to store recast HEU ingots.

To ensure ongoing secrecy, the HEU was sent from Circle to Pelindaba at night. Initially, Armscor had military guards patrolling the road, but stopped when the guards attracted the attention of people living in the area. One person demanded to know what was happening. Subsequent shipments aroused less curiosity.

Soon after sending the last material to the AEC, the Circle building was completely decontaminated and the equipment that had been used for the re-melting and casting of HEU sent to the AEC. The main uranium processing section of Circle was also decontaminated: walls were removed and the concrete floor was jacked out.

In the process, radioactive contamination was reduced to background levels. An Armscor official said that they wanted the room clean enough so that they could plausibly deny the existence of the programme. Indeed, several did not believe that the weapons programme would ever be revealed.

Although all the HEU had not gone to the AEC when South Africa acceded to the NPT on 10 July 1991, all of it had been sent before the safeguards agreement entered into force on 16 September 1991. The first IAEA inspection team arrived in South Africa in November 1991.

All major non-nuclear components of the weapons, detailed design drawings, as well as photos of components, remained. Destruction of many of these items began in 1992. By 24 March 1993, when de Klerk announced the programme's existence, most of the classified documents had been shredded and the sensitive weapon components destroyed or damaged beyond repair. Destruction of less important components continued into 1994.

Conclusion

South Africa's renunciation of nuclear weapons was a major success for international efforts to stop the proliferation of nuclear weapons. Its programme, however, shows how difficult it is to thwart a country that has a certain level of technological sophistication and is determined to build nuclear weapons.

South Africa's nuclear weapons production complex remained a secret for many years. Circle and Advena were essentially invisible to prying intelligence. Although the purpose of the Y-plant was widely suspected when the government announced its construction in 1970, no one knew when it started to produce HEU or how much it produced. The Y-Plant's visibility reinforces the view that the refusal to apply safeguards to a nuclear facility should be construed as evidence of weapons intentions.

However, South Africa also reminds us that political isolation can increase the incentives to built nuclear weapons (as we are observing today with North Korea).

It can lead a country to greater technological self-sufficiency and make it prone to take extreme acts in self-defence. International sanctions cannot always be relied on to stop a technologically capable country, but sanctions can slow down a country's programme. Linked to incentives, sanctions can reduce the political will of a country to remain isolated.

The South African case demonstrates the need for aggressive international and national efforts aimed at early detection of nuclear weapons programmes. Monitoring must include machine tools and other important equipment not covered by export control lists. If the international community had obtained clear evidence of South Africa's weapons programme, South Africa might have found its nuclear weapons far less political useful and been more vulnerable to international pressure.

South Africa's nuclear research centre at Pelindaba, on the outskirts of Pretoria.

Storage bunkers in Pretoria for the six atom bombs built by South Africa prior to the entire nuclear weapons programme being dismantled before President de Klerk handed over power to Nelson Mandela and his ANC. (Photo David Albright)

David Albright, head of Washington's Institute for Science and International Security. (ISIS) – or as he likes to say, 'the Good ISIS'.

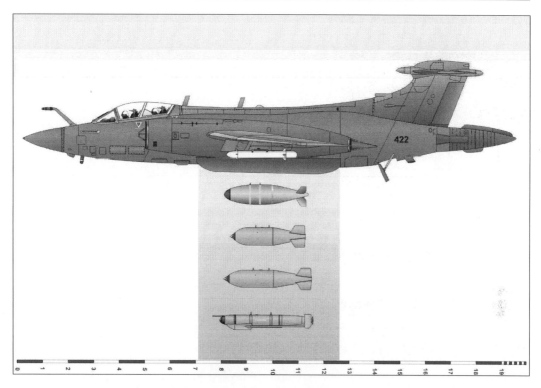

SAAF British-supplied Buccaneer bomber with envisioned potential nuclear weapons loads which never reached fruition. (Sourced to Pierre Louw Victor)

Pretoria – South Africa's capital city. The country's seat of Parliament is in Cape Town.

KEY EVENTS IN PRETORIA'S NUCLEAR WEAPONS PROGRAM

Year	Activity
1950s and 1960s	Scientific work on the feasibility of peaceful nuclear explosives and support to nuclear power production efforts
1969	AEB forms group to evaluate technical and economic aspects of nuclear explosives
1970	AEC releases report identifying wide applications for nuclear explosives
1971	R&D for gun-type device approved for "peaceful use of nuclear explosives"
1973	AEC places research priority on gun-type design over implosion and boosted weapon designs
1974	PM Vorster authorizes funding for work on nuclear device and preparation of test site
1977	AEC completes assembly of nuclear device (less HEU core) for "cold test" in the Kalahari Desert Soviet Union and United States detect preparations for the nuclear test and pressure South Africa into abandoning the test AEC instructed to miniaturise device; groundwork laid for ARMSCOR to take program lead
1978	Y-Plant uranium enrichment facility produces first batch of HEU Three-phase strategic guidelines established for nuclear deterrent policy P W Botha "Action Committee" recommends arsenal of seven nuclear weapons and ARMSCOR formally assumes control of program
1979	"Double-flash" event detected; first device with HEU core produced by AEC.
1982	First deliverable device produced by ARMSCOR; work continues to improve weapon safety and reliability
1985	ARMSCOR strategy review expands original three-phase strategy to include specific criteria to transition to next deterrent phase
1987	First production model produced; total of six weapons built with a seventh under construction at program termination
1988	ARMSCOR revisits Kalahari nuclear test site and erects a large steel hangar over test shafts and prepares the shafts for a possible nuclear test. Angola, Cuba and South Africa formally agree on Namibia's independence and schedule for Cuban troops to withdraw from Angola
1989	FW de Klerk elected President and orders weapon production halted
1990	Y-Plant formally shut down and nuclear weapons dismantlement begins
1991	South Africa signs the NPT and enters into a comprehensive safeguard agreement
1993	President de Klerk publicly discloses details of former South African nuclear deterrent program

Source ISIS, Washington D.C.

Key Events in South Africa's Nuclear Weapons Programme.

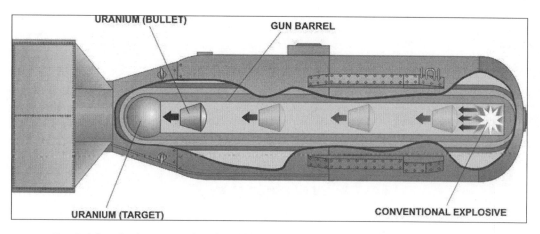

South Africa built six atom bombs, all 'Gun-Type' and similar to 'Little Boy' dropped by the Americans on Hiroshima.

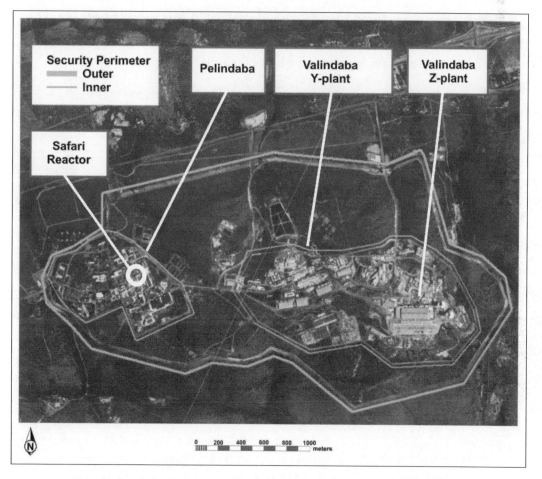

David Albright supplied this aerial annotated photo of the Pelindaba facility.
(Washington's Institute for Science and International Security)

11

Stoking the Forge of Fire: South Africa's Medium Range ICBM Programme

Israel and South Africa had a long and productive record of military coopera-tion, though neither would ever admit to working together on nuclear weapons or long-range missiles. Strong evidence of missile cooperation surfaced in 1989 when a powerful rocket blasted off from South Africa's Overberg Test Range and flew nearly 1,500 kilometres. It turned out to be a South African version of Israel's Jericho-2 missile, locally known as the RSA missile, in various configurations.

United States officials confirmed later that the CIA had evidence of a full-scale partnership between Israel and South Africa to develop, test and produce long-range missiles and rockets.

An American authority who tracked missile proliferation told the Wisconsin-based *Risk Report* – the leading source of unclassified information on companies around the world suspected of building weapons of mass destruction – that South Africa's space launcher, the RSA-4 (the upper stages, at least), was built around the same engines that power Israel's Jericho-2 missile and its 'Shavit' space launcher.

In tandem with the South African nuclear weapons programme, Pretoria – with strong support from Israel – launched one of the most sophisticated medium- to long-range missile programmes yet embarked upon outside the Great Power ambit. It was certainly the most extensive in all of Africa – Egypt included – as well as the Southern Hemisphere.

For a relatively small country like South Africa, the programme had substantial financial and personnel input. By mid-1992 more than a thousand engineers, technicians, and scientists in the Western Cape were involved with what was colloquially termed the 'space' programme. That was in addition to almost 5,000 more people indirectly linked including subcontractors.

Israel's involvement was critical to the final outcome, though these days Jerusalem does not like to be reminded about the close links it maintained with the old apartheid regime, something that went on for decades.

With Israeli scientists involved, the focus was more with the missiles component of South Africa's weapons of mass destruction programme than the construction of that country's atom bomb. For a start, only South Africans born in the country were permitted to be involved and those with dual nationality were not; the prime reason why the country's nuclear weapons programme was never penetrated either by the CIA or Britain's Secret Intelligence Service.

One South African scientist made the point that while the Israelis were helpful – some of the developments were later included in their own missile and launcher programmes – a lot of these developments were, as he put it, 'homegrown'. He did concede that the State of Israel was indeed pivotal to the entire venture.

What we do know is that very early on a deal was reportedly struck when Prime Minister John Vorster visited Israel in April 1976 which, in all likelihood, finally gave South Africa access to a broad range of Israeli missile technology. Two years before, that groundbreaking Israel-South Africa agreement – otherwise referred to as the ISSA Agreement – had already been signed, and in all probability, paved the way for Vorster's deal.

These developments were not unusual either for the difficult times or the threats faced by both countries. According to Seymour Hersh, South Africa and Israel had already started cooperating on nuclear matters 'in earnest' after the Six Day War in 1967.

There were a number of missiles built in South Africa. Apart from three test-fired, another is on display at the South African Air Force Museum at Swartkop Air Force Base in Pretoria (see photos and diagrams) and one more ceremoniously destroyed during a low-key ceremony in the spring of 1994, an event attended by a few foreign dignitaries as well as local media.

Still, we are aware that a variety of individual components did subsequently find their way abroad, specifically to several Asian and Islamic states then working on similar projects, and, indeed, still engaged on this kind of research. According to Charles Vick, erstwhile Fellow at GlobalSecurity. org, 'RSA-4 and RSA-3 technology have shown up in the four stages Chinese DF-31 (long-range ballistic missile) along with the precursor solid propellant two stage JL-1 SLBM.'

I was living in the United States at the time doing research and writing for Britain's Jane's Information Group and over time, I developed close ties to Vick, even visiting him at his home in Richmond, Virginia. He also provided diagrams and illustrations for my book on Tehran's purported nuclear programme, *Iran's Nuclear Option*, published by Casemate in the United States.

That was more than a decade ago, and as he said, 'all these missile-related technology transfers are expected to culminate in a satellite launch vehicle for Pakistan Shaheen-II derived SLV/ LRICBM and Iranian Ghadr-110A IRBM/LRICBM/SLV have a striking resemblance to the original South African RSA-4/Shavit follow-on, the Chinese DF-31/KT-1 as well as the altitude version of the upper two stage JL-1, heritage.'

Citing photos and specialist evidence, Vick maintained that 'there was real evidence of technology transfer to China (in the apartheid era) on those solid propellant ballistic missile programmes from South Africa, with Russian improvement additions introduced later.'

How successful then was South Africa's missile programme? Even Washington conceded in the early 1990s that it had progressed a lot faster than anybody gave Pretoria credit for, which was why the US demanded that the entire ballistic missile programme be shut down, and at very short notice. Washington held out the threat of punitive economic sanctions if Pretoria did not comply. Not long afterwards the entire programme became history.

The original South African concept had been to develop a series of weapons systems that, if it became necessary, would totally obliterate any aggressive enemy based on a modest-sized, but successful ballistic missile programme. Instead, the opposite happened. Once word had come down from Washington, much of what was developed by South African defence establishments working on missile components were clandestinely or otherwise dissipated to a host of other countries, none favourable to American interests.

Clearly, somebody in the American capital had not done their homework and the fallout as a consequence of this over-hasty act has been substantial.

But then there have been other, more recent examples of strategic lapses on the part of the American defence planners, not least what is going on with the Taliban again taking over vast swathes of Afghanistan, some of which had cost a lot of American, and in that country's Helmand province, British lives.

Current data available indicate that while the missile-launcher programme was ongoing, there were three South African launches from the Overberg Test Range near Cape Town. These included a single-stage test vehicle (RSA-1) on 1 June 1989, followed by a pair of two-stage potential (RSA-2 types) missiles on 5 July 1989 and 19 November 1991 respectively.

The July 5 launch, initially claimed to have been that of the single-stager, actually appears to have been a two-stage test missile proved to have traversed just more than 1,450 kilometres.

The Circle Error Probable (CEP) splashdown values of the respective front-ends on these occasions are not known but may be demonstrated by the manner that Armscor (South African Armaments Corporation) – which had overall responsibility for the project – informed the South African Cabinet in 1987, that it could build a missile that might be based on an Israeli design and which could strike a target in Nairobi within a CEP of 275 metres.

Since Nairobi is about 2,600km from the nearest South African border (roughly the distance from London to Moscow) Armscor described the potential of a two-stage (RSA-2) missile for a given range/CEP. Nuclear warhead weight, if indicated at all, did not survive transcription or any of the files available to researchers today.

What becomes apparent when researching the South African medium- to long-range missile programme is that help was not only forthcoming from Israel but from China, France and the United States, all of which allowed certain technical inputs. As was subsequently revealed, this developed into a multi-directional flow with subsequent Israeli–South African developed missile wherewithal heading to China and on to Pakistan and, more recently, to Iran's theocratic regime.

South Africa's apartheid-orientated regime seems to have had a lasting interest in missiles. This is evidenced by the establishment of the National Institute for Defence Research (NIDR) in Pretoria during 1954.

According to James P. McWilliams, the NIDR played an important part in missile development from the early 1950s to the late 1960s.[1] NIDRs activities, he maintains, appear to have been complemented by the National Institute for Rocket Research (NIRR – also known as the Rocket Research Institute, or RRI), which was established in 1964. It became substantive at the Council for Scientific and Industrial Research (or more commonly, the CSIR).

NIRR was specifically concentrated on activities such as atmospheric research and the development of guided missiles. Additionally, it already had its own testing range.

At roughly that time then, the Federal Republic of Germany came into the picture, having lent Pretoria's all-white government a generous helping hand, first by facilitating NIRRs rocket and missile research through a cooperation agreement with the West German defence industry, and second, by establishing a rocket research and ionosphere centre at Tsumeb in what was then still South West Africa (now Namibia) during 1963-64. This was achieved in close association with South African scientists.

The Washington-based Nuclear Threat Initiative (NTI) reported that the Herman Oberth-Gesellschaft (an academic organisation whose members created a network of approximately 30 private West German firms involved in the rocket industry) and Waffen und Luftrüstung AG, actively participated in early rocket construction in South Africa. In truth, a 1991 United Nations

---

1   James P McWilliams, *ARMSCOR South Africa's Arms Merchant* (Brassey's (UK) Ltd., London, 1989), p. 18.

report holds that RRI was actually a transitional stage or a 'build up', linked to assistance from several organisations in that European country.

What is notable is that both the NIDR and the NIRR operated under the auspices of the CSIR (and in NIRR's case, also in conjunction with the University of Pretoria).

According to the Nuclear Threat Initiative, South Africa's Rocket Research Institute (NIRR) was the primary agency responsible for research and development in the missile technology field. The above-mentioned United Nations report records that most of South Africa's research and development (R&D) organisations – relevant to long-range rocketry – were located within the framework of South Africa's National Institute for Defence Research.

The first solid indication of the kind of future role that the South African missile programme might ultimately play had already been given in 1963 by Andre Fouché, Minister of Defence. He told Parliament that the country needed 'rockets' to replace some of the other weapons then being produced and which were fast approaching obsolescence. The same year, Dr Abraham 'Ampie' Roux – the so-called 'father' of South Africa's nuclear weapons programme – commenting on the establishment of NIRR – noted that current events in an increasingly belligerent Africa had forced his country to enter the missile field.

The Nuclear Threat Initiative also sourced a secret CIA report of 8 December 1989 (since partially declassified and released under the Freedom of Information Act) which noted that South Africa's missile development programme had already begun in 1963 under the direction of the Armaments Production Board.[2] Since that body was only officially established in 1964, this programme, in all likelihood, was directed from within existing defence structures such as the Defence Resources Board, Defence Production Office, and possibly the NIDR.

By then, notes McWilliams, Defence Minister Fouché had already requested finance for research into rocketry. In fact, he'd already done so the previous year. That early development phase focused on surface-to-air (SAM), air-to-air (AAM), and eventually, the all-encompassing cruise missiles (CM) that were envisaged by Pretoria.

The country's first known missile venture was initiated in 1964: a short-range SAM system developed in conjunction with various French concerns. Referred to locally as the Cactus Missile, it was marketed elsewhere as the Crotale EDIR (*Ecartométrie Différentielle InfraRouge*/InfraRed Differential Ecartometry) an all-weather short-range anti-air missile used to intercept low-flight anti-ship missiles and aircraft (including Iraq in its lengthy war with Iran).

At issue here is the fact that it was South African money that played a major role in putting the system on the map.

Missile-related occurrences of note during the rest of that decade seemed to be restricted to 1968. On 9 October that year, Defence Minister P.W. Botha announced that a missile test range was to be established at Lake St Lucia on the Natal coast, about 300km north of Durban.

The Chief of Staff of the Army, General H.J. Martin, declared shortly afterwards that South Africa was also pursuing the development of ballistic missiles. This, to the author's knowledge, was the first time that ballistic missiles had specifically been mentioned in any defence-related context.[3]

---

2   Nuclear Threat Initiative (NTI) is a Washington-based non-profit organisation with a mission to strengthen global security by reducing the risk of use and preventing the spread of nuclear, biological and chemical weapons, and to work to build the trust, transparency and security which are preconditions to the ultimate fulfilment of the Non-Proliferation Treaty's goals and ambitions.

3   Leonard S. Spector, with Jacqueline R. Smith, *Nuclear Ambitions: The Spread of Nuclear Weapons 1989-1990* (Westview Press, Boulder, 1990), p. 270.

Another notable event that year was the first successful launching of a rocket from the Lake St Lucia rocket range, which took place on 17 December 1968. This fully-instrumented test establishment had been built for the NIRR with assistance from an unnamed European concern, in part because it formed a useful adjunct for firings across the Indian Ocean, something in which Israel was also very much interested. Bear in mind that because of geographical and political constraints, the Jewish State has always been unable to test its missiles along the customary west-to-east axis, in conformity with the rotation of the earth (along which all European, American and Russian missiles are launched).

The year 1973 saw a new development. That was the establishment by the NIDR of a Propulsion Division at Somerset West in the Western Cape, together with the initiation of serious work on the development of ballistic as well as aerodynamic missiles. The idea was for NIDRs Propulsion Division to be engaged in missiles, warheads, propellants, and propulsion systems. That would involve all aspects, from initial development all the way up to the production phase.

A year later, under the ISSA Agreement mentioned above, South Africa was to gain a measure of access to Israeli missile technology.

More recent research indicates that it is probable that the South African-Israeli connection with regard to missile cooperation may have begun earlier.

Profiling South Africa's missile chronology, the NTI notes in its entry for the 13-year period – from 1954 to 1967 – that the two countries cooperated closely on missile development over the next three decades.[4] In retrospect, this might not have been unexpected: South Africa was the first nation in the world to congratulate Israel when it declared itself an independent state in May 1948.

In the broader concept of basic missile cooperation between the two countries, while much was delivered, we are still not certain whether Israel's Jericho missiles and their special 'Chalet' (nuclear) warheads were ever delivered to South Africa according to the tenets of the ISSA Agreement.

British authors Hounam and McQuillan note in their book, which deals with South African weapons of mass destruction, that South Africa fielded medium- to long-range missiles in the early 1980s, some of which were nuclear-armed as long ago as 1982-83. These missiles were reportedly deployed at the army's battle school at Lohatlha in the Northern Cape – in silos dug deep into the side of a mountain.[5]

The type referred to also remains a mystery as the Jericho-1 (YA-1) missile, at best, was certainly a short-range ballistic missile or SRBM. They may well have been referring to another Israeli missile, namely the Jericho-1 (or 2) YA-2 which had a probable payload/range curve of 750kg/1,500km. While exchanges were made, specifics remain obscure.

Nonetheless, by November 1977 after the UN Security Council had imposed a mandatory arms embargo on South Africa, a missile that would ultimately be capable of delivering (nuclear) warheads over intercontinental ranges – and even satellites into orbit – was already on the cards with the two ISSA partners. Of relevance here is the fact that one of the objectives of the 'official' 1979 Armscor-run nuclear weapons programme was the study of implosion and thermonuclear technology, as well as long-range ballistic missile delivery systems (for both 'Gun-Type' as well as 'Implosion' nuclear weapons systems).

One of the most reliable time indicators of this anomaly remains the South African Air Force itself at the SAAF Museum at the Swartkop Air Base, where two of the presumed products of the alleged South African-Israeli cooperation – the RSA-3 SLV and Greensat satellite – are on display.

4   Nuclear Threat Initiative, Country Overviews: South Africa Profile: Missile Chronology: 1950s–1968, <http://www.nti.org/e_research/profiles/SAfrica/Missile/1622_1642.html>.

5   Peter Hounam and Steve McQuillan, The Mini-Nuke Conspiracy: Mandela's Nuclear Nightmare (Faber and Faber Ltd., London, 1995), pp. 172, 262.

A plaque there reads that due to the fact that the southern African sub-continent was being flooded by Soviet bloc weaponry, advisers and surrogate forces in the 1970-1980 period, a programme was initiated to develop and deploy a surveillance satellite as well as a suitable launch vehicle for this purpose. Development of a missile and launcher system in South Africa roughly paced what Armscor was achieving with its nuclear weapons programme.

Consequently, the National Institute for Defence Research became the National Institute for Aeronautical Systems Technology during 1978. The minister of defence announced in February that year that the missile issue would be transferred from the CSIR (and include facilities, research projects, and some NIDR personnel) to Brimstone Projects, a wholly owned affiliate company of Armscor. Brimstone eventually became Kentron in April 1978.

Another pointer was the announcement in March 1983 that the missile test range at Lake St Lucia would finally be closed. Another more extensive testing facility would be built to the east of Cape Town near Bredasdorp. It became known as the Overberg Test Range (OTR) or, more commonly in Afrikaans, *die Overberg Toets Baan* (OTB).

Significant at this stage was a 1983 UN study conducted by the Special Committee Against Apartheid. That noted that the Reagan Administration had authorised the sale to South Africa of vibration test equipment that could be used to establish the reliability of nuclear warheads.

It was probably as a consequence that Washington completed a report late 1989 since declassified and titled 'Africa Review – South Africa: Igniting a Missile Race?'[6] It noted that there were two sites built for producing solid propellants: one situated in Somerset West in the Cape and the other at the Irene Missile Component R&D and Production facilities (*sic*) outside Pretoria, which was expanded after 1983.

Mention was also made in the report of the fact that South Africa had in 1986 built new facilities at Somerset West capable of producing 'ballistic-missile sized' engines. The following year the Houwteq high-technology concern came into being near Grabouw, also in the Cape.

The main South African concerns involved with the development and testing of large launchers (whether RSA ballistic missiles or RSA SLVs) were Houwteq (design; assembly; integration of the launcher with its payload), Somchem (engines; solid propellants), Denel OTB (launch facilities), Kentron (guidance); Eloptro (electro-optical components), and Pelindaba Technology Solutions (satellite reactive control systems) with Houwteq being the prime contractor.

Missile research and development was also handled at a Pretoria facility situated roughly halfway between the Advena Circle and new Central Laboratory complexes. Its proximity to the nuclear weapons manufacturing/storage facilities that handled fissile material wasn't lost on the Americans either.

What eventually emerged from the reported 1974 Israeli–South African 'Project Burglar' effort was a reasonably versatile family of similar solid-propelled missiles such as the (Israeli) two-stage Jericho-2/YA-3 IR/LRICBM; three/four-stage Shavit/1 SLV's; the subsequent four-stage Next/Shavit-2 SLV, as well as another reported ICBM iteration.

Mark Wade, author of *Encyclopedia Astronautica*, a comprehensive internet-based knowledge base accords the designations RSA-1 and RSA-2 to the single and two-stage variations of South Africa's RSA-3, whether actual or conjectural. In this context, the South Africans did not appear to have developed an equivalent of the more powerful Israeli missile iteration known as Shavit-2. Alternatively, it might have been that their missile launcher programme was prematurely terminated.

---

6   See U.S. Central Intelligence Agency, Directorate of Intelligence, *Africa Review – South Africa: Igniting a Missile Race?* – 8 December 1989. Case No. F-1992-00809, Pub. 7/12/89, release date 27/4/97.

What we are aware of is that Pretoria did have a larger four-stage missile in mind, which we'll come to later.

In retrospect, we know too that Pretoria might have been able to use the single-stage RSA-1 missile (utilising the first stage of the RSA-3 – and thus resembling a single-stage Jericho-2) and the two-stage RSA-2 (utilising the first two stages of the RSA-3 – and thus essentially identical to the Jericho-2/YA-3) to deliver (nuclear) strikes against targets in the region.

RSA-2 would have had a length of roughly 14 metres, base/body diameter in the vicinity of 1.5/1.35 metres and a launch weight of around 21,000kg or 23 tons.

Delivering strikes (not necessarily nuclear) by such means had already been mooted at by then Armscor Chairman Piet Marais in 1985. He'd spoken in general terms about the value of developing a missile able to hit targets that were quite a few hundred kilometres distant. The following year he spoke of a local missile that might be able to strike targets in neighbouring countries, though none were named.

Conservative range/payload estimates for the RSA-1 and the RSA-2, with ranges and payload capacity of 1,000km/1,500kg and 900km/1,500kg respectively would have enabled strikes to be made from mobile launchers against a variety of fixed targets on the African continent. Consideration had already been given to missile attacks in Angola where South Africa was fighting a limited ground war, specifically against massed invading Cuban, Pan-African as well as Warsaw Pact troops.

This would have covered an arc that stretched from southern Angola, across the Democratic Republic of Congo to southern Tanzania.

Such wide-ranging applications of these missiles had already been alluded to by Wade. Their warheads would presumably have been the country's bomb/missile-deliverable nuclear gun-type atom bombs, even though these were initially designed to also be fitted to the country's so-called glide-bomb. In this mode of delivery, the bomb might have weighed in at anything between three-quarters of a ton to a ton-and-a-half.

Significantly, the lower weight estimate of three-quarters of a ton, or 750kg, was the same as that claimed by Israel for the 20kT Jericho-1 (YA-1) warhead.

The South African missile re-entry vehicle (RV) which would have carried its gun-type nuclear explosives charge would likely have had a length of 1.74 metres and a diameter of about 37cm. Its shape was reminiscent of the Mk-1 RV used on America's Polaris A1/A2 SLBMs, albeit without the flaring base but coupled to a straighter, somewhat pointy sharp end.

The American Institute of Aeronautics and Astronautics and the BTG Group published an extensive online informative piece called the 'Space Launch Mission Planner ToolKit' that detailed the development of the proposed LeoLink family of launchers (based on the Israeli Shavit family). It is important to accept that the 'Toolkit' claimed that the Jericho-2 (from which the Shavit space launch vehicle was derived, thus the Jericho-2/YA-3) was first tested in 1986.[7]

Its first *detected* test launch took place from Palmachim when it was fired into the Mediterranean in May 1987 with a range that extended to something like 800 kilometres. Obviously, South Africa must have been privy to all this because by then its scientists were cooperating at a fairly elevated level with their Israeli counterparts.

In this context, Professor Peter Liberman of the Department of Political Science, Queens College, University of New York observed that Armscor had originally informed the South African Cabinet in 1987 that it could build a missile, based on an Israeli design, which could strike a target in

7   *Space Launch Mission Planner ToolKit*, Version 3.0. LeoLink LK-2: Vehicle Evolution, <http://ltk.stacinc.com/ltk3/LeoLinkLK2/LeoLinkLK2_VehEvo.htm> (accessed 7 April 2001).

Nairobi within 300 yards[8] (about 275 metres). Apart from revealing a rather respectable CEP over a range of at least 2,600km, the identity of a missile capable of such a range suggests the RSA-2.

Considering that the first detected launch of Israel's Jericho-2 (YA-3) took place in the same year, it is probable that the missile Armscor had informed the South African Cabinet of later that same year was the local iteration of the aforementioned Israeli missile.

Going a step further and assuming domestic RSA-2/Jericho-2 availability, it would suggest that by the end of the 1980s, South Africa might have possessed the capability of launching a nuclear device (the first of which was completed in August 1987) to a range of roughly 2,000km (with a warhead that weighed a ton-and-a-half/1,500kg) or nearly 6,000km with a warhead of about 750kg respectively.

It should be mentioned that these figures represent conservative and optimistic guesstimates garnered from unrelated sources. However, it must be assumed that the most optimistic range/payload interval would have involved using the small, hydrazine-propelled, final stage of the Shavit/RSA SLV.

Peter De Ionno, writing in the *Sunday Times*, noted that two all-terrain mobile launchers intended to carry the country's ballistic missiles were built and tested at Armscor's proving ground at Advena in 1988 and 1989.

The eventual production TELs (Transporter-Erector-Launchers) had a length of 17 metres and a main vehicle height of 2.8 metres or 4.48 metres overall and were apparently dubbed *Beestrok* (Cattle Truck in Afrikaans). These were constructed by Lyttelton Engineering Works near Pretoria at its Special B Vehicles (or 'Spes B') facility.

Burrows and Windrem also claim that Israel launched three Jericho-2s from OTB near Bredasdorp even before South Africa itself had launched its first missile from that facility in July 1989. Johannesburg's *Weekend Star* actually ran a report that several Israeli-built Jericho IRBMs and that Shavits were launched from OTB in the 1980s and early 1990s.

The significance of Israeli missiles and launchers (specifically Shavits) being sent to South Africa for testing, is that such shipments could easily have included other missiles (i.e. more Shavits) intended for operational deployment or for different applications by their South African allies, whether as ballistic missiles (ICBMs) or SLVs.

Local availability of the Shavit, for instance, might have endowed them with the theoretical capability of being able to launch their nuclear warheads to a distance of roughly about 2,500km, or 8,000km respectively, that year. Though these figures remain speculative, they are based on existing data. The last-mentioned range/payload interval indicated would presumably again have meant utilising the hydrazine-propelled final Shavit stage as a means of propulsion to increase range.

More to the point, however, is the suggestion that Israel actually did supply their South African friends with details of a process to transform a SLV (in this case assuming an Israeli-supplied Shavit or Shavits) into a nuclear ballistic missile[9] (thus, the three-stage RSA-3).

In a military guise, such a missile has been classified as an intercontinental ballistic missile or ICBM, that was capable of delivering a nuclear warhead at a distance of 5,500km or more.

These details are realistic. It is interesting that the Washington-based Federation of American Scientists in one of its reports declared that a small ICBM capable of delivering a 500kg payload to a distance of something like 9,000km would weigh between 16 and 24 tons (15,000 and 22,000kg).

---

8   Peter Liberman, 'The Rise and Fall of the South African Bomb'. *International Security*, Volume 26, Number 2, (Fall 2001), p. 54 *n.* 29.

9   Peter Hounam and Steve McQuillan, *op. cit.*, p. 67.

Obviously, said the FAS, a lot would depend on the efficacy of the design as well as the sophistication of the technology involved.

Wade calculated that if the three-stage RSA-3 vehicle had been used as a ballistic missile, it would have been able to carry a 400kg payload from South Africa to Moscow and a 340kg payload all the way across the Atlantic Ocean to Washington.[10]

Even the lesser of these two payloads would have been sufficient to accommodate a small, relatively modern, nominal- to medium-yield warhead and its RV.

A payload of 340kg would suggest a nuclear warhead of about 200kg which appears to have been well beyond South Africa's best efforts of the late 1980s. However, General P.J. 'Tienie' Groenewald, a former member of the State Security Council (and also an erstwhile head of Military Intelligence) reportedly claimed that within the timeframe under consideration, South Africa had already 'miniaturised' nuclear devices for ballistic missiles.

By inference, therefore, Pretoria's ability to implement an intercontinental deterrent capability, as described, by the late 1980s consequently lay well within the technological grasp of the country.

Also of note was a revelation made by David Albright, head of Institute of Science and International Security (ISIS) another of Washington's weapons of mass destruction 'think tanks' that Advena's 'integration building' had storage vaults containing space suitable for one small re-entry body. That would appear to support General Groenewald's claim, especially since the Advena structure had a central bay large enough to accommodate a ballistic missile, which presumably was a reference to the massive TEL missile-carrying vehicles.

Extremely thorough in his approach to all his research, much of Albright's work on the South African nuclear weapons programme – which subsequently appeared on the ISIS website – were done inside South Africa with the cooperation of Pretoria.[11]

By the end of the 1980s, South African's own missile/launcher-fabrication infrastructure had progressed to a point that the 'booster rocket' launched from the Denel OTB in July 1989 may have made use of a locally-fabricated propulsion system.

To this end, *Africa Review* claimed that South Africa ' … may have produced at least the solid propellant motors … ' used in the July test launch, and also, that the country was apparently preparing for series production of solid motors that could be used in both ballistic missiles and space launch vehicles[12] (thus Israeli ATSM-9 equivalent units).

This 'booster rocket' (whether RSA-1 or RSA-2) covered a distance of 1,450km when launched in a south-easterly direction across the Indian Ocean towards Prince Edward Island group, which includes the adjacent Marion Island with which many South Africans are familiar since this is a long-standing meteorological station.

Professor Helen Purkitt notes that by the end of the 1980s the country's new mid-range launchers were coming on-line.[13]

For its part, Washington's Nuclear Threat Initiative (NTI) made the point that during 1989 South Africa had substantially increased its defence budget for 1990. It noted that half of this

10   Mark Wade, *Encyclopedia Astronautica*, Launch Vehicles, RSA-3, <http://solar.rtd.utk.edu/~mwade/lvs/rsa3.htm> (accessed 23 August 1999).

11   Institute for Science and International Security (ISIS), <www.isis-online.org/>.

12   U.S. Central Intelligence Agency, Directorate of Intelligence. *Africa Review – South Africa: Igniting a Missile Race?, op.* cit., p. 4.

13   Purkitt, Helen E., *'The politics of denuclearization: The case of South Africa.'* Paper presented at the Defense Nuclear Agency's Fourth Annual International Conference on Controlling Arms, Philadelphia 21 June 1995. (Earlier draft presented at Institute for National Studies [INSS], U.S. Air Force Academy, Colorado, November 9, 1994), p. 22.

proposed budget was what was termed 'a secret allocation', which some foreign analysts believed might have included funds for ballistic missile development. In this light, it might have suggested that the deployment of locally produced long-range ballistic missiles would have occurred in the foreseeable future in South Africa had the missile facility not been arbitrarily terminated by the Americans.

Indeed, it had been suggested to one of the authors that 39 'systems' were to be acquired. These would have equipped five flights (six TELs/missiles per flight), with the remaining nine, presumably intended to serve as a strategic reserve in the event of mishap or breakdown. It was furthermore suggested that the missiles involved would be RSA-2 – types. Those TELs would also have been able to deploy with three-stage RSA-3s. All of these systems would probably have been based at an ultra-secure site that housed 22 large 'hangars'.

The site boasted six substantially larger hangars as well. More on this below. By the time the plug had been pulled on South Africa's WMD programmes, altogether seven TELs had been built and six deployed, which was adequate for a single flight.

Exact dates that pertain to South African launches from the OTB launch facility in the South Cape are another issue that appears to be in dispute.

Early information indicated that a launch of a single-stage missile occurred on 5 July 1989. That was followed by a pair of two-stage missiles (RSA-2 types) in mid-November 1990 and in 1991 respectively.

Regardless, the South Africans were not yet done. There are indications that they were also working to produce their version of the more powerful Israeli Shavit-1 launcher. This contention appears to be supported by the ongoing engine tests at the Hangklip static motor test facility at Rooi Els during 1992 and 1993. These tests may also have been in support of a substantially more significant missile – the RSA-4.

A background paper, *Technologies Underlying Weapons of Mass Destruction*, published in 1993 by the US Congress, Office of Technology Assessment,[14] claimed that a test of the RSA-4 was planned for 1996. It would have a length of nearly 23.5 metres, a base diameter of about 2.4 metres and a launch weight of nearly 88 tons (80,000kg).

RSA-4 would feature four stages, the most significant being a large new solid-propelled first stage motor (being approximately equivalent to that used in the American LGM-118 Peacekeeper ICBM).

Wade estimates that this vehicle would have been capable of delivering a single 700kg warhead to any target on earth. Furthermore, he suggested that RSA-4s fourth stage was clearly adapted from an ICBM MIRV post-boost missile platform.

With these details in mind, the question needs to be asked: exactly where did everything needed for the RSA-4 missile programme originate?

In the broadest terms, its general layout appears to have been rather similar to that of the Taurus, a four-stage 27-metre solid-fuel launch vehicle built by Orbital Sciences Corporation (OSC) in the United States.

Taurus made its first flight (utilising a Peacekeeper first stage) in 1994. Subsequent vehicles would make use of the Castor 120 engine (based on that of the proven Peacekeeper first stage).

RSA-4s fourth stage could have been gleaned from that of the Peacekeeper ICBMs MIRV-dispensing Post Boost Vehicle (PBV) which, in the early 1990s, was being considered for civilian space application.

---

14   U.S. Congress, Office of Technology Assessment, *Technologies Underlying Weapons of Mass Destruction*, OTA-BP-ISC-115: Washington, DC: U.S. Government Printing Office, December 1993, p. 209.

Using RSA-4 as a point of departure the South Africans could eventually have turned out a launcher that would have been roughly equivalent to ICBMs such as the already-noted Peacekeeper and FSU/Russian RT-23 15Zh60 (SS-24 Mod 1, Scalpel). Such an iteration would probably have been named RSA-5.

With a variety of potential delivery systems at their disposal, it is possibly not surprising that towards the end of the Border War period, Pretoria appeared to have plans afoot to deliver their warheads by other means. While ordinary ballistic trajectories were very much the mainstay of the programme by then, there were several additional options.

That much had come to light in 1994 during the saga of 16 disgruntled South African scientists who claimed that Pretoria had initiated a multi-million rand deal which involved acquiring 'a system of explosives' from Israel that could stop a missile in mid-flight at a predetermined point. That, it was alluded, allowed the warhead to be dropped onto a target city with an accuracy of fractionally more than half-a-mile.

Whether all this was in any way connected to the subsequently-claimed 'Hanto' programme, described by one scientist as 'a sophisticated launching device for the South African ballistic missile developed by Israeli scientists with Israeli technology',[15] or the small, final stage Shavit/RSA-3 post-boost bus, is not known. The existing consensus is that it might be the latter.

Hannes Steyn, Richardt van der Walt and Jan van Loggerenberg note in their privately published work on the South African nuclear programme – *Armament and Disarmament South Africa's Nuclear Weapons Experience* that South Africa's TELs/missiles would have been controlled from the SAAFs central Command and Control Centre in Pretoria.[16] The head of Armscor's WMD efforts (nuclear as well as missile-related) appears to have been Deon Smit.

In all likelihood, all these missiles would have been deployed at Lohatlha and in the vicinity of Hammanskraal at a base called 'Rooi Lig' (Red Light) where the secure 'hangars' noted above were also sited. There was also a small underground base situated near the Kalahari Gemsbok Park in the Northern Cape.

More missiles were deployed at other sites in underground silos or on platforms that could be raised for firing, throughout the Transvaal.

Clearly, by the early 1990s, the South Africans were in the process of both developing and building a remarkable variety of nuclear-armed ballistic missiles.

15 *Sunday Independent*, Conventional weapons, unconventional methods: SA's arms trade with Israel, <http://www.inc.co.za/>.
16 Hannes Steyn, Richardt van der Walt and Jan van Loggerenberg, *Armament and Disarmament: South Africa's Nuclear Weapons Experience* (Network Publishers, Pretoria 2003), p. 79.

Factory where South Africa's MRBMs were assembled. (Pierre Louw Victor)

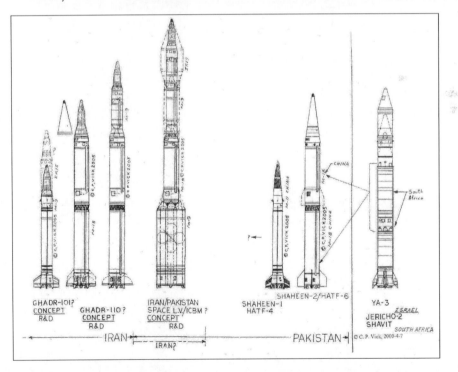

Charles Vick of GlobalSecurity demonstrated how much of the South African missile programme ended up in foreign hands after the ANC took power. The entire missile blueprint went to Iran and aspects were subsequently shared with Pakistan and North Korea.

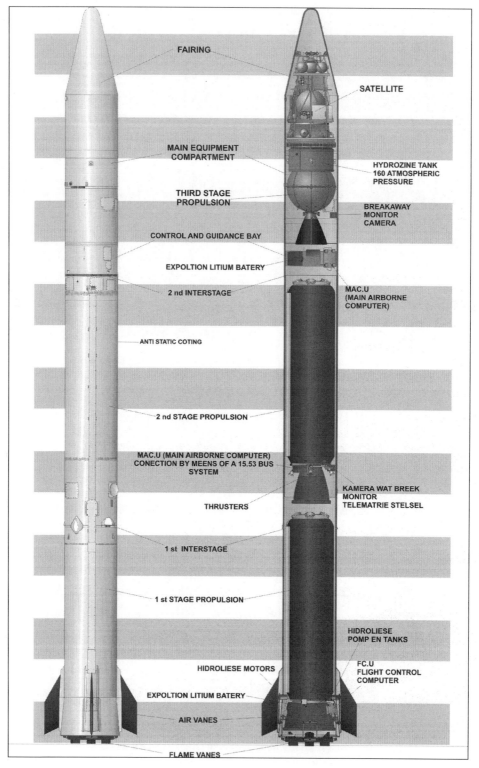

FAIRING

SATELLITE

MAIN EQUIPMENT
COMPARTMENT

HYDROZINE TANK
160 ATMOSPHERIC
PRESSURE

THIRD STAGE
PROPULSION

BREAKAWAY
MONITOR
CAMERA

CONTROL AND GUIDANCE BAY

EXPOLTION LITIUM BATERY

2 nd INTERSTAGE

MAC.U
(MAIN AIRBORNE
COMPUTER)

ANTI STATIC COTING

2 nd STAGE PROPULSION

MAC.U (MAIN AIRBORNE COMPUTER)
CONECTION BY MEENS OF A 15.53 BUS
SYSTEM

KAMERA WAT BREEK
MONITOR
TELEMATRIE STELSEL

THRUSTERS

1 st INTERSTAGE

1 st STAGE PROPULSION

HIDROLIESE
POMP EN TANKS

FC.U
FLIGHT CONTROL
COMPUTER

HIDROLIESE MOTORS

EXPOLTION LITIUM BATERY

AIR VANES

FLAME VANES

Cutaway of South Africa's RSA-3 missile.

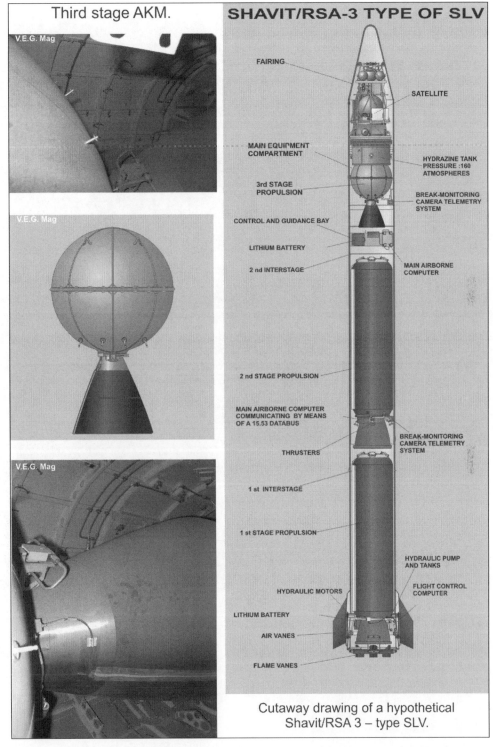

RSA-3/Israeli Shavit Medium Range Intercontinental missile – arguably the most successful built in the late 20th century outside the ambit of the Major Powers. (Sourced to Pierre Louw Victor)

Various shots of an RSA 3 launcher.

Jericho-2/RSA 2 – type of missile on a generic TEL.

South Africa's medium range ICBM Missile.

12

Operation Askari: Angola and Its Cuban Allies Take a Beating

During the course of a brilliant career with Britain's Fleet Air Arm, South African Air Force Brigadier General Dick Lord was always regarded as a most unusual man; competent in the extreme, a remarkable innovator and most of all, an achiever. As a fighter pilot, he was instrumental in the development of America's Top Gun fighter pilot academy (made famous by the film of the same name).

The eminent Dick Lord went on to play a leading role in planning some of South Africa's most critical attacks in Angola and quite a few were hugely successful in spite of the SAAF having lost air superiority over Angolan airspace.

The Soviets pumped hundreds of modern, sophisticated warplanes into their Angolan sphere of operations – mostly flown by Cubans as well as quite a few Soviet 'volunteers' – and Pretoria, crippled as it was by United Nations arms embargoes, simply could match either the sophistication or the volume of those weapons.

For all that, reckoned Dick Lord, our 'Fly Boys' managed pretty bloody well, as is borne out by some of the events we saw in Chapter Nine.

Before he died in 2011, Brigadier Dick Lord was good enough to give me this assessment (subsequently published in *Scientia Militaria*, South African Journal of Military Studies). It covered Operation Askari, the SADF's biggest cross-border strike in the post-Savannah phase and for those not familiar it's a bit of an eye-opener because our pilots did astonishingly well, not all the time but most of it.

To start with, Washington did not offer much hope that the South Africans would come out on top, but they proved that they could and they did …

Launched in December 1983, the prime objective of Operation Askari was to disrupt logistical support as well as command and control capabilities of SWAPO's military wing, the People's Liberation Army of Namibia (PLAN).

The fighting lasted almost a month and took place deep inside Angola, with FAPLA (the Angolan Army) getting powerful support from Cuba and the Soviets. In fact, had Moscow not been involved, it probably would never have happened.

During the course of that campaign, 21 South Africans were killed in action which was a great tragedy for the nation, but minimal compared to the loss of 426 Angolan Army and 45 PLAN troops. In fact, Cuba claimed that only five of its soldiers were KIA, though subsequent disclosures in Havana underscore Fidel Castro's vigorous efforts to deprive his own people of the truth; the real figure according to more recent disclosures in Cuba was closer to 60.

One also needs to factor in recent Cuban revelations uncovered by Austrian historian Tom Cooper, one of the leading military chroniclers of the epoch. As Cooper revealed in 2018, Havana always maintained that it never had more than 50,000 troops in Angola. His research – backed by reliable Havana sources (including a senior Havana military man who defected to the US with bundles of secret documents in his baggage) – maintains that the figure was more than double that. It was actually closer to 110,000 mainly men, all of whom served militarily in Angola over almost a decade and a half.

Cooper also disclosed that in the final stages of the Border War, the Angolan Air Force had two squadrons of Soviet MiG-23s – each of 12 aircraft – deployed exclusively in the deep south of that country, specifically to counter SAAF incursions, all flown by Cubans. From that action alone, Havana clearly, regarded the SAAF as an extremely potent threat and Dick Lord goes on to explain why this was so.

He explains why:

By 1983 the war in SWA/Angola had developed a predictable cyclical pattern. The seasonal variations allowed SWAPO – the guerrilla movement opposed to a South African military presence in what was to become Namibia – to take up the offensive during the summer passage of the Intertropical Convergence Zone (ITCZ) across northern South West Africa.

The ITCZ is a low-pressure belt of unstable moist air, that traverses southwards to the latitude of Rehoboth during late October and November and returns northwards across Ovamboland in late January through to April. Its passage gives rise to the phenomenon of the 'small rains' before Christmas and the 'big rains' from February to April.

These rainy seasons provided SWAPO insurgents' attempts to infiltrate the country from the north with good mobility. They offered the water they required for their trek to the south, while foliage on the trees and bushes provided concealment from the security forces and the showers obliterated tracks.

Most of these infiltration routes tended to criss-cross water-saturated pans (in local lingo 'shonas') to make things difficult for security force trackers trying to run them down. As a consequence, SWAPO's insurgency usually started late January each year and continued until the end of April or early May when the water started to dry up.

The onset of the dry season also brought about tactical changes. SWAPO withdrew its forces to bases in Angola for so-called 'rehearsals' – which meant regrouping and retraining their members prior to the next year's incursion. With the guerrillas concentrated in their bases, it became cost-effective for the SADF/SWATF to launch counter-offensive operations into Angola during the winter months: the mobility of vehicles in the torrential rains of summer was always a restricting factor.

For many years, up to the spring of 1983, this had been the rotating pattern of the war. A summer incursion by SWAPO/PLAN and a conventional/semi-conventional offensive by the SADF into Angola in the months that followed.

The consequences of these activities were overwhelmingly in the favour of South Africa's security forces, as can be deduced from the following table of operational losses:

Year	SWAPO	SADF Security Forces
1981	1,494	61
1982	1,280	77
1983	913	96

At the same time, the economic and socio-political effects on South West Africa and the SADF were appreciable. A war requires the deployment of a large number of forces and it was no different on the border.

Obviously, the direct cost factor was considerable, as was the insidious effect of keeping able-bodied men out of the country's economic workforce back home. An additional factor was a cumulative war-weariness of the population which got worse the longer hostilities lasted. As things progressed, the war became so predictable that it was difficult to foresee how this process could be halted.

The Portuguese in their colonial wars in Angola, Mozambique and Portuguese Guinea (which lasted from 1961 until an army mutiny in Lisbon put an end to it all) were faced with the same quandary.

In South Africa's Angola war, it eventually reached a stage to try to surprise the enemy with something totally unexpected in a bid to alter the pattern of predictability. Thus was Operation Askari planned.

Bearing in mind the piercing difficulties of mobile operations in the wet season, it was decided that this new attack (which was actually a subtle variation of the old) would be a semi-conventional operation using conventional arms. It would be ranged against the might of SWAPO's guerrilla force, specifically while they were massed in their training bases before the start of their 1984 insurgency campaign. The timing of the operation proper was therefore set to commence just after the 'little rains' in mid-December 1983.

Planning for Operation Askari's ground forces was carried out at Sector 10 at Oshakati, headquarters for Brigadier 'Joep' Joubert's ground forces. Dick Lord, then still a colonel, was responsible for the Air Plan.[1]

From conception, the overall arrangement was a joint operation; air force involvement totally committed to the support of ground forces objectives.

Simply put, the objective was 'to disrupt a SWAPO infiltration towards the south', which meant that South African intervention had to kick off in November 1983.

Among the general guidelines were the following:
- The enemy had to be stopped externally
- Deep reconnaissance coupled to offensive actions was to be commenced at an early stage
- Maximum use of mobile elements for follow-ups
- Security forces were to operate proactively, not reactively
- South African forces had to maintain the initiative throughout
- A guerrilla infiltration during 1984 had to be stopped at all costs[2]

1   This plan should have been initiated at the strategic level of planning, i.e. Army/Air Force HQ in Pretoria. It should have been part of the SADF military strategy, which in turn should have evolved out of the national strategy.
2   In retrospect this guideline was totally impractical and should therefore not have been included.

South African Air Force aims for Operation Askari were as follows:

1. Firstly, to gain and maintain a favourable air situation over Cahama-Mulondo-Cuvelai
2. Secondly, to prevent the expansion of enemy air defence capabilities in the Mulondo-Quiteve-Cuvelai areas
3. Finally, to expand the SAAF interdiction programme:
   a) All the way north to Chibemba
   b) North of Mulondo
   c) As far north as Cassinga
   d) Also factored into the equation would be extending *Maanskyn* operations (Impala night search and destroy sorties north of the 150km line), with preference given to joint attacks on SWAPO targets[3]

The plan was divided into four phases:

Phase 1: Deep reconnaissance by Special Forces followed by a SAAF attack on SWAPO's 'Typhoon/Volcano' base close to Lubango (between 1 November and 30 December 1983)

Phase 2: Offensive reconnaissance/isolation of the Angolan towns of Cahama, Mulondo and Cuvelai from 16 November to mid-January 1983. The objective was to cut enemy communication and logistic lines in the deep area and to 'terrorise and demoralise FAPLA to such an extent that they would withdraw'

Phase 3: To establish a dominated area from west of the Cunene River, through Quiteve, Mupa, Vinticet and eastwards through Ionde, by the beginning of February 1984

Phase 4: Final stopping of SWAPO's incursion, internally if necessary

Operational Approval

The joint Army-Air Force plan was presented to GOC SWA and OC Western Air Command and approved without major alterations. It was then presented at Army HQ Pretoria to the Chief of the Defence Force. Present in the audience that day were a dozen generals as well as an admiral. The army plan was accepted *in toto*.

In contrast, the Air Plan was only accepted after much discussion and a good deal of compromise and alteration. Reasons for changes are not open for discussion, but the fact remains that the Air Plan was altered.[4]

Limits and restrictions were placed on the deployment of SAAF aircraft, which did not coincide with the limits of action of the ground forces. In addition, the deception strike on Caiundo was taken out of the initial plan.

Once the revised Operation Askari plan had been approved – though I did not realise it at the time, neither did the twelve generals and the admiral – that what had started life as a combined plan, now no longer had the balance originally envisaged. What should have resulted was for us to go 'back to the drawing board' and rehash the situation and come up with a more functional arrangement: a vital lesson indeed.

---

3   An additional Air Force aim was a night strike by Impalas on Caiundo. Although the FAPLA garrison stationed there was no real threat to our planned operation, the idea was to sow confusion in the minds of the FAPLA high command as to what our exact intentions with Operation Askari were. This option was not authorised.

4   It is my opinion that there was a personality clash between the head of the SADF and OC Western Air Command. This, I believe, was the only reason the air plan was changed.

Reconnaissance Activities: Phases 1 and 2

While I do not intend to go into detail about all the involvement of the Recces, there are a few points that need highlighting since Operation Askari, from the outset, called for the largest reconnaissance effort of the war.

A total of five Reconnaissance Regiment teams of varying sizes were sent into Angola, some quite deep behind enemy lines. These were deployed both to the east and west of Cahama, in the vicinity of Mulondo, towards the outskirts of Cuvelai and these ground operators were also tasked to reconnoitre the Lubango area.

All provided basic tactical intelligence on which our battle plans were formulated and in general terms, those boys performed a difficult task well. Their command and control, however, became something of a problem from the air force point of view because each team operated as a separate entity (with an overall tactical headquarters at Xangongo on the Kunene River) but each in a separate locality.

The air force provided a Mobile Air Operations Team (MAOT) to be co-located with the army headquarters, also at Xangongo. Air support promised to each of the reconnaissance teams was consequently disjointed. A problem that might have arisen centred on priorities: if all teams suddenly found themselves compromised by the enemy, who would decide on the priority for air support?

I felt at the time that a joint operational headquarters was the only answer, with a representative of all involved parties present.[5]

At 0920B hours on 29 December 1983 four Buccaneers attacked the Tobias Hanyeko Training Centre (THTC) which lay just outside Lubango. This SWAPO facility, for a long time, had been responsible for training SWAPO recruits.

From THTC they were posted directly to the various frontline headquarters and the aim of the Askari strike was to demoralise these young men even before they had left the safety of their training base.

Altogether 32 bombs (each weighing 460kg) were dropped on the target area. Approximately half of the bombs exploded on contact, the others fitted with delay fuses from one to 36 hours, resulted in rendering the centre uninhabitable.

The air strike was bang on time, on target and most important, suffered no losses.

Round One to the *Boere*!

Offensive Actions: Phase 2

Cahama: For the duration of the Border War, Cahama had always been a formidable obstacle. The Angolan Army's 2nd Brigade had ensconced themselves in fortified positions in the periphery of this little town, both to the north and south of the Caculuvar River.

Numerous forays and probes by our ground forces over the preceding years had been undertaken against Cahama's perimeters. The air force had attacked radar as well as anti-aircraft artillery sites there on many occasions but none had succeeded in dislodging FAPLA or even making a dent in the enemy's peripheral defences of that stronghold. My analysis of the situation was that

---

5   All arms of the service, particularly the Recces, tend to be parochial. That is, they plan within the limits of their own involvement. Although the security of an operation is a definite factor, especially with clandestine operations, joint planning is always the best solution.

we never really made a concentrated joint effort to take the place and had that been the objective, I am certain we would have succeeded.

FAPLA's analysis of the continual assaults in contrast was that they had always succeeded in chasing the *Boere* away and would be able to do so again. They were therefore pretty confident of being able to hold Cahama. Contrary to our own widely disseminated intelligence on the troops that held the town, their morale was high.

On the ground during Operation Askari, 61 Mechanised Battalion Group (plus artillery) were ordered to pressurise FAPLA's 2nd Brigade by probes, feints and artillery bombardments. At the same time, offensive recce teams were tasked to cut FAPLA's logistic lines between Cahama and Chibemba, while the air force carried out strikes against identified targets within the defensive perimeter of the town.

The combined results of these actions were expected to dislodge FAPLA and SWAPO forces to such an extent that they would either withdraw or hopefully have their soldiers desert from Cahama. In terms of our planning, it was envisaged that this *uitmergeling* (grinding down) would take place between 16 November 1983 and mid-January 1984. Obviously, sufficient time had to be allowed for the desired actions to take effect.

In the event, the planning was naive in the extreme. Between mid-November and mid-December, our reconnaissance forces were indeed active, but a brigade garrison (which in their view had successfully and repeatedly beaten off the Boere) would simply not be disturbed by the activities of two small Recce teams.

The real offensive pressure started around 16 December, with the advance of 61 Mechanised Battalion from the Quiteve area, an approach that must have been detected by the defenders in Cahama very early on. Also, air bombardments had already begun and continued around the clock and must obviously have had a detrimental effect on the defenders.

Had the time limit of mid-January been open-ended, then the plan might have been successful because, by the end of December, the morale of the 2nd Brigade was still reasonable. We were aware that Angolan SA-8 anti-aircraft batteries were positioned about two kilometres south-west of the town, close to the road to Ediva.

A sub-operation within Operation Askari was Operation Fox. This called for a combined effort of ground and air forces to bomb the area so that these Triple-A batteries would be forced to change position by moving south. The intent was to drive them out of the protective ring surrounding Cahama and into the vicinity of FAPLA's defensive sites around Ediva.

Once in this area, a concerted effort by the ground forces (both Army and Reconnaissance Regiment), was to attempt to capture an entire SA-8 system intact; an aspect of the overall Operation Askari plan that was given top priority. More to the point, this plan was well on the way to succeeding. Angolan SA-8 batteries were eventually forced to move their position twice, both times towards Ediva, exactly as anticipated.

By the end of December, international media that had been seriously censuring South Africa's military because of its presence in Angola had reached a crescendo. A political decision was then made to cease all activities on the Cahama front by the end of the year.[6] As a consequence, all forces were withdrawn, FAPLA breathed a sigh of relief, and the status quo around Cahama returned to normal.

Once again, in the minds of those pulling the strings in the Angolan capital of Luanda, their 2nd Brigade had beaten off a determined assault by the Boere.

We lost that round!

---

6   Maintenance of the aim is a fundamental principle of war. All the effort put into the Cahama operation was not only wasted, it actually reinforced enemy morale.

Mulondo: The aim was:

a)   To isolate and demotivate the Angolan Army in both Quiteve and Mulondo to the extent that their troops would withdraw or desert

b)   To monitor the route Matala-Mulondo-Quiteve, to establish whether SWAPO was using the road as an infiltration route. The time frame for this sub-operation was to be 16 November to 15 January 1984. Ground forces would be the same that were involved at Cuvelai and the air force was briefed to carry out speculative bombing against selected targets in and around Mulondo, the intention being to heighten the tension prior to the final assault by the ground forces

On their advance towards Cahama, 61 Mech took Quiteve almost without firing a shot. This phase was so successful that it was decided to send a small fighting group with artillery support northwards on the western side of the Cunene River, to begin the process of isolating Mulondo.

As a result of the high state of alert throughout Angola, FAPLA's 19th Brigade in Mulondo had sent out their own recce teams to protect their increasingly vulnerable front. These troops performed an excellent task for FAPLA in that they were able to pinpoint the position of our fighting team.

When it was all over, we realised that Luanda never used that intelligence to engage offensively but, whenever we moved our artillery into range, they proceeded to bombard those positions with their D-30 cannons. Their guns outdistanced our artillery by three to four kilometres and that resulted in the South Africans having to withdraw after firing just a few salvoes.

This diversion from the original Operation Askari plan had its own set of repercussions on the air plan. Support had to be flown for the ground forces in the area, thus utilising aircraft hours and weapons that were set aside for the Cahama and Cuvelai battles. It had a further tactical disadvantage in that the element of surprise that was to have been gained with our air attacks on Cahama was lost.

After our Mulondo strikes the entire air defence system of southern Angola was placed on the highest possible alert.[7]

On 23 December 1983, two Impala jets attacked targets in the Mulondo area using their 68mm rockets. The weather was atrocious with large cumulo-nimbus clouds. After the fourth strike on that target area, the wingman took a hit from a SAM missile in the tail, but he managed to land safely back at Ondangua.[8]

The preamble to the plan for forcing FAPLA to leave Mulondo was consequently unsuccessful.

Political considerations in early January 1984 were such that the SADF did not continue with the original Operation Askari plan for Mulondo and in the eyes of FAPLA's 19th Brigade; they had succeeded in beating off a pretty determined attack.

We lost that round!

Caiundo

This small stronghold on the eastern bank of the Cubango River was never a part of the original Askari army plan. The air plan, however, had included a strike on its HQ unit; part of the overall deception plan, but this request was never approved. Consequently, no operational or logistical planning was carried out for operations in this eastern sector.

---

7   Surprise, as a principle of war, has become even more important with the advent of SAM defences.
8   Repeat attacks in the same target area are recipes for disaster …

Offensive actions, as detailed in the Operation Askari plan, commenced around 16 December. Both air and ground forces were engaged offensively in the Quiteve-Mulondo-Cahama areas.

Imagine my surprise, shortly thereafter, when I was casually informed that one of our army groups had been deployed within 20 kilometres of Caiundo, on the western bank.

When I enquired about their presence, I was told that they had been ordered to act as a deception force in that area and that they were troops from Sector 20, who would otherwise not be utilised in Operation Askari. This was never part of the joint Operation Askari plan, and as such, it had a detrimental effect on the outcome of this military action.

To everyone's consternation, this force was attacked on the night of 19-20 December. A FAPLA reconnaissance unit had discovered that one platoon of this force was deployed outside the main defensive perimeter and was much closer to Caiundo than they should have been and the result there was that the Angolan Army that night sent out a company to attack the intruders.

This they did successfully, killing five and capturing one SWA Territory Force soldier. They also seized 13 light machine guns, three rifles, three radios, a 60mm mortar as well as a Unimog.

It was clearly a setback and resulted in a switch of air activities from the Cahama and Mulondo fronts, to the unplanned-for Caiundo area, which continued uninterrupted for the remainder of Operation Askari. As a result, there was a substantial reduction in the air effort over the planned Operation Askari key points. That reduced pressure and allowed FAPLA to remain in control of both their troops and their morale, in Cahama and Mulondo.

In spite of a large air effort over a period of 21 days, Caiundo was not taken. Despite a heavy air bombardment and a determined ground assault, all FAPLA minefields and defensive bunkers remained intact. FAPLA's 53rd Brigade had reason to celebrate their successful defence of Caiundo against the Boere.

We lost that round!

Cuvelai: Phase 2 of the original army operational plan called for the isolation of Cuvelai, planned to be put into action between 16 November 1983 and 15 January 1984.

The aim was threefold:

1. To isolate, grind down or *uitmergel* and terrorise Cuvelai, to the extent that FAPLA would either leave on their own accord, or their soldiers would desert on a large scale
2. To carry out operations against SWAPO elements such as the Moscow, Alpha and Bravo battalions in the Cuvelai area.
3. To give early warning of a SWAPO incursion

The air force plan thus called for:
a) Extensive photo-reconnaissance of Cuvelai
b) Speculative bombing day and night of SWAPO targets in the vicinity
c) Air attacks on AAA sites that had a direct bearing on ground force operations

In mid-December photo-reconnaissance (PR) was flown and up-to-date images of all the AAA sites in Cuvelai were obtained. It must be remembered that in the history of our activities in Angola, PR flights were always understood by the enemy to be the precursor of an attack, which suggests that we lost Round One of the psychological battle.

On 27 December at 1405B hours, two Impalas dropped ten 120kg bombs on a SWAPO target in the area. At 1628B hours on the same day, four SAAF Canberra bombers dropped 600 Alpha bombs, a pair of 460kg bombs and a total of sixteen 250kg bombs on targets in and around the town.

The following day at 1335B hours, two Impalas carried out a further recce of the AAA sites in Cuvelai. At 1439B hours the Canberras carried out attacks on targets close to the Cuvelai airstrip, dropping seventeen 250kg, two 460kg as well as 300 Alpha bombs, which obtained a 90 percent coverage of the target. At 1610B hours eight Impalas dropped a total of thirty-two 250kg bombs on various targets in and around the town.

All these flights were undertaken with the intention of achieving tactical results against the enemy's AAA defences, as well as obtaining the psychological advantage while attempting to grind down FAPLA.

The South African Army meanwhile had sent in a battle group consisting mainly of citizen force troops to engage the SWAPO headquarters and logistic base five kilometres north-east of the town and this group came under heavy attack from FAPLA's 11th Brigade and were in a perceived danger of being cut off.

It was then decided to reassign 61 Mech under the command of Commandant van Lill – then on the outskirts of Cahama – to aid the endangered battle group.

In a little over 16 hours, 61 Mech, under battle conditions, moved from the Cahama area across the temporary bridge over the Cunene River to the outskirts of Cuvelai. This 'forced march' was clearly an epic of determination and perseverance, especially as those troops had to go straight into battle at Cuvelai when they arrived on 3 January 1984.

On the afternoon of 3 January, when the attack took place, it commenced with a coordinated air assault aimed at all known AAA and artillery sites. Each pilot was equipped with up-to-date enlarged photographs of his particular target and altogether ten Impalas led the raid, followed by four Canberra bombers. Between them, they dropped sixty 120kg, eighteen 250kg, two 450kg and 600 Alpha bombs.

A second wave of Impalas dropped a further thirty-two 250kg bombs. This was arguably the most effective strike flown by the SAAF, throughout the history of the war in Angola. On completion, an intercepted message from the military commander of Cuvelai to his Lubango headquarters was picked up, the gist of which declared his need for urgent help.

'You better send help, 75 percent of my artillery is out of action as a result of the SAAF bombardment.'

The air force played yet another important role while supporting ground forces as they attacked the town following the air strike, but the army was still faced with two major problems – navigation through fairly extensive minefields and the destruction of the last remaining resistance.

Two Alouette gunships, led by Captain Carl Alberts provided the assistance the army needed, doing so against all doctrine and at great risk. He was awarded the *Honoris Crux* (HC) decoration for his dedication to his task.

After bogging down and losing a Ratel in the minefields, ground forces entered Cuvelai to find that both SWAPO and FAPLA had fled, In fact, 32 Battalion who had troops in the Tetchamutete area, used their men as stoppers to capture a large number of FAPLA who were trying to escape northwards.

The battle for Cuvelai was a success, Large amounts of military hardware were captured and the reason was basic: this was the only time during the four major battles that comprised Operation Askari that air power had been correctly utilised, followed by a determined assault by the ground forces.

The objective was maintained and the concentration of forces, adopting a joint plan, finally overcame the enemy, Measured against the principles of war, this sub-operation was bound to succeed.

We won that round!

International Pressure

By the first week in 1984 the pressure on the South African government to pull their forces out of Angola reached a peak, particularly from Washington.

Our military presence and operations in Angola were being condemned from all quarters, with threats of even greater sanctions and boycotts. This pressure, coupled to the relatively slow progress of the weather-hampered operation, forced Pretoria to decide to call a halt to Operation Askari on 10 January 1984. Captured equipment was removed to South West Africa and all participating forces stood down.

> **Phase 3:** A dominated area was established by February 1984 and that included all the territory between the Cunene and Cubango rivers as far north as a line running east-west through Tetchamutete. The area west of the Cunene was still 'Injun country', but for purposes of Operation Askari it can be assumed that the *Boere* won that round.

> **Phase 4:** This phase was to be the final stopping of the incursion internally, if necessary. This always seemed to be a contradiction of the guidelines set for Operation Askari. A study of the results of operational losses for 1984 is a good indication of whether this phase was successful or not. SWAPO suffered 916 dead in 1984, of which 361 were killed during Askari, the remainder as a result of the normal summer incursion.

One positive factor was the reduction in security force deaths, down from 96 in 1983 to 39 in 1984. A total of 13 of those 39 were killed during Operation Askari.

Nevertheless, a SWAPO cross-border incursion did occur, so it must be inferred that we lost that round.

Summary

Over the years Operation Askari has been viewed as a major success. This perception began from the first debrief held at Oshakati, headquarters of Sector 10 in February 1984.

Certainly, we did capture Cuvelai along with masses of war materiel. Also, FAPLA suffered a severe defeat in terms of men and equipment and last, apart from their successful attack on a platoon of ground forces outside Caiundo, Angolan forces (heavily bolstered by Cubans) never achieved any other offensive success.

Still, the question remains: Was Operation Askari was a success? The Rhodesians were fond of stating the fact that, 'they never lost a battle' in their bush campaign. But they certainly lost their war …

Did the same happen during Operation Askari? One needs to carefully examine the facts:

> Our acknowledged enemy was SWAPO. They used Angola as a 'safe haven' from where they launched their attacks into South West Africa. After the initial large-scale raid by the SADF into Cassinga during Operation Reindeer, SWAPO realised the inherent dangers of establishing permanent bases that could be attacked by the SADF.
>
> To protect their headquarters and training establishments, they moved these facilities behind the umbrella protection provided by the Angolan Army, which effectively made FAPLA a 'legitimate' target.

During December 1983 to January 1984 we lost 32 soldiers compared to the 407 SWAPO terrorists killed; a ratio of nearly 13:1.

Overall figures for 1983 were: 96 security forces killed compared to SWAPO's 913, a ratio of just under 10:1. In 1984 the ratio increased to 23:1. In that respect Operation Askari reaped rich benefits and, as a matter of record, this ratio stayed over 20:1 for the remainder of the war.

SWAPO's military never succeeded in regaining the offensive capability it had achieved prior to Operation Askari. The overall aim of that operation was to prevent an infiltration to the south in 1984.

During 1984, a total of 555 enemy troops were killed, in addition to those who died during Operation Askari, indicating that although they suffered losses, the pattern of the insurgency war continued. We failed to achieve the main aim.

The second phase of the plan called for offensive action against FAPLA strongholds. We comprehensively beat the 11th Brigade at Cuvelai, but we did not achieve that goal at either Cahama or Mulondo. In addition, we never succeeded in dislodging FAPLA forces out of Caiundo.

Seen from the Angolan perspective, they lost Cuvelai but won the battles for Cahama, Mulondo and Caiundo.

Thus, Operation Askari became the watershed in the course of the Border War. SWAPO's military wing was reduced in strength and from then on, the People's Liberation Army of Namibia no longer posed a major threat.

On the other hand FAPLA – the Angolan Army – grew in stature and evolved into the major factor in the pursuance of our war against SWAPO. Our readiness to attack, wherever or whenever they protected SWAPO, provoked them into acquiring a series of extremely effective air defence systems to protect their national interests, second only to that assembled in the Warsaw Pact countries.

Two significant events occurred following Operation Askari. Firstly, initiatives were taken to bring the South Africans and the Angolans to the negotiating table. South Africa, being in a clear position of strength, welcomed this proposal, as did the Angolans, who by then, were taking knocks militarily and psychologically. In fact, the country had become 'war-weary'.

For its part, Pretoria saw this as an opportunity for peace in the region. Angola, on the other hand, seized the moment as little more than a tactic.

Communist-inspired organisations – as have observed often enough in the past – have a history of going to the negotiating table whenever they are in trouble, and then utilising that breathing space to re-plan, re-organise and re-equip. This is precisely what they did during the protracted life of the Joint Monitoring Commission (JMC) created specifically for the purposes of negotiations.

The second occurrence of significance was the subtle change in the whole structure of the war. FAPLA gradually replaced SWAPO as our main enemy and the war entered a phase of greater sophistication. Concurrently, the low-intensity counter-insurgency Bush War escalated over the next four years to a high-intensity undeclared conventional war between the armed forces of South Africa, South West Africa and UNITA on the one hand, and FAPLA, their Cuban allies plus their Russian advisers, on the other.

By then the war was no longer a regional conflict. It had become fully international with all the ramifications linked to such a development. As a result, the solution was no longer in the hands of either SWAPO or Pretoria. Also, it meant that an international solution had to be sought with all the accompanying implications.

Conclusion[9]

It can be fairly stated, that as a military strike against SWAPO, Operation Askari produced results that effectively eliminated SWAPO's military wing PLAN (People's Liberation Army of Namibia) as a major element in the struggle. While the organisation continued in its role as a guerrilla force and went about its business, PLAN's designated efforts by SWAPO's supreme command had lost momentum and its efforts were easily countered.

Although the South Africans required a large economic outlay to maintain this status quo, SWAPO had come to accept that the South Africans could not and would not be beaten militarily by their insurgent forces. In this aspect, Operation Askari was successful.

At the same time, I do not believe that the consequences of that brief cross-border campaign were originally envisaged in terms of factors other than drawing SWAPO into defending its integrity. The four years, from 1984 to the culmination of hostilities outside Cuito Cuanavale and Calueque in 1988, our reserves and capabilities were severely stretched.

The wholesale build-up of Soviet arms, within this time period, created a situation that was becoming daily more difficult to handle and the cost factor alone – in terms of men and materiel – was placing a critical burden on the country's resources.

Moreover, the 'internationalisation' of this conflict led to us become increasingly involved with extricating UNITA from situations they simply could not handle. Fundamentally, this was brought about by UNITA's guerrillas' inability to counter advanced military hardware such as Soviet main battle tanks as well as the most sophisticated helicopters and artillery that the Luanda government had acquired specifically to counter South African attacks.

These factors lend support to the belief that the conventional attacks on FAPLA during Operation Askari had long-term repercussions that affected the entire future of the war.

At the same time, there are several lessons that can be extracted from the limited success of those relatively modest (by international standards) infantry and light armoured strikes, some of which affected all levels of authority in South Africa.

For a start, an operation of the magnitude of Operation Askari requires both vetting and authority to be granted at sector, theatre, chief of staff as well as cabinet level. War is ugly: it possesses the potential to escalate beyond imagination, sometimes even before you become aware of what is actually taking place on the ground.

Consequently, in any conflict – before forces are committed to battle – it must be ensured that the operation is in accordance with the military strategy of the country involved. That, in turn, must be part of the national strategy.

---

9   This complete assessment also published by *Scientia Militaria*, South African Journal of Military Studies, Volume 22, Nr 4, 1992, <http://scientiamilitaria.journals.ac.za>.

A SWAPO Arms and food cache destroyed by SA troops in across-border raid. (Author's photo)

Operational briefing and church parade prior to the launching of Op Protea 1981 – Ruacana D minus 1.

Russians and Cubans on operations were always on the periphery during southern Angolan hostilities. As soon as things got hot, they scrammed. (Photo sources to Roland de Vries)

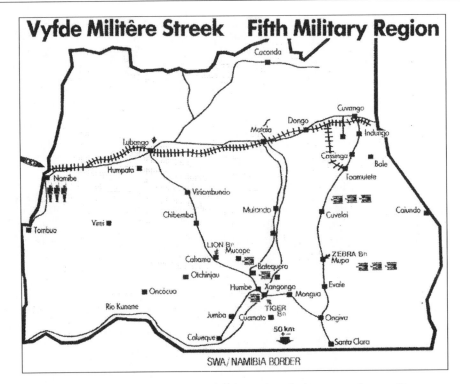

Op Askari operational map – it ended up a bit of a lemon, as these military adventures went because the enemy were tipped off.

Enemy troops KIA and brought back to base for identification. (Author's photo)

Kunene, Southern Angola, where parts of Op Protea took place, is a harsh, unyielding arid terrain in which to fight a war. (Author's photo)

Самолеты и вертолеты ВВС ЮАР летали над Анголой, как правило, с закрашенными опознавательными знаками
Usually the insignia of the airplanes and helicopters of AF of Republic of South Africa used in operations over Angola were painted over

The French-built Puma troop-carrying helicopter was acknowledged by the Russians for its capabilities operating under harsh conditions. That resulted in this Soviet ID image being circulated among Angolan and Cuban troops in Angola.

Forerunner to the Ratel in the Bush War was the AML-90 Eland armoured vehicle, totally outclassed by modern Soviet weapons and which ultimately led to the development of a range of infantry combat vehicles.

Sharp end of a Ratel 90 of Charlie Squadron.

Angola had many Soviet MiG-21s to begin with but these were soon supplanted by more sophisticated jets like the MiG-23s and the more advanced Sukhois.

13

How Washington Viewed Angola's Transition

As active as the Soviets were in changing the status quo in Angola, the United States played a few hands of its own. Jonas Savimbi was handed Stinger anti-aircraft missiles together with American military specialists who taught UNITA cadres how to use them. That was in addition to a handful of military instructors, vehicles and other equipment, all of which went towards attempting to cripple Luanda's Marxist government. The Soviets invested billions of dollars annually and Washington only a fraction of that amount.

Yet, for all that, there were quite a few Americans on the ground in various parts of Angola towards the end of 1975. John Stockwell, CIA Station Chief in the Democratic Republic Congo – where the tyrant Mobutu Sese Seko eventually installed himself as supremo – was among the most active and went on to become a vociferous critic of Langley's efforts, or lack of them, which was when he resigned.

Stockwell wrote a remarkable book that covered just about everything that occurred at the time. Titled *In Search of Enemies: A CIA Story* it covers his role while working for American intelligence during this critical phase. In exposing the naive futility of Washington's efforts in that part of Africa, he was able to observe the South African role during the course of the Angolan war and all its ups and downs, the latter principally.

What comes strongly across is that by a long chalk, Pretoria's forces were the most efficient and cooperative in all departments. If they said they were going to do something or make a delivery or take action, the South Africans responded appropriately every time. Stockwell's book is a compelling work and well worth a read.[1]

Another operative, as we have already seen was George Bacon, also a CIA operative who, we suspect, was sent incognito to establish what was going on. He operated solo, which was unusual, but then that was George Bacon. He'd knocked on my door in Johannesburg and asked whether I could help him with contacts in Angola. I couldn't, but he went ahead anyway.

Details about Washington's role in Luanda in the final stages of the handover are sketchy. Some material was provided by Robert Hultslander, the last CIA station chief in Luanda from July 1975 through to the evacuation of US personnel early November 1975 when MPLA security forces moved to overwhelm rival factions.

---

1   John Stockwell: *In Search of Enemies: A CIA Story* (W. W. Norton and Company, 1984).

In 1998, as part of his research for *Conflicting Missions*, Piero Gleijeses – Professor of United States Foreign Policy at the Paul H. Nitze School of Advanced International Studies – sent a set of questions and drafts of sections of his book to Mr Hultslander regarding CIA analysis and operations in the Angolan conflict.

Below, in précis, are Hultslander's responses, today filed in the National Security Archives and in the public domain.

For a start, this American intelligence agent who was posted to Luanda a short while before independence had absolutely no experience of Africa. This is strange considering that the country, about to become independent, had become a major factor in East–West Cold War diplomacy.

In essence, whoever took over in Angola would achieve an enormous advantage for its backers, which, in Cold War terms was momentous. The country straddled a huge swathe of Africa along the eastern shores of the Atlantic, and this is exactly what took place once the MPLA took over. Because Washington was half asleep about what was going on in Africa and the Democrats too busy scoring points against the Republicans in Congress (or vice versa), the Soviets ended up having free rein in every one of Angola's harbours and airports.

Moscow's planes and electronic monitoring ships were able to range far into the South Atlantic and the Indian Ocean. I was to go on several reconnaissance sorties by SAAF Shackletons and took numerous photos of Soviet 'fishing ships' with arrays of protruding aerials off the Cape coast that would not have looked out of place on the Mount Hebron foothills, one of which can be seen in this chapter.

Considering the CIA's intelligence prerogatives, one can only speculate why Robert Hultslander was pushed in at the deep end. Broadly speaking, that was roughly equivalent to putting a novice in charge of monitoring El Salvador's Farabundo Martí National Liberation Front during that country's civil war. This was worse because the security stakes in Angola were much higher.

Which begs the question: which dolt at Langley left Angola so exposed? Part of the answer may lie with Gerald Ford, arguably one of the most lacklustre American presidents of the previous century; it all took place on his watch.

To be fair, this new CIA station chief told Professor Gleijeses that 'in the interest of candour', he had some serious run-ins with US Consul General Tom Killoran in Angola while he was there, 'even if I came to share [his assessment] that the MPLA [communist or not] was the best-qualified movement to govern Angola.'

> Hultslander:
> I must admit that Killoran and I were frequently at loggerheads over what I initially perceived as his MPLA bias. The briefings and orientation I received prior to arriving in Luanda emphasised the communist orientation of the MPLA also and convinced me of the urgent need to stop [Agostinho Neto] from taking power. I fully agreed with the US policy objectives as articulated to the Senate Foreign Relations Committee in December 1995. Since the MPLA was receiving Soviet assistance, I believed we had no choice but to counter with our own assistance to its opponents. It was only after three months in Luanda, that I realised what was really happening …

Hultslander also told the professor that he had very little time to 'read in', prior to assuming the Angola command in August.

> I had less than one week with the Angola Task Force in Washington and spent two days on my way into Luanda with officers involved in the Angolan programme. My mind was not

clouded by many facts, and I had few preconceptions prior to hitting the ground. Since I would not be directly involved, I also had an only rudimentary knowledge of our covert action programme.

I volunteered to remain in Luanda after Angolan independence (11 November 1975), although the consulate was ordered to close. Initially approved at the highest levels of State and CIA, Kissinger – afraid of a potential hostage situation – decided on November 3 (the day of the last refugee flight) that every American diplomat had to leave Luanda.

Hultslander maintains that he strongly disagreed, and pointed out that the MPLA desperately wanted to keep an official US presence and would protect anyone who stayed behind.

I lost the argument. The consulate's convoy to the airport departed without me; I arrived by motorcycle only minutes before the flight left for Lisbon. I was only in Angola a few days over three months but continued to follow events from Lisbon for more than three years.

On America's future relations with the UNITA leader, Dr Jonas Savimbi, potentially a major force among the three liberation movements, the measure of bias was palpable and I quote:

Savimbi (according to Hultslander) was not to be trusted because of his Chinese communist contacts and his flirtation with Maoist philosophy, something we all knew about. The Luanda Consulate had already reported in mid-1974, 18 months before the handover – that Savimbi was ideologically sympathetic to Maoism.

The United States Embassy in Lusaka also reported that 'Savimbi is pro-Chinese and a racist.' The CIA took issue with these reports arguing that Savimbi was a nationalist exploring various means to gain assistance for his own liberation movement. The Luanda Consulate General subsequently modified its critical report but continued to believe that the UNITA leader was, in their words 'paranoid and self-pitying.'

A question was put to Hultslander regarding his own assessment of Agostinho Neto and the MPLA and the FNLA. He replied as follows:

I came to share Consul General Killoran's assessment that the MPLA was the best-qualified movement to govern Angola. Many of its leaders were educated at the University of Coimbra and a few at Patrice Lumumba University in Moscow. Although many outwardly embraced Marxism, they were much closer to European radical socialism than to the Soviet Marxist-Leninism dogma. Lucio Lara, a mulatto intellectual, was probably a convicted communist (in the old, Cold War sense).

However, Agostinho Neto, the undisputed leader of the MPLA was more moderate. A Protestant minister, he was married to a Portuguese and had many close Portuguese friends. His trusted doctor and unofficial adviser Armenio Ferreira was Portuguese and lived in Lisbon. Other senior MPLA leaders were impressive, inter alia, Lopo do Nacimiento, Paula Jorge, Nito Alves, Carlos Rocha and Iko Carreira were all smart political operatives. Chieto and Dangereux were good military commanders ...

In addition, the MPLA was the least tribal of the three movements. Neto and most of the top cadres were Mbundu, but the MPLA welcomed many different tribes, unlike the FMLN (Bakongo) and UNITA (Ovimbundu).

Despite the uncontested communist background of many of the MPLA's leaders, they were more effective, better educated, better trained and better motivated. The rank and file were also more motivated (particularly the armed combatants, who fought harder and with more determination). Portuguese Angolans overwhelmingly supported the MPLA.

Unfortunately, the CIAs association with the FNLA and UNITA tainted its analysis. As is frequently the case when intelligence collection and analysis are wedded to covert action programmes, objectivity and truth become victims of political expediency and I believe this was the case in Angola. No one wanted to believe the consulate's reporting, and Killoran's courageous and accurate analysis was ignored.

Following Angola's independence, there were numerous changes – some good and all too many bad – and most took place as the country headed towards the 1980s and thereafter. Initial, heady post-independence celebrations rapidly gave way to a civil war that evolved into one of the most intense and (after the Sudan and the Congo, both of which defy categorisation) the longest lasting conflict on the African continent.

Numerous American institutions have published assessments of what went on in Angola after 11 November 1975, but few have been quite as comprehensive as an American military-related Angola Study, a masterly piece of research published at Quantico in the early 1990s and titled *US Marines Angola Study 5*.

In one of my earlier books, I used their reflections on Nigeria's civil war in the rebel enclave of Biafra and that too, was a comprehensive, thorough and all-encompassing academic research, to be expected of such a venerable US institution.[2]

The United States Marine Corps is no lightweight in such matters. In the 2010 American census, the US Marines Quantico Station had a working population of almost 4,500 and included the Marine Corps Combat Development Command as well as its Systems Command, the Warfighting Laboratory and several academic bodies. At the top of this list was the Marine Corps University, the US Marine Corps Air-Group Task Force (Staff Training Programme), Officer Candidate's School, Basic School and several others.

The Quantico study paper on Angola during that crucial transitional period, while dealing with a period a few years after Lisbon's handover, was specific about several issues; one suggested that most African governments maintained generally cautious support of the Luanda regime during most of its first 13 years in power.[3]

African leaders, it said, recognised Luanda's right to reject Western alignments and opt for a Marxist state (following Angola's long struggle to end colonial domination). This recognition of sovereignty, however, was accompanied by uncertainty about the MPLA regime itself, shifting from a concern in the 1970s that spreading Soviet influence would destabilise African regimes across the continent, to a fear in the 1980s that the MPLA might be incapable of governing the country in the face of strong UNITA resistance.

The large Cuban military presence came to symbolise both Angola's political autonomy from the West and the MPLA's reliance as a Soviet client state to remain in power. By 1988 the party's

2   Al J. Venter: *Biafra's War: The Nigerian Civil War that Left a Million Dead*, (Helion, 2015).
3   The original document was titled *US Marines Angola Study 5* and ran to more than 20,000 words, of which these excerpts comprise more than a third of the original report. Also, the fact that it was published prior to Angolan hostilities with South Africa being settled at the negotiating table, tended to colour some of the observations. Once a peace treaty had been signed between the two African states, Washington and Luanda entered into a comfortable, mutually-beneficial relationship centred on Angola's oil resources. Throughout, Quantico refers to the MPLA as MPLA-PT (MPLA-*Partido de Trabalhon* in domestic parlance). For the sake of simplicity, we have reverted to the original MPLA.

role in the struggle against South Africa had become its best guarantee of broad support across sub-Saharan Africa.

The treatise went on: Pretoria's goals in Angola were to eliminate SWAPO as well as any South African ANC bases from Angolan territory, weaken MPLA support for Pretoria's foes through a combination of direct assault and aid to UNITA and reinforce regional dependence on South Africa's own extensive transportation system by closing down the Benguela Railway which linked the port of Lobito with the copper mines in the Congo.

At the same time, however, South Africa's right-wing extremists relied on Marxist rhetoric from Angola and Mozambique as evidence of the predicted communist onslaught against Pretoria.

The political ties of Angola and Mozambique to the Soviet Union also bolstered South Africa's determination to strengthen its security apparatus at home and provided a rationale for the continued occupation of South West Africa. Knowing this important prop for Pretoria's regional policies would diminish with the Cuban withdrawal from Angola, South Africa actually prolonged Angola's dependence on Soviet and Cuban military might by derailing negotiations for Namibian independence.

Angola was wary of attempts at African solidarity during its first years of independence, an attitude that gave way to a more activist role in southern Africa. President Neto rejected an offer of an OAU Peacekeeping Force in 1975, suspecting that African Union leaders would urge a negotiated settlement with UNITA. He then declined other efforts to find African solutions to Angola's instability and also to reduce the Soviet and Cuban role in the region.

A decade later, Angola had become a leader among the Frontline States (the others were Botswana, Mozambique, Tanzania, Zambia, and Zimbabwe) seeking Western pressure to end regional destabilisation by Pretoria. Additionally, Luanda coordinated efforts by the Southern African Development Coordination Conference (SADCC) to reduce Frontline States' economic dependence on South Africa.

Angola's relations were generally good with other African countries that accepted its Marxist policies and conversely, strained with states that harboured or supported rebel forces opposed to the MPLA. The most consistent rhetorical support for the MPLA came from other former Portuguese states in Africa, including Mozambique and Guiné-Bissau, the Cape Verde Islands as well as Sao Tomé and Principe).

Nigeria led the OAU in recognising the MPLA regime in1975 and went on to seek a leadership role in the campaign against South Africa's domination of the region. But the Nigerian government never forged close ties with Angola. Its own economic difficulties of the 1970s and 1980s, as well as close relations with the West and other cultural and political differences, prevented Luanda and Lagos from forming a close alliance. They were friends of course, in the diplomatic nature of things, but never close.

The Congo's (Zaire's) relations with Angola, in contrast, were unstable during this period. Zairean regular army units supported the FNLA in the years before as well as just after Angolan independence. Also, Angola harboured anti-Zairean rebels, who twice invaded Zaire's southern Shaba region (formerly Katanga Province). But Zaire's President Mobutu Sese Seko and President Neto were able to reach a rapprochement before the Angolan leader's death in 1979, which was when Zaire curtailed direct opposition to the MPLA.

Nonetheless, throughout most of the 1980s, UNITA operated freely across Zaire's south-western border; also, Western support for UNITA was channelled through Zaire.

Complicating relations between these two nations were the numerous ethnic groups whose homelands had been either ignored or split by the boundary between Zaire and Angola a century earlier. The Bakongo, Lunda, Chokwe, as well as many smaller groups, maintained longstanding cultural, economic and religious ties with relatives in neighbouring states. Holden Roberto, the sclerotic FNLA leader backed by the CIA for instance, was Mobutu's brother-in-law. These links quite often extended to support for anti-government rebels.

President Kenneth Kaunda's Zambia had officially ousted UNITA bands from its western region in 1976 and went on to voice strong support for the MPLA at the same time that it turned a blind eye to monetary and logistical support for UNITA by Zambian citizens. Without official approval (but also without interference) UNITA forces continued to train in Zambia's western region, part of the great Barotse Kingdom which sits on Angola's eastern frontier.

Lusaka's ambivalence toward Angola during the 1980s took into account the possibility of an eventual UNITA role in the government in Luanda. Both Zambia and Zaire had an interest in seeing an end to Angola's civil war because the flow of refugees from Angola had reached several hundred thousand by the mid-1980s and posed an enormous drain on Lusaka's budget. Also, everybody knew that peace would enable Zambia and Zaire to upgrade the Benguela Railway as an alternative to South African transport systems.

Elsewhere in the region, links with the Luanda regime varied. Strain would come at times with the Congo, where both FNLA and Cabinda rebels had close cultural ties and some semi-official encouragement. Senegal, Togo, Malawi and Somalia were among the relatively conservative African states that provided material support to UNITA during the 1980s.

Throughout most of that decade, UNITA also got assistance from several North African states, including Morocco, Tunisia, and Egypt, and these governments (along with Kuwait and Saudi Arabia) pressured their African trading partners and client states to limit their support of the Marxist MPLA.

The Soviet Union supported the MPLA as a liberation movement long before independence and then formalised its relationship with Agostinho Neto's government through the Treaty of Friendship and Cooperation and a slew of military agreements beginning in 1975. Once it became clear that the MPLA could, with Cuban support, remain in power, the Soviet Union provided still more economic and technical assistance and went on to grant Angola 'Most Favoured Nation' status.

This support included diplomatic representations at the UN and in other international forums, while military hardware and advisers were all part of it. Still, more direct military support in the face of South African incursions into Angola followed.

Civilian technical assistance extended to hydroelectric projects, bridge and road building, agriculture, fisheries, public health, and a variety of educational projects. Technical assistance was often channelled through joint projects with a third country – for example, the Capanda Hydroelectric Project entailed cooperation between the Soviet Union and Brazil.

But Soviet-Angolan relations also became strained at times during the 1980s, in part because Angola sought to upgrade diplomatic ties with the United States which, in Moscow's eyes, was a transgression of faith. Soviet leadership factions were also sometimes divided over their nation's future role in Africa, and some Soviet negotiators objected to Angolan President dos Santos's concessions to the United States on the issue of 'linkage'.

The region's intractable political problems, and the cost of maintaining Cuban troop support and equipping the MPLA, undeniably weakened the Soviet commitment to the building of a Marxist-Leninist state in Angola, as it was eventually to do in other guerrilla conflicts in which Moscow was involved.

Angolan leaders, in turn, complained about Soviet neglect, low levels of assistance, poor quality personnel and military hardware as well as derisory responses to complaints. Angola shared the cost of the Cuban military presence and made some efforts to reduce these expenses, in large part because many Angolan citizens felt the immediate drain on economic resources and rising tensions in areas occupied by Cuban troops.

Moreover, dos Santos complained that the Soviet Union dealt with Angola opportunistically, purchasing Angolan coffee at low prices and re-exporting it at a substantial profit, over-fishing in Angolan waters and as a consequence driving up local food prices.

For the first decade after independence, trade with communist states was not significant, but in the late 1980s, dos Santos sought expanded economic ties with the Soviet Union, China, and Czechoslovakia and other nations of Eastern Europe, as his government attempted to diversify its economic relations and reduce its dependence on the West. In October 1986, Angola signed a cooperative agreement with the Council for Mutual Economic Assistance (Comecon or CMEA), a consortium dedicated to economic cooperation among the Soviet Union and its allies.

As part of the Comecon agreement, Soviet support for Angolan educational and training programmes was increased. Thus, in 1987, almost 2,000 Angolan students attended institutions of higher education in the Soviet Union and Moscow also provided about 100 lecturers to the Agostinho Neto University in Luanda as well as a variety of Soviet-sponsored training programmes in the African state, most with Cuban instructors.

Approximately 4,000 Angolans studied at the international school on Cuba's renowned Isle of Youth and still more Angolan students were scheduled to attend the Union of Young Communists School in Havana in 1989 so, clearly, ties were strong.

Cuba's presence in Angola was more complex than it appeared to outsiders who viewed the Soviet Union's Third World clients as little more than surrogates for their powerful patron. The initiative in placing Cuban troops in Angola in the mid-1970s was taken by President Fidel Castro as part of his avowed mission of what was termed 'Cuban Internationalism'. Facing widespread unemployment at home, young Cuban men were urged to serve in the military overseas as their 'patriotic duty', and veterans enjoyed great prestige on their return.

Castro also raised the possibility of a Cuban resettlement scheme in southern Angola, and several hundred Cubans received Angolan citizenship during the 1980s. As a consequence, Cuban immigration to this part of Africa increased sharply in 1988.

In addition to military support, Cuba provided Angola with several thousand teachers, physicians, and civilian labourers for construction, agriculture, and industry, all desperately needed as most of the Portuguese who filled these roles had fled back to their roots in Europe. It is also worth mentioning that Angolan dependence on Cuban medical personnel was so invasive that during the 1980s Spanish became known as the language of medicine in that part of Africa.

China's relations with Angola were complicated by Beijing's opposition to both Soviet and United States policies toward Africa. Beijing supported the FNLA and UNITA after the MPLA seized power in Angola, and the Chinese provided military support to Zaire when its troops clashed with Angolan forces along their common border in the late 1970s. China nonetheless took the initiative in improving relations with the MPLA during the 1980s.

Throughout most of the civil war period, the United States aided both the FNLA and UNITA and blocked Angola's admission to the UN. Almost until the 1990s the two nations lacked diplomatic ties.

Throughout, and in spite of these links, United States representatives pressured Luanda to reduce its military reliance on Cuba and the Soviet Union, made necessary in part by the United States and South African opposition to the MPLA and support for UNITA.

In 1988 Angola's government news agency quoted Minister of Foreign Relations Afonso van Dunem (*nom de guerre* Mbinda) as saying the United States was stuck with what he termed a

'Cuban psychosis' and suggested that it prevented the Americans from engaging in talks about Namibia and Angola. However, after the December 1988 regional accords to end the Cuban military presence in Angola, United States officials offered to normalise relations with Angola on condition that an internal settlement of the civil war with UNITA be reached.

Political and diplomatic differences between the United States and Angola were generally mitigated by close economic ties. American oil companies operating in Cabinda provided a substantial portion of Angola's export earnings and foreign exchange, and this relationship continued despite political pressures on these companies to reduce their holdings in Cabinda in the mid-1980s.

The divergence of private economic interests from United States diplomatic policy was complicated by differences of opinion among American policy-makers, again hampered by differences within Congress by opposing political agenda between the Republicans and Democrats.

By means of the Clark Amendment, from 1975 to 1985, the United States Congress prohibited aid to UNITA and slowed covert attempts to circumvent this legislation. With President Reagan, and after the repeal of the Clark Amendment in 1985, trade between Angola and the United States continued to increase, and Cuban and Angolan troops attempted to prevent sabotage against United States interests by UNITA and South African commandos.

Western Europe – like the United States – feared the implications of a strong Soviet client state in southern Africa, but in general, European relations with the MPLA were based on economic interests rather than ideology, that country's huge oilfields and colossal natural resources always being a powerful motivator.

France and Portugal, in spite of providing financial assistance for UNITA, tended to maintain good relations with the MPLA and allowed its representatives to operate freely in their capitals. It helped too that Portugal was Angola's leading trading partner throughout most of that period and Brazil – another Lusophone state – went on to continually strengthen its economic ties with Angola, as it still does today.

Since the 1960s, Angola had experienced, sometimes simultaneously, four types of war: a war of national liberation, a civil war, a regional war, and the global struggle between the Super Powers. Angola had won its independence from Portugal in 1975 after a 13-year liberation struggle, during which the externally supported African nationalist movements splintered and subdivided. However, independence provided no respite, as the new nation was immediately engulfed in a civil war whose scope and effects were compounded by foreign military intervention.

Although the MPLA eventually won recognition as the legitimate government, it did so only with massive Soviet and Cuban military support, on which it remained heavily dependent until their military forces went home.

Despite the party's international acceptance and domestic hegemony, Angola in the late 1980s remained at war with itself and its most powerful neighbour, South Africa. Additionally, the insurgency led by UNITA, bolstered by growing foreign support, spread from the remote and sparsely populated south-east corner of the country throughout the entire nation. South African interventions on behalf of UNITA and against black South African and Namibian nationalist forces in southern Angola also escalated.

Luanda's reliance on the Soviet Union, Cuba, and other communist states for internal security and defence increased as these threats intensified. Intermittent diplomatic efforts since the late 1970s had failed to end the protracted war; indeed, each new initiative had been followed by an escalation of violence.

Accordingly, FAPLA was organised and equipped to fight both counter-insurgency and conventional wars and to deploy abroad when ordered; it had engaged in all these tasks continuously since independence. Its main counter-insurgency effort was directed against UNITA in the south-east, and its conventional capabilities were demonstrated principally in the undeclared war with South Africa.

FAPLA first performed its external assistance mission with the despatch of 1,000 to 1,500 troops to Sao Tomé and Principe in 1977 to bolster the socialist regime of President Manuel Pinto da Costa. During the years that followed, Angolan forces conducted joint exercises with their counterparts and exchanged technical operational visits. The Angolan expeditionary force was reduced to about 500 in early 1985. It is probable that FAPLA would have undertaken other 'internationalist missions, in Mozambique for example, had it not been absorbed in a war at home.

In 1988 the strength of the Angolan armed forces was estimated at 100,000 active duty and 50,000 reserve personnel, organised into a regular army and a supporting militia; air and navy defence forces. he active duty forces had expanded greatly since independence as UNITA's insurgency spread throughout the country and South African interventions increased in frequency and magnitude.

As of late 1988, Lieutenant General Antonio dos Santos Franca (*nom de guerre* Ndalu) was FAPLA chief of the general staff and army commander. He had held these positions since 1982.

Ground Forces

The regular army's 91,500 troops were organised into more than 70 brigades ranging from 750 to 1,200 men each and deployed throughout the ten military regions.

Most regions were commanded by lieutenant colonels, with majors as deputy commanders, but some regions were commanded by majors.

Each region consisted of one to four provinces, with one or more infantry brigades assigned to it. The brigades were generally dispersed in battalion or smaller unit formations to protect strategic terrain, urban centres, settlements, and critical infrastructures such as bridges and factories.

Counter-intelligence agents were assigned to all field units to thwart UNITA infiltration. The army's diverse combat capabilities were indicated by its many regular and motorised infantry brigades with organic or attached armour, artillery, and air defence units; two militia infantry brigades; four anti-aircraft artillery brigades; ten tank battalions and six artillery battalions.

These forces were concentrated most heavily in places of strategic importance and recurring conflict: the oil-producing Cabinda Province, the area around the capital, and the southern provinces where UNITA and South African forces operated.

Special commands, military formations, and security arrangements were also created in extraordinary circumstances. For example, 'in June 1985 the provincial military authorities in the Tenth Military Region established a unified command to include both FAPLA and the People's Vigilance Brigades (*Brigadas Populares de Vigilencia* – BPV) to confront UNITA's expanding operations in the region.'

Similarly, special railroad defence committees were formed in the Ninth Military Region to protect the Luanda railway between Malanje and Luanda. These municipal committees were composed of party, government, FAPLA, JMPLA, and BPV units.

In 1987 FAPLA was reported to be recruiting regional defence forces to assist the regular army against the UNITA insurgency.

FAPLA was equipped almost exclusively by the Soviet Union.

In early 1988, it was reported to have at least 550 tanks and 520 armoured vehicles, more than 500 artillery pieces and multiple rocket launchers, 500 mortars, at least 900 anti-tank weapons, and more than 300 air defence guns and surface-to-air missile (SAM) batteries. However, in view of continuous losses and the influx of new and replacement materiel, these figures were only approximate.

For example, the South African minister of defence reported in late 1988 that Angola's inventory of T-54 and T-55 tanks had increased from 531 to 1,590 between September 1987 and September 1988. Moreover, FAPLA and UNITA exaggerated successes and underestimated losses in military actions.

In the major battle of Mavinga in 1986, UNITA claimed to have killed 5,000 FAPLA troops and to have destroyed 41 combat aircraft, 202 tanks and armoured vehicles, 351 military transport vehicles, 200 trucks, and 40 SAMs; figures that represented 15 percent to 25 percent of FAPLA's inventory which, of course, is nonsense.

In addition to combat troops and equipment, logistical support units and extensive headquarters organisations, the armed forces established a growing infrastructure to service, repair, and manufacture defence equipment.

In 1983 the government created a new company under the Ministry of Defence to rehabilitate and repair armoured military vehicles, infantry weapons and artillery.

A maintenance and repair centre for Soviet-made light and heavy vehicles, located at Viana near Luanda, was turned over to Angolan authorities by the Soviet Union in 1984 to strengthen Angolan self-sufficiency. This centre, reportedly capable of servicing 600 military and commercial vehicles a day, was one of the largest of its kind in Africa.

Viana was also the site of an assembly plant for commercial vehicles as well as military trucks and Jeeps. In June 1986, the government signed a contract with the Brazilian company Engesa for the purchase of military trucks and construction of a facility with the capacity to repair about 30 percent of the country's heavy trucks, military vehicles foremost.

The regular army was also supported by a 50,000-member citizens' militia, the Directorate of People's Defence and Territorial Troops, an organisation under the minister of defence that had both counter-insurgency and police functions. The directorate was established in September 1985 as a successor to the People's Defence Organisation or ODP, formed in September 1975 as an adjunct to FAPLA to defend against Portuguese settler resistance and attacks by anti-MPLA insurgents.

After the civil war, it retained its territorial defence and counter-guerrilla supporting roles but served more as a reserve than as an active paramilitary force. Indeed, some 20,000 ODP militias were inducted into the regular army in the early 1980s, apparently to satisfy an urgent requirement to expand FAPLA.

In 1988 the Directorate of People's Defence and Territorial Troops was organised into 11 'Guerrilla Force' brigades, two of which (about 10,000 members) were to be on active duty with FAPLA at any given time. They were deployed in battalion and smaller formations, and they often operated in proximity to or jointly with FAPLA units, defending factories, farms, and villages and maintaining vigilance against insurgents. Although some estimates put the troop strength of the Guerrilla Force as high as 500,000, such figures were probably based on data from the late 1970s or reflected the inclusion of reserve components.

Lieutenant Colonel Domingos Paiva da Silva was the commander of the Guerrilla Force from 1978 until his death from natural causes in July 1987.

Air and Air Defence Force

The People's Air and Air Defence Force of Angola (*Forca Aérea Popular de Angola/Defesa Aérea y Antiaérea* – FAPA/DAA), officially established on 21 January 1976, was one the largest air forces in sub-Saharan Africa.

Colonel Alberto Correia Neto became Vice Minister of Defence and FAPA/DAA commander in September 1986. He succeeded Colonel Carreira, who had held that post since 1983.

The 7,000-member FAPA/DAA included about 180 fixed-wing combat attack and interceptor aircraft; an equal number of helicopters; several maritime patrol, reconnaissance, trainer, and transport aircraft; five air defence battalions and ten SAM battalions. Seeking voluntary enlistment was initially the sole form of recruitment, but in the 1980s conscription was increasingly employed until volunteerism was restored in 1988.

Angola's army had about 15 years to develop an organisation and gain combat experience prior to independence. In contrast, FAPA/DAA had to acquire personnel, experience, and equipment immediately, and in the context of a civil war. These unusual circumstances affected both recruitment and force development. FAPA/DAA's pilots, mostly in their mid-twenties, got combat experience immediately. Moreover, given FAPA/DAA's virtually instantaneous creation, its long-term dependence on external assistance was inevitable.

Soviet, Cuban, and other communist forces provided pilots and technicians to fly and maintain FAPA/DAA's growing, diversified and increasingly complex air fleet. The principal tasks of this new branch of the Angolan military were to protect the capital, guard major cities and military installations in the south against South African air raids, and extend the air defence network and combat operations southward to confront UNITA forces and South African invaders.

According to a 1987 press report, FAPA/DAA was reorganised into three regiments: a light-bomber regiment headquartered in Lubango, a transport regiment in Luanda, and a helicopter regiment in Huambo. In addition, FAPA/DAA aircraft and air defence units were deployed in strategic locations throughout the country. Of Angola's 229 usable airfields, 25 had permanent-surface runways, 13 of which exceeded 2,440 metres.

The capabilities and effectiveness of FAPA/DAA increased markedly following its creation. FAPA/DAA's expanded capacity to provide air cover and supplies to forward ground forces, strike at UNITA bases and interdict South African aircraft, evacuate wounded personnel – as well as perform reconnaissance and liaison missions – became particularly apparent during combined offensives after 1985.

Like the army, FAPA/DAA developed modern facilities to repair and service both military and civilian aircraft for Angola and other African states.

Angola's Navy

The People's Navy of Angola (*Marinha de Guerra Popular do Angola* – MGPA) remained a relatively unimportant branch of the armed forces because of the exigencies of the ground and air wars in the interior. The navy's fortified headquarters and home port, as well as major ship repair facilities, were at Luanda.

Although there were several good harbours along Angola's coastline, the only other ports used regularly were Lobito and Namibe and then only to support temporary southern deployments. The latter two ports were located near railheads and airfields. Lobito had minor repair facilities as well.

The navy's mission was to defend its 1,600-kilometre coastline and territorial waters against South African sabotage, attacks, and resupply operations to UNITA; to protect against unlicensed fishing in Angolan waters and to interdict smugglers.

In early 1985, President dos Santos transferred responsibility for protecting the rich offshore fisheries from the coast guard to the MGPA to provide more effective enforcement of fishing regulations. After Lieutenant Colonel Manuel Augusto Alfredo, Vice Minister of Defence and MGPA commander was killed in a road accident in June 1985, he was succeeded by Rear Admiral Antonio José Condessa do Carvalho (*nom de guerre* Toka), who had spent the previous four years in the Soviet Union studying military science.

The MGPA officially dates from 10 July 1976, when late President Agostinho Neto visited the naval facilities at Luanda. Its senior officers had actually begun training in 1970, during the war of liberation, when the MPLA sent the first cadre of 24 naval trainees abroad for a three-year training programme.

However, there was no navy awaiting their return.

The MPLA inherited a small number of Portuguese ships at independence, which was subsequently augmented by various Soviet warships and support craft. In 1988 the MGPA was reported to have 1,500 personnel (thought to be volunteers) and a fleet of about 50 vessels that included guided-missile fast patrol boats, torpedo boats, inland-water and coastal patrol vessels, mine warfare craft, and amphibious landing craft. The independent merchant marine fleet had about 100 vessels that could be impressed into service.

Most of the navy's maintenance, repair, and training were provided by Soviet and Cuban technicians and advisers; Portugal and Nigeria also provided training assistance.

Despite extensive foreign support, in late 1988 the serviceability of many of the vessels and equipment was in question. Moreover, naval recruitment and the proficiency of MGPA personnel remained problematic; indeed, the MPLA and Ministry of Defence leadership repeatedly appealed to the youth (the JMPLA in particular) to join the navy.

14

Unita and the Post Independent Phase in Angola

The third member of Angola's 'Liberation' triumvirate was UNITA – the Union for the Total Liberation of Angola or *União Nacional Para a Independência Total de Angola*. It were led by a burly Geneva-educated Maoist by the name of Jonas Malheiro Savimbi who began by marshalling his insurgents in the remote south-east of the country, the tribal homeland of his own Ovimbundu people.

British foreign correspondent Fred Bridgland has had an interest in African conflicts for almost as long as he has been a scribe. His revelations with regard to Cuba's role in the Angolan conflict are graphically detailed in what many buffs regard as his best book, *The War for Africa*.[1]

He recalls that it was not until 1979 that it dawned on Havana (having by then pushed tens of thousands of troops into Angola), that the war was never going to be an easy slog. More likely, some of Castro's advisers concluded, they faced a tough, protracted military struggle, blighted by an inordinate number of casualties (compared to what was suffered by South Africa).

Cuban General Rafael del Pino Diaz, one of the enduring brains behind Castro's adventures in Africa and who later defected to Washington, told Bridgland during his American debrief that that revelation came 'when UNITA guerrillas – for the first time – shot down one of our helicopters.' It happened at a place called Maria Delida, near Mussende, about 400 kilometres south-east of Luanda.

The Mi-17 (Codenamed Hip in NATO parlance) had been firing rockets at a small group of guerrillas who for once, did not scatter when the transport helicopter started hovering and shooting at ground targets nearby (most Angolan Mi-17s were fitted with rocket pods and had side-gunners armed with RPD or PKM Soviet light machine guns).

Though there were casualties on the ground, their insurgent compadres stood fast and returned fire, penetrating the helicopter's fuel tank. When another rocket was fired, its flame ignited some of the leaking fuel and the machine exploded in mid-air. All Cubans onboard were killed: one report said there were ten deaths, another spoke of a dozen.

Commented another source: 'It meant that we now faced a very difficult situation and it was likely that we would possibly be bogged down in Angola for years.' He explained: 'that particular UNITA group clearly demonstrated that they had lost their inherent fear of aircraft – something that takes both time and courage – and that they were prepared to answer an air attack with fire of their own.'

---

1   Fred Bridgland: *The War For Africa: Twelve Months That Transformed a Continent* (Casemate, 2017).

Conflict in Angola had never been a one-way street. While stuck with many of the foibles of a typical African liberation movement, rebel UNITA troops were sometimes incredibly brave, yet often foolhardy and scarcely the perfect insurgent force. Its guerrilla units – invariably operating far from home – lacked equipment and supplies and this soon became apparent on long-range penetration operations when ammunition was almost always in short supply, food ran short and not many wounded survived under conditions that could hardly be rated as sanitary.

A sad but interesting sidelight here is that many guerrilla cadres because they lacked many basic medicines, were infected with 'crabs', slang for body lice, which are parasitic insects that infest in the genital area of humans. I was to see this often enough during the Rhodesia war on the bodies of dead insurgents that had been stripped of their uniforms. More salient, their nether regions were crawling with the pests.

I saw it again while operational in Angola, which suggested that the problem was endemic and anybody wounded below the belt would have the injury suppurating in almost no time at all.

In contrast, these irregular bush fighters, in spite of being regarded by their adversaries as unprincipled, unruly, often ill-disciplined and more-often-that-not prone to doing exactly that which they had been ordered not to do, did very well when there was a serious need.

For instance, during my sojourn in the mid-1970s around Nova Lisboa (today Huambo) while attached to another rebel group that called itself *Chipa Esquadrao*, there were constant reports coming into the local HQ of dissident groups of UNITA soldiers firing indiscriminately, usually at anybody or anything took their fancy.[2] But those were early days and conditions improved as hostilities progressed.

Certainly, by the time the Cuban and Soviet forces had left Angola, UNITA proved itself to be a formidable guerrilla force. Its soldiers were committed and well trained (usually by South African Special Forces instructors) and, when the occasion demanded, these men could fight, as one journalist described it, 'like demons'.

For example, a series of battles spanning several weeks took place when Savimbi's men tried to stop an Angolan armoured column from reaching the disputed Cafunfo diamond fields. The attacking force was headed by a group of South African mercenaries under the command of former Recce commander, Colonel Hennie Blaauw.[2]

UNITA's losses during the course of that three-month campaign were appalling. Unofficial sources spoke of upwards 60 percent killed.

From the start of post-independence hostilities in Angola in the mid-1970s, Pretoria gradually came to regard UNITA as its principal ally in the war against Angola's Marxist regime.

By then the Americans also clandestinely took this rebel group under its wing – to the extent, as we have already seen – that substantial numbers of Stinger missiles were handed over to Savimbi's forces. The 'package' came with scores of US Army technicians who were detached from their units and sent to Africa to teach the recipients how to use them. In a sense, it was similar to the Mujahideen situation that had evolved against Russian occupation forces in Afghanistan in the 1980s.

Once the parameters had been delineated in this African theatre of hostilities (which included the all-encompassing command structure as well as language), training started in earnest. The best South African military specialists and technicians were sent north to train Savimbi's guerrilla army. Other than primary coaching, there was extensive and ongoing instruction in a number of

2   Al J. Venter: *Battle for Angola – The End of the Cold War in Africa c1975-1989* (Helion, 2017).

units, which included, inter alia, UNITA's Logistical Corps, its Technical Services Corps, Medical Corps, Military Police and Intelligence Corps.

Leadership training took place at all levels; from platoon, all the way through company, battalion and brigade commander level. Additionally, there were combat teams as well as group leadership courses.

As one of the South African officers linked to this development pointed out, training was provided 'by the finest available from the full South African military gambit.' This included specialists from the Infantry School, Artillery School, Anti-Aircraft School, School of Engineers (which specialised in some remarkably sophisticated landmine techniques) and a variety of other top-line establishments.

'At the same time, it was not enough just to be superior in order to become accepted in those roles. In order to become part of the Directorate of Special Tasks personnel instructing UNITA, you had to have significant above-average skills as well as the ability to display the requirements for a top secret security clearance. At the same time, you were expected to complete a selection process.'

In addition, there was a contingent of personnel at the training camps that comprised former members of elite units such as Special Forces, 32 Battalion Reconnaissance Wing, the Parachute Battalion and others – which, other than providing advanced training – often accompanied UNITA battalions into battle. As the source suggested:

'At the end of a training cycle, such UNITA units were integrated – together with artillery, anti-air and other specialist units – into regular infantry battalions. Where possible, with the provision of troop carriers (the vehicles being adapted for mounting battalion support weapons and invariably captured in battle from the Angolan Army) some cadres were formed into motorised infantry units.'

While South Africa, Germany and the United States provided some of this hardware, the bulk of it was captured. Ground-to-air missiles were mainly American Stingers (FIM-92 man-portable air defence systems).

'After each training cycle, there would be a practical integrated exercise with dummy targets assigned and attacked. Thus, various UNITA units – which included Special Forces, Penetration Battalion, Regular infantry and semi-regulars – learned to conduct "appreciation and planning" in an integrated manner. Specific actions were planned with the intention of launching full brigade-scale attacks against government forces.'

The main objective here was integration: getting the insurgent army accustomed to working along integrated lines with various units and, in so doing, bringing their specialities optimally to bear.

It was axiomatic, he declared, that in the low-key Angolan environment, such actions would produce results. One consequence was that this concerted South African training programme eventually turned a revitalised and combined UNITA army into what one of the CIA operators who worked with Savimbi, 'among the best guerrilla armies in the world.'

Additionally, there was much help from outside. Some UNITA elements would be put through their paces in other locations, primarily in Zaire (the DRC Congo today) by the US Army and in Morocco. But those soldiers were not subjected to the same standards and disciplines as those handled by the South Africans and, as a consequence, were neither as effective nor as dedicated as their 'home-brewed' counterparts.

Notably, semi-regular troops serving with UNITA received exactly the same duration and standard of instruction as regular South African national service infantry troops – the only difference being that their regular infantry and specialist forces got 'double doses' in terms of operational duration.

With time, the Angolan civil war steadily escalated, to the point where Savimbi was able to take hostilities directly to the enemy; at that stage, the conventional FAPLA Angolan Army, as well as Cuban military elements and those Soviet forces, ensconced in the country.

At no stage, after Castro had committed his army to 'defend Angola', were there ever less than 45,000 Cuban combatants in this West African Marxist state and that figure eventually topped 110,000. Peculiarly, that took years to emerge because it was almost impossible for outsiders to penetrate Havana's KGB-style security screen and eventually only came to light when a senior Cuban Army defector arrived in Washington with a tranche of sensitive documents.

Although a preponderance of Soviet heavy weaponry and air power precluded UNITA from attacking cities and anything that was heavily fortified, the guerrillas were comfortably able to take on many smaller outlying towns and garrisons. Indeed, these irregular fighters were efficient enough to rapidly overcome both fixed positions and forces in conventional battles and in this way, took quite a few towns, though Luanda would always quickly rally to oust the newcomers.

Concurrently, UNITA conducted an effective guerrilla campaign against a far larger military force that had been bolstered by foreign personnel, equipment and aircraft.

One immediate consequence was that Luanda and its allies were unable to make serious headway against the insurgents at source. They tried often enough to attack Savimbi in his heartland in the south-east in a bid to drive him out of his Jamba headquarters (where most of the Americans were based), something that took place on an annual basis after the rainy season but they never succeeded.

That, in turn, led to what some observers refer to as 'The Great Battle for Africa', the massive Soviet offensive in 1987. It lasted nine months and eventually took the war across a vast swathe of Angolan territory to the east of Cuito Cuanavale.

There, in the expansive Lomba River valley – hardly a 'valley', because the terrain was flat rather than undulating – a huge Angolan Army armoured battle force, backed by a substantive number of Cuban troops as well as Soviet Union advisers and senior officers launched the largest single land battle to have taken place in Africa since the end of the Second World War. It was a desperate final bid to destroy Savimbi's military machine and failed dismally.

The battle resulted in a total withdrawal of all Soviet, Cuban and Angolan forces towards the north and aspects of this confrontation are detailed in Chapter 25 of the author's *Battle for Angola*.

Through the decades that followed, until in 2002 when Savimbi was betrayed and killed after he had been lured into an ambush, the UNITA leader continued to notch up successes against the Luanda government of President Eduardo dos Santos.

Let it also be said that these were not isolated victories. Following the withdrawal of Cuban and Soviet forces in 1990-91, UNITA was eventually able to overrun government forces almost wherever they were encountered outside the country's larger urban areas, to the point in 1992, when the rebel leader was effectively in command of about four-fifths of the country.

Only Angola's primary cities (and the more traditional Kimbundu tribal regions) remained firmly in government hands – though some larger centres, including Angola's second city of Huambo (formerly Nova Lisboa) – ended up being brutally contested. There were colossal casualties on both sides of an episode that is every bit as vicious as the Battle for Beirut at its worst.

By now, it had become clear to the major powers that it was only a question of time before UNITA made a direct bid for Luanda and possibly the country's leadership which suggested that militarily, Savimbi was short of neither manpower nor initiative; more importantly, time was on his side.

Significantly, it was at that point in the history of the Angolan civil war that the Luanda regime was approached by a group of British friends headed by former SAS officer Tony Buckingham who offered President dos Santos the services of a private South African military company that would effectively counter Savimbi's advances. Within weeks, Executive Outcomes had been hired by Luanda to fight its war, something I deal with at length in *War Dog: Fighting Other People's Wars,* one of my earlier volumes.

It is also noteworthy that Buckingham was subsequently involved in the Valentine Strasser army coup d'état in Sierra Leone in 1992 and where Executive Outcomes again went to war.

Drawing largely from his tribal roots among the Ovimbundu people, Savimbi – who had spent time in China and spoke seven languages, four of them European – waged a series of guerrilla campaigns for almost 40 years; first against the Portuguese and thereafter, with strong South African military support, against what he liked to refer to as 'the hated communist MPLA-led government in Luanda.'

There is no question that UNITA – which still operates as a political not a military entity in present-day Angola – left its mark on the populace like no other liberation group, even though Savimbi was never able to achieve his ultimate goal.

His guerrillas carried out their first tentative attacks late in the 1960s while attempting to prevent freight and passenger trains passing along the Benguela railway at Teixeira de Sousa (Luso today) on the border with Zambia. The rail link was the main export route of Congolese copper mines from Katanga.

It was also UNITA irregulars who twice derailed trains in 1967. That infuriated the landlocked Zambian government which depended on the link to get its cargoes to the coast for shipment abroad through the Angolan port of Lobito. Zambia's President Kenneth Kaunda responded by kicking all UNITA's 'freedom fighters' out of his country, about 500 of them. Savimbi moved to Cairo, Egypt, where he lived for a year before secretly returning to Angola (again through Zambia) where word had it, he worked with the Portuguese military against the established government order in that country.

The website of the Federation of American Scientists – which hosts more about international movements and disputes than most – in detailing UNITA's first guerrilla attacks in eastern Angola – resulted in a flurry of interest abroad. In fact, his railroad attacks put his guerrilla movement effectively on the map. It caused Europeans to sit up and take notice of what was happening in that part of Africa.

Early reports indicated that the maverick insurgent leader – a burly academic who was educated first by missionaries in Angola and then sent to Switzerland – was the man to watch, the same 'upstart' incidentally, that got his doctorate from Lausanne University. At an early age, Savimbi's political visions of an egalitarian society gelled, reinforced by his experiences of becoming a revolutionary under the mantle of Mao Zedong.

In Beijing, he and several of his followers received four months' training in various military disciplines and possibly the strongest impact the Chinese leader had on Savimbi was that he imparted his principle of self-sufficiency in waging a guerrilla war, a la 'to be as a fish in the water …'

It was to be a valuable lesson and the budding revolutionary proved an enthusiastic pupil; he always had Mao's little red book to hand and as a consequence, Luanda paid a heavy price.

Once back in his native Africa, Savimbi, now with Chinese backing, emerged as the principal political representative of his own Ovimbundu people. For a while, Savimbi held the post of foreign minister within GRAE, the Revolutionary Government of Angola in Exile (*Govêrno Revolucionário de Angola no Exílo*) whose disagreements over policy issues led to his resignation in July 1964. That was three years after Portugal's war in that country started.

An immediate effect of his return to his roots was that Savimbi turned down an invitation from the MPLA to join its organisation as a rank-and-file member. Instead, he moved his guerrillas into the bush and UNITA began its unconventional long march to war. By then, a small amount of Beijing's military aid had already reached him overland through Tanzania and Zambia.

Although UNITA lacked the educated cadres and arms of the opposition (a proud African, Savimbi deplored the role of a large group of *mestiço* 'intellectuals' and policy-makers within the MPLA hierarchy) his movement attracted the largest following of the three movements because it was tribally based; the Ovimbundu comprised almost a third of the country's population.

Also, unlike the MPLA and FNLA, his rebel army enjoyed the benefits of a unified and unchallenged leadership directed by a single individual in supreme control, Savimbi himself.

A distinctive trait of Savimbi's control was his insistence that in contrast to the mixed-blood-dominated, urban-based MPLA, he liked to present his movement as a 'worker' or 'peasant' force. In effect, UNITA was seen to be representative of ordinary folk, most of them from the bush. This was underscored by its constitution, which proclaimed that the movement would strive for a government proportionately representative of all ethnic groups, clans, and classes.

Always reflecting an underlying Maoist-oriented disposition, Savimbi spent a lot of effort on raising what he liked to refer to as the 'political consciousness of the ordinary people', almost all of whom were unsophisticated and, more often than not, illiterate. This was one of the problems facing South African instructors since most modern weapons require a modicum of reading (and in the case of mortars, for range etc) or calculation.

This largely rural community was dispersed over an area about a quarter the size of Western Europe.

Among the masses, Savimbi's theme was consistent with the environment of the people. The creed of self-reliance was dominant and to this end, he founded cooperatives for food production and village self-defence units. It was no surprise consequently – as he went from strength to strength within a society that had had been all but ignored by the Portuguese for centuries – that his arrival as a leader was likened by some of his followers as something of a 'second coming'. Indeed, as reflected in his mién – coupled to his message to his people – *he*, the African revolutionary messiah had arrived.

This could very well be one of the reasons why Jonas Savimbi, though dead for a few decades, continues to enjoy a cult status among many Africans in black communities abroad rather similar to what Che Guevara achieved in South and Central America. The fact that many of his more brutal excesses have since been exposed and were every bit as vicious (though not as expansive as those of Mao), has had little effect on his broadly-based popularity.

The fact is, Savimbi's politics, throughout, were grassroots: no-holds-barred fundamental and functional.

In regions in which he held sway, he set up pyramidal structures of elected councils. These grouped up to 16 villages that – at least in theory – articulated demands through a political commissar to a central committee, whose 35 members were chosen every four years at a national congress.

In the early 1970s, UNITA began infiltrating the major population centres, slowly expanding its areas of influence westward beyond Bié, Nova Lisboa (Huambo), Sa da Bandeira (Lubango) and other centres. There, overnight, this new order collided with a concurrent eastwards and southwards thrust by Luanda, which was sending its Soviet-trained political cadres to work among the tribal folk and, specifically, within the Chokwe, Lwena, Luchazi, and Lunda communities. It was a shrewd move because the MPLA vigorously exploited ethnic antagonisms.

On the eve of independence in 1975, UNITA controlled many of the rich, food-producing central and southern provinces and was, therefore, able to regulate the flow of food to the rest of the country. At the time, it claimed the allegiance of about 40 percent of the masses, and as hostilities dragged on, this figure increased exponentially.

The civil war (following the colonial uprising) started in earnest on 11 November 1975, when the MPLA (with Soviet and Cuban collusion, discreet at first and then quite blatant) seized power in a well-planned and coordinated putsch orchestrated from Luanda. Up to that point, all three factions had been each other's throats, but prior to independence – and as part of the 'negotiated' withdrawal of the Portuguese – they had agreed to work within the framework of a tripartite power-sharing alliance. It seemed that everything was going fine but in reality, it was a hall of mirrors.

Everything changed on that momentous November day when Lisbon finally abrogated its responsibilities in Angola, truly one of the enduring tragedies of that century, considering the lives that were subsequently lost.

Without blinking, MPLA commanders trashed the agreement and together with a large and very well equipped and armed Cuban force that been surreptitiously flown into the country, attacked both UNITA and FNLA cadres wherever they were found. Thousands of unsuspecting political hopefuls were massacred.

Unilaterally – and stealthily – the Marxists in Luanda had achieved power by force, and, it says much that they have never relinquished it.

Important about this development is the fact that by its actions (with powerful communist support) it rendered the MPLA an illegal faction, not as a government but as the maxim goes: *to the winner, all the spoils.*

Things stayed that way for the first two decades, until after the 1992 elections which, independent European observers averred, were also rigged. Things have continued unchanged ever since including the looting of national resources by senior members of the government.

Washington has consistently pointed, year after year, to the disappearance of about a billion dollars of oil revenue and the government has never responded. The money has gone, who knows where and as one anonymous source within that same government has said (had he been identified, he would have had an 'accident') that it was enough each year, to build a new clinic and school in every single village and town in the country.

Former President dos Santos and his family know exactly where all that money went and sadly, all he has to show for it is Africa's richest woman: his daughter …

Earlier, the MPLA had created its own military wing, the People's Armed Forces for the Liberation of Angola or FAPLA, which, as we have seen, became the core of the government's post-independence army.

There was enough common sense among those opposing Luanda to accept that both Holden Roberto's Congo-based FNLA and Savimbi's UNITA – were aware that their separate and independent military forces, even jointly, were not nearly beefy enough to take on the full might of the MPLA. How could they, with Moscow and Havana pumping in arms and men at will?

Consequently, both opposition factions formed a largely ineffectual military alliance. Loose it was too, for apart from fighting the MPLA, it was not uncommon for them to cross swords whenever and wherever their forces made contact, either in the bush or in some of the towns where they both had an interest. The early days of conflict were characterised by roving bands of insurgents shooting at just about anything that moved.

What had also happened when the split came, was that both 'outsider parties' withdrew their ministers from the provisional government in Luanda – at least those that had managed to survive the initial bloodletting (and there were not too many of them). Some sought shelter in foreign diplomatic legations, others headed for the jungle because these were exceedingly brutal times and the often mindless shock tactics of the newly entrenched MPLA government heralded the country's first full-scale civil war.

The CIA meanwhile, by now alarmed at what was taking place, initiated a covert programme of its own. Washington turned a blind eye when a small body of American and European mercenaries arrived to serve with the FNLA. Among the first to be hired under this arrangement was that old French warhorse Bob Denard who later invaded and took over the government of the Comores Archipelago where he remained for almost a decade.

In Angola, Denard did not stay long. He told me later when we met again in Pretoria, this time through the good offices of former SADF military intelligence operative Fiona Capstick, that he saw the writing on the wall in Angola's civil war very early on. Also, he was not sure he would get paid, which in Denard's mind – apart from doing good work for French Intelligence – was what it was all about.

In fact, within UNITA, the mercenary influence was short-lived, if only because Savimbi – proud African traditionalist that he was – always made it clear that he did not need a bunch of Europeans directing military operations in a region about which they knew absolutely nothing, and, in a sense, he was right.

Obviously, he said nothing of the kind to the South Africans supporting him. In any event, the vast majority of mercenaries brought into the country by foreign influences devoted their efforts towards the FNLA and MPLA.

As one commentator noted, UNITA in the 1980s was 'a state within a state. 'Under Savimbi's leadership, it survived defeat during the civil war, retreated to the remote south-eastern corner of the country, regrouped, made Jamba its home base and continued fighting.

From Jamba – an expansive base stretching over a vast stretch of bush country in some of the most primitive regions on the continent, he launched his campaign to overturn the Luanda regime. Failing that (he conceded to some of his American friends, of which he had many, despite his Mao rantings) he was prepared to force the Angolan government to accept UNITA in a coalition or possibly, even something that might have resembled a federation.

With increasing international support and military aid, particularly from South Africa, and after 1985, from the United States, UNITA extended its campaign throughout the country.

It enlarged its military forces and the scope of its operations and in so doing, withstood about a dozen major FAPLA offences into which the Soviets poured billions of dollars worth of arms and equipment.

The idea then – as far as Pretoria was concerned – was that Savimbi would be given the wherewithal to escalate his insurgency in a bid to counterbalance Soviet and Marxist MPLA gains in that embattled country. Various meetings between US officials and Savimbi took place in southern Angola which even progressed to the UNITA leader being hosted at the White House. He was often to visit Washington in ensuing years.

One consequence of these cosy get-togethers was an agreement whereby the United States would support UNITA, both with funding and materiel, almost all of it channelled through Mobuto Sese Seko's Zaire. The CIA and American Special Forces units set up various training camps in a bid to train limited numbers of UNITA soldiers in southern Zaire, but overall, that assistance would consist mainly of financial and political support, together with the provision of arms and ammunition.

UNITA also secured assistance from various other NATO and Western-aligned countries opposed to Soviet expansionism. These included France, West Germany, Italy, Switzerland, Israel,

Morocco, Saudi Arabia, Kuwait, Egypt and others – all of which gave money, political support, training, weapons, ammunition, equipment, intelligence – or a combination of these. It was notable that France played with a double deck of cards, supporting Savimbi on one hand and selling military helicopters – including Alouette chopper gunships to Luanda on the other.

During the 1970s, UNITA soldiers were also being trained in Senegal, Tanzania, Zambia and other African countries. Subsequently, Egypt, Morocco, Senegal, Somalia, and Tunisia furnished financial as well as military aid.

Morocco's role in the war was pivotal. That Arab government in Rabat had supplied arms to the MPLA during the liberation struggle and then switched allegiances to become a major source of military training for FALA, Savimbi's military wing, especially for officers, paratroops, and artillery personnel.

This was in retaliation for Luanda embracing Comintern nations, Moscow especially. Israel was also reported to have provided military aid and training to UNITA soldiers at Kamina in Zaire.

At the start of 1986, the United States supplied UNITA with roughly US$35 million annually in covert military aid funded out of the budget of the Central Intelligence Agency, a procedure only halted at the behest of Congress in 1993.

The first acknowledged shipments of United States aid (as opposed to clandestine US shipments) consisted of non-lethal items such as trucks, medical equipment, and uniforms. Anti-tank and air defence weapons soon followed, as did Jeep-mounted 106mm recoilless guns and other hardware supplied by the US from 1981 onwards.

By February 1988, he announced the formation of his UNITA government in a region designated 'Free Angola', a large area directly under his control. While his intent was to regularise administration (rather than to secede from the Luanda central government or seek international recognition) this event marked a new stage in his organisational development and consolidation. By then, several Africans states maintained at least informal ties to the guerrilla movement, which underscored its efficacy.

Savimbi's strategy and tactics were designed to raise the costs of foreign 'occupation' (as he referred to MPLA domination of areas under its control) through what he termed was 'maximum disruption and dislocation' and at the same time minimising his own casualties.

His forces infiltrated new areas and contested as much territory as possible, quite often wresting it from government control. Consistently, the rebels sabotaged strategic targets of economic or military value. Then they would ambush Angolan Army units when they attempted to retake what they had lost. Bridges were favourite targets – UNITA explosives engineers having been trained by South African Army specialists.

It was also an era when mine-laying came into its own, the rebels having been given supplies of both anti-tank and anti-personnel landmines captured by South African forces just about every year when they did battle with Soviet and Cuban-backed FAPLA forces. The laying of landmines obstructed extensive government access along various lines of communication, including roads, jungle and bush tracks, approaches to settlements as well as infrastructure sites.

To undermine support for government forces, UNITA routinely attacked or took hostage hundreds of expatriate technicians and advisers and Pretoria was hard-pressed by Western governments to get their nationals released.

Savimbi also repeatedly threatened multinational companies with retaliation for their support of what he termed the 'illegal government in Luanda.' Throughout, with an almost fanatical determination and the hope of an eventual military victory, this Ovimbundu leader sought to strengthen UNITA's bargaining position in demanding nothing less than direct negotiations with Luanda for the establishment of a government of national unity. The Angolan government would not hear of it; Savimbi was a criminal, they declared and Luanda would not negotiate with a felon.

But what does emerge from a study of Savimbi's role in the almost quarter-century civil war that followed independence from Portugal in Angola, is that UNITA, as British writer Fred Bridgland observed in his own research, 'runs like a thread through every South African soldier's or airman's story.'

For a long time, this burly leader denied that Pretoria was at the core of his many tactical achievements in the field. In fact, as Bridgland reports, 'he claimed the entire military credit for his struggles, and there is no doubt, they were significant.' But then it is also true that he could never have done it on his own.

To uncover the real truth as to what took place in south Angola at a critical time in the war, Bridgland turned to those who had been closest to him. A lot of what he writes came from SADF Colonel Fred Oelschig, who worked for South Africa's Chief of Staff Intelligence (CSI). Throughout the years 1986-89, this extremely capable military specialist was Pretoria's senior liaison officer with Savimbi.

The SADFs surrogate-force operations in the 1980s fell under the Directorate of Special Tasks (DST) in the office of the Chief of Staff Intelligence.

What is of relevance here is that the DST had its origins in the 1976 decision to channel assistance to UNITA (Operation Silwer) which resulted in a special office being established in Rundu in Namibia's Caprivi and headed by Colonel (later Major General) Marius Oelschig, brother of Fred Oelschig.

In the early 1980s, DST operated as a secret project in Pretoria, its first head being Colonel (later Brigadier) 'Cor' van Niekerk, who was also responsible for managing what became known as the RENAMO project in Mozambique in the early 1980s.

By the mid-1980s, DST had been incorporated into the Operational Intelligence Directorate headed by General Niels van Tonder. It was Oelschig that subsequently commented:

> I had fought extensively in Angola, notably in Operation Savannah in 1975 and in Operation Protea in 1981. In 1986 I was appointed as the chief SADF liaison officer working with the rebel force. My job was two-fold; first to liaise between Savimbi and the SADF general staff and second, to provide UNITA with good training and to show exactly how to fight a conventional war.
>
> My team taught them to realise the limitations of conventional warfare. We got them to climb into captured T-54 tanks and BRDM armoured cars to see how little their commanders and gunners could actually observe the surrounding terrain.
>
> UNITA is one of the most remarkable foot-slogging armies since the Romans. It meant that they thought mainly in terms of four kilometres an hour to carry out a conventional offensive, which was roughly as fast as a fit man can walk. Instead, we had to get them to think in terms of 40km an hour, and that wasn't easy because it involved vehicles.
>
> I left towards the end of 1986 but was back again in May 1987 with two other CSI liaison teams under my command, led by Commandants Bert Sachse and Les Rudman to assist UNITA in getting to grips with the coming offensive. I was also required to report back on the ability of UNITA to counter MPLA efforts.
>
> Then followed the eight conventional brigades put onto the offensive by Luanda's FAPLA and that was more than any of us had expected.
>
> A largely guerrilla army together the two multiple rocket launchers I had with me were hardly enough to stop them. So we agreed with the general staff that UNITA pursues a series of delaying tactics, the aim being to ensure that (the Angolan Army) arrived at the Lomba River in a position of weakness rather than of strength, by which time our conventional forces would be ready to deal with them.

Both Rudman and Commandant James Hills of 5 Reconnaissance Regiment organised some quite remarkable delaying tactics, working mainly with the three most prominent UNITA generals; Desmosthenes Chilinguitila, Ben-Ben Arlindo Pena and Bok Sapalalo. Ben-Ben was a particularly active thinker on how to disrupt the advance.[3]

Savimbi frequently came up to the front-lines, so there was a constant interaction and joint decision-making. The UNITA leader conducted a nine-week course for his commanders every year, putting great emphasis on the use of personal discretion on the battlefield.

At that time we were fighting a real and extremely exacting guerrilla war. We would hit the enemy and then bombshell [disperse] in every direction. Throughout, UNITA performed very well, but the enemy's tanks and BM-21 Stalin Organs on tracked vehicles won them a lot of space.

At the very beginning, when tanks appeared on the horizon, I ran and the UNITA men ran. These [Soviet] tanks were being used in a long-range, pre-emptive role, firing into the bush from considerable distances and keeping the BM-21s firing throughout the night. We were often nailed down by Soviet MiGs as well.

But we quickly worked out ambush tactics to delay them. With UNITA we laid mines across their lines of advance. As we progressed, we hammered them with 120mm mortars, American LAW anti-tank missiles and from the French, Apilas anti-tank missiles, delivered to UNITA at the beginning of 1987. At night, when they *laagered*, we kept them busy with our 81mm and 120mm mortars: they lost a lot of sleep and suffered much damage to their soft-skinned trucks.

It was a really interesting period. Only one of the UNITA soldiers was captured. He'd escaped and told us that a Cuban officer had ordered an Angolan Army soldier to shoot him. The FAPLA soldier took him away and then told him to run for his life.

There were probably about 8,000 UNITA fighters opposing 10,000 Angolan government forces, said Oelschig.

We used the 1st, 2nd, 3rd and 4th UNITA Regular Battalions, with the 5th in reserve. There were also eight semi-regular battalions with much lighter weapons, as well as eight penetration groups that infiltrated enemy lines in conjunction with our 5 Reconnaissance Regiment teams laying anti-personnel mines.

---

3   Unita's General Ben-Ben, a distinguished and much respected UNITA leader died under mysterious circumstances in a Bloemfontein hospital while receiving treatment under the auspices of Nelson Mandela's ANC government. Sources have indicated to the author that he was poisoned; an evil 'thank you gesture' for the help the ANC had been given by the Luanda government over many years of the struggle.

Veteran African guerrilla leader, Swiss-educated and Maoist propagator Dr Jonas Savimbi who ran rings around the Luanda regime for decades.

Rebel troops cross a waterway carrying their gear, food, medical supplies as well as weapons. If needs be, they would also bring their wounded back to base, often days from where a contact took place.

A UNITA sabotage team laying mines on a railway bridge early in the war.

The US Stinger missile, supplied in quantity to UNITA together with instructors who taught rebel cadres how to field them. This was the same MANPAD deployed by the Americans in Afghanistan.

Angolan Soviet-supplied jet fighter aircraft (probably a MiG-23) brought down by one of the American Stinger missiles while operating in Eastern Angola.

South African and UNITA troops on joint ops in the south. (Photo Dion Cragg)

A UNITA squad examines a Soviet bomb that had failed to detonate near their HQ in Eastern Angola.

Jonas Savimbi, Angola's flawed but enormously successful guerrilla leader.

A ragged bunch of UNITA troops on parade.

Rebel UNITA troops take a closer look at a captured Soviet amphibious tank taken in battle
in South Angola.

15

Veteran of Africa's Skies: The Venerable Douglas Dakota

The first of these remarkable old aircraft took to the skies more than 80 years ago. Quite a few are still flying today, obviously with strengthened airframes and upgraded turbine engines; including, until quite recently, a handful in the South African Air Force. In June 1983, I wrote a feature for _Scope_ magazine titled 'Game Bird', focusing on the role of this aircraft in South Africa's Border War. Much of what I said about this remarkable aircraft remains valid today, but even better, judge for yourself ...

But first, a word about what the Americans in Vietnam called the 'Gooney Bird', and before that, a war-time version that was labelled 'Skytrain'. Officially it came from the Douglas Aircraft Corporation stable of aircraft and was listed in American inventories as the Douglas DC-3.

For its time, this was no ordinary aircraft: its cruise speed of 207mph or thereabouts (333km/h) and a range of 2,400 kilometres revolutionised air transport in the late 1930s and 1940s. Many of the movies we have seen of Allied D-Day landings in Normandy had fleets of these old planes taking men to war and they did so to great effect. When films were made three, four, sometimes five decades later, first in line was always the trustworthy old 'Dak', as some like to call it.

Its lasting effect on the airline industry as well as on the Second World War makes it one of the most versatile transport aircraft ever made.

Civil DC-3 production ended in 1942 with 607 aircraft coming off production lines. However, together with its military derivative, the C-47 Skytrain (designated Dakota in RAF Service), with Russian and Japanese versions, over 16,000 were built.

Following the Second World War, the airliner market was flooded with surplus C-47s, as well as a host of other transport aircraft and attempts to produce an upgraded super DC-3 resulted in failure. American Airlines inaugurated a passenger service in June 1936, with simultaneous flights from Newark, New Jersey and Chicago and, as we now know, that was only the start of it.

This remarkable aircraft also enjoys a folklore culture that is all its own. The most common axiom among aviation enthusiasts and pilots is that the only replacement for a DC-3 is another DC-3 and the aircraft's legendary ruggedness is enshrined in the light-hearted description of the plane as 'a collection of parts flying in loose formation.'

Perhaps the most heartening comment came from former President Dwight Eisenhower who, during the most critical period of the Second World War, was the supreme allied commander in Europe. Years later he commented: ' ... four pieces of equipment that most senior officers came to regard as among the most vital to our success in Africa and Europe were the bulldozer, the Jeep, the 2½-ton truck and the C-47 airplane.' He added that it was curious that none of those was actually designed for combat.

Unquestionably, this is a most remarkable plane. In an article *'Flight Test: Douglas DC-3 – Dakota Skies'*, Peter Collins made the point that the military transport version was, as he phrased it; 'A beast to handle on the ground that becomes a beauty to fly once level in still air.' He goes on:

> There are still scores of 'Daks' operating commercially around the world, some with more than 100,000 hours on their clocks. The secret of the DC-3's longevity, he suggests, lies in the fact that it has no main wing spar, just a complete mid-fuselage section manufactured as one piece, including inner wing and engine nacelles, onto which the outer wing sections are attached externally using more than 200 bolts per wing. In my walk-around check, first impressions of the Dak was how big it was for a tail-wheel aircraft, and how high the cockpit was off the ground.
>
> I was much taken by the crew escape hatch on the left-hand fuselage side, just behind the cockpit bulkhead, because if during an evacuation, the still-turning left propeller (the tips just missing the hatch by inches) didn't kill you, the 25ft (7.6 metre) drop certainly would.
>
> The other impression was of a surface finish that wouldn't have gone amiss on a battleship. In these days of high-speed flight and carbon fibre composites, you forget just how basic structures were in that era and how akin they were to the cars and trucks of the time.
>
> The aircraft sits on the ground at an angle of almost 12 degrees nose-up so, after entry via the rear door, the pilot is faced with a climb to the cockpit that would put a scramble up the slopes of Mount Snowdon to shame. But after overcoming vertigo and getting there, the true character of the cockpit became evident.
>
> It reminded me of my father's Austin 7 (which had the same windscreen wipers): it seemed to have levers everywhere (12 just for the two engines) and was all done out in a delicate shade of black on black.
>
> The sliding cockpit side windows looked like they had been pinched from an old Land Rover and my pilot seat (1930s tractor-style) had a vertical adjustment for which the only direction was down. Having made myself comfortable in the left seat, I finally got to look out of the front windscreen to see – not much at all. Field of view to the side and back behind the wingtip on that side was excellent, but visibility forward while on the ground, with such a nose-up attitude, was poor and through the opposite right-hand front windscreen bordered on non-existent (I made a mental note: taxi using left turns only).

My article below was written when this aircraft was still very much a part of the Border War and was headed *'Game Bird'*. *In peace and war, few aircraft can match the impressive record of this amazing flying machine.* It was published in *Scope* magazine on 3 June 1983:

We took off early, just as the first hint of tropical dawn was piercing the gloom of south Angola. Having cleared the ragged row of Makalani palms at the southern end of Ondangua airport, the left wing of our Dakota dipped and the plane swung abruptly to port.

The so-called 'Rum Run' – a delivery of supplies to outlying operational bases – was never a favourite chore for SAAF aviators, especially when they were required to hug the deck nearly all the way to their destination at an average height of perhaps 20 metres. By the time we'd settled into our bucket seats on board, our Dak was doing exactly that and a few of the passengers, having checked their whereabouts out of the aircraft windows, were clearly not happy.

Too many C-47s, we all knew, had returned to base with holes in their fuselages, the majority made by AKs toted by SWAPO insurgents keen to claim the distinction of being the first to down an operational 'Dak'.

But it wasn't the distinction of being onboard an aircraft that might break the enemy's Dak duck, even if that prospect bothered me, which it did. Rather, what worried everybody was the fact that we would be required to land on at least two extremely short bush strips and the first time in it would be with maximum weight on board…

We'd been cautiously advised before heading out that one of those primitive airstrips had been 'blessed' that bright and sunny morning with a crosswind of about 20 knots: it was going to be hairy. But the guys on the ground needed supplies (and their precious mail) and we had to go in.

Our pilot, Major Dries Pienaar had calculated the load factor while we drank coffee in the Ready Room, and even with only 2,000 litres of fuel, he told us, we were going to be lifting 3,000 kilograms of cargo, myself included. Under normal circumstances these figures were reasonable, but with a crosswind … ?

Still, it didn't seem to bother Major Dries.

We weren't shot at that day. Nor did we plough into one of the huge camel thorn trees that are so much a part of the south Angola landscape or any of the clusters of goats that seemed to be everywhere before our wheels touched down. What did happen was that my fear of flying – which had been building steadily during the past 20 or 30 years of covering the African beat – took another knock.

During those formative decades, I had crisscrossed the continent, often in aircraft that probably couldn't sell as scrap in most Western countries. But airborne that day, over what seemed to be about half of Africa and almost within touching distance of the Mopani and camel thorn trees below gave a new meaning to the word trepidation, even if Major Dries was at the controls.

Nor were my spirits raised by reports that one of these ageing Gooney Birds had attempted to land on a too-short runway and hit a tree, which had torn off about a metre of wing-tip, something that had taken place only a month or two before. Undaunted, the flight engineer responsible for keeping the old bird flying, simply trimmed off the rough edges and bound up the splintered tips with tape. Soon, that battered Dak was again in the air and finished its mission.

That's just one of the many stories flying people tell about the Dak, a latter-day legend in every far-flung corner of the globe.

At the time of the war, the Douglas DC-3 was used extensively by the SAAF in support and supply roles in the operational areas adjacent to the Angolan and Zambian borders and in later phases into Angola itself. In fact, while hostilities lasted, the South African Air Force was one of the world's largest C-47 operators, mainly because a United Nations-imposed arms embargo prevented Pretoria acquiring more advanced military transporters in economically feasible quantities.

But those who flew 'Methuselah with Wings' – one of the many fondly and irreverent nick-names for a Dak – also liked to say that there was no other plane quite as rugged. In Vietnam, they sometimes took an awful lot of punishment and still limped back to base.

South Africans are not alone in their love of the Gooney Bird. Even in well-supplied Europe, the DC-3 has not been forgotten. A 'sentimental journey' by a Dak between London and Tangier was inaugurated in the late 1980s and people were queuing up to book their seats once the news was made public. You could possibly do the trip today, but it wouldn't be easy – too many regional wars bar the way.

But a quarter century ago, the trip down Africa took three days, so everybody had a leisurely chance to become thoroughly acquainted with 'Old Fatso'.

Very few of those sentimentalists would possibly recall the words of CBS reporter Charles Collingwood as he described the skies over England on the morning of 6 June 1944.

I quote: 'The sky is darkened with swarms of cargo planes and the roar of their engines is like the thunder of the war gods,' was the phrase that greeted an America waking from a good night's sleep that day.

The nation was told by Collingwood that there were over a thousand Daks en route to Hitler's Europe and a week later he was able to report something along the lines that in the first 40 hours of the invasion these planes ferried more than 20,000 troops and their equipment across the Channel.

Astonishingly, a few of the aircraft that took part in that airlift are still flying. One of these old-timers, bedecked in the colours of the Rhodesian Air Force, took part in the paratroop drop on the Dutch city of Arnhem not long ago. It will be recalled that Arnhem was the focus of Cornelius Ryan's great book *A Bridge Too Far* and immortalised in 1977 as one of the best films of the period to emerge after the war.

What is also little known is that this remarkable aircraft had its origins in the uncertain period before the Second World War. The first 'Douglas Commercial' as it was called, or DC-1 – a controversial product of a small amount of money and a tiny rented room behind a Los Angeles barbershop – never got beyond the prototype.

Its successor, designed in 1934, was found to be seriously underpowered. Nonetheless, its potential was spotted by William Littlewood, head of powerful American Airlines, still operating flights world-wide today. He proposed that the aircraft be adapted for commercial service, but suggested a few changes. It was made wider and fitted with bigger engines.

The first DC-3 – serial number DST 14988 – made its maiden flight on 18 December 1935. A new passenger service was inaugurated, complete with sleeping compartments and meal service. Thereafter, many thousands were built. So many, that even though they were adapted for passenger and cargo use by most of the world's civilian airlines then operating, the Douglas Aircraft Corporation was never obliged to re-open its production lines. There were enough spares to adequately cope with demand.

Other countries built their own versions: the Russians constructed more than 2,000 under licence and called them the *Lisunov* Li-2. The Japanese did likewise. Almost 500 eventually bore the emblem of the Rising Sun, though the Americans always differentiated between their own 'Gooney Birds' and the Japanese 'Tabby'.

Over the years, the aircraft set one record after another. In April 1965, North Central Airlines in the United States was reported to have logged 83,000 hours of accident-free flying across America and Canada. Then, in Texas, another airline came up with 100,000 hours without serious hitches.

The Vietnam War saw the re-emergence of this distinguished old flying machine in a potent new guise – this time as a heavily-armed gunship. Re-designated as the AC-47, a number of Daks were fitted with three multiple-barrelled 7.62mm Gatlings poking out of what used to be windows on the port side and each one capable of saturating jungle targets with a devastating 6,000 rounds-a-minute.

Attached to the 1st Special Operations Wing and dubbed 'Puff the Magic Dragon' AC-47s were a welcome sight to many a beleaguered foot soldier pinned down by Viet Cong fire in that South East Asian war. Elsewhere in that theatre of operations other Dakotas were pushed into a variety of ancillary roles, including service with tactical electronic warfare squadrons and designated the EX-47 to become airborne radio posts or electronic counter-measure craft.

Interestingly, when the author was covering the guerrilla war in El Salvador he spotted and photographed several of these gunships at that country's Ilopango Air Base. Referred to locally as 'Spooky', these planes with their triple banks of Gatlings were deployed nightly against Cuban and Nicaraguan-backed insurgents and apparently caused a lot of damage.

I took quite a few photos of these planes and even went up for a flip. Later I passed on what I knew to some pals in Pretoria and a month later, I'm told, quite a few specialists from the old country arrived in San Salvador to see for themselves. That could be one of the reasons why 44 Squadron SAAF eventually came into being ...

Some were even used in America's abortive psychological 'hearts and minds' offensive, scattering propaganda pamphlets over the jungle or stooging around local villages with recorded messages blaring from an impressive array of loudspeakers mounted under the fuselage.

The Dakota's involvement with Asia goes back even further than the Vietnam era (a generation earlier) to the Japanese war with China. One classic story relates how, in early 1941, a Dakota on a flight between Hong Kong and Chunking on the mainland was forced to land in a field because of engine trouble. Repair work began but suddenly the area was strafed by Jap fighters. When it was over, the Dak had been peppered by bullets and one of its wings completely shattered.

The pilot radioed back to base for spares but none were available, no spares whatever, he was told. But there was a derelict DC-2 wing somewhere behind one of the nearby buildings ... it might just work, it was suggested, even though it was a good couple of metres shorter than the DC-3s usual wingspan.

An airdrop was made by parachute and the replacement wing carefully bolted onto the fuselage. With holes patched as efficiently as possible under the circumstances, the lumbering monster took off again and finally landed at its original destination. In the record books, the hybrid is officially recorded as a DC-21/2.

A year later, another notable Dakota event took place. This time the celebrated United States Colonel (later General) Jimmy Doolittle found himself stranded in China with Japanese forces blasting at his heels. He had been bombing Jap targets for months with a force of B-25 Mitchell bombers and had he been caught, Tokyo would unquestionably have adequately rewarded him ...

Stuck on an airfield with a single operational Dakota, Colonel Doolittle was faced with the problem of getting 74 people – every one of whom faced internment and possible execution – into an aircraft that the instruction manual specified was only able to handle 21.

It was a tight squeeze, but he managed it. First, all the side arms of the seats were removed and that allowed three adults to sit in double seats, increasing passenger capacity to 28. Another 22 people sat in the laps of those 28. A further 10 squeezed into the cargo space – six more in the forward mail compartment and four in the cargo bin. The remaining 14 just stood in the aisles.

Incredibly, the aircraft flew, not very far, but sufficient for them all to reach safety. In later years Doolittle recalled, 'I wasn't worried about the number of people on board, I was more concerned about running out of fuel.'

Once again, the good old 'Gooney Bird' came up trumps.

Some interesting facts about the legendary DC-3

Sourced to Herman van Kradenburg – with grateful thanks.

Impossible Feats
The DC-3 has been known to do some absurdly improbable feats. Built to carry 21 passengers, one routinely carried 40 in the Philippines. On flights from Australia to New Guinea, Qantas rigged its DC-3s with slings and carried 50 people.

In 1949, a DC-3 carried 93 people out of an earthquake-ravaged Bolivian village. Many were small children, but it is still a feat that defied the designer's slide rule.

Then 25 years later, the DC-3 broke its own record again. On 23 March 1975, a Continental Air Services DC-3 flew from Ku Lat, Vietnam to Saigon with 98 orphan children, five attendants, and three aircrew: a total of 106 people.

Flying Hours
Eastern Airlines DC-3s accumulated 2,227,863 hours of flying time, logging 83,584,318 miles, the equivalent of 3,343 times around the world or the distance between the earth and moon, 350 times.

North Central Airlines estimates that its DC-3 '728' spent more than nine and half years in the air hauling passengers and freight and covered over 12 million miles, the equivalent of 25 trips to the moon and back.

During its career, 'Old 728' had 136 engine changes, its landing gear was replaced 550 times and it used over 25,000 spark plugs, to burn eight million gallons of fuel. This DC-3 taxied more than 100,000 miles and carried 260 million passengers in its 36-years of service.

Although many 'old timers' had their share of bumps and bruises, 'Old 728' never suffered even a minor mishap. Today, it is sitting quietly at the Henry Ford Museum in Dearborn, Michigan. Critics have said that everything but its shadow has been replaced. However, this is not true. 'Old 728's' airframe was still 90 percent factory issue when it retired.

Aircrew of the Dakota hit by a Soviet Strela-2 ground-to-air missile. From left: National Service Private Walsh, loadmaster; Captain Colin Green, aircraft commander and Lieutenant Mark Moses, his co-pilot. (Photos by Justin de Reuck)

Herman van Kradenburg in his blog 'Aircraft Nut' tells us

In 1986, a Dakota while on a flight to Ondangua at about 8,000 ft was hit by a Soviet SA-7 missile. The explosion ripped off most of the aircraft's tail. More serious, the Dakota was on a special mission, with a number of important military VIP passengers including the Chief of the Army.

The pilot Captain Colin Green slowed his DC-3 down to about 100 knots in order to keep it under better control and radioed for help. There was a helicopter in the area which flew in formation with the stricken plane and was able to relay the extent of damage to the pilot, also in the process, taking pictures.

Apparently, he ordered the passengers to sit in specified positions in the cabin so as to regulate the aircraft's centre of gravity before landing. Using flaps and power to control the pitch (up and down), he greased his machine onto the tarmac.

Captain Green was later awarded The Chief of the South African Defence Force's Commendation for his exceptional flying skills.

Some comments on the tale: Captain Green did not shift individuals in the cabin around to adjust the centre of gravity: instead, that was instructed to facilitate the trim. With much of his elevator and its trim tab missing, Green and his co-pilot, Lieutenant Mark Moses had a lot of back pressure to maintain on the control column.

Nor did he use his flaps to control the pitch. Any amount of flap usage would have caused the nose to pitch down, which would have required more elevator input which he simply did not have. Instead, he performed a flapless landing and not a 'normal' power-off landing.

Last, the crew were lucky that the airfield to which they were headed was not more distant because as they progressed, they sensed that they were losing more rudder and elevator components. Still more would be lost the longer the Dakota remained aloft.

It is interesting that though the stricken parts involved were constructed of fabric and not metal, the Dakota was always regarded as an unusually 'tough' plane, often able to take an astonishing amount of damage under fire and still remain airborne.

Also, the Strela-2 that did the damage was not the most potent weapon. Indeed, it was the view of both Captain Green and Lieutenant Moses that the hit was quite a lucky shot considering the IR output of the aircraft's two Pratt and Whitney 1830s at 8,000ft.

Peter Wonfor took this striking action shot of a
SAAF Dakota lifting off from a dirt strip in the
operational area.

For decades Dakota DC-3s played an active role in
maritime patrols.

Side-on view of an operational Dak.

50th anniversary with 24 Daks on the taxiway at Swartkops Air Force Base.

Rhodesian Air Force Daks on their way to attack Chimoio in Mozambique, one of the major guerrilla staging points in that war

DC-3 Cockpit.

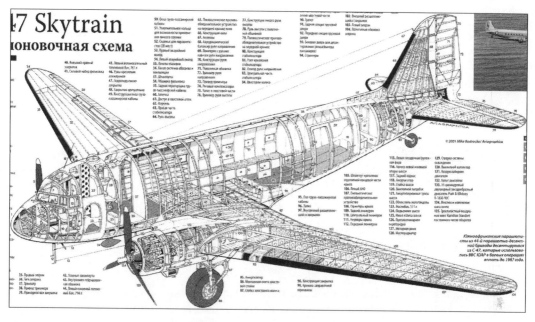

DC-3 Diagrammatic from Russian sources.

Today a popular Scuba tourist attraction in the eastern Mediterranean – a DC-3 underwater.

16

Russia's 'Twin Terrors': The Mi-17 Hip and the Mi-24 Hind Chopper Gunship

The Former Soviet/Russian Mi-17 helicopter (NATO designation Hip) is a military version of the Mi-8 – basically the same airframe – but with different model engines. While the Border War lasted, they were 'big time' active in Angola. And while hardly ever in direct combat with the SAAF (except for a single Impala ambush in which six Soviet helicopters were 'mysteriously' shot down) the South Africans sometimes spotted these Soviet choppers while operational across the cutline.

Well aware of the threat posed by these helicopters – which were armed, though not as extensively as the Soviet Hind/Mi-24 gunship (which had rocket pods mounted on their winglets as well as a four-barrelled 12.7mm Gatling in the nose), Mi-17s were routinely tasked to take part in limited ground operations in Angola.

The main role of the Hip involved logistics and troop movements and – being rugged machines – they were as well-suited for Angolan conditions as they were for the Soviet war in Afghanistan. Customarily they had Soviet light machine guns protruding both to port and starboard (and also towards the rear if their clamshell doors were removed). In some instances, there was also a pair of rocket pods.

From the start, it was clear that Soviet helicopters played a significant role in ongoing hostilities against South African forces: they could haul more than 20 troops into action (more recent Mi-8AMTSh variants can lift off with 37 paratroopers with all their gear). Working jointly with Hind gunships, they gave the Soviets and Cubans in Angola a distinct advantage over the SAAF.

As a result, the South African Air Force had to do something to curb this activity which had gone unchallenged for several years. A good deal of deliberation went into what exactly could or could not be done until somebody in Pretoria came up with a plan.

The idea was formulated that the SAAFs Impala jets would launch an extremely sophisticated ambush of both Hips and Hinds over south Angolan air space. The plan was both complex and dangerous and was obviously top secret and very well planned mission. Several of the jet trainers would go into Angola air space – literally hugging the deck to avoid being detected by Soviet radar and see what they could accomplish. In the process, the SAAF destroyed six Soviet choppers in a single air strike: two Mi-17s and four Hinds, one of the biggest losses to Soviet aircraft since the end of World War Two.[1]

Though it took a while and several wars, both the Hip and the Hind emerged as among the most versatile frontline helicopters ever produced by Moscow and its surrogates. More than 12,000 twin-turbine Mi-17/8s were produced over the years and have seen service in 60 countries, superseded in later phases by the military version of the same aircraft, the Mi-8, the '8' being the civilian version, while the military version is the '17'.

In contrast, the Mi-24 turbo-shaft attack helicopter, of which more than 2,600 were built, first flew in the late 1960s and eventually entered service in 30 countries (more, if mercenary use is taken into account, because Executive Outcomes, the South African private military company had use of them both in their time spent combating Savimbi in Angola and afterwards, battling rebels in Sierra Leone).

An international leader in heli-borne transport, the Mi-17 originally came fitted with Klimov TV3-117MT engines whereas the Mi-8 (a more advanced version) had the Klimov TV3-117MTV and during the Cold War epoch there were also sensors for chemical and nuclear warfare. Nowadays, the MT seems to have fallen out of favour and the choppers currently have the MTV engine, better suited for 'hot and high'.

The earlier version of the Hip was also designated the Mi-8, but had the lesser powered Klimov TV2-117 engines, whereas the TV3 series engines allowed for a substantial increase in power and developed for the Russian military during the latter stages of their war in Afghanistan.

On armaments carried by the Mi-17/Mi-8 range of helicopters, fired from the cargo space behind the cockpit, the mercenary air wing in Angola were using the 7.62mm PKT machine gun, essentially a PKM but designed for chopper use with an electrical firing system. The Mi171Sh (the export model of the Mi-8AMTSh) has two stubby winglets fitted with a total of 12 hardpoints and can carry up to 1,500 kg of weapons.

Mercenary chopper pilot Neall Ellis who flew both Hips and Hinds for the Sierra Leone government for the duration of its civil war and played a major role in destroying the rebel effort, used Soviet PKMs mounted on an antiquated Mi-17 dubbed 'Bokkie'. When he needed more firepower he would equip with a DsKh 12.7mm mounted to port and for firing out the chopper's side door. The original mounting was made by Executive Outcomes flight engineers prior to his arrival.

While flying 'Bokkie' operationally after the EO days, former British SAS operator Fred Marafono who joined forces with Nellis, tended to prefer the British GPMG as his weapon-of-choice.[1]

In terms of value for money the Soviet – and now the Russian-Hind Mi-24 helicopter – is regarded by both East and West as one of the best combat choppers on the open market. There are still a lot of them around, especially east of Suez and in the air forces of several African countries. Overall, mercenary units preferred them above all other rotorcraft.

There are several reasons, both good and bad. For a start, Mi-24s are readily available, but not 'second-hand' as such. You do not find Hinds waiting for buyers in a Ukrainian or Russian arms dealer's warehouse. If one is on offer, it is hardly likely to be in good condition and is certain to require a major overhaul and that, basically, is why it is up for sale. Parts can be expensive; a newly-overhauled Hind engine can cost US$500,000 or more.

At the same time, used Mi-24 helicopters are difficult to locate because governments who have them in their inventory will not readily let them go; they are both difficult and expensive to replace and there is also the legal requirement for a buyer to produce a legitimate government EUC (End User Requirement).

1   Al J. Venter: *Gunship Ace*; Protea Bookhuis, Pretoria 2013.

There are no privately-owned Hinds and no newly-manufactured Mi-24s, but when the intention is to purchase one, an airframe stored at the manufacturer or overhaul facility will be completely stripped and refurbished. Finally, when the Hind is released to service, all the major components will have zero hours.

The term zero hours refers to the timing of the next overhaul, as many of the major components have seen previous use. But each component has a life and when 'total life hours 'is reached after successive overhauls, the component is discarded.

Consequently, a fully overhauled 'battle-ready' Mi-24 these days will cost around seven or as much as ten million dollars (this is for the airframe alone and weapons costs extra) which is still good value for money when you cannot expect a new Apache to cost anything less than $35 million at today's inflated prices (and then again without armaments or high tech equipment).

On the negative side, the Hind is a fighting machine and cannot haul a full load of fuel, armaments as well as troops: so it is either armaments or troops, avgas being the common denominator.

Also, The Mi-24 is not a good trooping helicopter because landing away from base onto an unprepared LZ in the jungle (or remote bush areas) can be problematic. The helicopter's armour protection (a titanium 'bath' that surrounds the cockpit area) does not allow for good external visibility for the pilot to monitor reference points on the ground when bringing her down.

Of interest here, is that while flying combat as a mercenary in Sierra Leone, Indian Air Force pilots with that country's United Nations component in that West African country regularly told mercenary aviator Neall Ellis that he was foolish to carry out confined landings away from base. Yet he was doing it just about every day while on ops in West Africa.

The official Indian Air Force doctrine, as he was to discover while part of the joint force combating Sierra Leone's Revolutionary United Front rebels, only allowed for movement at prepared airstrips where their pilots could carry out rolling take-offs and landings.

To South African mercenary ace Neall Ellis, the 'Star of the Show' has always been the Hind attack helicopter which he piloted over several years while countering rebels in Sierra Leone. As Ellis tells it, the Mi-24 is certainly the most remarkably efficient helicopter he has piloted.

So far, I've had one in-flight engine failure with the Hip in over 2,000 hours' flying time and that happened while flying support missions for three years in Southern Afghanistan. It took place fairly close to the Pakistani frontier and had things not turned out the way they did, it might have become a pretty hairy experience.

The terrain we were traversing at the time was inhospitable. There were valleys and gorges just about everywhere with very little flat country in-between that might have allowed us to put down should we have been forced to do so. Also, you didn't know which areas were dangerous (a Taliban presence) and which were not. Anyway, nobody goes anywhere near the place totally 'blind'.

We had our first warning of impending problems just as we crossed a ridge at an altitude of about 10,000 feet. As expected, the mountains were almost sheer and from a quick look at the options, I realised that there was nothing that even vaguely resembled a suitable landing place, which was another reason why I chose to fly over the rougher areas.

My take on that grim war was that the insurgents preferred to operate in more inhabited areas, which are usually coupled to less-formidable mountain trails.

But the MTV is a very powerful helicopter, and its single-engine performance again proved phenomenal. So, with all the weight onboard, we were able to stabilise single engine level flight at 8,000 feet, maintaining a healthy clearance between us and the mountains all around. And while we were aware that that specific valley was under strong Jihadi control, we were eventually able to land at a military base in the interior.

We established afterwards that the cause of the malfunction was a failure of certain moving parts in the FCU (fuel control unit). With time, it had disintegrated into small particles, which basically became iron filings; these, in turn, ended up blocking the helicopter's fuel filters and caused fuel starvation. Had it affected both engines at the same time, we'd have gone down.

By the time we realised what was going on, we'd lost power to the point where the malfunctioning engine suddenly became totally useless. And because we were unsure of the cause, we decided to shut it down anyway and rely totally on the remaining good engine. That way we prevented further damage to the damaged one.

We eventually managed to touch down at a friendly forward operating base and using our radio, requested a new FCU. Once the replacement arrived and had been installed by our flight engineer, we were able to fly back to Kabul.

After South Africa's Border War had ended, Luanda's government relied heavily on both Hips and Hinds when the South African mercenary group Executive Outcomes (EO) became operational out of the diamond-rich town of Saurimo in the north-east of that vast country close to the Congo border. One incident stands out.

EOs commander at Saurimo received an urgent call from Simon Witherspoon, a former Recce and in his day and one of best operators in any man's army who had been dropped in a particularly hostile area in a bid to harass UNITA supply lines.

What emerged later was that Witherspoon, Rich Nichol and their two trackers were running hard from a UNITA follow-up team through an unusually-dense stretch of jungle. The undergrowth was so thick that they could barely manage to cover 500 metres an hour. Worse, they were making little headway in a black night and the enemy was gaining on them, which was unusual because these were among the fittest men in the unit.

It didn't take Witherspoon long to realise that his rebel adversaries were closing in. And since the South Africans weren't familiar with the area, there was the distinct possibility of them being ambushed by other enemy soldiers deployed further out. As he was to argue afterwards, they all had radios so they knew exactly what they were doing.

At that point several members of the chase team were about 300 metres behind, close enough for the South Africans to spot the reflections of their pursuers' torches off the wet foliage. He admitted afterwards that they had considered an ambush, but from the noises being made, they were hopelessly outnumbered. Whenever Witherspoon stopped he could clearly hear enemy scouts slashing away at the undergrowth behind him.

At that stage, they were near the village of Sacassambia, about 30 kilometres north of where an earlier group of mercenaries had disappeared not long before. EOs policy in these matters is clear: if the men in the field ask to be extricated, it had to be assumed that the situation was critical. Such requests were serious and the unit reacted accordingly.

In any event, all these men had years of combat experience and always looked seriously at all their options. 'So,' said their EO commander Hennie Blaauw, 'when the call came, we reacted as fast as we could. I sent somebody to wake our pilots.'

Consequently, at four in the morning, a pair of Mi-17s left Saurimo and arrived at the pre-planned designated LZ at first light. A heavy mist obscured visibility, which – according to the aviators, all experienced men – was scary because the region was undulating and a mountain or two in the immediate area hardly helped. Since the cockpit crews hadn't brought night vision goggles, they were forced to rely on the fleeing party's strobe light. Finally, using GPS, they were able to close in and establish comms.

With J.C. Linde at the controls and Charlie Tait's machine offering what support it could, the drama that followed was about as treacherous as it gets. Though it soon became light, a heavy mist still clung to the slopes of all surrounding hills.

'It was really tough,' recalled "Juba" Joubert. 'We would feel our way across the top of the jungle and then suddenly a mountain would sort of appear out of the mist right in front of us. At last, Charlie spotted the strobe and he gave me bearings.'

As he tells it, the hillside sloped from left to right and the bush there was almost impenetrable. Meanwhile, the guys below had reached a small clearing but as he could see from where he hovered, it really wasn't big enough for his rotors to make a clear descent. There had to be some kind of damage in such narrow confines.

The South Africans took the helicopter in anyway and Joubert used his rotors to carve a passage through the bush. It would have worked, but for one tree that was sturdier than the rest and caused a bit of buckling to the blades. Had the blades sheered clean off, that would have been that!

Joubert recalled:

> But we still weren't down on the ground. In trying to hover, I found that the machine had become seriously unstable. Meanwhile, Witherspoon and the boys had emerged from the bush and shouted that we were still too high, so I beat the trees for a few more seconds and finally, we were able to get them onboard.
>
> As I pulled power, the chopper began to vibrate and it was quite violent. The shaking continued as I gained altitude and I was forced to lower collective to decrease power and it was then that I decided to put her down. If I didn't, I was pretty bloody sure that the old bird would break up.

Just then he spotted a stretch of water ahead. To buy time from his UNITA pursuers – they must have been well within RPG range by the time they lifted off – he decided to put his wheels down on the far side of a river. The moment they touched, he knew that he'd brought the helicopter down in water: they'd landed in a swamp.

> My tail boom immediately began to sink. With Charlie Tait still circling nearby and having been given time to inspect the damage, the crew decided that they might just be able to make it back to base, almost 200 kilometres away. Finally, the men set about extricating the machine from the mud and though it took time, they got it clear in the end. At least they were able to lift off.
>
> We had to fly at reduced speed the rest of the way. Anything over 90 knots and the helicopter began to vibrate almost uncontrollably and yaw all over the place. Obviously, our light load helped.

Another equally unlikely survival story to come out of the war also involved 'Juba' Joubert, who was later to fly combat in Sierra Leone with Neall Ellis.[2]

With John Viera as his co-pilot on a supply run to Cafunfo, a remote diamond-producing area just taken by the mercenary force under the command of former Recce Colonel Hennie Blaauw (the same man who had sent choppers to rescue Simon Witherspoon and his group) their Mi-17 took a hit from a ground-to-air missile – probably a Strela MANPAD – a few days after the column had finally taken Cafunfo.

---

2   Al J. Venter: *War Dog: Fighting Other People's Wars*, Casemate Publishers, US 2006

It was a two-ship haul, and though the aircrews were assured that the area around the diamond town was clear of threat, including missiles, these veterans of several wars always tended to remain a little circumspect: it was just as well they did. When they were required to head for the sharp end, they flew in high and came down fast – invariably in a spiral and as steep as their rotors would allow. It was the same on the way out again: straight up and then a swing away when the required altitude had been achieved.

Cafunfo presented the same problems as anywhere else in that ongoing war. The pilots noticed that as soon as they got anywhere near Cafunfo, Savimbi's guns and mortars across the river would open up and the firing could sometimes be really vicious. The rebels would shell the landing strip and would keep hammering away as long as there was a helicopter on the ground.

On that day, 'Juba' decided that he would make a change and they should put down at an old disused airstrip on the south-western side of town.

His Hip had just delivered its two-and-a-half ton load and taken on board about a dozen casualties when he prepared to lift off. The two helicopters took off again and, as he ruminated afterwards, 'There was no hanging about when you had people throwing things at you.'

The two machines were about 600 feet in the air when several people on the ground saw the brilliant white flash of a missile being launched from the opposite bank.

'SAM!' somebody shouted, pointing at a contrail heading straight for the circling choppers.

Joubert's wingman saw it first, but things happened so fast there was no time for evasive action. At Mach-2, the missile shot right past his nose and headed for Joubert, hitting his chopper's exhaust just above the starboard engine. The pilot recalled an enormous blast above his head.

Talking about the incident afterwards, both aviators extolled the ruggedness of that Soviet-type helicopter for not being immediately knocked out of the sky. Arthur Walker, one of the veteran merc pilots was always of the opinion that no Western helicopter would take that kind of punishment and come out of it still airworthy.

Having got down onto the deck again, shaken but safe, the aircrews were able to examine the damage. Altogether five pockets on one of the rotor blades had been blown away and the blast actually missed the main spar by a single finger's-width.

Had any one of the Mi-17's five blades been sheared, it would have resulted in the gearbox being torn out and they would have crashed. Exactly what had already happened to 15 other Angolan Air Force Mi-17s in the war by the time that incident took place. Worse, there was not a single survivor among any of them.

Nor did Hip crews get out alive when three more SAMs destroyed Angolan Air Force choppers in the following six months.

Mi-24 chopper gunship bring prepared for a strike in the Sierra Leone interior. The Angolan Air Force operated the same Hind helicopter gunships against South African forces in Angola. (Author's photo)

Mi-24 rocket pod over the African jungle. (Author's photo)

Former SAAF Colonel Neall
Ellis at the controls of an
Mi-24. (Author's photo)

Soviet-built Mi-24 rocket salvo homes in on rebel position. (Author's photo while on ops with Neall
Ellis in Sierra Leone)

Reloading Mi-24 rocket pods. (Author's photo)

In later years many South African mercenaries used the Hind to good advantage in attacks on terror bases, such as from Freetown's Aberdeen HQ in Sierra Leone, seen here. (Photo Cobus Claassen)

Author Al Venter in a Mi-24 Hind gunner's seat during West African mercenary ops. He flew on numerous combat missions in Sierra Leone with former SAAF pilot Neall Ellis who also took the photo.

17

Buccaneer Rescue Mission off the West African Coast, 1965

The 1960s was a difficult period for South Africa. The United Nations arms embargo had begun to bite, the Portuguese were fighting three widely dispersed wars in their African territories and the Rhodesians were on full alert militarily. That was when Pretoria negotiated a deal to buy 16 Spey-powered Buccaneer jet bombers from Britain. However, the aircraft had to be delivered by air down the west coast of West Africa, all the way across the north and south Atlantic.

On a warm October morning in 1965, an Avro Shackleton long-range maritime patrol aircraft from SAAF 35 Squadron Ysterplaat took off from DF Malan Airport, Cape Town on its way to Air Force Station Rooikop, on the outskirts of Walvis Bay in present-day Namibia.

Designated Shackleton 1722, and originally developed by Avro – the British aircraft manufacturer – from the Avro Lincoln bomber of Second World War fame, it was one of a pair of these planes tasked for a West African standby mission should something go wrong with the delivery flights.

It was an obvious choice. The SAAF already possessed the aircraft and the Shackleton was always regarded as versatile aircraft. It could fly long distances and was ideal for maritime surveillance work in the early stages of the Cold War. On anti-submarine warfare patrols in 1949 peacetime manoeuvres, a Shackleton showed that it could detect a surfaced submarine at a range of 30 kilometres.

On the 1965 standby mission, the aircraft commander was Major Pat Conway and his co-pilot was Captain Johan Kruger. Navigators were Lieutenant Henning Els, Commanding Officer Knoppies Coetzer (who provided all this material) and Commanding Officer Bokkie van der Merwe. The electronics leader was Lieutenant Wynand Bloemhoff. He later saw the light and switched to navigation.

Orders were to fly to Bissau, capital of Portuguese Guinea (later Guiné-Bissau) and stand by for possible search and rescue missions for the first eight Buccaneers acquired for the SAAF from Britain. Nothing untoward was expected, but the jets were about to be ferried across a huge stretch of open water from the UK, all the way down the west coast of Africa.

Indeed, it was the single longest delivery flight ever attempted by that remarkably versatile two-seater warplane that first entered service with the Royal Air Force in 1965. The 'Bucs' as they were termed by aircrews, remained militarily active with the RAF for a quarter century, when they were stood down in 1991.

As Commandant Coetzer recalls, the range of the Buccaneer in the days before mid-air refuelling became effective was 3,700 kilometres (2,300 miles), remarkable for a medium-sized jet bomber of the time that 'empty' weighed more than 14 tons. At best, it could clock up speeds in excess of 1,000kms/hour, relying on its two Rolls Royce 168-1A Spey Mark 101 turbofans and it came with a Bristol BS 805 twin-chamber rocket engine. In fact, as everybody who had anything to do with the plane said, it was quite something!

The Buccaneer ferry flights were scheduled to depart Britain on 30 October that year, and the route to be covered by our standby search and rescue aircraft were the two legs; first from Ilha do Sol (Sal Island in the Cape Verde Archipelago) to Ascension Island and then from that British base (which also played a seminal role in the Falklands War) to Luanda, like Bissau, still staunchly Portuguese.

Shackleton 1722 flew to Rooikop three days before the second search plane departed from Cape Town. It refuelled and waited for nightfall before heading out into the mid-Atlantic for Ascension Island shortly before midnight. The other Shackleton was supposed to follow but it encountered various snags and only joined us in the air, way out over the sea due west of Bissau four days later.

Our late evening departure from Rooikop was carefully planned to arrive at Ascension Island just before sunrise the next day, clearly to avoid being spotted and possibly photographed by any intrusive news gatherers who may have been around. There had been considerable opposition to the sale of the planes in the British Parliament, specifically from the staunchly leftist Labour Party because of Pretoria's apartheid policies. But it was a valuable export order and the deal went through.

Coetzer: Navigation during the course of all flights on that operation entailed serious Astro fixing techniques, aided by the ADF (Airborne Direction Finder) tuned to the 10 KW NDB (Non-Directional Beacon) installed on Ascension Island. Cruising altitude to Ascension was 5,000ft, which was 'full throttle height' for the Shackleton under those semi-tropical atmospheric conditions over the mid-Atlantic.

On reaching cruising altitude, I tuned in to the NDB, call sign AW, on Ascension Island and lo and behold, the ADF needle jumped to the 12 o'clock position on the compass rose, almost as if the beacon was 100 nautical miles directly ahead. In fact, it was something like ten times that distance, possibly more, a clear demonstration of sky waves at that time of night (the ATC Tower call sign for Ascension Island incidentally was 'Wide Awake Tower').

Our Astro fixes soon became more refined, making the accuracy of the navigation better than five nautical miles. The NDB bearing from AW would periodically disappear as we flew into the skip distances of the sky waves and then it was steady again, dead ahead of the aircraft.

From 400 nautical miles out from Ascension, the bearing was dead steady and we were able to home in on the Island. After a flight of more than ten hours, Shackleton 1722 landed at Ascension Island shortly after five local time on the morning of 28 October. The next leg – Ascension to Bissau – was scheduled for the following day but since the pub and canteen at the airport never closed, meals and drinks were available 24/7.

One of the most memorable things about our stay there was that because the South African rand was fractionally stronger than the American dollar, we could buy a case of Bacardi Rum or a case of a dozen bottles of any whisky for ten rands from the American PX. It also stocked various electronic devices which were not available in South Africa and of course, *Playboy magazine*, then banned in South Africa.

After Ascension, we headed back towards the West African coast and after a seven-hour flight, finally landed at the main airport in Portuguese Guinea, only too well aware of the murderous ITCZ (Inter Tropical Convergence Zone) that straddled the equator where massive thunderstorms could occur with the tops reaching 75,000 feet. In fact, so far out at sea, there was no sign of any of these.

The only 'big bump' that occurred was when Bokkie van der Merwe counted down the latitude before crossing the equator. On 'zero' Pat Conway induced a massive bump that sent some of the wireless operators flying out of their bunks in the galley where they had been sleeping off the after-effects of Ascension Island. It was a first time for most of us.

The approach into Bissau was marked by a language barrier as the ATC was not informed of our arrival. Eventually, word came from the control tower: 'Shackleton 1722 please land', which we did.

Once on the ground in friendly Portuguese territory – Bissau was the capital – we were met by Commandant Wally Black, then Staff Officer Operations at SAAF headquarters. In Portuguese Guinea, he was the head of the Rescue Coordination Centre, but how he got to Bissau, I still don't know.

Airport formalities done with and passports checked, we checked into the hotel in the kind of heat and humidity to which none of us was accustomed and which obviously suggested a great thirst.

Come supper time in the hotel and we were in for another new experience. The main course was white steak and something. When I cut into my steak and the blood shot into my eye, I was quite pissed off. A *boereseun* does *not* eat raw meat. Language was a great problem because none of us was conversant in Portuguese.

I called the waiter over to tell him to put my steak back on the fire until it was done, stabbing the steak with my fork to make my point. With my other hand I got out my Zippo lighter to show the man that the steak needed more fire. I flicked open the Zippo, hit the flint, but that was one of the rare occasions that the trusty old Zippo did not light. The waiter's face brightened up and he disappeared, but without taking my steak, returning shortly afterwards with a small box of matches ...

The following day, 30 October, was the long-awaited moment: our Buccaneer ferry flights would be in full swing. We got up bright and early because sleep in that stupefying heat and humidity where mushrooms sprouted on the carpet in your hotel room was impossible and anyway, air conditioners were not an option because Bissau was already subjected to load-shedding.

After breakfast, we started a bridge game in a well-ventilated area with a bunch of fans cooling the surroundings. Lunch followed and the bridge game continued. Meantime, Wally Black was in and out doing his best to keep us informed of the progress of the Bucs. The planes, we'd been told, flew in two four-ship formations, roughly an hour apart.

Shortly after two that afternoon with the bridge game still ongoing, Wally entered the room clearly in a sombre mood. In a serious voice that suggested trouble, he told us that one of the Buccaneers had gone down in the sea and that we had to scramble immediately. It was a joke; of course, we chuckled and went on with the game. But he was not laughing ...

Then suddenly things started to happen and Wally began by rolling open on our bridge table a complete map of the oceanic area to the west of Bissau. That was serious because nobody interrupts a 35 Squadron bridge game. We navigators had all our planning instruments and maps with us at the hotel and the word was to quickly prepare for the transit to the search area and file a flight plan with Wally. He meanwhile did his thing with Air Traffic Control at the airport. Shackleton 1722 got airborne at 1600 hours and headed out of Bissau towards the search area.

According to Commandant Black's briefing, one of the accompanying Buccaneers relayed the downed Buccaneer's crash position back to Sal Island oceanic control centre on Cape Verde. They, in turn, informed a TAP Portuguese airliner overflying the area to keep their eyes peeled for any sign of wreckage, or possibly a life raft.

Other Buccaneer pilots that had been flying with the downed aircraft picked up a distress signal on the 243 MHz emergency frequency and spotted a red flare in the area, marking the position as best they could and relaying latitude and longitude to us. In our Shackleton, by now well clear of the African mainland and over the sea, we updated the search area and proceeded in that direction.

Onboard, Wynand Bloemhof was manning our Search And Rescue And Homing (SARAH) equipment, a primitive J-scope system that gave a straight line on the Cathode Ray Tube (CRT) running from left to right. Should a SARAH signal be received, it would provide a spike and we would turn the plane in that direction.

In those days aircrew personal locator beacons were SARAH equipment, transmitting a carrier wave only on frequency 243 MHz, but with no speech facility. That meant of course that there was no way we would have been able to communicate with the downed airmen. Also, they would have no way of knowing that we were onto them.

We'd worked out by then that the transit time for us to the search area for the missing aircrew was about four hours from Bissau, due west and that did not bode well because an hour before we reached the Buccaneer's last known position, it would be dark. We were flying at 1,500ft AMSL which is the normal operating altitude over the sea.

With about 30 minutes to go before we reached the missing plane's last known position, Wynand Bloemhof came through and he was explicit: 'SARAH Contact!' he reported several times to the cockpit and others on board listening. He also told us that the signal strength was very weak but it held until in a hoarse voice he shouted 'On Top.'

We were over our boys floating on the ocean below us and if we were elated, they must have been over the moon. There is no way they would have missed the combined roar of our four giant Rolls Royce Griffon 57 liquid-cooled engines. That was the good news, but there was now much to do.

We marked that position on our maps and estimated the accuracy as approximately one nautical mile. In doing this, one has to remember that as aircrew, we were thoroughly familiar with particular aircraft equipment accuracies. Indeed, we could refine the Doppler and GPI (Ground Position Indicator) positions with great accuracy and obviously the two pilots down below were very much aware of that. Naturally, our hopes ran high.

On getting Bloemhof's 'On Top' call, we marked the position with flame floats and with marker marines which would provide a highly visible flame for about four hours, but the problem just then was that there was no SARAH contact with the downed aircrew; both their locator beacon batteries we discovered afterwards were dead.

After a brief debate in the aircraft, we decided to drop a set of Lindholme equipment to the downed two-man crew. This consisted of three canisters: one with fresh water, another containing a large 10-man dinghy and the third with rations. All three canisters were connected by a floating rope to make recovery easy, especially for anyone floating in a small life raft. Trouble was, it was almost dark, but right then there was no time for prevarication.

We first made a pass illuminating the area with flares and moments later, two sets of eyes in the cockpit spotted a couple of one-man dinghies tied together ... we carefully marked the position again.

We then turned in for the Lindholme drop but height, as well as our speed, was wrong, and with flares illuminating the position and our pilot distracted by searching for the survivors, we almost joined the downed aircrew in the water.

While going into the drink with a fully operable Shackleton might sound unlikely, it had already happened to an RAF flight in June 1952.

Shackleton MR.1 VP261 of 120 Squadron RAF crashed into the sea near Berwick-on-Tweed. The aircraft was making dummy attacks on Royal Navy submarine *HMS Sirdar* when it lost height and hit the water. All eleven crew members were killed.

Fast reaction on the part of our commander (Pat Conway, bless his soul) rescued the situation and the Lindholme was released.

The 10-man dinghy deployed prematurely and in the process, its bottom got damaged. Luckily the two airmen in the water managed to get hold of the joining rope and pulled themselves towards the dinghy. With that, they pulled their modest little one-man dinghies into the new 10-manner and, as we were to learn later, settled in for the night.

It was just as well that things happened as quickly as they did because we'd allowed 150 minutes over the search area and were just about on Bingo fuel by then; it was time to head back to Bissau. But not before the area was well spotted with marker marines. We'd actually dropped a pattern, with some of the markers fitted with delayed igniters to light up the markers after specific time intervals. Meantime, there was a second SAAF Shackleton on its way to the search area from Ascension Island.

It was now well into the dark hours and on our way back to our temporary base in Portuguese Guinea. Once there, we had to land, refuel and return as soon as possible.

Fortunately, we had good VHF comms with the second aircraft and briefed them over the air with positions and other information provided. They estimated to be over the position about two hours after we had left it, yet, there was still the problem of us not being able to tell the downed Buccaneer aircrew that they were not being left to their fate and that another search aircraft was on its way. That must have been two pretty tense hours.

We landed at Bissau military air base at 0130 hours on the last morning of October 1965, refuelled, got airborne again less than three hours later and headed back to the search area. But before we got airborne, the last Shackleton had landed at Bissau: they were ordered to remain on standby. We would call them if needed since there was no point in having two large aircraft in the rescue area in the darkness.

Shortly before sunrise we finally reached the search area and were astonished at the spectacle: all our marker buoys were spread out across the ocean and parts of it resembled a small maritime village. But we still needed to wait for 30 minutes for sunrise before we could start looking for our 24 Squadron comrades.

As visibility improved, we could see all the marine markers but there was no 10-man dinghy. Had the lifesaving craft sunk? If not, where were the two pilots? We'd actually physically spotted them at last light in their tiny dinghy. The life raft and marker marines were supposed to all have the same drift rate, but we'd forgotten that the floor of the 10-man dinghy had been damaged during the drop; obviously, that changed its drift rate.

Now we were faced with having to execute a brand new search. We decided on a cloverleaf type pattern which starts in the centre and covers an area shaped like a cloverleaf to a distance estimated to be the extreme distance the dinghy might have drifted. Obviously, it involved quite a few quick calculations, but it worked out well in the end.

On our eighth and final turn at the extreme of the clover insert space leaf pattern, co-pilot Johan Kruger spotted the missing dinghy below the starboard wingtip.

'Mark! Mark!' he ordered, and two flame floats were launched. Thereafter, we made it our business not to lose sight of the dinghy again.

After that it was time for a celebration, especially since the wireless operators, their jobs all but done, could turn out a mean breakfast in the small galley of the Shackleton. With one pilot, a navigator and an engineer at their posts, the rest ate and the position was then reversed, the way things worked in those big aircraft.

Not long afterwards I took up prime position in the nose gunner position to keep the dinghy in sight and take some photos. By now we'd done numerous passes and could radio that both crew members appeared to be alive and well. A few hours later that morning we made contact with the first of two SAAF C-130s on their way to the rescue area. They radioed that they were busy vectoring the *Randfontein*, a Dutch cargo and passenger ship to the rescue area.

But the Herc crews were not sure exactly where the dinghy was, so we headed out to the ship and overflew it in the direction of the 10-man dinghy, rocking the Shackleton's wings in the process. The *Randfontein* altered course and we returned to a position over the downed crew. Not long afterwards the Dutch steamer was alongside the elusive dinghy and the pick-up completed.

We returned to Bissau and landed early afternoon and every one of us totally bushed. By this time our crew has been on the hop for an unbroken 32 hours. We were joined by the second Shackleton crew for a celebration at the hotel in Bissau but the beer and the wine were warm and both affected us quite quickly.

The next day both Shackletons departed for Ascension Island after lunch and arrived shortly after nine that evening where the crew members of the remaining seven Bucs awaited us. Their reception was so buoyant that when our doors opened and ladders were in place, we were unable to get out of the aircraft, totally overwhelmed by Buccaneer air and ground crews hauling crates of beer.

The party went from the aircraft to the canteen and then on to the pub: we got to bed at about nine the following night.

The next day all seven Buccaneers lifted off Ascension Island for Luanda, but we had to sit tight until the last of the jets had arrived safely in the Angolan capital.

It is worth mentioning that the presence of South African Air Force Buccaneers in Luanda, Angola on 3 November 1965 was the first and last time that those British-built bombers flew over or entered Angolan air space in a non-menacing role ...

SAAF Buccaneer – one of several bought from Britain prior to the Border War.

HAWKER SIDDELEY BUCCANEER S MK 50

ON 27 OCTOBER 1965 EIGHT BUCCANEERS TOOK OFF IN TWO FORMATIONS
FROM RNAS LOSSIEMOUTH, SCOTLAND FOR SOUTH AFRICA, AFTER THEY
HAD BEEN BOUGHT IN TERMS OF THE SIMON'S TOWN AGREEMENT.
BUCCANEER 412, PILOTED BY CMDT R.H.D. ROGERS SM, DSO, DFC,
(LATER CHIEF OF THE AIR FORCE), AND MAJ J.J. MURPHY, WAS THE
FIRST TO TOUCH DOWN ON SOUTH AFRICAN SOIL AT AFB WATERKLOOF ON
03 NOVEMBER 1965 AT 15:00B.

THE BUCCANEERS OF 24 SQUADRON TOOK PART IN TWENTY SIX
OPERATIONS DURING THE HOSTILITIES IN SWA/ANGOLA OF WHICH OPS
REINDEER ON THE 4TH OF MAY 1978 WAS THE FIRST. FURTHER
WELL-KNOWN OPERATIONS WERE OPS COTTON, REKSTOK, SMOKESHELL,
PROTEA, DAISY, RONDEBOSCH, WELDMESCH AND MODULAR/HOOPER.

ON 28 MARCH 1991 THE SAAF BUCCANEERS FLEW THEIR LAST OFFICIAL
SORTIE, WHEREAFTER BUCCANEER 412 WAS HANDED OVER TO
AFB WATERKLOOF TO SERVE AS A STATIC DISPLAY TO COMMEMORATE
25 YEARS OF GLORIOUS SERVICE TO THE SOUTH AFRICAN AIR FORCE.

Aerial view of Portuguese Air Force base in Bissalanca, on the outskirts of Bissau, capital of Portuguese Guinea, from which SAAF rescue teams operated while the jets were being flown down the west coast of Africa on their delivery journeys. (Photo John P. Cann)

One of the SAAF Shackletons used in the West African rescue bid.

Buccaneer cockpit view.

SAAF Shackletons were based in Cape Town for decades and their role – operating out of Portuguese
Guinea – was seminal in the search for crew members of the ditched Buccaneer in the Atlantic.

18

South Africa's 'Olifant' Main Battle Tank: Bloodied in the Angolan War

The heavy armour displayed in some of the images in this chapter is South Africa's main battle tank; the same fighting machine that gave the Angolans and Cubans such a drubbing at the Battle of the Lomba River in the final years of the Border War.

Based on Britain's Centurion tank, the remarkably versatile *Olifant* (Afrikaans for elephant) – which went on to distinguish itself against Soviet armour in the final stages of the Border War in Angola – was the most effective armour deployed by the South African Army since 1957. The manner in which they were acquired and entered service is instructive, if only because of all the devious international skulduggery involved.

Initially, there were 250 Mark 2 and Mark 3 Centurion main battle tanks bought directly from the UK but in later years, South Africa surreptitiously acquired from India and Jordan a number of Mark 5 Centurions (also originally British) that had been scheduled for scrapping. It was all very hush-hush, neither country aware of the true purpose of the sales; in a very short time these derelict, rusty hulks were being offloaded in Durban harbour.

Starting in 1970, the UN imposed ever-more-restrictive arms embargoes on South Africa due to its apartheid practices and human rights violations. This forced the Pretoria government (with clandestine help from Israel, France and the United States) to develop a significant arms industry of its own, which included a variety of modern weapons, aircraft and naval craft.

The programme included a significant upgrade of its armoured capability and the design and production of a range of new equipment. That included a revolutionary new brand of wheeled mine-protected infantry combat vehicles (ICVs) including the Ratel, which features elsewhere in this volume.

First upgrades to the Centurions were primarily for test purposes. In 1972, the machines were fitted with V-12 fuel-injected petrol engines that developed 810 horsepower coupled to a new three-speed (two forward and one reverse) automatic transmission. The project was dubbed 'Skokiaan', but only eight such versions were completed.

That was followed by what was known as the 1974 Semel Project, which involved fitting the eight 'Skokiaan' vehicles (as well as several unconverted Centurions) with modified engines and other improvements listed as Mark 5As or Semel. A total of 35 were produced and quite a few deployed in South West Africa (now Namibia). That was followed by a far more ambitious upgrade programme two years later, producing a more versatile Olifant main battle tank (later the Olifant Mark 1 after further-upgraded versions were built).

The Olifant Mark 1 entered service with the South African Armoured Corps in 1978, a controversial period when Israel was closely involved with the development of advanced South African weapons. The country's controversial medium-range ICBM missile programme also entered the picture.

What we do know is that what was being done to the Olifant benefited markedly from Israel's *Sho't* Programme (the Israeli rebuild of the Centurion that included several new features including laser sighting devices). Other features involved an upgraded engine, improved suspension, turret drive, and night vision equipment. The commander was able to operate with a hand-held laser range-finder, another contribution from the Jewish State.

The Olifant Mark 1was later further upgraded when the Mark 1A entered production in 1983 and went into service two years later.

The reason for these additional enhancements followed the discovery that the Mark 1 and its 20-pounder main gun could not match the weapons' capability of the Soviet T-55 MBT then being made available to armed forces in substantial numbers to the Angolan Army. Production of the earlier version was halted in the mid-1980s, because the Mark 1A was intended to become an interim solution for use until the advent of the Mark 1B version.

As a consequence, the tank's main weapon was replaced by a 105mm L-7 rifled gun. Also, eight smoke grenade dischargers were installed on either side of the turret; further improvements included a new engine and the upgrading of the tank's armour. By now, the laser range-finder was incorporated into the gunner's sight with night vision equipment also upgraded.

The Mark 1B was a new production vehicle, rather than an upgrade of existing Centurions or Olifants. Thereafter, its development was started in 1983 and the new tank entered production in 1991.

Notably, the revised design produced a more refined fighting machine than before, with the tank carrying 68 rounds of ammunition for its 105mm L-7 rifled main gun, fitted with a thermal sleeve. The tank is also fitted with a co-axial 7.62mm general purpose machine gun and a 7.62mm anti-aircraft machine gun, while the driver's station has a day and a night sight. The gunner's station was similarly laid out, together with an integrated laser range-finder.

According to Paul Mulcahy's website, night commanders' machine guns were replaced with MG-4s chambered for the 7.62mm NATO calibre. The driver could (and can still, in some versions) replace his forward vision block with an infra-red vision block and has a new cupola, which manually-rotated independently of the turret. Additionally, its front hull allowed attachments to be fitted which allowed the tank the use of mine rollers or anti-mine ploughs.

Fuel tank capacity was also increased, but by then the smoke grenade mortar had been removed.

The enormous number of landmines deployed in neighbouring African countries played a seminal role in upgrading the tank's defensive capabilities. For instance, its belly armour was doubled and new side-skirts added. The glacis plate and nose of the hull were strengthened with the addition of passive armour and the turret fitted with sturdier stand-off armour.

In its present state the armoured vehicle can generate a smoke screen by injecting fuel on the engine's hot exhaust: also added was a fire suppression system to the crew fighting compartment as well as a searchlight over the main gun.

In October 2003, some years after the Border War had ended, Alvis OMC was awarded a contract for the upgrade of a number of Olifant Mark 1B MBTs: that included improvements in the power pack, fire control and training systems.

Until the end of 1987, South Africa was involved in a fully interventional role during the latter stages of the Angolan civil war. Olifant tanks were dispatched into full combat in numbers and, as we have seen, participated with a good success rate in several skirmishes against the far more numerous Angolan armoured units that faced them: one source – unsubstantiated because of the usual Soviet secrecy about numbers, but it makes good sense – puts the ratio at something like 20 to one, to South Africa's disadvantage.

In September that year, a major tank battle took place when a squadron of Olifant tanks ran into several squadrons of Soviet T-55 (as well as some outdated T-34/85) tanks and destroyed almost all of them. That was followed by what took place in the savannah plains to the east of Cuito Cuanavale when Olifant tanks and Ratel infantry fighting vehicles took on almost 100 Soviet main battle tanks. The only losses suffered by South African armour resulted from mines.

The Cuban Revolutionary Armed Forces claimed afterwards that during the battle, the 50th Cuban Division T-62s had 'halted South African tanks at the Chambingi River,' but this is nonsense. By the time those hostilities ended, the entire Angolan-Cuban-Soviet mechanised force had been cut off, following the only connecting bridge to safety having been destroyed and all their equipment abandoned.[1]

It is worth mentioning that the Olifant Mark 2 has an up-armoured and fire control equipment turret which can be fitted with a 120mm smoothbore cannon on the Mark 1B chassis.

Major General Roland de Vries, former deputy head of the South African Army and the architect of a series of mobile victories against combined FAPLA, Cuban and Soviet armoured units in Angola has his own view of the nature of tank warfare that evolved during the course of the Border War.

He heads Chapter Three of his book *Eye of the Firestorm* – which devotes large sections to his legendary 61 Mechanised Infantry Battalion Group – with a simple premise: quoting Napoleon, he declares that ' ... swiftness is an elemental factor ... making up for numbers on the battlefield by the quickness of marches ... aptitude for warfare is aptitude for movement ... '

In a section headed '*The Olifant Main Battle Tank's debut ... Shock Tactics Unveiled*' he declares the obvious: ' ... the primary role of the MBT is aggressive mobile action in the enemy's rear areas; the deeper it penetrates the greater its leverage.' Yet, he points out, that was not the way the enemy deployed its armour. They dug in their tanks and created a series of static defensive structures, reducing almost every one of them 'to being simply an expensive pill box.'

General de Vries explains that by the late 1980s, the South African Army had about 172 operational Olifant main battle tanks, though clearly, because of servicing and other mechanical issues, not all were operational at any one time. Consequently, when it came to some really serious encounters that erupted in southern Angola on 9 November 1987, his people were more than ready for action: 'They were actually looking for a scrap, he reckoned ... going strictly by combat results, our boys in their tanks proved their worth.'

A month before, a South African battle group comprised mainly of soft-skinned Ratel IFVs destroyed FAPLA's 47 Brigade in the historic 'Battle of the Lomba River'. This was a decisive encounter that ended up totally dislocating the Luanda government's overwhelming offensive against Mavinga, UNITA's window to the outside world. Soon afterwards, a dozen Olifant tanks arrived with the same number in reserve and the several battles that followed represented the first time South African heavy armour had been seen in action since 1945.

---

1   Details of this battle are to be found in the author's latest book on warfare in Africa. *Battle for Angola: End of the Cold War in Africa*, published by Helion in the United Kingdom in 2017. See Chapter 23, which details how a dozen operators with South Africa's Reconnaissance Regiment blew the bridge. All those Special Forces operators survived, even though several were attacked by crocodiles and each one of whom was decorated with the *Honoris Crux* medal for exceptional bravery under fire.

De Vries: '... [in that battle] FAPLA fielded more than 150 [Soviet T-54/55] main battle tanks, while at no stage were more than two Olifant squadrons deployed. The Olifants joined forces with our G-5 artillery pieces (which fire a 155mm base-bleed shell almost 50 kilometres), SAAF Mirage ground attack fighters and Hannes Nordmann's "Hunting Group". By the time the fighting ended, 94 enemy tanks had been knocked out.' Large quantities of enemy hardware were destroyed or captured.

'From personal experience, I can attest to the fact that that handful of battle tanks made a vast difference to the morale of the relatively few South African soldiers at the fighting front.'

He added that the only significant South African loss was three Olifant tanks, which were not lost in combat but rather, were damaged when they entered a minefield towards the east of Cuito Cuanavale. Those armoured remnants were abandoned when the main South African combat force withdrew behind its own lines towards the end of April 1988.

'Considering what had been accomplished, it was a small price to pay,' concluded the general.

Obviously, the three crippled Olifants resulted in great play being made afterwards by both the Luanda government – and by the Cuban military – when the South African tanks were put on display in the Angolan capital. Newspaper headlines in Luanda trumpeted the event as proof of 'a great and glorious victory against the racist South Africans.'

That lie continues to be propagated in both Havana and Luanda and is often used as evidence by the ruling African National Congress in South Africa that the *Boere* suffered a great defeat in the final stages of the Angolan War ...

The corollary is never mentioned: the loss of three South African tanks in a single battle against the 94 lost by the Cubans and the Angolans.

C'est l'Afrique ...

A fascinating story emerged from the pen of Johan Schoeman, then a youthful *dienspligte* in the SADF and attached to a cross-border unit fighting the Angolans and the Cubans north of the Cutline. It was titled *'Trying to Destroy the Olifants'* and I quote:

> I was deployed for the upcoming attack of 82nd Brigade on the Tumpo Triangle on 23 March 1988 in what was termed an 'anchor observer' (call sign 35A) with 2nd Lieutenant 'Pikkie' Prinsloo and a Lance Bombardier acting as a technical assistant. My position on the Chambinga high ground (directly east of Cuito Cuanavale) gave me a panoramic view of the entire triangle as well as the Cuito and Cuanavale Rivers and the town of Cuito Cuanavale beyond.
>
> I also commanded a good view of the east slope of the Cuito high ground to the west and my primary task was counter-bombardment of FAPLA artillery batteries and rocket launchers which were deployed there in great numbers. I was unable to see any of the actual defences of the Tumpo Triangle itself and therefore engaged very few targets of opportunity there. Only when I saw the occasional vehicle dart about in the dense bush did I attempt [hitting those targets].
>
> I could clearly see the high ground in the 'Delta' north of the Cuito-Cuanavale confluence, where another anchor observer was deployed. He was protected by the UNITA 118th Semi-Regular Battalion. We also had a section of UNITA soldiers protecting us.
>
> A third discreet observation post was deployed south of the Tumpo Triangle who had a direct line of sight on the Cuito Bridge and the Tumpo Triangle itself. This one offered the best opportunities for organising direct engagements.
>
> Just after 0500 hours on that morning, we were shelled by FAPLA. A 130mm shell went right through the branches of our observation tree where 'Pikkie' was perched, ready to engage the pesky Soviet-supplied BM-21 multiple rocket launchers which responded every

morning to our 'wake-up' call. They would hurl ripples of rockets at us from their MRL troop deployments to the north-east of our position.

This was fast becoming a ritual. I was busy brewing some coffee in our make-shift kitchen the UNITA soldiers had constructed for us. I feared the worst when I headed out towards the tree to see if Pikkie was all right. Shaken, but intact, he was climbing out of the tree obviously shocked. Treatment consisted of a cup of coffee and both of us were ready to respond in kind.

Quietly we reported the shelling by DET (Data Encryption Terminal) because we had no intention of letting FAPLA know how close they came to hitting us. Clearly, our training had instilled a strict discipline that prevented us panicking and shouting on the radio, which was usually the case with many of the enemy when we struck at them!

When the third attack on Tumpo went in later that morning, we were in a rather fortunate front row seat watching one of the biggest military showdowns of the war. While I was engaged with registered targets of known artillery positions on the Cuito high ground and watching out for opportunities to take out a single BM-21(which kept reappearing in different positions all the time) I was able to see the progress of the battle.

The volume of dust, detritus and noise generated by the tanks and Ratels during their approach towards battle that morning was awesome and frankly, I was at first puzzled by the lack of any kind of response from our adversaries. Normally FAPLA would retaliate with a massive show of force, usually artillery. Surely, I thought, just about everybody within a 10-kilometre range would have seen what was going on ...

Until about 0830 hours nothing happened, but shortly afterwards, more than 60 enemy guns opened up with indirect fire on the advancing South African armour from just about every stretch of high ground in the area as well as from the Tumpo Triangle itself.

I sent in some counter-battery fusillades as best as I could with the three remaining G-5s, but I don't believe they made even a dent in FAPLA's artillery assault. By 1000 hours the attack was in full swing and several Angolan T-55 tanks had joined the fray. Then our attack stalled in an enemy minefield.

We brought G-5 fire down on the positions of the enemy tanks and I think the southern OP reported a tank knocked out with a direct hit. As I was unable to directly observe all the goings on, I couldn't tell whether it was as a result of our reporting or his (not that it made any difference).

At one stage during the morning, Captain Rendo Nel, an observer deployed at the Cuito-Cuanavale confluence reported that the UNITA battalion to which he was attached was being driven from its position when a FAPLA division launched an attack on the 'Delta' to clear it. Rendo had attended a number of artillery courses with me before and also studied with me at the Military Academy in Saldanha Bay so I knew him well.

It was unnerving to hear the panic in his voice as his group were routed from their observation post with the rest of the UNITA unit.

I could actually clearly pick up the snap of bullets on his radio as he maintained a steady report of their progress. This fire was sustained on the South African force for a number of hours, increasing in intensity each time the force tried to force its way through several minefields. Eventually, by about 1400 hours, there was a reversal movement when our tanks started pulling back, but then, unknown to us, the three Olifant tanks that were damaged in the minefields were left behind.

Commandant Gerhard Louw – he had been my course leader when he was a captain during my formative training at the Military College in Pretoria in 1981 – was in command of the two squadrons of tanks, and he tried to recover the immobilised tanks, but unsuccessfully.

By 1500 hours several MiGs were in the air attacking our force, though as usual they came in high and delivered inaccurate fire. How it was possible to miss such an incredible massed target creating enormous volumes of dirt and dust and I will never understand. As a result, their bombs fell way off target!

It became clear not long afterwards that the Angolan Army attack was a failure, but more importantly, we suffered no real casualties in any of those bombardments. It would be interesting to know how much ammunition was expended on both sides: it would have been a sizeable number of tons ...

Certainly, UNITA took many casualties; they were simply riding on top of our tanks and Ratel ICVs and got the worst of the bombardments. We were actually never given their losses. Only much later, talking to some of the tank crews that were there, did I learn of the subsequent horrors of cleaning the tanks and tracks, almost all of which were covered in blood, body parts and intestines. Still more died while when they were run over by withdrawing tanks.

A family member who was there at the time – actually a tank driver – is still today unable to hold either a job or a relationship. He put me in the picture years later. Yet he was never sent for counselling for PTSD treatment – as most of us, who were there. The majority of us survived, but he was unable to recover from constant nightmares and his life now revolves around the bottle.

I later heard that UNITA lost over 1,200 men in the three Tumpo battles but cannot substantiate any of it. My own sentiments are that that figure was much higher.

However, the next day, in the calm and quiet of the aftermath of the battle, Pikkie and I took the opportunity to explore the old Angolan Army 59 Brigade position just a few hundred metres north-east of our original observation post. There were a number of T-55 tanks left, abandoned where they had taken hits in their hull-down positions around the perimeter.

We investigated some of the HEAT hits on the turret and clambered over them like a couple of school kids. The UNITA section assigned for our protection was showing us around and even led us into the main bunker which housed the brigade headquarters and that of their Soviet advisers. We were astonished at the effort put into constructing bunkers four of five metres underground – some as vast as two large rooms.

Additionally, these were covered by three or four layers of tree trunks, each at least half a metre thick.

The Soviets obviously had a very high regard for the ability of the South Africans, but neither they nor their Cuban allies stayed long enough to see the outcome of it all. Every one of them was airlifted out of the area by helicopters – even before the first shots were exchanged.

SADF bush ops in Angola.

Longa, in south Angola – where one of Africa's major tank battles was fought, though in the end it
was the Ratels that outgunned and outpaced Soviet T54/55s. (Sourced to Roland de Vries)

The South African Army's Olifant-Mk1A main battle tank.

Versatile fighting machine the Olifant – based on the chassis of a British Army Centurion tank –
originally sold as scrap to India, then surreptitiously acquired by South African agents to be refigured
into the formidable main battle tank that saw action in Angola during the final phases of the Border War.

South African armour, with tanks at the vanguard and supported by Ratel Infantry Combat Vehicles, move into battle.

A T54/55 Russian main battle tank (MBT) knocked out on the road between Menongue and Caiundo on one of the roads in south Angola. (Photo AR Turton 2014)

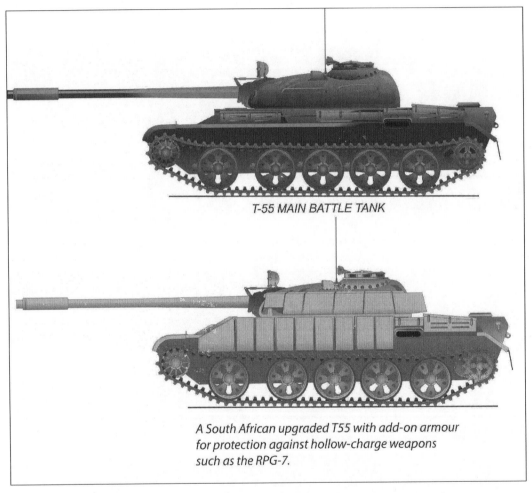

T-55 MAIN BATTLE TANK

A South African upgraded T55 with add-on armour
for protection against hollow-charge weapons
such as the RPG-7.

Variants of Soviet main battle tanks, some subsequently modified by South Africa.

19

The Arthur Walker Story

Mark Twain once said something about all friends being precious. As he appropriately phrased it: 'In each of us there are a few who are **really** special.' By the time Arthur Walker took that last long flight in 2016, he had been my good friend for almost 40 years. To me, this remarkable aviator was one of those 'Special Few'.

It was fairly early in the Border War that I first met a youthful South African Air Force lieutenant by the name of Arthur Walker. I'd spotted him with some of his mates in a pub in Rhodesia but thought nothing of it: 'Fly-boys' tended to do their own thing when out and about in town and in any event, South Africans flying Ian Smith's helicopter gunships were something not generally bandied about in Salisbury, or anywhere else in a beleaguered country fighting for its survival.

A few years later at the so-called Long Bar in Ondangua's Air Force base it was different. He was just one of a great happy family of pilots and ground crews in that operational area and the wry smile of partial recognition Arthur gave me was friendly enough for me to offer my hand. He had apparently just returned from a successful gunship sortie in the bush that included a few kills.

Being one of the scribblers – I was working for *Scope* magazine at the time – I was eager to know more. But Arthur suggested that he buy me a beer instead and we talked of other things. That, basically, was the Arthur Walker I came to know; modest and self-effacing no matter how intense the war or the bush contact from which he had just returned. He was always reluctant to talk about himself.

In time, after we became house friends, I flew combat with him and his mates quite often. In 2015 he even helped me with material I needed for a series of TV documentaries on mercenaries and private military companies that we were working on for Discovery Channel. As usual, his interviews were little more than the kind of characteristic understatements for which he was known.

For instance, Arthur would never talk about being twice awarded South Africa's highest military honour, the *Honoris Crux* decoration in gold for extreme valour. Or that he had been involved in numerous scrapes in half a dozen wars after he had left the SAAF to pursue a career 'in other things' – about which he was equally vague.

Several things invariably stood out and first on the list was that all of Arthur's women – lovers, and afterwards his wives – were 'top of the range' strikingly beautiful and it was probably his laid-back insouciance that did it. Also, Arthur was never far from his pack of Camel cigarettes and, after hours, the requisite few tots of Jack Daniels, his bourbon of choice.

'Good man that Walker fellow,' one of his commanders told me when I'd returned from a particular hairy flip where he took his helicopter gunship in low and gave fire support to some of the boys on the ground who had been following up a squad of SWAPO insurgents. The army had been after this group of insurgents for about a week and, at the controls of an Alouette gunship

– he finally managed to tie them down in an overflowing *shona* (a large water-logged pan) near the Angolan border.

Clearly, as I was to see for myself at the Battle for Cuamato, the man was one of the best pilots to emerge in the SAAF since the end of the Second World War.[1]

He had the medals, and if he was reluctant to talk about his exploits, there are many stories told by air force colleagues to prove his mettle: coupled to the *Honoris Crux* and Bar for two remarkably brave exploits under enemy fire. It is worth mentioning that during the course of the 23-year-long Border War, only six *Honoris Crux* in Gold were ever awarded and Arthur Walker was awarded two of them.

As both skill and a remarkable succession of events were to prove, Arthur could sometimes be mindlessly bold.

Take one example, an event that took place not very long before he died. When not 'on the road' Arthur lived with his family in an expansive Pretoria suburb that fringed on Waterkloof Air Base. As usual one afternoon, he'd left home in his car to fetch his teenage daughter from school and had just pulled up in front of his home when two cars suddenly veered off the road behind him. Very effectively he was boxed in.

Moments later, three men brandishing handguns emerged and surrounded his vehicle. One of the thugs opened the far-side door and manhandled his daughter onto the road before putting the muzzle of a gun against her head. In recalling this event afterwards, Arthur stressed: 'One needs to bear in mind that South Africa has one of the highest murder rates in the world and hijacking cars is almost as commonplace as road accidents … hell, this is Africa!'

Totally unfazed by the presence of a hijacking gang, all armed, Arthur reacted instinctively. He had already exited from his side of the vehicle – with his own handgun drawn – and by the time everything had come to a halt, he had his daughter's assailant clearly in his sights. 'Let's face it,' he remonstrated afterwards, 'when that happens, you are dealing with one of the critical moments of your life – I had perhaps two or three seconds to make the ultimate decision … '

At this point, clearly emotional while recollecting an event that had obviously scarred his mind, he stopped talking for a moment or two.

> So I took the only course open to me, aware that there were three attackers and any one of them could drop me at any time. I lowered my right hand which held the gun and placed it on the roof of my car. Then I said quietly: 'OK guys, let's cool it! You want my car, you take it.' At which point, without waiting for any kind of acknowledgement from his attackers, he ran around to the other side of his vehicle and pulled his daughter away from the man who had been holding her.
>
> The bastards wasted no time. Two of the attackers jumped into my car: I hadn't even had a chance to switch off the engine. The third man backed away the vehicle in which they had all arrived and drove off. Seconds later my car was high-tailing in its wake to God knows where …
>
> I reported the attack to the police, but in South Africa in those days, it was and still is a pretty useless exercise … when I explained everything to the cop in the charge office he didn't

---

1   The author went into battle at Cuamato with Charlie Company, a crack Parabat unit. The event is detailed, with photos, in Chapter 20, *Battle for Angola: The End of the Cold War in Africa c1975-89* (Helion, 2017), pp. 304-320.

even bother writing it all down, never mind following up on a potentially violent crime that could have resulted with somebody dead ...

This Pretoria attack was unusual in another respect because what does set Arthur apart from the others in his league is that once at the controls of his gunship, he never allowed anything to impede the need to 'finish the job.'

Another example of his gung-ho approach was the rescue of 22 sailors held hostage by pirates aboard the Panamanian-registered freighter *Iceberg* for three years off the coast of north-east Somalia. Walker was operating on contract to a private military company in Puntland at the time, a semi-autonomous state that had broken away from the Mogadishu government some years before because it claimed the country was 'ungoverned and ungovernable'.[2]

In that ongoing drama, he played a key role in a series of firefights over several days, piloting the country's only gunship doing circles around the target which was lying beached on an open stretch of shoreline. Throughout, the pirates constantly fired at his helicopter, with the machine taking quite a few hits. But that did not deter Arthur Walker from retaliating.

Several crew members had died during the three years they were incarcerated, with several others savaged and tortured by their Somali guards. The *Iceberg's* chief engineer had had his ears cut off because his brutal captors told him 'you do not listen to what we are saying'. They then crushed his leg with a steel bar so that he could not escape even if he'd wanted to.

Working closely with Colonel Roelf van Heerden, the mercenary commander of the unit's ground forces that eventually forced the pirates to yield, Arthur used his gunship – with a Soviet-era PKM machine gun mounted at the port door – to maximum effect.

Van Heerden, having brought some heavier weapons to the stand-off – including a Soviet 82mm smoothbore B-10 recoilless gun, as well as three or four RPG-7s – the onslaught ended almost two weeks later when the pirates, using mobile phones, called their leaders in the Yemen Republic to negotiate a truce through diplomatic channels. The Puntland government agreed to exchange the hostages for the freedom of the pirates who had been holding them. That was the first time in recent history that an independent military group headed by mercenaries had rescued a group of hostages from captivity while still at sea.

Arthur was also involved in one of the most savage ground-air battles of the entire Border War period in south Angola, where he won the first of his medals in gold at Cuamato. It was his job to provide 'top cover' for the troops on the ground with his helicopter and it was an enormous coincidence that I was with the Parabat (Paratrooper) company deployed that was the first go into battle against a fairly well-equipped and organised Angolan Army battle group. We were dropped into position by Puma helicopters.

However, to quote the famous maxim, 'no battle plan survives contact with the enemy'. The 1981 fight for Cuamato ended up providing a slew of unpleasant surprises for both South African ground and air forces. Basically, the intention was to use the deserted village as a forward logistics base from where, shortly afterwards, an area operation was mounted to seek and destroy a suspected guerrilla camp. The target included SWAPO's western headquarters.

On the afternoon of 15 January, six Alouette helicopter gunships and four Pumas flew 120 kilometres to a position roughly 35 kilometres north of the Angolan border, the intention being to set up for the operation due to commence the next morning. Apart from the Parabats, there were also

---

2   A more comprehensive account of events is contained in Chapter xx of the author's *The Chopper Boys*, a new, enlarged and revised edition of the original version published in the UK in 2016 by Helion.

troops from 32 Battalion, the elite army unit that accounted for more enemy losses than any other in the South African Defence Force.

With the Parachute Battalion's Charlie Company, everybody on the ground was busy securing the perimeter and checking out the surrounding area when the call went out; contact had been made with a fairly large enemy force and there had been casualties. One of the patrols had come across a previously unknown Angolan Army strongpoint just miles north of the village that gave its name to the battle.

That first contact was just before last light, and as Arthur recalled; 'There was no idea that this base even existed … it certainly wasn't on any of our maps, so clearly, our intelligence was fundamentally lacking,' he told me years later. That first call was soon followed by another, together with more details of the initial clash; two of the reconnaissance troops had been wounded and one man killed. A helicopter extraction was requested.

Walker: 'Captain Mike McGee and I went off in our two 20mm gunships to secure a landing zone for a Puma (already arrived at Cuamato from Ondangua) and it would be tasked to extract the casualties. But we were hardly properly orientated when Mike and I came under extremely heavy anti-aircraft fire, both 12.7mm and 14.5mm heavy machine guns backed by clusters of RPG-7s – dozens of them.'

> We'd already observed in our approaches that the open ground below all sandy soil with light grass cover was traversed by numerous Soviet-style zigzag trenches, straight out of the Red Army manual. Also, we spotted quite a few firing emplacements as well as positions for 82mm mortars and sandbanks that appeared to provide extra cover … there were underground bunkers all over the place.

As he explained, a complex mesh of tracks traversed the entire area showing where the Angolans had moved back and forth, making it all the more surprising that the strongpoint had never been identified from the air on earlier reconnaissance flights. Thorn trees that were normally dotted haphazardly across the bush had mostly been cleared to provide fields of fire … or for fuel, leaving only occasional clumps of bush.

> Our troops on the ground threw yellow smoke markers to identify their positions and then Mike and I went straight in to attack the base to suppress what was now a hellova lot of Triple-A fire coming up at us. Essentially, our role was supposed to soften up enemy defences so that a Puma could come in and uplift the wounded but this was obviously a very dangerous situation and it was only a question of time before one of us would be hit.
>
> But it was now getting dark, the sky filled with tracer … all quite dramatic, especially for anybody watching from the ground. Walker estimated that there were something like 120 to 150 Angolans dug in around this previously unknown base and it was pretty evident to everybody involved that the buggers were very well armed, with some of the larger automatic guns firing an effective 300 rounds-a-minute.
>
> We'd see the muzzle flashes and tracers would follow; a powerful barrage of fire and it all seemed to be headed in our direction almost in slow motion, just like you see in the movies. Then suddenly, the stuff was whooshing past our heads … all quite desperate stuff.
>
> Of course, we'd be firing back at them, aiming 'down their tracers' towards their muzzle flashes – it wouldn't have worked in the daytime, though.
>
> My gunner was Sergeant Danie Brink, and he took on the anti-aircraft guns until we ran out of ammunition. (The gunships normally carried 150 rounds each) which was when

I broke off out of orbit and called Mike to tell him that I was going down to re-arm. In my mind, we hadn't yet given up the battle, even though it was already twilight.

Then Mike suddenly came through on the radio and said that he was under heavy fire and was going to crash. We had been hovering at about 500 feet while we were still in orbit but that was a mistake – under those conditions it would have been best to get down low and fast.

However, as was established days later in the debrief back at base, McGee, in his rapid descent must have become disoriented, which is why he thought he was headed into the dirt.

'In the half-light, I couldn't really see him,' said Arthur, 'so I turned around to look for his chopper, put on all my lights and told him to fly towards me. But hell, that had the immediate effect of us attracting enemy fire from just about everywhere.'

But it did give the wingman the opportunity to recover, and Walker began escorting him clear of the battle zone.

As the two gunships moved away, Arthur remembers, it was time for some serious evasive manoeuvring. He used a succession of sharp turns and altitude changes to maximum effect and it worked.

Mike followed me back to the base where we landed and shut down to re-arm and re-fuel. More importantly, we had to reassess the whole situation and I soon realised that it was point-less to head out again because we couldn't have a bunch of gunships orbiting the area in the dark. At the same time, the position where the South African casualties were lying was too close to the enemy, a mere 200 metres or so from their lines.

While all this had been going on, reckoned Arthur, 'we still hadn't assessed what exactly was down there or been able to make a reasonably accurate guess about total enemy strength. Obviously, the target base was not a simply low-key guerrilla camp in the bush, but a strategic discreetly placed and very well equipped Angolan Army base. Big mistake on our part!'

Later that same night, the South Africans determined that their forces would move on the enemy position at first light and that was when the next surprise arrived. Judging by past behav-iour, FAPLA (the Angolan Army) could confidently have been expected to evacuate the base during the dark hours, but that did not happen. Those manning the defences were waiting for the South African attackers the following morning.

Once the South Africans went in shortly after dawn, the majority dropped into position by relays of Pumas, the battle went on for several hours until all enemy positions had been overrun. There were more casualties, including this author who took a blast next to his face in the melee and lost all hearing in his left ear.

Arthur's family background and history are interesting. His grandfather, also named Arthur Walker originally founded Walkerville, a small but quite prominent town south of Johannesburg. His only son inherited a large property which he was in the process of developing into a memorial garden. Arthur Walker Senior had been a Springbok golfer.

Born in February 1953 in Johannesburg the young Arthur went to King Edward VIII School, which curiously, was only a couple of clicks from where I spent my school years at Marist Brothers College in Observatory.

He got his pilot's wings in the SAAF in 1977, from where he went north under a still-unex-plained military aid scheme to assist the rebel Ian Smith government and flew for Rhodesia's 7 Squadron before re-joining the South African Air Force in 1980. Like other South Africans who joined the Rhodesian war effort, that period of service in an intense guerrilla war provided valuable experience and a good insight to what was to follow not long afterwards along the southern frontier of Angola.

It was while flying Alouette helicopter gunships based at AFB Ondangua in 1981 that Walker was awarded his first *Honoris Crux* Gold.

The citation for his decoration reads:

> During December 1981 Captain Arthur Walker was again requested to provide top cover for the evacuation of a seriously wounded soldier. On take-off, with the evacuee, his number two helicopter was hit and crash-landed. Without hesitation and with total disregard for his personal safety, Captain Walker landed near the wrecked helicopter and immediately searched for the crew.
>
> Eventually, the situation became suicidal, compelling Captain Walker and his crew to withdraw. When he was airborne he spotted the missing crew and yet again, without hesitation and despite the fact that virtually all enemy fire was now [aimed] in his direction, he landed and lifted the crew to safety.
>
> Through this courageous deed, he prevented the loss of two men. His distinguished actions, devotion to duty and courage make him a credit to the South African Defence Force in general, the South African Air Force in particular and makes him a worthy recipient of the Bar to the *Honoris Crux* Gold.

What the South African public was rarely told was that pilots like Arthur Walker, Neall Ellis, Heinz Katzke, 'Juba' Joubert, Mark von Zorgenfrei and many other distinguished aviators operating in the northern reaches of what was then still South West Africa – and later, Angola – would often land in hazardous terrain, pick up the army or Koevoet section commander and his black team leader. They would then go airborne to make an assessment, perhaps directing flushing fire at a position in a bid to unsettle an insurgent group waiting in ambush.

More often than not, they would put down in an area that had not yet been properly cleared and drop them off if another contact appeared imminent.

In Arthur's words, 'Koevoet section leaders would never rush blindly into a contact.' Nor, he told me, 'would he let things drag on so that the enemy had time to regroup or reorganise – the Koevoet guys were marvellous operators and they would usually stay right on their tails of their adversaries and when they believed the moment was right, they'd go for it!'

Getting into the final phase of a full-blown contact with well armed and increasingly well-trained SWAPO insurgents was something salutary to those who went out with any Koevoet unit. If you understood the basics of military interplay, it was certainly an exercise in skill that came from a lot of experience: an event combined with an almost intuitive cunning that sometimes fringed on the atavistic.

Once the Border War had ended, Arthur Walker, like so many of his mates began looking for opportunities where they might be able to earn a reasonable crust by employing their skills of trade. Africa, just then, was in a state of flux and there were a number of wars where experienced helicopter gunship pilots were needed. Essentially, mercenaries were in demand in Africa, South America, the Middle East and Central Asia.

Some South African aviators went to the Congo, quite a few to Uganda and still more further afield, to the Sudan and elsewhere.

Following Angola's independence from Portugal in November 1975 that vast country erupted militarily and one of the most brutal and expansive civil war followed. The Marxist MPLA government in Luanda was forced to call on some of its foreign supporters – the Soviet Union, Cuba

Yugoslavia, Moscow and others – for help, but when that did not work, a South African group of mercenaries in what was termed a private military company (with the unlikely title of Executive Outcomes, or EO) came to the rescue.

It took a while, but combined South African ground and air elements eventually forced the UNITA rebel Angolan leader Dr Jonas Savimbi to the negotiating table. That much achieved and the government of Sierra Leone – also seriously threatened by a rebel uprising and having observed EOs way of doing things – requested the services of this maverick group of combatants, the majority with years of Special Forces expertise.

If anything, Freetown's need to counter a festering guerrilla war in its jungle interior was even more urgent than Angola's.

Among the first of the gunship pilots to be hired was Arthur Walker. Now, with skills acquired in Angola, he was at the controls of a Soviet Mi-24s helicopter gunship ('Hind' in NATO phrasing).

Back in South Africa, Eeben Barlow and his group of operators had put together a team and produced a working blueprint for a fairly sophisticated military operation against the rebel Revolutionary United Front (RUF), then active in faraway West Africa. This was rushed to London and Freetown, the Sierra Leone capital by EO commander Lafras Luitingh for consideration. It took only days to get the go-ahead and the War Dogs went in.

Already the first elements of a RUF advance guard – headed by Foday Sankoh, a cunning and brutal psychopath who had served in the national army and dismissed in disgrace – were camped on the outskirts of Freetown. The newly-arrived South Africans were very much aware that they were up against a movement that relied on bludgeon, long knives and intimidation to achieve its aims. The cutting off of hands and legs of children and the elderly was all part of it …

Until this South African bunch arrived, nobody from EO had been able to assess the situation because none of them had been any further into the interior of the country than Freetown's city limits. Also, just about everything they had been told about the rebels – the nature and intensity of the insurgent war, the circumstances surrounding the death of the previous mercenary commander, American Bob MacKenzie (who had served in both Vietnam and Rhodesia's SAS) as well how the rebel army went about their business, came from State House.

Sierra Leone's already-desperate President Valentine Strasser – a heroin and cocaine hardliner – was hardly likely to level with the newcomers about what was really going on because, in his mind, he did not want to frighten them off …

At that point, former SAS operative Fred Marafano – who had been living in Freetown until a short while before – offered his services and EO wasted no time offering him a job. This Fijian national who had originally been recruited by the British Army was of enormous help. Indeed, he was not only familiar with what was going on in Sierra Leone, but he'd also been living there, on the periphery of some of the earlier fighting and knew many of the players personally. He could also tell you what made Foday Sankoh and his men tick …

What he had to say about the rebels was sobering. The situation, he told the EO commanders, had all the ingredients of a long-term guerrilla struggle. Being ex-SAS, and having been faced with this kind of insurrection for a good part of his professional life, Fred Marafano would know.

Heading the South African mercenary force was a former South African Reconnaissance Regiment veteran with years of service in the Angolan war, Major Lafras Luitingh. He formed two combat groups: a Mobile Group and a Fire Force Group and instructions were passed down the line to his field commanders to prepare for action. Heading the EO mission in Freetown was Bert Sachse, a former Rhodesian SAS and Selous Scouts veteran who, until approached to head that mission, he had, like Luitingh, been a serving officer in South Africa's Reconnaissance Regiment, the Recces.

As Sachse told me when we met later in Cape Town; 'I didn't even think about it. I'd made colonel in the South African Army and when the offer came, I resigned my commission.' He took six weeks leave of absence and a couple of days later Sachse was fighting a war in West Africa and once he had returned to Freetown, hostilities went into overdrive. It did not take him long to turn this conflict around.

With EO combat teams in place in Freetown – each with their respective commanders – it was agreed that as soon as contact with the enemy was made, EO would react in strength with their newly acquired Soviet-built Mi-17 helicopters taking the men in. The helicopters would then provide 'top cover' and, if necessary, shift some of the combat elements around and, when necessary, pull out the wounded. That was distinctly Arthur Walker's metier.

As one of the South African section leaders commented at the time, 'It was all classical bush war stuff that we'd been involved in scores of times before when operational during Border War days, and also subsequently, inside Angola against UNITA.'

The basics involved in getting to grips with the enemy, even in an ambush (which was invariably the case) was using the unit's Fire Force to maximum advantage, something that completely befuddled the rebels. Until then, RUF commanders had become accustomed to the lackadaisical approach of the country's regular army, who was probably two notches worse than they were since both liked to use liquor and drugs to bolster courage.

The South Africans, in contrast, once contact had been made, were taken into action by the Hips immediately afterwards. They would invariably have improvised plans in hand to attack from the front and rear (where possible) and to cut off any line of retreat. Follow-ups would result until the rebels were dispersed or had fled.

According to Arthur, involved throughout much of the campaign, it was more of a game plan than any kind of set-piece action. This was when his South African Air Force experiences, as well as time spent with EO fighting against UNITA in Angola, came into play.

> In Sierra Leone, our boys had no option but to act of their own volition: it was classic initiative, instinct and reaction in the true *Wehrmacht* tradition. Individual squads, more often than not, were essentially "lone operators". In effect, he reckoned, the EO force was an extremely versatile fighting group and then only because they remained flexible in their approach to the kind of problems that might arise. Each situation was handled piecemeal – nothing predetermined or fixed.[3]
>
> If needs be, we could and sometimes would make a 180-degree change of plan in full flight and the platoon leaders would know exactly what to do. They'd been in the thick of it often enough in the past, so it was nothing new.'

It soon became obvious that the rebels knew that the South Africans were coming and they were making a few plans of their own. In all likelihood details about numbers, armour, helicopter support and so on would have been passed back to rebel command in Benguema, a small town in the jungle interior.

---

3   A reading of James Lucas' *The German Army Handbook* provides a good insight to many of these tactics where, in essence, the objective is paramount and the means to achieve success is adaptable to circumstances or deployment. Being Special Forces, the majority of these operators would have spent a lot of their own time studying other wars, World War Two and South East Asia especially.

Then, without ado, the call would go out from EO section leaders for a Fire Force to be deployed. Shortly afterwards the Mi-24s would drop men in two groups, well within radio communication with each other in anticipation of a contact.

It was a difficult war, remembered Colonel Duncan Rykaart, another of EOs senior commanders. Movement was almost always impeded, often severely by the kind of terrain that was so furiously overgrown that it sometimes reached right over and onto the road. 'Also', he explained, 'it encroached on both sides: a man could be standing metres from you and you'd miss him completely. That worried us all because it limited our options and then there could be casualties.'

To the majority of South Africans fighting that war, this was not quite what they'd experienced in Angola, even though adaptation to West African jungle conditions was easy enough. Some of the men did find the brooding triple-tier forests intimidating, particularly the Southern African blacks fighting with the unit and sometimes making up half its strength.[4]

Everybody was also aware that the rebels must have had a pretty good idea of the size of the force they were up against.

Colonel Bert Sachse (elevated soon thereafter to Brigadier) explained that the rebels very often used the dark hours to prepare for ambushes, usually at cuttings alongside the road, though they would avoid actual night actions. The moment a contact took place, the South African phalanx would go onto the offensive and turn directly towards where the enemy had positioned themselves in the undergrowth. At the same time, Arthur Walker and his gunships would be summoned and shortly afterwards, sometimes within minutes, the South Africans would be on the offensive.

In quite a few subsequent debriefs, it was established that EO squads would gain the advantage even before the rebels had even begun to realise their predicament. Those who could flee did so at double pace, the Hind gunships, meanwhile – always operating in pairs – having been called in to provide top cover as soon as the action began.

The Mi-24 gunships would often arrive about the same time the rebels were pulling out and though heavy bush often precluded the pilots from following everything going on down below, clumps of rebels running through the jungle would present Arthur and his associates with marvellous targets of opportunity.

To help the aviators differentiate friend from foe, the government forces were issued with strips of orange 'Day-Glo' that they stuck onto the tops of their bush hats, another well-worn tradition from South Africa's Border War.

Rykaart: 'Our casualties were never serious. There were quite a few shrapnel wounds from RPG rockets, though one of the men, Henry Engelbrecht, lost an eye and he was lifted out to Freetown by helicopter. His wounds were first dressed by our doctors and the same night he was flown to London on a commercial flight.'

Duncan Rykaart had originally told me in Angola that psychologically, it helped that EO was never afraid to trade blows: as he declared 'it's basically our operational style.'

Thus, his men would take the war to the enemy and that too was a first-timer. Also, the rebels had never been confronted either as doggedly or on such a scale before. Nor had it experienced such a series of defeats, one after the other, with the rebels never able to recover the kind of initiative they had enjoyed for some years before the South Africans arrived.

---

4   Black soldiers from the old SADF who had served in Special Forces units like the Recces, Koevoet and 32 Battalion played a prominent role within the ranks of Executive Outcomes. Initially, their numbers were sparse – during the early EO days in Angola – but with time, because they were all remarkably competent combatants, they would be approached by their former white commanders and invited to join the ranks with their old associates. By the time the Sierra Leone operation and a subsequent little-known EO effort in Kabila's Congo had taken place, black soldiers made up more than half their number.

Naturally, said Rykaart, our gunships made an enormous difference. As Arthur Walker would always proclaim, 'the Hind is still the ultimate killing machine in any Third World War.'

Once back home in Johannesburg, Arthur was able to take a long hard look at what had taken place. He stressed that the tactics that Executive Outcomes employed were actually pretty basic. It was all classic, counter-insurgency stuff, he reckoned, coupled to superior discipline.[5]

Arthur walker's citation for his first *Honoris Crux* Gold decoration for 'bravery beyond the call of duty' at Cuamato makes for interesting reading. It states:

> During January 1981, two Alouette helicopters with Lieutenant Arthur Walker as flight leader carried out close air support operations resulting in the helicopters coming under intense enemy artillery and anti-aircraft fire. He only withdrew when ordered to do so. Later Lieutenant Walker returned to the contact area to provide top cover for a Puma helicopter assigned to casualty evacuation. Again he was subject to severe enemy anti-aircraft fire. During the withdrawal, the second helicopter developed difficulties and called for assistance. Yet again Lieutenant Walker returned to provide top cover, drawing virtually all the anti-aircraft fire. His courageous act prevented the loss of an Alouette and crew.
>
> Lieutenant Walker's actions were not only an outstanding display of professionalism, devotion to duty and courage, but also constitute exceptional deeds of bravery under enemy fire and makes him a worthy recipient of the *Honoris Crux* Gold.

Having been tried and tested in battle many times in half-a-dozen wars, including The Balkans, Arthur was never seriously wounded in action.

He died of cancer, his family by his side in Pretoria in 2016.

---

5   The almost complete Executive Outcomes story in both Angola and Sierra Leone can be found in the author's first book on the subject *War Dog: Fighting Other People's Wars*. Published by Casemate in the United States in 2005, it went into several editions but is now out of print. An inferior pirate version of *War Dog* was published in South Africa but that work was a third shorter than the original and of inferior quality.

Chopper Pilot Arthur Walker with unit award for Excellence. Arthur garnered a pair of Honoris Crux in Gold decorations for bravery during the Border War – two of only six in gold that were ever issued.

Arthur's medals – the Honoris Crux in Gold, with Bar – is in prime position on the left.

Arthur, working as a mercenary, took this shot while flying his erstwhile SAAF Alouette over a pirate hostage ship in Somali waters. After a lengthy stand-off, the criminals eventually yielded their captives.

Alouette gunner over the Angolan bush – Arthur Walker was one of the SAAF gunship pilots that developed remarkable skills – a master of ground support operations in that war. (Author's photo)

Arthur and Suzette at their home in Pierre van Ryneveld on the outskirts of Pretoria, often visited by the author.

Rhodesian gunships in a forward operating base. (Photo Chris Cocks who was serving in the RLI at the time)

Arthur Walker and colleagues at Angola's Saurimo air base while flying for the mercenary group Executive Outcomes. He can be seen standing, on the right.

Rhodesian Alouette chopper gunship (like that flown by Walker) with twins heavy machine guns mounted. Arthur spent good time during the course of his early career flying gunships in Rhodesia.

Attack on guerrilla positions in Sierra Leone where Arthur played a seminal airborne role. (Author's photo, while flying combat with Neall Ellis)

Arthur Walker and the Puntland Alouette helicopter where he flew as a mercenary in anti-pirate operations out of the Bosaso air base in Somalia's extreme north-east. (Photo Roelf van Heerden)

20

The Ubiquitous RPG-7: A Formidable Soviet Offensive Weapon

The RPG-7 is indisputably the 'ground forces weapon of its time'. There are almost no contemporary wars, insurrections or revolutions where it has not or is not deployed – and that in an era when Jihadi groups like Islamic State and Al-Qaeda have been most active. It is sometimes used in an anti-aircraft role (RPG-7s were used to down two American Black Hawks in the historic October 1993 'Battle of Mogadishu'). They are seen every day in conventional attacks against UN and other forces in Somalia, in Al-Qaeda's ongoing war in Mali as well as other troubled regions of the world.

I have fired RPGs many times, both on the range and in action in Lebanon when caught in a tight spot. I've also handled French Army Strim M52 rifle grenades, outdated Second World War generation American bazookas as well as M60 anti-tank rifle grenades and I rate the versatility of the RPG-7 ahead of them all. In experienced hands, the RPG-7 is a truly formidable weapon.

Probably the narrowest scrape I had with the RPG-7 was not in wartime, nor being targeted by this weapon. My closest call came in Maputo, the Mozambique capital, a few years after that country's independence.

I had taken my three sons on a diving holiday on Inhaca Island, a pleasant little resort at one of the entrances to the great Maputo Bay. We reached Mozambique by road in the family Landcruiser and it was on our return to South Africa that we were almost caught short.

Because of the civil war with RENAMO, then still very active, there were quite a few roadblocks in and out of the city and we were ordered to stop at one of them all. No problem. I pulled up each time and would reach across to get our passports and vehicle documents from the cubbyhole, the usual routine.

Then, at the very last roadblock, a military vehicle approached from the opposite side of the road and pulled up sharply immediately ahead. There were three or four FRELIMO soldiers on the rear of the truck, one of whom shouted a greeting at his mates manning the stop, at which point he hurled a large plastic bag to the ground. At first glance, it appeared to contain a nondescript array of machine parts.

The man who threw the bag must have been drunk because his aim was wobbly. The 'parcel' bounced off my front wheel, rebounded onto the road and came to a halt next to my window on the driver's side. At that point, I was able to see that what had been casually thrown from the military transport were eight or ten brand new RPG-7 grenades, hardly missable because of their bulging, triangular warheads and lengthy exhaust tubes that extend from the rear of every one of them.

In the Maputo incident I could see quite clearly that all the grenades in the bag were tied together with twine, which made the package an unusually lethal load: had a single RPG detonated, all four of us would have been history.

Thank God the RPG7 has a built-in safety factor. Its arming system – under normal circumstances – is made active by the propellant explosion that drives the grenade out of the launcher and needs a gravitational force (or more commonly G-force) of two or more before it will detonate on contact.

But then, as with so many Soviet weapons, RPGs included, *you never really know* …

I had fired RPG-7s several times during the Border War, not on actual operations with the South African Army, but rather, to get a feel of how the weapon performed. That meant that I was well aware that impact grenades are unarmed until they have actually been fired, for the very good reason that in wartime things are often thrown about or might be dropped and accidental contact might set them off. Those eight or ten that were hurled at my car – hitting metal in the process – could just as easily have exploded.

Each of the grenades is usually loaded with a charge of about two kilograms of high explosive, gathered together towards a shaped charge in the front of each grenade. That meant that there was probably 10-something kilograms of HE in that pile.

Since the deployment of the RPG-7 is so widespread, it is worth knowing that numerous variations have been developed over several decades. When fired, the grenade develops a velocity of 115 metres a second (in the initial boost) and 300 metres a second in flight.

There is the PG-7V baseline 85mm High Explosive Anti-Tank (HEAT) rocket, which *Military Today* tells us penetrates around 26 centimetres (almost a foot) of rolled homogenous armour, while the PG-7VS is a 73-mm HEAT rocket with similar destructive power.

More recent variants include the TBG-7V, a 105mm thermobaric rocket, which has an awesomely devastating explosive effect and has seen extensive service in recent Middle East conflicts.

The RPG-7 has seen such wide and varied service that it is nearly impossible to list all of the wars in which it has been deployed.

It is certainly combat proven and continues to be produced in countries such as Iraq, Romania, China, and Bulgaria. While it will continue to serve in low-budget forces for years in a fire-support role, the weapon is being phased out by most militaries from its anti-armour role due to its limited effectiveness against today's main battle tanks.

Its low cost is possibly the primary reason why the weapon is so popular. You can buy the weapon on the periphery of just about every Third World conflict from anything between $500-$2,000 American dollars for a launcher and perhaps $100-500 per rocket.

Moreover, it boasts a commendable history. One of the first times the weapon was used by international militants (aka terrorists) was on 13 January 1975 at France's Orly Airport. That was when the still-elusive 'Carlos the Jackal', together with another member from a Palestinian terror group, used two Soviet RPG-7 grenades to attack an Israeli airliner. Both missed the target, one of the grenades striking a Yugoslav passenger airliner instead.

So much for that evil man's claim to be one of the best guerrilla fighters in the world, currently in prison, probably for the rest of his life.

Not long afterwards in Afghanistan, Mujahadeen guerrillas were regularly deploying RPG-7s to destroy Soviet vehicles after Moscow had invaded that Central Asian country in 1980. They were also used more often than any of us believed possible again Soviet warplanes, with reports at the time suggesting that supplies came from one of Moscow's staunchest allies.

While making a film for the CIA about this war in 1985 – it was timed for release on the fifth anniversary of hostilities (five years after the invasion) – my teams were able to film in some of the guerrilla training camps on the outskirts of Peshawar in northern Pakistan. The Soviet rocket grenade featured high on the agenda and we joked at the time that it was ironic that a really brilliant Soviet weapon was being deployed by every Mujahadeen squad in the country, every man jack among them blood enemies of the same people that had developed and manufactured them.

Also, with a little prodding from American technicians and instructors in their ranks, the Mujahadeen were using the weapon to extremely good effect. We actually filmed the RPG-7 featured in demonstrations right alongside American Stinger missiles that were responsible for an inordinate number of Russian aircraft losses, helicopters especially.

The way it was explained to us was that the Islamic guerrillas worked according to a series of attack systems, some devised by their then American allies, and it is sardonic that the very same tactics would be put to use a couple of decades later by Islamic State in Iraq and Syria.

In Afghanistan then, to assure a kill, two to four RPG shooters would be assigned to each of the Mujahadeen vehicles, usually a pick-up truck and it says something that those vehicle-orientated hunter-killer teams could fire as many as a dozen or 15 RPGs in a single attack that would perhaps last a minute or two.

In areas where vehicles were possibly confined to a single (path like a mountain road, snow-covered terrain or urban areas) RPG teams often trapped convoys by destroying the first and last vehicles in line, halting the movement of all the other vehicles in the column.

This tactic was especially effective in cities. First the Soviets and then the Americans and British quickly learned to avoid approaches with overhangs and to send their infantrymen forward on foot in hazardous areas in bids to detect rebel groups fielding RPGs. Obviously, the attrition rate of those 'scouts' was high.

Similarly, as I was also to observe a few years later in Somalia, the RPG-7 was as much the favourite weapon of choice then as it is today, half a century after it was first deployed in combat.

Interestingly, during the Border War, the South African Army captured massive supplies of these grenade launchers during their cross-border raids into Angola and eventually incorporated them among some of their own Special Forces strike groups, 32 Battalion especially.

Large numbers of the weapon were also passed on to the UNITA guerrilla group.

In truth, the RPG-7 – the veteran fin-stabilised, rocket-propelled anti-tank launcher – actually changed the face of warfare when it was first introduced in 1961. It also went on to capture the imagination of game studios and became a go-to Hollywood prop. So too with the classic 1980s film *Red Dawn* which portrayed ordinary American high school students blowing up Soviet tanks with captured RPGs. You can hardly make it through a lot of video games these days without tripping over the weapon.

In the real world though, the RPG-7 is one of the deadliest weapons on the planet because of its sheer destructive power for its size. Perhaps the only other single weapon more widely available is the Kalashnikov assault rifle.

My old friend Lester Grau, an analyst with the US Army's Foreign Military Studies Office at Fort Leavenworth and author of *The Bear Went Over the Mountain: Soviet Combat Tactics in Afghanistan* reckons that the RPG-7 anti-tank grenade launcher is one of the most common and most effective infantry weapons in contemporary conflicts. He comments:

> Whether downing Black Hawk helicopters in Somalia, blasting Russian tanks in Chechnya or attacking government strongpoints in Angola, the RPG-7 is the weapon of choice for many infantrymen and guerrillas around the world.
>
> For American soldiers, the weapon is responsible for their single deadliest day in Afghanistan. On 6 August 2011, Taliban insurgents fired up to three RPG rounds at a CH-47 Chinook heavy-lift helicopter.

Following US Defence Department investigations into that historic Afghan battle that left many American soldiers and airmen dead, officials who examined details of the Jihadi attack concluded that it was the second RPG round that struck one of the three aft rotor blades of the helicopter and did the necessary; it destroyed the helicopter's rotor assembly. The twin-rotor Chinook heavy-lift crashed less than five seconds later, killing all 38 people including 25 American special operators, five US Army National Guard and Army Reserve crewmen. Also killed were seven Afghan commandos and an Afghan interpreter.

That loss of life surpassed the 19 deaths during the 2005 Operation Red Wings – the engagement portrayed in the film *Lone Survivor*.

The RPG-7 is a simple weapon to handle. Without much practice, a user can hardly miss a vehicle-sized target at 100 metres. More practice enables engagement of targets at extended ranges, which obviously provides better relative safety to the user if he comes under fire.

At its maximum range of 920 metres, RPGs self-explode (4.5 seconds from firing) and that is why the weapon is sometimes used as a form of air-burst 'artillery', spraying shrapnel over troops huddled together, military installations, or slow, low flying or hovering helicopters. Anti-personnel grenades also have good destructive power.

Following the conflict in Afghanistan, new anti-personnel grenades have been added to today's arsenal. A modified version, PG-7BR (VR for the RPG-7V1) is also designed to defeat reactive armour. It uses a precursor charge to eliminate any reactive coating on an infantry fighting vehicle and a propellant charge to penetrate the main armour.

The rocket launcher is easy to handle, sitting comfortably on the shoulder and with the weapon's iron sights directly in sight. As a squad weapon, it is slightly larger than average, so there can be no mistake who or what you might be aiming at. Once you've checked that there is nobody standing immediately behind you (during the firing process a mighty sheet of flame is emitted that can stretch back 15 or 20 metres), you aim and pull the trigger.

It is actually the launch detonation that intimidates most of those who haven't handled RPG-7s before because the blast is enough to burst an eardrum; hearing protection is essential.

What I found notable the first time I fired the weapon was that for all the noise and back-blast, there was absolutely no recoil. A moment after firing, you are able to very briefly track your grenade as it heads in towards the target at close to the speed of sound.

The best indication of what it is like to use the device has come from the film *Black Hawk Down*, the book by that name originally written by Mark Bowden with whom I exchanged notes after I had returned from Somalia. He agreed that the Somali warlords that were targeted by the American Special Forces team knew exactly what they were doing when the Black Hawk choppers – Sikorsky UH-60s – arrived over the scene.

Suddenly there were scores of rebels on the ground, each one equipped with RPG-7s firing at the helicopters as quickly as they could reload their tubes. One of the pilots is said to have commented after it was all over that there were so many RPG grenades self-destructing around them – which happens if there is no hit – that it was like something out of one of the old Second World War films about Allied bombers taking flak over Nazi Germany.

Subsequent intelligence that came from Washington suggests that those warlords had been planning the attack for months and had actually shipped in containers of RPG launchers and grenades from their friends in Yemen, clandestinely, of course. It was a clever tactic and it worked ...

Many stories have emerged over the years about the weapon, including some remarkably narrow escapes from those at the receiving end.

One event that made the news at the time concerned a South African soldier who had taken a hit in his chest by an RPG grenade. He survived because it did not detonate. Stuck with an RPG grenade embedded in his body he was taken to the military hospital in Oshakati where a team of surgeons – working behind sandbags and armour-plated glass – eventually succeeded in removing the bomb. The entire procedure was done at great personal risk to those brave doctors and theatre assistants.

Whether it was actually ever activated on being fired or not we will never know. It was taken to the range and detonated by army engineers shortly after the operation.

I was always curious about the weapon and spent quite a bit of time with some of my Koevoet friends discussing the RPG-7, which happened to be – apart from boosted Soviet anti-tank mines – the biggest single threat their units when on the move and susceptible to ambushes.

Obviously, they took some hits but the Casspir was pretty secure and could most times survive even a boosted (double) blast from a Soviet TM-57 anti-tank mine. Among most Koevoet veterans, a direct hit from an RPG was more feared.

Something that emerged early on was the fact that part of the process of constructing the business end of the grenade was that the Soviets had made it 'tamper proof'. You simply do not fiddle with it (I was warned) when we went over some of the intricacies involved.

And yet, Frans Conradie, who achieved the highest individual kill rate in the war – his units hunted down and killed or captured hundreds of SWAPO insurgents each year – thought otherwise. He was quite candid about having explored the 'innards' of dozens of RPG-7 grenades, carefully disassembled many, breaking them down into their component parts without one ever having been accidentally detonated.

He actually gave me one of the disarmed grenades which I kept for years (together with a launcher that followed afterwards) until I left South Africa permanently for the United States. I handed over both to Colin Ainsworth Sharp, owner and publisher of *Habitat magazine* in Johannesburg and he mounted them over his bar.

Notably, Conradie's personal tally of enemy killed in roughly 150 contacts – in a career that spanned more than a dozen years (including time spent in the Rhodesian War) – is said to be about 1,000 killed. Frans died in a road accident when he overturned his vehicle after a run ashore with his boys in Sector 10.

Another very lucky man was American soldier Private Channing Moss who also survived after having an unexploded RPG stuck in his stomach following an ambush in Afghanistan.

His story was originally carried by the London *Daily Mail* under the heading 'Remarkable Man' on 31 May 2011.

Private Moss was on patrol in Paktika Province in eastern Afghanistan a few months prior when his unit was attacked – likely by Al-Qaeda or Taliban insurgents – in a mountainous region that bordered on Pakistan. A couple of dozen men from the crack 10th Mountain Division's Alpha Company were driving a convoy of five Humvee armoured vehicles and a pick-up truck, containing Afghan National Army troops when they were hit first by gunfire, followed by a hail of rocket-propelled grenades.

The pick-up truck exploded, killing two Afghan soldiers and, as the rockets struck Moss's Humvee, the gunner recalls being thrown against the interior bulkhead of the vehicle.

'I smelled something smoking and I looked down ... *and it was me that was smoking*,' he told ABC News in a documentary.

The team called for a medical evacuation (MEDEVAC) and soon afterwards a helicopter based at Salerno base arrived at the scene of the contact. But his colleagues said nothing to the aircrew about Moss having a still-unexploded rocket grenade lodged in his abdomen because they feared that if they knew, the chopper boys would refuse to transport him. It had entered through one of his hips and the tip of its grenade was protruding from his opposite hip.

Somehow the bomb had not detonated on impact, but if it had, it would probably have killed or wounded just about everyone within a 10-metre radius.

In the first of two major strokes of luck, the convoy's only medic, Jared Angell who was in the vehicle with Moss and able to treat him immediately, bandaging his wounds and stabilising the RPG to ensure that it did not move around.

But even after the extraction chopper arrived, its crew had to wait for the fighting on the ground to cease before they could land. That meant, considering the circumstances, an inordinately long delay. It also entailed Moss exceeding the 'Golden Hour' for trauma treatment that saves so many combat wounded.

When the helicopter did eventually land the crew could see immediately what had happened. Moss knew then that there was little likelihood that they would lift off with him on board.

United States Army policy in such a situation states very clearly that anyone who is wounded and who might subject his rescuers to serious risk, should not be handled. In Moss's case, it could have led, had the device exploded, to the deaths of the four members of the rescue medical team, with possibly another three other wounded, if not killed, as well as the potential loss of a helicopter. However, the flight crew conferred and they agreed to take Moss up with them.

The chopper boys flew him to the nearest field hospital at the Orgun-E base, but again crucial unexploded detail of his injury was omitted.

Once within the confines of the hospital the medical team, led by surgeons Major John Oh and Major Kevin Kirk, were confronted with this horrific wound together with all its implications.

'The wound had fins coming out of the left side of his body and had a big bulge in the front of his right thigh,' recalled Major Kirk. Again, US Army policy is clear: Moss should not be operated on because of the risk to medics and other patients.

Moss's second stroke of luck came when it was revealed that an army bomb disposal expert, Staff Sergeant Dan Brown, was on the base. He carefully examined the patient where he lay on his stretcher, gingerly felt around the wound and then explained all the possible scenarios to the medical team. One of his comments was that they could all become 'pink mist' if the grenade exploded. The medical team briefly discussed the issue and they agreed to treat him.

At this point, Moss's heart had stopped due to massive blood loss and the medics had to administer epinephrine to restart the organ before they could operate.

Thereafter, Staff Sergeant Brown went to work, using a hacksaw to remove the RPG's tail fins and very slowly easing the rocket back out through the entry wound. The senior NCO then 'walked' the unexploded bomb out of the operating theatre to a bunker and had it detonated.

Private Moss was transferred to hospitals in Afghanistan and Germany en route to Walter Reed Army Medical Centre in Washington DC, where he was reunited with his wife Lorena and his daughters Yuliana and Ariana, then six and four.

The after-effects of this remarkable episode were severe. Moss' internal organs were severely damaged and he suffered a shattered pelvis, leaving him unable to walk. Thereafter, he had four major operations and years of gruelling physiotherapy that took him out of a wheelchair, onto a walking frame and, finally, to walking with a cane. But his determination did allow him to walk up to the podium when the time came and collect his Purple Heart, the award given to all American soldiers wounded in combat.

'I wanted to walk and get my medal, I wanted to stand up, to let them know I fought hard to get to this place, considering where I came from,' he said.

The soldiers and medical team who helped save Private Moss were also honoured.

The RPG-7 has seen such wide and varied service that it is nearly impossible to list all of the conflicts in which it has been involved. From the Vietnam War to the Gulf War and Islamic State – as well as many other conflicts worldwide, the RPG-7 is remarkably combat proven.

Powerful, cheap, simple and exceptionally robust, the RPG-7 is undoubtedly the most famous anti-tank rocket launcher ever devised since its introduction in 1961. It remains in production with more than 9 million units come off many production lines to date and continues to serve with over 40 countries, plus a large number of irregular military groups that include rebel groups in dozens of countries.

A few facts about one of the most versatile weapons ever produced

The RPG-7 is a reusable single-shot smoothbore steel tube with a diameter of 40 millimetres. This recoilless, shoulder-fired, muzzle-loaded launcher can shoot a variety of rockets. Optical and iron sights generally come standard, though night vision sights can be used.

RPG stands for the Russian *Ruchnoy Protivotankovvy Granatomyot* or hand-held anti-tank grenade launcher (although it is more frequently called a Rocket Propelled Grenade or RPG). It is a further development of the 1949 RPG-2, itself based on the Second World War German Army *Panzerfaust* and the American Bazooka. Its chief advancement over the RPG-2 includes much-improved range and increased armour penetration.

The central part of the barrel is covered in wood to protect the operator from heat. There are also the two handles located close together in the centre of the weapon.

Another advantage of this weapon is that it can be fired from inside a building if sufficient open space is available for its vicious back-blast. This weapon also gives off a highly noticeable flash, noise, and smoke, a disadvantage if deployed in open ground where patrolling helicopter gunships might spot the origins of a strike.

After 10 metres, the rocket's internal rocket motor ignites and four stabilisation fins fold out, giving it a maximum muzzle velocity of 300 metres per second.

Normally, the RPG-7 is operated by a gunner and an assistant who holds extra rounds and defends the gunner from attack.

The RPG-7 has a maximum range of 920 metres at which point the rocket detonates. Nevertheless, it is only considered effective up to about 200 metres, at which range it is estimated to have about a 50 percent chance of hitting a slow-moving target.

During its almost six-decade service life, the RPG-7 has been used to knock out tanks, destroy armoured personnel carriers, buildings, fortifications, attack infantry, and shoot down low-flying helicopters. Indeed, the simple RPG-7 has succeeded in bringing down more helicopters to date than most man-portable air-defence missile systems.

Also, insurgents have made extensive use of 'small boats' armed primarily with RPG-7s and machine guns.

Al Venter in a 'before and after' sequence of firing an RPG-7 while operational with the
SADF in Angola

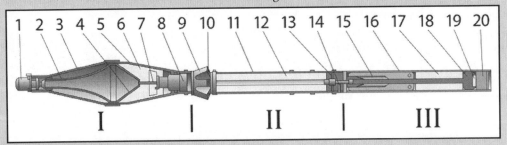

RPG-7: 1 – trigger, 2 – conductive cone, 3 – aerodynamic cover, 4 – conical liner, 5 – body,
6 – explosive, 7 – conductor, 8 – detonator, 9 – nozzle block, 10 – nozzle, 11 – rocket motor
body, 12 – powder propellant, 13 – rocket motor; rear part, 14 – ignition primer, 15 – fin, 16 –
paper cartridge, 17 – powder charge, 18 – turbine, 19 – tracer, 20 – foam wad.

RPG-7 rocket launchers are to be found just about everywhere in Africa's ongoing wars, as they have been for almost half a century. Child soldiers are very much part of conflict in Africa. This Ugandan youngster was barely 12 years old.

AKs and RPGs aplenty in this rebel group going to war in Angola.

Al-Qaeda RPG-7 grenades on a vehicle with a French Air Force Puma as a backdrop at Timbuktu in Mali's ongoing insurgent war.

Aerial view of Mogadishu as a US helicopter flies over this vast and troubled conurbation. When the American Army went into Somalia in the early 1990s, they found that the rebels had been well supplied from Yemen with RPG-7s which they used in their hundreds to bring down two US Choppers, as described by Mark Bowden in his book *Black Hawk Down*.

Batches of RPG-7 grenades recently captured from Al-Qaeda Jihadis in West Africa.

Angolan rebel soldier with RPG-2, forerunner of the more versatile RPG-7.

South African mercenaries serving with Executive Outcomes in Angola and a selection of rebel arms that included a range of Soviet weapons, like RPG-7s, RPD machine guns and AKs. (Author's photo)

Russian poster depicting the ubiquitous RPG-7 and instructions for its use.

Former rebel and a clutch of RPG-7 warheads. Photo taken from Al Venter's book on the Jihadist insurgency in West Africa's Mali: *Al Qaeda in the Islamic Maghreb*. (Pen and Sword Books, 2018)

21

Puma Helicopter Operations

At the end of 1977, former SAAF helicopter pilot, the late Peter 'Monster' Wilkins was serving as flight commander at 16 Squadron in Bloemfontein. He received orders to prepare for a posting to Puma helicopters. After a final bush tour on Alouette IIIs at Rundu, he was appointed flight commander on Pumas in Pretoria early 1978; a squadron deployment to the Angolan border followed. Brigadier Wilkins – who later served as his country's air force attaché at the South African Embassy in Washington – recounted:

We finished our three-week Puma conversion in mid-February 1978 and then completed our operational conversion by the end of the month. I went on my first tour along the Angolan border as a co-pilot a month later with Ralph Platte as commander.

Though I was with 19 Squadron for two years, I managed to accumulate nearly 900 hours on Pumas and that meant that the pace was furious. This was actually true for all Puma and Alouette crews at that time, which was heavy on their families because we aviators were often away from home for the duration.

Bush tours on Pumas consisted largely of ferrying troops into forward positions, re-supplying those already in the field coupled to casualty evacuations or, in the lingo, casevacs: we were on standby around the clock for any of the above.

While Windhoek was the regional headquarters for the war, the main operational area was at Sector One Zero at Oshakati, the biggest town in the homeland of the Ovambo people, South West Africa's largest tribe. In contrast, Air Force elements with their helicopters – and later, with Mirage fighter jets – were stationed at Ondangua, the biggest air base in the operational area, only minutes' flying time to the south-east. Occasionally some of the helicopters might be deployed elsewhere, like Rundu to the east or south to Grootfontein.

The much larger SAAF French-built Super Frelons were based in the Caprivi Strip at Rundu's Mpacha air base because of their engine-to-weight ratio they never performed well at 'hot and high'.

Chopper boys – wherever they might be found – have never been shy about making things comfortable for themselves, so our base at Ondangua boasted a swimming pool and what was certainly the biggest and busiest pub in that corner of 'Darkest Africa'. For all these shenanigans, duty came first and casevac standby was a serious matter in this combat zone that fronted onto an extremely hostile Angola.

It was also a region where the war sometimes went conventional and involved large Soviet and Cuban-led armoured thrusts from the Luanda regime in its bid not only to topple Dr Jonas Savimbi, the UNITA leader but to make things uncomfortable for us.

Going through my logbook – it listed all the flying I did on my first tour while operating out of Ondangua. During that phase, I'd registered 40 missions, of which a quarter was linked to transporting the wounded or injured to the main hospital at Oshakati and some of those experiences were sobering …

With time, the level of conflict started to escalate and the SADF was eventually faced with combat operations that involved SAAF jet fighters as well as British-built Buccaneer and Canberra bombers giving back-up to ground forces who from early on had been heavily involved against Cuban and Angolan armoured thrusts.

Our boys would sometimes take the war deep into Angola and when that happened the Angolan Air Force responded with Soviet strike aircraft that were much more versatile and advanced than our Mirages. These included MiG-23s and Sukhois: it was axiomatic that casualty evacuations became both more frequent and urgent.

Whenever there were SAAF fighters on missions over enemy territory, standby Puma crews would wait by their machines or in our ops room where radio reports were coming in. The crews would go airborne the moment a call came in, and though it rarely happened, this might entail retrieving a pilot who had been shot down.

Paul Kruger earned an *Honoris Crux* medal for bravery by picking up one of our colleagues in an extremely confined bush area where, because of heavy foliage cover even the tiniest miscalculation would have spelt disaster. He achieved that in the face of barrages of enemy fire.

Flying a Puma with an overall rotor diameter of 15 metres, it was generally accepted that this larger helicopter needed a cleared space of about 50 metres in order to bring the machine in and take off safely. In the heavy bush country – of which Angola had a lot – that kind of ground area was not always available and when Kruger came in to retrieve the downed aircrew he had to do a substantial amount of 'tree cropping'; his rotor blades slashing a way in and out of the improvised LZ. Though the chopper suffered damage and the rotors had to be replaced, the rescue was a success.

April 1978 saw Peter 'Crow' Stannard and I finish our instructor conversions and the squadron was ordered to prepare for upcoming bush operations. An early operation involved our Pumas providing support when our army attacked an enemy headquarters camp at Cassinga in Angola. It lay more than 100 nautical miles north of the border, which suggested that the guerrillas deemed it safe from attack by the South Africans. They were wrong.

Just a few clicks south of the target lay a village occupied by the Cubans. To the west flowed a river and eastwards there was nothing but bush: no settlements, no villages and no roads, so the South Africans decided to attack from the north, the idea being that a paratroop [Parabat] contingent would jump in from C-130 and French-built C-60 transporters. This attack turned into the largest airborne operation in the history of the SADF.

But first, several squadrons of air force jets had a clearing job in hand, the first South African hostile action since the Korean War ended in 1953. Additionally, about 20 helicopters – mainly Pumas and several Super Frelons – got involved in troop uplifts as well as handling any casualties needing urgent attention.

It was all classic stuff while it lasted. 12 Squadron's Canberra bombers emulated their Second World War motto of 'First Into Action' by launching the initial aerial onslaught. They hit the enemy with 1,200 Alpha bombs, specifically designed for what is known in artillery technology as 'air burst'. The Alphas would strike the ground and bounce back into the air before exploding, causing serious damage. The weapon was designed specifically for use in the kind of sandy, arid terrain that characterises almost all of southern Angola: bedrock sometimes lies hundreds of metres below the surface and more often than not desert sand would stifle blast on impact.

Having arrived over the target at Cassinga, our pilots observed a thousand or more enemy troops on the parade ground; they had just been mustered for the morning parade. Some of them actually waved at the SAAF planes as they approached, believing them to be friendly having come in from the north. SAAF Buccaneers followed in short shrift with 1,000-pound gravity bombs and the Parachute Battalion completed its insertion.

Prior to the jets going in, a Puma flown by John Church was the first to become airborne. His role was to set up a mobile navigating beacon about 15 nautical miles east-north-east of the target which would be used by the bomber crews to get an accurate fix prior to commencing their run-ins. The same position was also used as an assembly point by our chopper crews and to uplift troops when the order was given to pull out.

Earlier clandestine insertions by squads of No 1 Reconnaissance Regiment – the Recces – suggested that this was the most secure area for a Helicopter Administration Area (HAA) because the only real access was by helicopter. There were no roads that would allow the enemy to approach, only sandy tracks which tended to impede large vehicles, armour especially.

Meantime, backed by Johan Ströhme at the controls of Puma 169, I led the chopper formation in from Omaone. On reaching the HAA, we off-loaded dozens of drums of fuel and shortly before midday started to prepare the choppers for the first uplift of Parabats, but by then things were running a little behind schedule.

Once the combat area was reached, where the firing was sporadic, we flew directly towards the most prominent landmark and put our machines down on the enemy's main parade ground. There was no missing evidence of what must have been a vicious battle, underscored by battered buildings, smoke still hanging low and scores of jagged craters that scarred the area all of it surrounded by still-burning vehicles scattered about haphazardly.

From the air, we spotted a series of trenches – zigzagging everywhere – according to the way the Soviets did things. In fact, these fortifications surrounded the entire town, which had all the hallmarks of a military base with well-defended strongpoints at all the extremities, supported by more heavy weapons than we cared to count, many now made inoperable by our troops.

The bodies of enemy soldiers killed in the initial strike were everywhere. So much for Cassinga being a peaceful little town where only civilians and refugees from the war lived, the thrust of arguments subsequently put out by both Angolan and Cuban propaganda machines.

South African military intelligence had known from the start that the place was well defended and all aircrews involved in the attack briefed accordingly, as were the troops that went in. Early reports estimated that Castro's soldiers had only four armoured vehicles, so when radio reports from the men on the ground started coming in about a column of about 30 Soviet tanks and armoured personnel carriers heading up the only connecting road towards our landing ground in the target area, sectional heads got together and a rapid change of plan formulated.

The Buccaneer jets and the 'Bats' immediately took the initiative and accounted for the spearhead of the Cuban column; three of the four Soviet tanks were knocked out in the first strike and the fourth made a run for it. Shortly afterwards, about two dozen BTR armoured vehicles were spotted heading south and they too were successfully targeted by 2 Squadron's Mirage IIIs.

John Church meantime had also been active and earned himself an *Honoris Crux* for remaining behind in his Puma to ensure that nobody was left behind. Together with 'Hojan' Cronjé – who had a twin .50-calibre machine gun mounted in his Puma – they provided covering fire so that some of our stragglers could depart. By the time we all got airborne and were on our way out of Angola, it was dark. We took our formation up high, to about 8,000ft, more than a little concerned about enemy anti-aircraft fire.

The final 'score' was lopsided. We lost four of our boys, all paratroopers KIA, with well over a thousand enemy killed and about double that wounded.

Pumas Under Heavy Fire

In September 1979, a total of 13 Puma and two Super Frelon helicopters headed out of Pretoria for a short 'cross-border' operation of about a week's duration, all of which would take place from Rhodesia, into Mozambique.

Altogether ten of the choppers took battle damage with one Puma shot down with the loss of all 17 men on board, the ground fire intense throughout. Approaching an enemy road convoy, there were so many RPG-7s being fired at us that the barrages could easily have been confused for AAA fire.

On some of the sorties there also SAM-7s – Soviet Strela hand-held MANPADs – fired at our attacking force but no hits were registered.

While stiff opposition had to be expected by the aircrews, there was some consternation when the word went out, officially or unofficially (we were never to find out) that a helicopter or two might be lost in action. This was something that had never emerged on any of our pre-operational briefings and the tension was strong for a week. Still, this was war and the 'old guys' weren't perturbed. As one of them said, 'if it happens, it happens …'

On leaving Pietersburg for Rhodesia after refuelling, we had to get above cloud cover and continue on a distance and heading reckoning to get to Buffalo Range, the forward airfield at Chipinga Pools which lay in open country among the cane fields in south-eastern Rhodesia. Our Pumas had not yet been fitted with GPS, so the gaggle simply followed the squadron boss in the hopes that he would get us all there.

The next day, moving into hostile Mozambique air space, we flew a concerted operation of four and a half hours and the first of our choppers to suffer damage took a hit from an RPG-7 self-destruct burst. There was much more incoming, but nothing serious. We continued with the operation for four more days, with over 28 hours' combat flying, of which three hours were night ops.

Having established an HAA about 110 kilometres inside Mozambique, we spent only an occasional night in enemy territory, most times returning to Chipinga before dark to sleep on Rhodesian soil. This proved to be a wise decision because on one of the nights when we weren't there, the army ended up ambushing several dozen insurgents that walked into the camp one night. They accounted for 23 of them.

One advantage of flying over this south-western quadrant of what had been Portuguese East Africa for more than four centuries was that the terrain was relatively flat. We could transit at very low levels at night, always in pairs and occasionally flicking on our navigation lights so Number Two could get us visual and adjust accordingly.

Phil Meredith was my co-pilot and we teamed up with Rob Dean to make up our team. We would be indicating 140 knots and cruising at 100ft on the radio altimeter (Radalt), as the region gradually became more overgrown, with some forest giants that reached upwards 20 metres or more. Another problem was high-tension wires, which, we'd been briefed, were almost 50 metres at max. So on that faithful old 'time and heading', we would call 'pulling up for the wires' and would ease up to about 175 feet. The margin was slim and there was good reason.

One night while exiting guerrilla territory, I had just called for a pull-up when a string of green and red tracer came towards us from starboard, which was roughly where we'd expected Rob Dean to have positioned his chopper. He'd actually been there as planned and took some fire; when we landed back at base, we found six holes in his aircraft. Fortunately, the Puma's self-sealing fuel tanks had taken care of the hits and there was no serious damage. We had to wait until the end of the tour before we could remove the tanks and the bullets – our souvenirs!

Another of the Puma operational pairs was composed of Jonsson & Johnson as well as Ronnie and Tony. One of their helicopters was hit by a Soviet DshKa 12.7mm bullet and he was lucky enough to have it go straight through his chopper. It had entered immediately above the passenger cabin, just below the engines. Had one of the engines taken a hit (both are positioned alongside each other) the situation could have become critical.

The shedding of turbine blades by one of the chopper's motors – caused by any kind of bullet impact – would almost certainly have resulted in the other engine also being destroyed in-flight.

During the course of these cross-border raids, some of the troops that we hauled were fortunate not be hit when bullets passed through their cabin space, which becomes limited when you have so many men on board.

Other helicopters targeted and hit were those of 'Doc' Hawker, Paul Kruger and Vic Swanepoel. In fact, only 'Crow' Stannard and I came out unscathed for the entire week. However, because some of our exploits involved us going in extremely low, our two aircraft probably boasted the most scratches and missing paint on their fuselage undersides.

One job entailed trooping in the vicinity of the main railway line between Rhodesia and the Mozambique capital of Maputo. Pairs of Pumas would set off on different headings from our operational base to deposit troops at selected points. After the first drop, we'd come together at a temporary 'safe' area to stand by until the work was done before going in and fetch more army groups and those delays were always unnerving.

There was no question that the local populace in the area simply had to be aware we were there, compounded by the fact that they were hardly likely to be friendly. There was always a small detachment of 'browns' detached to protect the choppers, but, as one of the guys pointed out, had there been a concerted attack, we might have paid the price.

Throughout, we proceeded with caution, great speed and always hugging the deck. At one stage there was a motorcyclist heading out through a field immediately ahead of us and had he not aborted his run and taken a dive, he would probably have taken a knock. Looking back, it is hard to imagine that we were sometimes so low that we had to pull up even for ordinary fences on the ground.

We got to the target eventually but were more than a little disconcerted when we spotted a very large and ominous-looking concrete pillbox protecting the northern end of it. Meantime, we never discouraged the troops onboard from opening the chopper doors and, if they thought it appropriate, using their weapons to good effect.

That time we sneaked in low, using a river bank as an improvised protective buffer from the 'hot' side and got in and out as fast as I've ever done. The troops on board hardly needed encouragement to exit at speed. Later, when we were radioed for the pick-up, we came in from a totally different direction, guided that time by columns of smoke spewing from the target that had been demolished.

Because of a very substantial amount of anti-aircraft fire, other targets were more problematical. Commandant 'Breytie' Breytenbach, our squadron boss at the time and 'Crow' Stannard went into one extremely hazardous position and in the process, they earned a Silver *Honoris Crux* and an HC.

'Breytie' also did a casevac out of there when one of the Rhodesian Bell 205s was shot down, the chopper having been called for the evacuation of a wounded RLI soldier. At the controls was Dick Paxton but when he arrived at the pick-up zone, he was asked to 'move around a bit', which is never advisable in a hot zone. The next thing Paxton knew was that an RPG-7 grenade hit the Bell on the port side and the machine went down in flames.

Our guys were tasked to recover both the original casevac and the new one (because Dick Paxton was hurt) as well as the body of his engineer. In the end, 'Breytie' handled the task himself, even though our Pumas were a lot larger target than the average Bell.

I flew Dick out to Chipinga Pools after Breytenbach had returned to base and brought the dead and wounded to the HAA, from where they were all airlifted to hospital in a Dakota. Otherwise, the day was notched up as a success, but that was not the case with what followed ...

Early the next morning we took off with a bunch of troops for an air-landed assault on a large guerrilla camp, which intelligence had told us housed a few hundred soldiers. In fact, three figures soon turned into four and one informed military source spoke about 'thousands' of enemy troops waiting for us. Worse, all were very well armed, coupled to a surfeit of AAA. The jet jocks bombed and strafed the position almost all day, but it was still an extremely difficult job because there were enough anti-aircraft guns in position to keep them firing all day.

We'd arrived over the scene and were just turning for the last short leg to the drop point, when Paul Velleman, Nigel Osborne and their engineer Dick Retief were shot down in their Puma. They had taken up a position towards the rear of a Bell 205 formation when they were hit by a particularly heavy concentration of fire, including at least one RPG-7 that penetrated their cockpit.

The grenade exploded directly behind the pilot and the chopper went straight down and all 17 people on board were killed instantly.

A pall of thick black smoke rose up quickly, up to 800ft or more, with the Bell leader calling in the loss. That meant that we were all left with a sickly, hollow-gut feeling that aviators experience when they lose a comrade; in this case, several.

Only the previous day Paul had experienced a hairbreadth escape when his Puma hit some telephone wires as they approached their designated target. The chopper survived and took a few scratches, but there was no structural damage, so life went on ...

The pick-up was almost at last light. Because of a powerful enemy presence, all the troops were able to do throughout the day was move from the hotly contested area where we had dropped them to a relatively safe field where we could get to them about 35 kilometres miles away. It was dodgy ...

We eventually landed and uplifted the troops, all relieved that we'd managed to come in unscathed. Moments later we set our heading for the HAA flying directly into a rising full moon. There was only one road left to cross before we reached the border, but as luck would have it, there was an enemy convoy right in our path. Intelligence reports later suggested that they were looking for our temporary base.

The column below threw everything they had at us, from small arms and RPGs to vehicle-mounted 23mm anti-aircraft fire. 'Breytie' was out ahead, with 'Crow' following up close behind and about a kilometre ahead of us. Suddenly the lead Puma appeared to be enveloped in a web of tracer fire and the helicopter wavered a little, before resuming straight and level flight. It was that close.

Commandant Breytenbach called out that his co-pilot, 'Jakes' Jacobs had been hit, but he came back shortly afterwards and said it wasn't serious. He had two neat bullet holes in his helmet – an entry and an exit hole and which is now in the SAAF Museum.

The only damage that Jacobs suffered was a red mark over his left eye: the bullet had not even broken the skin! The 'blood' he'd felt, he realised afterwards, was sweat running down his face. The bullet exited immediately in front of the pilot, starring his windscreen, which was the cause of the momentary 'bounce' we'd noticed as he tensed up on the controls.

Because we were some distance behind, we'd had adequate warning of that reception committee; it would almost certainly have been waiting for us so took appropriate evasive action. We swung out wide towards the west and made a wide detour. But that did not discourage the bastards from throwing up a barrage of stuff, all the more visible in the early evening light.

One of the army officers onboard estimated that at one stage there were dozens of RPG-7 bursts all around us, which was quite something because those Soviet weapons self-destruct and there was also more than enough tracer!

That operation ultimately served its purpose: at the end of it, we were all more pensive about going in 'blind' into an extremely hostile Mozambique. But we were coming to the end of the deployment and were told after we'd landed that the next day would be the last.

Our role that final day was to go into Mozambique again and drop troops some distance in from their actual targets; as before, we'd pick them up again towards evening. The biggest issue facing us was that the target was 200 kilometres behind enemy lines.

With memories of the death of Paul Velleman and his crew still fresh, everything happened at ultra-low level, especially when we came in sight of the target, which lay on a slight rise. Again, some of us returned to base with helicopter underbellies and wheel nacelles needing paint jobs.

I brushed one tall tree with my right wheel nacelle while in a 60° bank towards port. From the cockpit, we could see it coming, but in a flash I decided it was better to hit it than become more exposed. The tops of the trees were soft and pliable enough not to cause structural damage to our machine.

Fortunately, there was no canopy perspex or glass impacted, though Rob Dean did have his HF 'bath rail' aerial torn off from under his fuselage.

Fire Force with the Pumas

I was deployed with the SAAF to Rhodesia many times – from 1967 through to 1976 – most times flying Alouette gunships.

In November 1979 I was sent north on a Puma tour with the so-called Fire Force Zulu, basically a South African operation in the south of the country using our own troopers (Pumas and Dakotas) as well as spotters (Cessna 185s) and Parabats.

The Rhodesians routinely supplied Alouette gunships as well as Cessna Lynx aircraft for top cover support, the latter fitted with twin over-wing machine guns as well as rocket pods. Rhodesian DC-3s also appeared a few times and if the operation became expansive enough, their Bell 205s would muck in with the trooping, though they were mostly too busy elsewhere to be deployed in the south of the country.

Fire Force Zulu became one of the more successful deployments, not least because the fighting ability and tenacity of the Parabats took some Rhodesians by surprise; it was unusual to have so many enemy troops shot in the head. Also, on that op, we mostly worked out of Buffalo Range in the east, towards the Bulawayo area further towards the west and south as far as the South African border at Beit Bridge.

Many small Rhodesian towns like Gulu and Gwanda became pivots, but our movements would occasionally take us operational from open areas or fields converted to temporary camps.

Throughout, the basic attack concept never changed. The need to spot, track and report on the movement of the enemy was inviolable, as was the ability to call in the fire force when it looked like a successful attack might be likely.

Rhodesian Cessnas had a 'Skyshout' capability, a bank of powerful speakers mounted into the door of the plane that was used to talk to crowds or villages suspected of harbouring insurgents. The device was an improvement over the original system employed onboard the Dakota and even tried experimentally on the Alouette.

The older system consisted of two massive speakers, one mounted to port and starboard of the Alouette or on the fuselage of the Dakota, while the more modern version contained a number of smaller speakers and was markedly much more powerful and clearer and consequently, easier to hear on the ground. There were a number of safety regulations as to how close these aircraft could be used to groups of people because of potential ear damage.

One morning one of the Cessna pilots tested his device on us. He had flown off on an early morning task and on his way back to Gwanda – where we were billeted on the periphery of the airfield – he climbed high, pulled back on the throttle and as quietly as possible, glided in over the airfield towards our temporary base.

When he reckoned he was directly over our billet, we suddenly awoke to an awesomely loud 'Come on you bastards! Wake up! Wake up all you f*@&% chopper pilots down there!'

SAAF Puma helicopter airlifting fighting squad into action in South Angola. (Author's photo)

Puma helicopter picking up recce group well inside Angola. (Author's photo)

Portuguese Air Force Puma rendezvous with Paras in the Chanada Cameia in the eastern regions of Lisbon's war in Angola. (Sourced to John P. Cann)

A soldier wounded in an attack on an enemy base receiving treatment back at a temporary holding position deep inside Angola. (Author's photo)

22

Covert Communications During South Africa's Border War

Walter V. Volker reports:
Earliest forms of 'Y Services' in South Africa during the course of the Second World War involved two entirely separate organisations that were established in South Africa to monitor and record enemy radio traffic. Radio direction finding techniques (DF) to accurately determine the position of those transmitters were also brought into play.

The first of these was formed by the Director of Signals, Colonel Freddie Collins. It followed a request from British Intelligence for South Africa to monitor radio traffic between Lisbon and the Portuguese territories of Angola and Mozambique.

Since Lisbon had declared itself neutral, that city was crawling with spies and intelligence agents – from both sides. There was concern in Britain that radio traffic to the German embassies in Luanda and Lourenco Marques was being transmitted from Lisbon.

In South Africa, meanwhile, it had been appreciated that a spy ring – possibly operated by the *Ossewa Brandwag* (OB) – was in contact with a German agent in Lourenco Marques. In addition, illegal radio broadcasts in the country, carrying decidedly pro-Nazi propaganda, were being run by the OB.

As a result, Colonel Collins ordered Lieutenant E.R. (Ted) Cook, an enthusiastic and knowledgeable radio amateur to set up a monitoring station at Roberts Heights (subsequently renamed Voortrekkerhoogte) so that all radio traffic to and from those Portuguese territories could be intercepted.

Another, even more, secretive organisation was created at the same time – but beyond the control of the Director of Signals. This grouping was so hush-hush that General Smuts decreed that it should not fall within the ambit of any government department for fear of its purpose and role being made known to the enemy. There was also concern that overt OB sympathies within some echelons at Defence Headquarters in Pretoria and elsewhere might compromise the whole scheme.

So what became known as the Price-Milne Organisation was instigated on the recommendation of Dr Hendrik van der Bijl, Director General of War Supplies who effectively functioned as Smuts' wartime scientific adviser. It appears that the operators' cabins and consoles were pre-fabricated to minimise installation work in the field and about 100 such stations were built.

In later years these basic 'Y' and related services were greatly expanded to embrace a more comprehensive range of electronic warfare capabilities – which have remained just as hidden from the general public as before. Few people are aware that a much-enhanced capability was utilised very effectively during the Border War and indeed, made a major contribution to the successes of the SADF against the enemy. This is a brief summary of how that capability was developed and utilised.

The Concept of Electronic Warfare

But first, a brief explanation is required of what exactly is meant by electronic warfare (EW). 'Normal' military communications (or 'signals', as it is known in the military) is an essential ingredient to the functioning of any military organisation if effective command and control are to be achieved. However, as we have seen in recent times it is possible to hamper, disrupt or even totally destroy the communications arm of the enemy.

This, in essence, is what is meant by EW – turning communications into an aggressive weapon.

Essentially, military communications and EW are two sides of the same coin. It is not possible to have the one without the other and still have an effective and well-balanced capability in service of the country. At the same time, these two dimensions are generally at arms-length from each other, to be moved about as two separate chess pieces on the wartime chess board.

There is obvious frequent interaction as well as mutual and continuous influence, but never really integration. Over time these two disciplines have diverged rather than converged and even the training process and approach is different; very few of the personnel work on both sides of the divide.

Basically then, EW is the military application of electronics to determine, exploit, and reduce or prevent the hostile use of the electromagnetic spectrum, while retaining its use by friendly forces. More salient, this battle is less tangible than a physical battle for territory but no less important and potentially, deadly. The implication of losing this battle can be more profound, under some conditions, than the loss of territory.

There is no question that military electronics and electronic warfare have been the two most significant force multipliers since the Second World War. As the saying goes, 'You are not going to win the war only by employing EW to your advantage, but you certainly are not going to win without it.'

Post-Second World War Development of EW by the SADF

The first EW related requirement of the SADF was focused on passive and static ESM, such as intercept and direction finding, during Operations Brush and Falcon (the decade from 1968 to 1978).

As this skill matured, progression was made to enable tactical and active EW measures; the first use of active ECM was in May 1978 during Operation Reindeer when jamming of enemy frequencies was most effectively utilised.

Prior to this development in the late 1960s, apart from the establishment of basic 'Y Services' located on General Kemp Hill at Roberts Heights during the Second World War, the capability of the Union Defence Force (and later the SADF) in terms of EW was rather limited in the immediate post-war era.

As it was regarded as an 'unnecessary luxury', only very basic monitoring and intelligence collection ability was maintained after the war – with Radio Uitkyk in Voortrekkerhoogte acting as the transmitter station and General Kemp Hill as a receiver station. The main 'customer' for these intercepts was the Directorate Military Intelligence (DMI).

Some Basics Concepts of the EW Task

The EW task can be grouped into two main categories:
- Passive – generally non-intrusive, non-detectable.
- Active – generally intrusive and therefore more detectable.

More comprehensively, the scope of the EW task can be summarised as:
- Offensive – ECM (Electronic Counter Measures)
  - * Passive ECM
    - » Monitoring/Interception (IC)
    - » Direction Finding (DF)
  - * Active ECM
    - » Jamming
    - » Deception
- Defensive – ECCM (Electronic Counter-Counter Measures). These could also be:
  - * Counter Passive ECM
    - » Minimised power output, etc.
    - » Communication security (COMSEC)
    - » Codes and cyphers
  - * Counter Active ECM
    - » Counter Jamming, e.g. Frequency hopping
    - » Counter Deception, e.g. Verification, Encoding systems, etc

The above measures can be deployed in a number of modes, depending on the requirements for movement:
- Static – when the capability is located at a permanent physical location
- Mobile – when the equipment can be placed at a semi-permanent location, but easily moved when required
- Tactical – when the capability (equipment and personnel) are able to provide the service on the move, e.g. EW equipment built into combat vehicles to go into combat for purposes of either jamming or monitoring.

During the early 1960s, there was an increasing realisation that the SADF had virtually no meaningful EW assets – as was also the case with independent electronics and telecommunications manufacturing at that stage. In the initial stages of re-establishing an EW capability, the authorities turned to the radio 'hams' (radio amateurs) for assistance, as well as a core team of individuals from Armscor and the Directorate Telecommunications.

The initiative, however, came from DMI in the early 1960s, which recognised the need for a reliable and effective source of electronic intelligence (ELINT).

The post-war initiator of EW prowess was Commandant A.J.C. (Tony) de Wit, who had a strong technical background and was the OC of the School of Signals (June 1965 to August 1966). He started developing an intense interest in EW and provided technical support to the DMI, to the extent that he was eventually transferred to the DMI in the role of what was eventually to become the Senior Staff Officer Telecommunications (SSO Tels); later changed to D Technology, a Directorate of DMI.

The role of the DMIs SSO Tels included telecommunications, agent communications and photo-analysis – and at the time reporting directly to the Director Military Intelligence (Brigadier Frits Loots).

At this stage, Commandant de Wit started offering EW courses and building up the general knowledge base in the area of EW. He had taken over this role from a SAAF officer, Captain Mike Venter, who had been involved in some basic monitoring while seconded to the office of the Chief Communications Officer at DHQ. At the time EW equipment was sourced primarily from C. Plath and Rhoode & Schwarz in West Germany.

Meanwhile, Gerrit Murphy was recruited by the South African Corps of Signals (SACS) from the SA Post Office in 1965. However, soon thereafter Murphy was seconded to the DMI to assist with their EW effort.

The EW team (de Wit and Murphy) built up a good personal relationship with the founder and owner of C. Plath, Dr Wächlter, who had developed his skills in Direction Finding (DF) during the Second World War, particularly in Naval DF.

During 1967 three DF systems – the SFP5000 – were purchased and mounted on VW Combi vehicles for mobile deployment. The (undercover) DMI officers that assisted with the sourcing process during these early years were P.W. van der Westhuizen (based in Paris and later to become Chief of Staff Intelligence) and Dirk Greyling (based in Frankfurt at the time, later to become a Director at DMI, and afterwards a professor at UNISA).

Operation Brush

The event that triggered an even greater urgency and drive to develop an EW capability even further came in late 1967 when the DMI Electronic Warfare team at General Kemp Hill near Pretoria intercepted a number of messages emanating from United Nations/United States sources that suggested that an invasion of South West Africa by a combined UN force might take place. This was no idle threat: a considerable amount of planning was already in the works at UN Headquarters in New York.

This intelligence was relayed to the Chief of the SADF and also to Brigadier Magnus Malan, Officer Commanding South West Africa Command. The immediate consequence was Operation Dikmelk in December 1967, followed by Operation Eksamen in January 1968 – together with a hasty build-up of a basic reaction force in Walvis Bay and elsewhere in the League of Nations Mandated territory.

Eventually, the planned UN invasion was cancelled (a development which was also monitored by the EW team), and the reaction force was stood down. However, it was also accepted at that point that the interception of those key messages was more a stroke of luck rather than due to any systematic monitoring of the radio spectrum, and as a result, a more effective EW capability – especially one located much closer to the threat – was urgently needed.

The result of these developments was the initiation of Operation Brush by the DMI at the end of 1967.

Katima Mulilo – the first EW or 'BRUSH' station

The first EW (or 'BRUSH') station established as a result of Operation Brush, was at Katima Mulilo in the Caprivi Strip of north-eastern SWA.

The first group was deployed in mid-January 1968, headed up by an infantryman, Captain 'Witkop' Badenhorst, with his 2IC Captain Wessel Kritzinger and WO1 George Beukes as the senior NCO in the SA Corps of Signals. (Badenhorst was destined to be appointed Chief of Staff Intelligence many years later in 1989.)

This was really a DMI team (as mentioned above), but they were deployed covertly under the guise of being a SABC team, investigating the possibility of setting up another radio transmission tower in the region. At that time the SADF was not supposed to have a presence in SWA, with all law and order maintained by the South African Police. The only 'accepted' SADF presence was at Windhoek itself, and in Walvis Bay – officially part of the Cape Province.

In the meanwhile, the young Lieutenant Gerrit Murphy was placed in charge of the EW personnel at these stations. For almost a full year during 1968, Murphy flew up to Katima Mulilo once a week on Tuesdays. This was done with two Dakota aircraft of the SAAF – one loaded with fuel (as there was no infrastructure for air traffic at the time) and the other loaded with provisions for the EW Section. From there on, Lieutenant Murphy started to play an increasingly prominent role in the development of the EW within the SACS.

While Tony de Wit can be called the 'Initiator of EW', Gerrit Murphy is generally recognised as the 'Father of EW' in the SACS.

After a few months, the infantry section commander at Katima Mulilo was replaced by a signals officer/DMI member, Captain Gerrit Ockerse. Not long thereafter, he was replaced by another signals officer Captain Dirk Verbeek, who was seconded by the DMI (and later became Chief of Staff Intelligence in the early 1990s, succeeding 'Witkop' Badenhorst).

Interference by the Bureau for State Security ('BOSS')

During this same period, while Brigadier Frits Loots, Director of Military Intelligence was away on leave, the staff at DMI headquarters were surprised one day when a strange tall man and some of his henchmen burst in to their headquarters building unannounced stating that they were taking over the office of the director and his second in command, Colonel Hein du Toit.

They then went on to remove personal effects and other related material of these two officers from their offices. It then emerged that these actions were the work of Lieutenant General Hendrik J. van den Bergh, head of the newly established Bureau for State Security (or as the media preferred, 'BOSS') and also known as *Lang Hendrik* or 'Tall Man'.

Lieutenants Murphy and 'Klein Pine' Pienaar were among those who witnessed this incident, which seemed to be a prelude to van den Bergh replacing both the DMI and the SA Police Security Branch with his own bureau, and with the personnel of both organisations reporting personally to him.

Having established himself in his new office of choice, General van den Bergh started interviewing his 'newly acquired' members of staff. The interview with Lieutenant Murphy lasted a brief two minutes, which he cut short with the observation that he did not understand a word of what Murphy had said and that in any case, if he (van den Bergh) was in need of intelligence, he was fully capable of sending out a policeman on a bicycle to collect what was needed!

Van den Bergh made it clear that he had every intention of closing down every EW station, including Katima Mulilo, declaring that he saw no need for them.

The Corps of Signals takes over EW operational functions from DMI

During this crisis period when the EW stations were in danger of being closed down by *Lang Hendrik*, Lieutenant Murphy appealed to the Director of Signals, Colonel Gert Boshoff, to intervene.

The result was that from that point on, the SACS took over the role and all EW stations from the DMI as a precaution, and was henceforth to play the leading role in static and tactical operational deployment of the army (and SADF) land-based EW efforts.

At this point, all EW functions were placed under command of the EW Troop of the Defence Headquarters (DHQ) Signal Squadron. Key operational EW functions, including the strategic photo-analysis section and all its equipment, was transferred from the DMI to the DHQ Squadron of the SA Corps of Signals.

As the DMI team at this stage was effectively non-functional, the SACS started sending the information collected at its BRUSH stations to the GOC JCFs (General Officer Commanding Joint Combat Forces), Lieutenant General 'Pop' Fraser and the SO1 Ops Dennis Earp (later Chief of the SAAF) located at Voortrekkerhoogte.

The first SACS officer, Lieutenant Denis Jelliman, was sent to Katima Mulilo in September 1968 to take over from the DMI commander Captain Dirk Verbeek. Jelliman was also the first in this role to wear his SADF uniform; up to that point, the covert roles of SABC personnel had been strictly maintained, and everybody worked in civilian clothes and drove civilian vehicles.

When DHQ Signal Squadron was upgraded to 2 Signal Regiment in 1972, the EW role was later taken over by 23 Squadron and eventually in November 1981, 5 Signal Regiment emerged from 23 Squadron, with an exclusive focus on EW.

As of 20 December 1968 the young Major Georg Meiring (the future head of the SADF) was appointed Commanding Officer of DHQ Signal Squadron, which then consisted of a handful of officers, eleven WO2s and four WO1s. With this modest team a very big task needed to be performed. The squadron consisted of a Long Distance Static Troop (which Meiring himself commanded with the assistance of WO1 Jack Shaw), while the EW troop was headed by Captain Gerrit Murphy.

Over time, with the tremendous task at hand, the numbers mushroomed, and DHQ Signal Squadron became larger, in terms of actual numbers than that of a regiment.

Rundu 'BRUSH' Station

Later in 1968, a second EW or 'BRUSH' station was deployed in SWA at Rundu in the Caprivi Strip. Due to the highly covert nature of these stations and the fact that even very senior officers were not allowed access, it was thought by many that 'BRUSH' was an acronym meaning 'Bush Reconnaissance Unit for Signal HQ'. The meaning 'stuck' in the minds of many a troop that was aware of the secretive nature of the EW efforts in the operational area, and especially the 'Recon' part, which confused some enough to think that these stations were part of the 'Recces' or were Special Forces (which they were obviously not). 'BRUSH' personnel were also sometimes referred to as 'Spec signallers' for the same reasons and regarded as 'untouchable'.

Each EW deployment had its own unique identity and circumstances, and in the future, each deployment would be allocated a name. For example, the deployment at Rundu would be known as Section A (Alpha). Consequently, Katima Mulilo was called 'Section B' (Bravo) of DHQ Signal Squadron. The first Section commander at Rundu was Lieutenant Martin Waring, who was also apparently the first SADF officer to wear an army uniform there.

Operation Falcon (1969 – 1976) in Rhodesia

The next electronic warfare-related project was initiated in 1969 and called *Operation Falcon*. The purpose was to set up EW stations in Rhodesia in a similar way to the 'BRUSH' stations in northern SWA, as close as possible to the frontier with the Frontline States.

The South West African and Rhodesian EW stations were placed more or less on the same degree of latitude, thus providing a wide range of EW coverage of the African sub-continent, while being as far forward to target areas as possible.

The combined efforts of the SWA and Rhodesian stations would provide excellent coverage for intercepts and also make for accurate triangulation for direction finding (DF). Three stations were planned as part of this next operation, namely:

- Romeo Troop – located in Salisbury and manned mainly by the Rhodesian Corps of Signals
- Zulu Troop – located at Binga and manned by members of DHQ Signal Squadron, although wearing Rhodesian Army uniforms and ID cards (named Section C of DHQ Signal Squadron, SACS)
- Victor Troop – located in Chirundu and also manned by SACS members (Section D)

The SACS only provided equipment to Romeo Troop, while personnel came from the Rhodesian Corps of Signals.

Meanwhile, EW coverage by DHQ Signal Squadron of the countries north of the Kunene and the Zambezi rivers was now quite comprehensive:

- Section A (Rundu, SWA) – which covered Angola and Zambia
- Section B (Katima Mulilo/Mpacha, SWA) – which covered the eastern parts of Zambia
- Section C (Binga, Rhodesia) – which covered primarily Mozambique and Zambia
- Section D (Chirundu, Rhodesia) – which covered Zambia, Tanzania and Malawi

Pietersburg EW Station

The first EW station within South Africa's borders was contemplated in the late 1960s. Initially, the trigger for such a station was a request from the West German intelligence agency – the *Bundesnachrichtendienst* (BND) – for South Africa to provide a facility for long-range HF communication with their agents in the field. This contact, once again, came through Tony de Wit, and the proposal was for the West Germans to provide the funds and equipment for the setting up of such a facility.

Equipment, including a 100-ton 'Log P' (Logarithmic Periodic) antenna and 100 kW transmitter, was then acquired and a suitable 4-5 hectare plot bought just north of Pietersburg and called *'Mimosa'*.

Unfortunately, just before the equipment was installed, political events relating to the Cold War intervened. During 1973, one of the closest aides of the West-German chancellor, Willy Brandt, was exposed as a STASI (Communist East German Security Police) spy and the fallout from the scandal caused him to resign. This crisis gave the West German authorities cold feet, and combined with possible pressure from the CIA and USA government, caused the Germans to withdraw from the arrangement.

As a result, the 'Log P' antenna equipment was never deployed as planned but actually used at Radio Uitkyk in Voortrekkerhoogte – although the planned 100 kW transmitter was swapped for a number of 1 kW transmitters.

The Pietersburg plot was retained and in later years even extended with additional purchases of a further five plots.

In the meanwhile, prior to this political drama unfolding, in January 1971, a young Lieutenant Sarel Kruger was sent to the new Pietersburg site to establish Section F of DHQ Signal Squadron. This station was re-designated 231 Troop when 23 Squadron of 2 Signal Regiment was established just over a year later in April 1972.

After the withdrawal of all EW troops from Rhodesia in early 1976, new stations needed to be found along the periphery of South Africa's borders and these new locations included:

- Jozini – in June 1976
- Lydenburg – in July 1976 a temporary location was found when an old road camp was evacuated
- Phalaborwa – in 1977 (the Lydenburg troop was moved here)
- Louis Trichardt – in 1979
- Boekenhoutskloof – in 1980

When Boekenhoutskloof was completed as part of Project Ebbehout, the main EW station was moved from Pietersburg to Boekenhoutskloof (Project Bowie) some kilometres north of Pretoria.

Each of these stations had a personnel of approximately 20 to 30 troops, except for Mimosa (Pietersburg) that had about 50 troops – and the headquarters itself, which had many more – making it more than 300 EW troops in total by the time 5 Signal Regiment was established at the end of 1981.

Louis Trichardt EW Station

In February 1979 a major new EW station was activated close to the SAAF base at Hanglip, Louis Trichardt. Second Lieutenant Stephan Fick was tasked with starting this station with 26 staff. Their role was EW-related coverage, mainly of Mozambique, though from time to time they would turn their attention to Botswana and Zambia.

For direction finding purposes in Mozambique, they were assisted by the Jozini and Phalaborwa EW stations. In turn, Louis Trichardt supported Pietersburg with covering Botswana (as did Boekenhoutskloof), while Katima Mulilo/Mpacha handled Zambia in those days. By the end of his stay in December 1980, the personnel numbers at Louis Trichardt had grown to a complement of 150 troops.

Early Border War Operations

Up to this point, the EW capability was mainly *static* in nature, which meant that the equipment and personnel were located at selected permanent structures.

Thereafter the *mobile* deployment of this capability was developed – including the ability to utilise the capability within enemy territory during operations. During the period from 1978 to 1980, the operational value of EW was further exploited and expanded, especially during operations such as Reindeer, Safraan, Rekstok and Sceptic.

Operation Protea, directed at SWAPO bases and headquarters in the Ongiva and Xangongo areas of Angola, took place from August to September 1981. It was the largest mechanised operation executed by the SA Army since the Second World War and was also the most successful in terms of EW support to combat forces in the history of EW in this country.

Tactical EW support and specifically HF and VHF ESM were provided to Task Force A and Task Force B with the assistance of tactical EW equipment installations in Ratel, Buffel and Samil 20 vehicles. Overall, EW support turned out to be exceptionally successful, but the absence of a tactical Direction Finding or DF capability was identified as a clear weakness – and subsequently developed.

Establishment of 5 Signal Regiment on 1 November 1981

The value of the EW weapon to obtain valuable intelligence about the enemy had by this time been fully appreciated, and there was a realisation that technological development in this area had become an urgent priority.

Projects to further modernise and expand the country's EW capability were consequently launched and by then *Project Molasses* had already started, with the objective to establish a fully *mobile* HF ECM capability.

Other projects which had come on stream by then included *Project Expanse* for the development of a mobile HF and VHF ESM and ECM capability. The results of both these projects, however, would only become available for use after the EW function had been transferred under the wing of 5 Signal Regiment.

On 1 November 1981, with the relocation of 2 Signal Regiment to the new base at Wonderboom to the north of Pretoria, the appropriate circumstances for the separation of 23 Squadron and the activation of the envisaged EW Regiment had arrived. The management of EW would henceforth no longer be the responsibility of 2 Signal Regiment but of the newly-created 5 Signal Regiment.

Thus ended the significant contribution of DHQ Signal Squadron and its successor, 2 Signal Regiment, in this field of warfare. The First Officer Commanding 5 Signal Regiment was Commandant S.J. (Sarel) Kruger and the first Regiment Sergeant Major was WO1 M.J. Marais.

Evolution and design of the 5 Signal Regiment emblem – by Colonel Sarel Kruger

Once while I was in America, I made contact with the *Association of Old Crows* – an organisation of former electronic warfare personnel. I became a member in 1976 and eventually used the crow as the basic design for the 5 Signal Regiment emblem during 1982.

The crow, as I was to learn, symbolises a creature which gathers interesting bits and pieces – just as we EW soldiers do when we listen to the radio frequencies. My original design was obviously adapted and corrected by the Department of Heraldry.

Redesignation of EW Signal Troop

With the transferring of the EW Signal Troop from 23 Squadron, 2 Signal Regiment to 5 Signal Regiment, the Troop was redesignated as follows:

EW Troop, DHQ Signal Squadron ('BRUSH' Stations)	23 Squadron, 2 Signal Regiment (EW Troop)	51 & 52 Squadrons, 5 Signal Regiment	Location(s)
A Section (1969)			Rundu, SWA
B Section (1968)	236 Troop	512 Troop	Katima Mulilo (later Mpacha), SWA
C Section (1969)	Sierra/Zulu Troop – 234 Troop (1976)	524 Troop	Binga, Rhodesia; Lydenburg, Transvaal
D Section (1969)	Victor Troop – 235 Troop (1976)	525 Troop	Chirundu, Rhodesia; Jozini, Natal
E Section (1974)	237 Troop	511 Troop	Oshakati (later Ondangua; later Grootfontein), SWA
F Section (1968-71)	231 Troop	522 Troop	Pietersburg
G Section			
H Section (1975-76)			Grootfontein
I Section			
J Section (1975)	234 Troop (1976)	524 Troop	Mariepskop (later Lydenburg; later Phalaborwa)
	232 Troop	521 Troop	Wonderboom; Boekenhoutskloof
	233 Troop	523 Troop	Louis Trichardt
		513 Troop (1983)	Ongiva; Oshakati; Rooikop

Personnel deployment during the late 1980s at 5 Signal Regiment typically included about 80 SADF Permanent Force members, 900 National Service members and about 100 Citizen Force members at any one time.

Further expansion of the EW Capability – some major projects

As may be seen from the preceding history, the initial focus of the SADF's EW efforts were confined to static/passive forms of ECM – mainly Intercept and Direction Finding. During the 1980s these capabilities were significantly enhanced and expanded. The sequence of projects and their respective tasks that were launched to cover the various aspects were as follows:

Project Name	Mobility			Mode		Frequency range		
	Static	Mobile	Tactical	Passive	Active	HF	VHF	UHF
Bowie	X			X		X		
Scoop	X				X	X		
Expanse		X		X		X	X	X
Molasses		X			X	X		
Lasciva			X	X		X	X	X
Lateral			X		X		X	

Project Bowie was the first of the series of projects to be initiated in 1978. The purpose and scope of Project Bowie was 'to establish a fixed-installation, passive ESM (Electronic Surveillance Measures) which will render a dynamic contribution to the defence of our country.'

At that time the key parties involved were the SADF, Armscor and Fedkom Systems, the latter the only civilian contractor who was willing to invest resources into a scheme that represented a totally new and unique technology in this country. At the time Fedkom Systems was a subsidiary of Federale Volksbeleggings, and most of the funding came from Volkskas Bank.

At the conclusion of the project in the late 1980s, the SADF had developed one of the most sophisticated and modern radio monitoring and DF systems capabilities in the world.

The first message intercepted by the new static electronic warfare system proved that most of the objectives were achieved. It came from a FRELIMO presence in Mozambique on 1 July 1986 at 1123 hours, was decoded and translated (from Portuguese) and sent to the intelligence and operational staff one hour and nine minutes later.

Military Intelligence Division and the Expansion of EW into other countries in Africa

As explained earlier, the initiative for post-Second World War development of EW within the Defence Force was taken by the Directorate Military Intelligence (as it was known then) in the mid-1960s.

Following the 'take-over' of DMI by BOSS, the EW stations were all transferred to the SACS or SA Army Signal Formation. Meanwhile, the South African Navy had also developed its own EW capability, with Silvermine on the Cape Peninsula as its main station. The air force had already developed the capability of aerial EW by means of specially equipped Boeing 707 aircraft and some ground stations.

All intelligence gathered by these three capabilities was fed into the electronic collections capability at the Directorate Technology of the Military Intelligence Division (MID). By the early 1970s, the Directorate Military Intelligence of DMI had been upgraded to a full division, namely the Military Intelligence Division of MID.

While the Army (SACS), SAAF and Navy EW efforts were all operated from within the borders of South Africa and SWA, as from 1980 MID established an extensive series of EW stations outside the borders of the country – called Project Insignia.

The Director Technology at MID was Brigadier 'Pine' Pienaar and the officer tasked with putting this project into effect was Major J.J. (Kosie) Needham. The first of these was established was on the Comoros, an island group in the Mozambique Channel and named Charlie Station (Alpha and Bravo being the two original stations established under Operation Brush in northern SWA in 1968-69). The network control station was located in Voortrekkerhoogte and called Delta Station.

When a second station was opened in Malawi, it was quite logically named Echo Station and also played a valuable role (obviously with the cognisance of that government).

The IC station in the Democratic Republic of the Congo (DRC) was established under Project Galery. Galery 1 resulted in an EW Station in Kinshasa, while Galery 2 was located in Lubumbashi, in the south.

The primary purpose of these stations was the electronic collection of intelligence – mainly by means of intercepts (IC) of radio traffic of the target territory. These fell under the control of the Section Electronic Collection in the Directorate Technology, although many were manned by members from the SACS, SA Navy, SAAF, or in some cases by soldiers of the host country.

They were generally referred to as '*ML Stasies*' (from the Afrikaans '*Meeluister*') or Intercept (IC), as their main function was exactly that.

Starting from the first 'BRUSH' station in the late 1960s, and the base station in Voortrekkerhoogte, the full complement of EW stations which were at some stage under the control of DMI/MID were the following:

- **Alpha Station:** Originally established by the DMI in Rundu, northern SWA, in early 1968. Handed over to the SACS in 1969.
- **Bravo Station:** Originally established by the DMI at Katima Mulilo, northern SWA, in early 1968. Handed over to the SACS in 1969.
- **Charlie Station:** Grand Comoros. MID set up the EW station and manned it with personnel from MID, SA Navy EW section and 5 Signal Regiment. This was during the time that Bob Denard (or Colonel 'Bako' as he was called) and his *Garde Presidentielle (GP)* was occupying the island. The SADF took over from the Rhodesians in 1980 to finance this private army at $6 million per annum but later, due to pressure from the French, 'persuaded' them to hand over to the French Army and they were given transportation back to South Africa by the end of 1989.
- **Delta Station:** Voortrekkerhoogte, Pretoria. A MID monitoring station dating back to the Second World War was operational until the end of 1993. Most world news agencies were monitored at Delta. FRELIMO military, police and government nets in the south of Mozambique were also monitored at Delta. A mobile monitoring unit (equipped Land Cruiser), was stationed at Delta and manned by MID personnel.
- **Echo Station:** Lilongwe, Malawi. Echo was stationed inside a Malawian military base in Lilongwe. FRELIMO nets in the Tete and Niassa provinces were monitored from Echo. The station was staffed by MID personnel as well as operators of the Malawi Army.
- **Galery 1 Station:** Kinshasa, Congo-Zaire. The MID established an EW station in a two-storey building along the banks of the Congo River. The aim was to do radio intercepts in Angola and also Congo-Brazzaville, to help their government in monitoring rebel movements and plans, as well as to assist the SA government in their intelligence-gathering efforts. The MID personnel installed the equipment and trained local staff; after this they only made regular visits. They were able to source their own equipment – mainly from Germany, including from Siemens and Rhoode & Schwarz. From 1989 the station in Zaire was manned permanently by MID personnel
- **Galery 2 Station:** Lubumbashi, Congo-Zaire. The result of the combined network of Galery 1 and 2 stations in the Congo – and the 'BRUSH' stations to the south in northern SWA (now Namibia) provided very effective coverage of most of Angola in terms of electronic intercepts of enemy radio traffic.

Tactical EW during Operations Modular, Hooper and Packer

Various elements from 5 Signal Regiment were also actively involved in EW support during the final phase of the Border War from late 1987 to mid-1988 in Angola.

These elements were an embedded and integral part of combat groups that were involved in the battles. For example, major EW successes were achieved in tactical EW during Operation Modular – specifically during the Battle on the Lomba River when massive jamming of enemy radio networks was achieved, rendering efforts of command and control between various formations and units of the enemy virtually impossible.

This put EW – specifically tactical jamming and intercepts – right at the sharp end of the battle as there were EW Ratels in the thick of battle, alternatively intercepting enemy communication and in turn jamming them in real time as the battle developed.

From both perspectives, this gave the battle group commander (in this case Commandant 'Bok' Smit) a decided advantage over enemy Cuban as well as Angolan FAPLA forces.

A few months later this type of battlefront involvement unfortunately also resulted in the first operational losses of 5 Signal Regiment in south-east Angola. On the 21 February 1988 Sergeant G.M. Maritz and Signalman Jacques de Lange (511 EW Troop) were killed during a MiG-23 attack in the operational area, together with another member from MID. A fourth member, 'Speedy' Goncalves was injured by shrapnel and taken to the military hospital in Rundu.

Conclusion

General Georg Meiring (last Chief of the SADF and first Chief of the SANDF), himself a former signaller, had the following to say with regard to EW and Intelligence …

> Our communications interception system was the best in the world at the time. Over 90 percent of the intelligence we operated on during the war came from interceptions. Electronic warfare is an exact but tiring science … While the South Africans were listening, so were the Cubans and Angolans. There is no doubt they intercepted us, but they were not as good as we were because our equipment at the time was much more sophisticated …

References

This chapter is based on extracts from the trilogy by Walter V. Volker:

Army Signals in South Africa. The Story of the South African Corps of Signals and its antecedents (Veritas Books, Pretoria, 2010).

Signal Units of the South (space) Africa Corps of Signals and Related Signal Services (Veritas Books, Pretoria, 2010).

9C – Nine Charlie! Army Signallers in the Field. The Story of the Men and Women of the South African Corps of Signals, and their Equipment (Veritas Books, Pretoria, 2010).

During the course of South Africa's border wars, effective communications dominated throughout, even when conditions were primitive. Combat vehicles were soon converted for comms with both aircraft in the immediate area as well as units serving in support of a particular operation. (Author's photo)

South African Defence Force base in Ovamboland. (Author's photo)

Comms maintained from a converted Buffel troop carrier in a SADF cross-border operation.
(Author's photo)

23

A Few of the Portuguese Special Forces Who Served the SADF with Distinction

Compiled by Stephen Dunkley and Manuel Ferreira

The number of Portuguese nationals who served in the SADF during the Border War was modest but each one of them, including quite a few women, made important contributions in their specific roles. Some like Danny Roxo was born in the Metropolis; others came from Lisbon's African possessions. There were also several hundred Angolan nationals who ended up in the ranks of the country's crack 32 Battalion.

Corporal Manuel Antonio Infante Ganhão

Like numerous Portuguese fathers, husbands and sons who joined the SADF after the collapse of the Portuguese colonies in the mid-1970s, Corporal Manuel Antonio Infante Ganhão gave his life to his adopted country when he was killed in action in the Gaza province, Mozambique.

He lost his life as a Special Forces operator during Operation Melon on 28 January 1978, the same 1 Reconnaissance Commando operation in which his commander Lieutenant Kokkie du Toit lost his life.

Like many of his predecessors, not much was known about this brave man until members of what South Africans like to refer to as 'Forgotten Portuguese Warriors' decided to do something about it. That happened after Manuel Ferreira posted a request for information on a number of websites. The following information came to light:

Manuel Antonio Infante Ganhão, the son of a former police chief, was a Portuguese Commando who served with the 3rd Commando Company of Mozambique after having completed his selection course in Montepuez in January 1971. With the collapse of Lisbon's authority in Africa in 1974 and shortly after arriving in South Africa, he completed his Reconnaissance Regiment selection course in 1976. In time, he was to become a proud and dedicated member of this elite unit.

A former Recce and comrade-in-arms remembers him as a great soldier and a good friend.

To the young South African men that had joined the SADF and Special Forces he was an inspiration and a good example as to how things should be done; much like the men who had come before him where names such as Daniel Roxo, Jose Ribeiro, Ponciano Soeiro and Carlos Ribiero come to mind.

Manny – as his friends knew him – was popular with many of the youngsters who had success-fully passed selection because he was both patient and willing to teach them, especially when it concerned the Portuguese language.

With his experience of having fought in several so-called liberation conflicts in Africa, he was able to impart valuable knowledge of the conditions of the ground as well as the capabilities of those against whom they would be matching skills.

He has been described by several of his colleagues as being, as the saying goes, 'hard as nails' and while generally a quiet and reserved individual, he was always willing to help. Even as a corporal he would make time for those under him and set exemplary standards about how he and they dressed. More pertinent, he always made an issue that they should understand the 'Recce tradition' and that nothing and nobody could take that honour away from them.

Manny would often say: 'Take nothing for granted because these are special times and at any moment everything can be taken away from you.' It was a lesson that many Special Force operators would learn with the loss of friends and comrades in future operations.

As with the late Staff Sergeant Danny Smith (ex-Rhodesian SAS), he would always inspect the men prior to going on parade to ensure that they adhered to their high standards.

A course instructor – with his speciality being the use of Bren or LMG machine guns – one former SF operator recalls how Manny would call him to his room to help him master the weapon. In the dark, he would make the soldier strip it and put the weapon together again.

On the range, Manny would ensure that those he taught could load, re-load and sort out stop-pages so that, when needed, they could react without thinking – possibly saving their as well as their comrades' lives. He was extremely fond of the LMG and wanted those using it to know that it would, as he would sometimes say, 'shoot them out of the shit if it came to that.'

There was little that would annoy Manny during the normal course of events back at base, except when those under his command would use water unnecessarily; then he would berate those about the importance of water discipline in the field.

Manuel Antonio Infante Ganhão is buried in Stellawood Cemetery, Durban and, unlike some other former Portuguese soldiers or DGS who joined the SADF, has a headstone to mark his last resting place. His funeral was attended by members of No 1 Reconnaissance Commando, as well as a former comrade-in-arms, who had decided to fight for the MPLA after Angola's independence in 1975.

Apart from being allowed to wear the Special Forces operator's badge, Manny was also para-chute qualified having completed his basic parachuting training in 1976 in Bloemfontein.

Manny was married with one child, Rubin Daniel Martins Ganhao, who was still an infant when his father died. At the time of his death Ana Paula Guerreiro Martins Ganhao, his wife, was pregnant with their second child, although she did not know that at the time.

Sergeant José Correia Pinto Ribeiro (Robbie/Carnaval)

José Correia Pinto Ribeiro was born in the former Portuguese colony of Guinea Bissau. After completing school, he joined the Portuguese Air Force and became a paratrooper in Guinea (BCP 12). He went on to distinguish himself as an exceptional airborne soldier in Portuguese Guinea.

When his former Officer Commanding in Guinea, Colonel Costa Campos formed the GEPs (*Grupos Especiais Pára-Quedistas*) 'Special Para Groups' in Mozambique, he arranged a transfer for Sergeant José Ribeiro to join the unit in that former Portuguese colony.

In Mozambique, while serving with the GEPs, Ribeiro became a specialist in pseudo insurgent operations, where he and his men operated on the terrain as 'FRELIMO insurgents'. He also operated for a while as a 'hunter' with the *nom de guerre* of 'Carnaval', where he excelled under primitive conditions.

He also worked closely with Adelino Serras Pires, the legendary safari operator in Mozambique, who was closely involved with 'Carnaval' in this clandestine phase against FRELIMO and who was actually part of the 'hunting front.'

Shortly after the Portuguese Communist Revolution of 1974, José Ribeiro joined the South African Defence Force. He completed the Special Forces selection course and became an operator with 1 Reconnaissance Regiment. In South Africa, he was fondly known to his friends and colleagues as 'Robbie' Ribeiro.

During Operation Savannah, he was seconded to Bravo Group as a platoon leader. He went on to serve with that force until 25 August 1976, the tragic day he died while evacuating battle casualties to a hospital in South West Africa. A week prior to Robbie's death, his younger brother Carlos also died in an ambush.

Sergeant Robbie Ribeiro was recommended for the *Honoris Crux* decoration for bravery and excellent leadership under combat by his commander Colonel Jan Breytenbach but the recommendation was never approved. According to his colonel, the fact that Robbie was non-white tended to influence the decision back in 1976.

Staff Sergeant Ponciano Gomes Soeiro

Ponciano Soeiro was born in Portugal in 1941 where, after completing his studies he joined the Portuguese State Police. He was transferred to Angola, early in his career with the DGS, and was stationed in the Uíge Delegation with the rank of Agent 2nd Class where he served as a *Flecha* operator.

He joined the SADF after the Portuguese revolution of 1974 and Soeiro completed his Special Forces selection course in September 1975 together with Roxo, Robbie Ribeiro and Mourão da Costa, where he became an operator with the Recces.

As with his compatriots, he was deployed to Angola during Operation Savannah as part of a Special Forces team attached to Bravo Group. On his return to South West Africa, with his Portuguese colleagues, he remained with the group of Angolans they had fought alongside in Angola, the core of whom were to form 32 Battalion. His experience as a former Special Forces operator was put to good use many times during Operation Savannah.

Staff Sergeant Soeiro was killed in combat on 23 August 1976 while serving with Bravo Group/32 Battalion: he was serving at the time with Daniel Roxo on an operational mission on the way to Derico in Angola. Unlike his friend Roxo, Soeiro did not die at the scene, but while being evacuated by road back to Woodpecker.

On 17 May 2015, Staff Sergeant Soeiro's name was appended to the unit Roll of Honour during the 32 Battalion's Veterans Association Annual Savate Memorial Service. Ponciano was married and left behind a daughter.

Staff Sergeant Almerindo Mourão da Costa, PMM

Almerindo Mourão da Costa was born on 19 August 1944, in a small village in the north of Portugal. After finishing school he joined the Portuguese Secret Police (PIDE/DGS) and was posted to Angola where he served with the *Flechas* until the Portuguese Army mutiny of 25 April 1974.

Like many other former Portuguese military or DGS personnel, he joined the SADF and successfully completed the Special Forces selection course and became an operator with 1 Reconnaissance Commando.

From August 1975, Mourão da Costa was deployed into Angola on deep penetration operations as part of Operation Savannah, As an instructor of Battle Group Bravo, he went on to join one of the 32 Battalion units. Since he was an explosives expert, he became an instructor with the South African Special Forces.

In January 1980, Staff Sergeant Mourão da Costa was awarded the *Pro Patria medal* for taking control of his unit after his assault commander had been wounded. Through good leadership and determined action, he pressed the attack through successfully. He played a leading role in re-organising the unit, arranging for the evacuation of casualties. His performance was an exceptional example of meritorious service and devotion to duty.

Mourão da Costa was killed in action on 24 February 1980 and the official SADF version of his death mentions a landmine explosion; that is not true because he was killed in a still-unnamed African capital while on a mission to destroy an enemy target. His body was never recovered.

On 30 August 2006 a number of servicemen and their families gathered at Voortrekkerhoogte to mark the 30th anniversary of the death of Staff Sergeants Daniel Roxo, Ponciano Soeiro and Jose Ribeiro.

General Swart paid a moving tribute to our fallen comrades including Staff Sergeant Almerindo Mourão da Costa, whose operator's badge and certificate were handed to his wife.

In due course, it is hoped that the true story with regard to Almerindo's contribution to the defence of South Africa and the circumstances of his death will emerge.

Staff Sergeant Francisco Daniel Roxo (*Honoris Crux*)

Francisco Daniel Roxo was born on 1 February 1933 in the village of Mogadouro in the Tras os Montes province of Portugal. It was there, as a child, that his father and grandfather installed a love of hunting and the outdoors.

In 1951 at the age of 18, Daniel left the familiarity of his homeland and travelled for a month by boat to the Portuguese colony of Mozambique. After a short period working on the railways as a foreman/hunter, he became involved with hunting in the Niassa province of northern Mozambique. It was during these years that Daniel honed his skills and learnt the moods of the bush that were to be put to good use in the war against insurgents in later years.

In 1963 Governor Costa Matos offered Daniel a job to officially assist with the census of the population of Niassa – at this time Daniel had stopped hunting and all of his men but nine had left his employ. Governor Costa Matos was obviously aware of Daniel's experience as well as his contacts in the province and with his intelligence background he was obviously looking to harness Daniel's expertise in the area.

Daniel accepted the job and was given both transport as well as a contingent of five black policemen (*Cipaios*). After the hunting teams were disbanded in 1963, Governor Costa Matos was totally behind Daniel and had trust in that man whom he regarded as 'a diamond in the rough.'

At the end of 1963, Daniel was asked to take ten armed *Cipaios* and visit the far north villages of the Niassa province and gather as much intelligence as he could, especially with regards to the numbers of locals that were leaving Niassa and joining FRELIMO. Daniel and his team – that at this stage numbered about 17 (not one with any military training) – became the first group that the government used to try and stop the local population from fearing and joining the guerrillas.

Indeed, they were not 'shock troops' – their role was as 'Soldiers in the Shadows'– to fight a silent war against insurgents that wanted to destroy Mozambique.

Daniel was to lead the Militia Forces in the Niassa province with great success, becoming feared by the FRELIMO cadres that operated in the north of Mozambique and for his actions in combat he was awarded the *Cruz de Guerra* (Portuguese Cross of Honour) as well as the *Medalha de Servicos Destintos* (Medal of Merit).

Daniel left Mozambique shortly after the unplanned and unsuccessful Lourenco Marques (Maputo) coup of 7-10 September 1974. Together with a number of other Portuguese nationals who had left Angola, Mozambique and Guinea Bissau he was recruited into the South African Defence Force.

At the age of 41, he was to show his resilience and hardiness by passing the tough selection course to join 1 Reconnaissance Commando as a Special Forces operator.

Soon after qualification in September 1975, he was seconded to Charlie Company of Bravo Group as a Platoon Leader. Soon after his arrival, Operation Savannah started, and Daniel's actions in combat against Cuban and Angolan Forces at Bridge 14 in Angola in December of 1975 resulted in his being decorated for bravery. Staff Sergeant Daniel Roxo was the first non-South African to receive this award. He was killed in action on 23 August 1976.

Tribute to the great Danny Roxo – KIA Angola in the service of the SADF.

Another view of Danny in command mode – a photo that appeared in the American
adventure magazine Soldier of Fortune

Index

INDEX OF PEOPLE

INDEX OF PLACES

INDEX OF MILITARY UNITS & FORMATIONS

INDEX OF MATERIEL

INDEX OF GENERAL & MISCELLANEOUS TERMS